CUCHULAIN OF MUIRTHEMNE

THE STORY OF THE MEN OF THE RED BRANCH OF ULSTER

CUCHULAIN OF MUIRTHEMNE

THE STORY OF THE MEN OF THE RED BRANCH OF ULSTER

LADY GREGORY

DOVER PUBLICATIONS, INC.
MINEOLA, NEW YORK

Bibliographical Note

This Dover edition, first published in 2001, is an unabridged reprint of the fourth edition of the work, originally published by John Murray, London, in 1911.

Library of Congress Cataloging-in-Publication Data

Gregory, Lady, 1852–1932.
    Cuchulain of Muirthemne : the story of the men of the Red Branch of Ulster / Lady Gregory.
        p. cm.
    ISBN-13: 978-0-486-41717-2 (pbk.)
    ISBN-10: 0-486-41717-4 (pbk.)
    1. Epic literature, Irish—Translations into English. 2. Heroes—Ulster (Northern Ireland and Ireland)—Legends. 3. Cuchulain (Legendary character) 4. Mythology, Celtic. 5. Tales—Ireland. I. Title.

PB1423.C8 G7 2001
891.6'2103208—dc21

00-052295

Manufactured in the United States by LSC Communications
41717405   2022
www.doverpublications.com

DEDICATION OF THE IRISH EDITION

TO THE PEOPLE OF KILTARTAN

My Dear Friends,

When I began to gather these stories together, it is of you I was thinking, that you would like to have them and to be reading them. For although you have not to go far to get stories of Finn and Goll and Oisin from any old person in the place, there is very little of the history of Cuchulain and his friends left in the memory of the people, but only that they were brave men and good fighters, and that Deirdre was beautiful.

When I went looking for the stories in the old writings, I found that the Irish in them is too hard for any person to read that has not made a long study of it. Some scholars have worked well at them, Irishmen and Germans and Frenchmen, but they have printed them in the old cramped Irish, with translations into German or French or English, and these are not easy for you to get, or to understand, and the stories themselves are confused, every one giving a different account from the others in some small thing, the way there is not much pleasure in reading them. It is what

I have tried to do, to take the best of the stories, or whatever parts of each will fit best to one another, and in that way to give a fair account of Cuchulain's life and death. I left out a good deal I thought you would not care about for one reason or another, but I put in nothing of my own that could be helped, only a sentence or so now and again to link the different parts together. I have told the whole story in plain and simple words, in the same way my old nurse Mary Sheridan used to be telling stories from the Irish long ago, and I a child at Roxborough.

And indeed if there was more respect for Irish things among the learned men that live in the college at Dublin, where so many of these old writings are stored, this work would not have been left to a woman of the house, that has to be minding the place, and listening to complaints, and dividing her share of food.

My friend and your friend the *Craoibhin Aoibhin* has put Irish of to-day on some of these stories that I have set in order, for I am sure you will like to have the history of the heroes of Ireland told in the language of Ireland. And I am very glad to have something that is worth offering you, for you have been very kind to me ever since I came over to you from Kilchriest, two-and-twenty years ago.

AUGUSTA GREGORY.

March 1902.

PREFACE

I

I THINK this book is the best that has come out of
Ireland in my time. Perhaps I should say that it
is the best book that has ever come out of Ireland;
for the stories which it tells are a chief part of Ireland's
gift to the imagination of the world—and it tells them
perfectly for the first time. Translators from the Irish
have hitherto retold one story or the other from some
one version, and not often with any fine understanding
of English, of those changes of rhythm for instance
that are changes of the sense. They have translated
the best and fullest manuscripts they knew, as accurately
as they could, and that is all we have the right to
expect from the first translators of a difficult and
old literature. But few of the stories really begin
to exist as great works of imagination until somebody
has taken the best bits out of many manuscripts.
Sometimes, as in Lady Gregory's version of Deirdre,
a dozen manuscripts have to give their best before
the beads are ready for the necklace. It has been
as necessary also to leave out as to add, for
generations of copyists, who had often but little
sympathy with the stories they copied, have mixed
versions together in a clumsy fashion, often repeating

one incident several times, and every century has ornamented what was once a simple story with its own often extravagant ornament. One does not perhaps exaggerate when one says that no story has come down to us in the form it had when the story-teller told it in the winter evenings. Lady Gregory has done her work of compression and selection at once so firmly and so reverently that I cannot believe that anybody, except now and then for a scientific purpose, will need another text than this, or than the version of it the Gaelic League is about to publish in Modern Irish. When she has added her translations from other cycles, she will have given Ireland its Mabinogion, its Morte D'Arthur, its Nibelungenlied. She has already put a great mass of stories, in which the ancient heart of Ireland still lives, into a shape at once harmonious and characteristic; and without writing more than a very few sentences of her own to link together incidents or thoughts taken from different manuscripts, without adding more indeed than the story-teller must often have added to amend the hesitation of a moment. Perhaps more than all she had discovered a fitting dialect to tell them in. Some years ago I wrote some stories of mediæval Irish life, and as I wrote I was sometimes made wretched by the thought that I knew of no kind of English that fitted them as the language of Morris' prose stories—the most beautiful language I had ever read—fitted his journeys to woods and wells beyond the world. I knew of no language to write about Ireland in but raw modern English; but now Lady Gregory has discovered a speech as beautiful as that of Morris, and a living speech into the bargain.

As she moved about among her people she learned to love the beautiful speech of those who think in Irish, and to understand that it is as true a dialect of English as the dialect that Burns wrote in.   It is some hundreds of years old, and age gives a language authority.   One finds in it the vocabulary of the translators of the Bible, joined to an idiom which makes it tender, compassionate, and complaisant, like the Irish language itself.   It is certainly well suited to clothe a literature which never ceased to be folk-lore even when it was recited in the Courts of Kings.

II

Lady Gregory could with less trouble have made a book that would have better pleased the hasty reader. She could have plucked away details, smoothed out characteristics till she had left nothing but the bare stories ; but a book of that kind would never have called up the past, or stirred the imagination of a painter or a poet, and would be as little thought of in a few years as if it had been a popular novel.

The abundance of what may seem at first irrelevant invention in a story like the death of Conaire, is essential if we are to recall a time when people were in love with a story, and gave themselves up to imagination as if to a lover.   One may think there are too many lyrical outbursts, or too many enigmatical symbols here and there in some other story, but delight will always overtake one in the end.   One comes to accept without reserve an art that is half epical, half lyrical, like that of the historical parts of the Bible, the art of a time when perhaps men passed more readily than they do now from one mood to another, and found it harder than we do to keep to the mood in which one tots up figures or banters a friend.

III

The Church when it was most powerful created an imaginative unity, for it taught learned and unlearned to climb, as it were, to the great moral realities through hierarchies of Cherubim and Seraphim, through clouds of Saints and Angels who had all their precise duties and privileges. The story-tellers of Ireland, perhaps of every primitive country, created a like unity, only it was to the great æsthetic realities that they taught people to climb. They created for learned and unlearned alike, a communion of heroes, a cloud of stalwart witnesses; but because they were as much excited as a monk over his prayers, they did not think sufficiently about the shape of the poem and the story. One has to get a little weary or a little distrustful of one's subject, perhaps, before one can lie awake thinking how one will make the most of it. They were more anxious to describe energetic characters, and to invent beautiful stories, than to express themselves with perfect dramatic logic or in perfectly-ordered words. They shared their characters and their stories, their very images, with one another, and handed them down from generation to generation; for nobody, even when he had added some new trait, or some new incident, thought of claiming for himself what so obviously lived its own merry or mournful life. The wood-carver who first put a sword into St Michael's hand would have as soon claimed as his own a thought which was perhaps put into his mind by St Michael himself. The Irish poets had also, it may be, what seemed a supernatural sanction, for a chief poet had to understand not only innumerable kinds of poetry, but how to keep himself for nine days in a trance. They certainly believed in the historical reality of even their wildest imaginations. And so soon as Christianity made their hearers desire a chronology that would run side by side with that of the Bible, they delighted in arranging their Kings and Queens, the shadows of forgotten mythologies, in long lines that ascended to Adam and his Garden. Those who listened to them must have felt as if the living were like rabbits digging their burrows under walls that had been built by Gods and Giants, or like swallows building their nests in the stone mouths of immense images, carved by nobody knows who. It is no wonder that one sometimes hears about men who saw in a vision ivy-leaves that were greater than shields, and blackbirds whose thighs were like the thighs of oxen. The fruit of all those stories, unless indeed the finest activities of the mind are but a pastime, is the quick intelligence, the abundant imagination, the courtly manners of the Irish countrv people.

IV

William Morris came to Dublin when I was a boy, and I had some talk with him about these old stories. He had intended to lecture upon them, but "the ladies and gentlemen"—he put a communistic fervour of hatred into the phrase—knew nothing about them. He spoke of the Irish account of the battle of Clontarf, and of the Norse account, and said, that one saw the Norse and Irish tempers in the two accounts. The Norseman was interested in the way things are done, but the Irishman turned aside, evidently well pleased to be out of so dull a business, to describe beautiful supernatural events. He was thinking, I suppose, of the young man who came from Aoibhell of the Grey Rock, giving up immortal love and youth, that he might fight and die by Murrugh's side. He said that the Norseman had the dramatic temper, and the Irishman had the lyrical. I think I should have said epical and romantic rather than dramatic and lyrical, but his words, which have so much greater authority than mine, mark the distinction very well, and not only between Irish and Norse, but between Irish and other un-Celtic literatures. The Irish story-teller could not interest himself with an unbroken interest in the way men like himself burned a house, or won wives no more wonderful than themselves. His mind constantly escaped out of daily circumstance, as a bough that has been held down by a weak hand suddenly straightens itself out. His imagination was always running off to Tir-nan-oge, to the Land of

Promise, which is as near to the country-people of
to-day, as it was to Cuchulain and his companions.
His belief in its nearness, cherished in its turn the
lyrical temper, which is always athirst for an emotion,
a beauty which cannot be found in its perfection upon
earth, or only for a moment. His imagination, which
had not been able to believe in Cuchulain's greatness,
until it had brought the Great Queen, the red eye-browed
goddess to woo him upon the battlefield, could not be
satisfied with a friendship less romantic and lyrical than
that of Cuchulain and Ferdiad, who kissed one another
after the day's fighting, or with a love less romantic
and lyrical than that of Baile and Aillinn, who died at
the report of one another's deaths, and married in
Tir-nan-oge. His art, too, is often at its greatest when
it is most extravagant, for he only feels himself among
solid things, among things with fixed laws and satisfying purposes, when he has reshaped the world
according to his heart's desire. He understands as well
as Blake that the ruins of time build mansions in
eternity, and he never allows anything, that we can
see and handle, to remain long unchanged. The
characters must remain the same, but the strength of
Fergus may change so greatly, that he, who a moment
before was merely a strong man among many, becomes
the master of Three Blows that would destroy an army,
did they not cut off the heads of three little hills
instead, and his sword, which a fool had been able to
steal out of its sheath, has of a sudden the likeness of
a rainbow. A wandering lyric moon must knead and
kindle perpetually that moving world of cloaks made
out of the fleeces of Manannan; of armed men who

change themselves into sea-birds; of goddesses who become crows; of trees that bare fruit and flower at the same time. The great emotions of love, terror, and friendship must alone remain untroubled by the moon in that world, which is still the world of the Irish country-people, who do not open their eyes very wide at the most miraculous change, at the most sudden enchantment. Its events, and things, and people are wild, and are like unbroken horses, that are so much more beautiful than horses that have learned to run between shafts. One thinks of actual life, when one reads those Norse stories, which were already in decadence, so necessary were the proportions of actual life to their efforts, when a dying man remembered his heroism enough to look down at his wound and say, "Those broad spears are coming into fashion"; but the Irish stories make one understand why the Greeks call myths the activities of the dæmons. The great virtues, the great joys, the great privations come in the myths, and, as it were, take mankind between their naked arms, and without putting off their divinity. Poets have taken their themes more often from stories that are all, or half, mythological. than from history or stories that give one the sensation of history, under-standing, as I think, that the imagination which remembers the proportions of life is but a long wooing, and that it has to forget them before it becomes the torch and the marriage-bed.

V

One finds, as one expects, in the work of men who were not troubled about any probabilities or necessities but those of emotion itself, an immense variety of incident and character and of ways of expressing emotion. Cuchulain fights man after man during the quest of the Brown Bull, and not one of those fights is like another, and not one is lacking in emotion or strangeness ; and when one thinks imagination can do no more, the story of the Two Bulls, emblematic of all contests, suddenly lifts romance into prophecy. The characters too have a distinctness one does not find among the people of the Mabinogion, perhaps not even among the people of the Morte D'Arthur. One knows one will be long forgetting Cuchulain, whose life is vehement and full of pleasure, as though he always remembered that it was to be soon over ; or the dreamy Fergus who betrays the sons of Usnach for a feast, without ceasing to be noble ; or Conall who is fierce and friendly and trustworthy, but has not the sap of divinity that makes Cuchulain mysterious to men, and beloved of women. Women indeed, with their lamentations for lovers and husbands and sons, and for fallen rooftrees and lost wealth, give the stories their most beautiful sentences ; and, after Cuchulain, one thinks most of certain great queens—of angry, amorous Maeve, with her long pale face ; of Findabair, her daughter, who dies of shame and of pity ; of Deirdre who might be some mild modern housewife but for her prophetic wisdom. If one does not set Deirdre's lamentations among the greatest lyric poems of the world, I think one may be certain that the wine-press of the poets has been trodden for one in vain; and yet I think it may be proud Emer, Cuchulain's fitting wife, who will linger longest in the memory. What a pure flame burns in her always, whether she is the newly-married wife fighting for precedence, fierce as some beautiful bird, or the confident housewife, who would awaken her husband from his magic sleep with mocking words; or the great queen who would get him out of the tightening net of his doom, by sending him into the Valley of the Deaf, with Niamh, his mistress, because he will be more obedient to her; or the woman whom sorrow has sent with Helen and seult and Brunnhilda, and Deirdre, to share their immortality in the rosary of the poets.

"'And oh! my love!' she said, 'we were often in one another's company, and it was happy for us; for if the world had been searched from the rising of the sun to sunset, the like would never have been found in one place, of the Black Sainglain and the Grey of Macha, and Laeg the chariot-driver, and myself and Cuchulain.'

"And after that Emer bade Conall to make a wide, very deep grave for Cuchulain; and she laid herself down beside her gentle comrade, and she put her mouth to his mouth, and she said: 'Love of my life, my friend, my sweetheart, my one choice of the men of the earth, many is the women, wed or unwed, envied me until to-day; and now I will not stay living after you.'"

VI

We Irish should keep these personages much in our hearts, for they lived in the places where we ride and go marketing, and sometimes they have met one another on the hills that cast their shadows upon our doors at evening. If we will but tell these stories to our children the Land will begin again to be a Holy Land, as it was before men gave their hearts to Greece and Rome and Judea. When I was a child I had only to climb the hill behind the house to see long, blue, ragged hills flowing along the southern horizon. What beauty was lost to me, what depth of emotion is still perhaps lacking in me, because nobody told me, not even the merchant captains who knew everything, that Cruachan of the Enchantments lay behind those long, blue, ragged hills!

W. B. YEATS.

March 1902.

CONTENTS

CUCHULAIN OF MUIRTHEMNE

I

BIRTH OF CUCHULAIN

IN the time long ago, Conchubar, son of Ness, was King of Ulster, and he held his court in the palace of Emain Macha. And this is the way he came to be king. He was but a young lad, and his father was not living, and Fergus, son of Rogh, who was at that time King of Ulster, asked his mother Ness in marriage.

Now Ness, that was at one time the quietest and kindest of the women of Ireland, had got to be unkind and treacherous because of an unkindness that had been done to her, and she planned to get the kingdom away from Fergus for her own son. So she said to Fergus: "Let Conchubar hold the kingdom for a year, so that his children after him may be called the children of a king; and that is the marriage portion I will ask of you."

"You may do that," the men of Ulster said to him; "for even though Conchubar gets the name of being king, it is yourself that will be our king all the time." So Fergus agreed to it, and he took Ness as his wife, and her son Conchubar was made king in his place.

But all through the year, Ness was working to keep the kingdom for him, and she gave great presents to the chief men of Ulster to get them on her side. And though Conchubar was but a young lad at that time, he was wise in his judgments, and brave in battle, and good in shape and in form, and they liked him well. And at the end of the year, when Fergus asked to have the kingship back again, they consulted together; and it is what they agreed, that Conchubar was to keep it. And they said: " It is little Fergus thinks about us, when he was so ready to give up his rule over us for a year; and let Conchubar keep the kingship," they said, " and let Fergus keep the wife he has got."

Now it happened one day that Conchubar was making a feast at Emain Macha for the marriage of his sister Dechtire with Sualtim son of Roig. And at the feast Dechtire was thirsty, and they gave her a cup of wine, and as she was drinking it, a mayfly flew into the cup, and she drank it down with the wine. And presently she went into her sunny parlour, and her fifty maidens along with her, and she fell into a deep sleep. And in her sleep, Lugh of the Long Hand appeared to her, and he said: " It is I myself was the mayfly that came to you in the cup, and it is with me you must come away now, and your fifty maidens along with you." And he put on them the appearance of a flock of birds, and they went with him southward till they came to Brugh na Boinne, the dwelling-place of the Sidhe. And no one at Emain Macha could get tale or tidings of them, or know where they had gone, or what had happened them.

It was about a year after that time, there was another feast in Emain, and Conchubar and his chief men were sitting at the feast. And suddenly they saw from the window a great flock of birds, that lit on the ground and began to eat up everything before them, so that not so much as a blade of grass was left.

The men of Ulster were vexed when they saw the birds destroying all before them, and they yoked nine of their chariots to follow after them. Conchubar was in his own chariot, and there were following with him Fergus son of Rogh, and Laegaire Buadach, the Battle-Winner, and Celthair son of Uithecar, and many others, and Bricriu of the bitter tongue was along with them.

They followed after the birds across the whole country southward, across Slieve Fuad, by Ath Lethan, by Ath Garach and Magh Gossa, between Fir Rois and Fir Ardae; and the birds before them always. They were the most beautiful that had ever been seen; nine flocks of them there were, linked together two and two with a chain of silver, and at the head of every flock there were two birds of different colours, linked together with a chain of gold; and there were three birds that flew by themselves, and they all went before the chariots, to the far end of the country, until the fall of night, and then there was no more seen of them.

And when the dark night was coming on, Conchubar said to his people: "It is best for us to unyoke the chariots now, and to look for some place where we can spend the night."

Then Fergus went forward to look for some place, and what he came to was a very small poor-looking house. A man and a woman were in it, and when they saw him they said: "Bring your companions here along with you, and they will be welcome." Fergus went back to his companions and told them what he had seen. But Bricriu said: "Where is the use of going into a house like that, with neither room nor provisions nor coverings in it; it is not worth our while to be going there."

Then Bricriu went on himself to the place where the house was. But when he came to it, what he saw was a grand, new, well-lighted house; and at the door there was a young man wearing armour, very tall and handsome and shining. And he said: "Come into the house, Bricriu; why are you looking about you?" And there was a young woman beside him, fine and noble, and with curled hair, and she said: "Surely there is a welcome before you from me." "Why does she welcome me?" said Bricriu. "It is on account of her that I myself welcome you," said the young man. "And is there no one missing from you at Emain?" he said. "There is surely," said Bricriu. "We are missing fifty young girls for the length of a year." "Would you know them again if you saw them?" said the young man. "If I would not know them," said Bricriu, "it is because a year might make a change in them, so that I would not be sure." "Try and know them again," said the man, "for the fifty young girls are in this house, and this woman beside me is their mistress, Dechtire. It was they themselves, changed into birds, that went to Emain Macha to bring you here." Then Dechtire gave Bricriu a purple cloak with gold fringes; and he went back to find his companions. But while he was going he thought to himself: "Conchubar would give great treasure to find these fifty young girls again, and his sister along with them. I will not tell him I have found them. I will only say I have found a house with beautiful women in it, and no more than that."

When Conchubar saw Bricriu, he asked news of him. "What news do you bring back with you, Bricriu?" he said. "I came to a fine well-lighted house," said Bricriu; "I saw a queen, noble, kind, with royal looks, with curled hair; I saw a troop of women, beautiful, well-dressed; I saw the man of the house, tall and open-handed and shining." "Let us go there for the night," said Conchubar. So they brought their chariots and their horses and their arms; and they were hardly in the house when every sort of food and of drink, some they knew and some they did not know, was put before them, so that they never spent a better night. And when they had eaten and drunk and began to be satisfied, Conchubar said to the young man: "Where is the mistress of the house that she does not come to bid us welcome?" "You cannot see her to-night," said he, "for she is in the pains of childbirth."

So they rested there that night, and in the morning Conchubar was the first to rise up; but he saw no more of the man of the house, and what he heard was the cry of a child. And he went to the room it came from, and there he saw Dechtire, and her maidens about her, and a young child beside her. And she bade Conchubar welcome, and she told him all that had happened her, and that she had called him there to bring herself and the child back to Emain Macha. And Conchubar said: "It is well you have done by me, Dechtire; you gave shelter to me and to my chariots; you kept the cold from my horses; you gave food to me and my people, and now you have given us this good gift. And let our sister, Finchoem, bring up the child," he said. "No, it is not for her to bring him up, it is for me," said Sencha son of Ailell, chief judge and chief poet of Ulster. "For I am skilled; I am good in disputes; I am not forgetful; I speak before any one at all in the presence of the king; I watch over what he says; I give judgment in the quarrels of kings; I am judge of the men of Ulster; no one has a right to dispute my claim, but only Conchubar."

"If the child is given to me to bring up," said Blai, the distributer, "he will not suffer from want of care or from forgetfulness. It is my messages that do the will of Conchubar; I call up the fighting men from all Ireland; I am well able to provide for them for a week, or even for ten days; I settle their business and their disputes; I support their honour; I get satisfaction for their insults."

"You think too much of yourself," said Fergus. "It is I that will bring up the child; I am strong; I have knowledge; I am the king's messenger; no one can stand up against me in honour or riches; I am hardened to war and battles; I am a good craftsman; I am worthy to bring up a child. I am the protector of all the unhappy; the strong are afraid of me; I am the helper of the weak."

"If you will listen to me at last, now you are quiet," said Amergin, "I am able to bring up a child like a king. The people praise my honour, my bravery, my courage, my wisdom; they praise my good luck, my age, my speaking, my name, my courage, and my race. Though I am a fighter, I am a poet; I am worthy of the king's favour; I overcome all the men who fight from their chariots; I owe thanks to no one except Conchubar; I obey no one but the king."

Then Sencha said: "Let Finchoem keep the child until we come to Emain, and Morann, the judge, will settle the question when we are there"

So the men of Ulster set out for Emain, Finchoem having the child with her. And when they came there Morann gave his judgment. "It is for Conchubar," he said, "to help the child to a good name, for he is next of kin to him; let Sencha teach him words and speaking; let Fergus hold him on his knees; let Amergin be his tutor." And he said: "This child will be praised by all, by chariot drivers and fighters, by kings and by wise men; he shall be loved by many men; he will avenge all your wrongs; he will defend your fords; he will fight all your battles."

And so it was settled. And the child was left until he should come to sensible years, with his mother Dechtire and with her husband Sualtim. And they brought him up upon the plain of Muirthemne, and the name he was known by was Setanta, son of Sualtim.

II

BOY DEEDS OF CUCHULAIN

IT chanced one day, when Setanta was about seven years old, that he heard some of the people of his mother's house talking about King Conchubar's court at Emain Macha, and of the sons of kings and nobles that lived there, and that spent a great part of their time at games and at hurling. "Let me go and play with them there," he said to his mother. "It is too soon for you to do that," she said, "but wait till such time as you are able to travel so far, and till I can put you in charge of some one going to the court, that will put you under Conchubar's protection." "It would be too long for me to wait for that," he said, "but I will go there by myself if you will tell me the road." "It is too far for you," said Dechtire, "for it is beyond Slieve Fuad, Emain Macha is." "Is it east or west of Slieve Fuad?" he asked. And when she had answered him that, he set out there and then, and nothing with him but his hurling stick, and his silver ball, and his little dart and spear; and to shorten the road for himself he would give a blow to the ball and drive it from him, and then he would throw his hurling stick after it, and the dart after that again, and then he would make a run and catch them all in his hand before one of them would have reached the ground.

So he went on until he came to the lawn at Emain

7

Macha, and there he saw three fifties of king's sons hurling and learning feats of war. He went in among them, and when the ball came near him he got it between his feet, and drove it along in spite of them till he had sent it beyond the goal. There was great surprise and anger on them when they saw what he had done, and Follaman, King Conchubar's son, that was chief among them, cried out to them to come together and drive out this stranger and make an end of him. "For he has no right," he said, "to come into our game without asking leave, and without putting his life under our protection. And you may be sure," he said, "that he is the son of some common fighting man, and it is not for him to come into our game at all." With that they all made an attack on him, and began to throw their hurling sticks at him, and their balls and darts, but he escaped them all, and then he rushed at them, and began to throw some of them to the ground. Fergus came out just then from the palace, and when he saw what a good defence the little lad was making, he brought him in to where Conchubar was playing chess, and told him all that had happened. "This is no gentle game you have been playing," he said. "It is on themselves the fault is," said the boy; "I came as a stranger, and I did not get a stranger's welcome." "You did not know then," said Conchubar, "that no one can play among the boy troop of Emain unless he gets their leave and their protection." "I did not know that, or I would have asked it of them," he said. "What is your name and your family?" said Conchubar. My name is Setanta, son of Sualtim and of Dechtire," he said. When Conchubar knew that he was his sister's son, he gave him a great welcome, and he bade the boy troop to let him go safe among them. "We will do that," they said. But when they went out to play, Setanta began to break through them, and to overthrow them, so that they could not stand against him. "What are you wanting of them now?" said Conchubar. "I swear by the gods my people swear by," said the boy, "I will not lighten my hand off them till they have come under my protection the same way I have come under theirs." Then they all agreed to give in to this; and Setanta stayed in the king's house at Emain Macha, and all the chief men of Ulster had a hand in bringing him up.

There was a great smith in Ulster of the name of Culain, who made a feast at that time for Conchubar and for his people. When Conchubar was setting out to the feast, he passed by the lawn where the boy troop were at their games, and he watched them awhile, and he saw how the son of Dechtire was winning the goal from them all. "That little lad will serve Ulster yet," said Conchubar; "and call him to me now," he said, "and let him come with me to the smith's feast." "I cannot go with you now," said Setanta, when they had called to him, "for these boys have not had enough of play yet." "It would be too long for me to wait for you," said the king. "There is no need for you to wait; I will follow the track of the chariots," said Setanta.

So Conchubar went on to the smith's house, and there was a welcome before him, and fresh rushes were laid down, and there were poems and songs and recitals of laws, and the feast was brought in, and they began to be merry. And then Culain said to the king: "Will there be any one else of your people coming after you to-night?" "There will not," said Conchubar, for he forgot that he had told the little lad to follow him. "But why do you ask me that?" he said. "I have a great fierce hound," said the smith, "and when I take the chain off him, he lets no one come into the one district with himself, and he will obey no one but myself, and he has in him the strength of a hundred." "Loose him out," said Conchubar, "until he keeps a watch on the place." So Culain loosed him out, and the dog made a course round the whole district, and then he came back to the place where he was used to lie and to watch the house, and every one was in dread of him, he was so fierce and so cruel and so savage.

Now, as to the boys at Emain, when they were done playing, every one went to his father's house, or to whoever was in charge of him.   But Setanta set out on the track of the chariots, shortening the way for himself as he was used to do with his hurling stick and his ball. When he came to the lawn before the smith's house, the hound heard him coming, and began such a fierce yelling that he might have been heard through all Ulster, and he sprang at him as if he had a mind not to stop and tear him up at all, but to swallow him at the one mouthful.   The little fellow had no weapon but his stick and his ball, but when he saw the hound coming at him, he struck the ball with such force that it went down his throat, and through his body.   Then he seized him by the hind legs and dashed him against a rock until there was no life left in him.

When the men feasting within heard the outcry of the hound, Conchubar started up and said: "It is no good luck brought us on this journey, for that is surely my sister's son that was coming after me, and that has got his death by the hound."   On that all the men rushed out, not waiting to go through the door, but over walls and barriers as they could.   But Fergus was the first to get to where the boy was, and he took him up and lifted him on his shoulder, and brought him in safe and sound to Conchubar, and there was great joy on them all.

But Culain the smith went out with them, and when he saw his great hound lying dead and broken there was great grief in his heart, and he came in and said to Setanta: "There is no good welcome for you here." "What have you against the little lad?" said Conchubar.

"It was no good luck that brought him here, or that made me prepare this feast for yourself, King," he said; "for from this out, my hound being gone, my substance will be wasted, and my way of living will be gone astray. And, little boy," he said, "that was a good member of my family you took from me, for he was the protector of my goods and my flocks and my herds and of all that I had." "Do not be vexed on account of that," said the boy, "and I myself will make up to you for what I have done." "How will you do that?" said Conchubar. "This is how I will do it: if there is a whelp of the same breed to be had in Ireland, I will rear him and train him until he is as good a hound as the one killed; and until that time, Culain," he said, "I myself will be your watch-dog, to guard your goods and your cattle and your house." "You have made a fair offer," said Conchubar. "I could have given no better award myself," said Cathbad the Druid. "And from this out," he said, "your name will be Cuchulain, the Hound of Culain." "I am better pleased with my own name of Setanta, son of Sualtim," said the boy. "Do not say that," said Cathbad, "for all the men in the whole world will some day have the name of Cuchulain in their mouths." "If that is so, I am content to keep it," said the boy. And this is how he came by the name Cuchulain.

It was a good while after that, Cathbad the Druid was one day teaching the pupils in his house to the north-east of Emain. There were eight boys along with him that day, and one of them asked him: "Do your signs tell of any special thing this day is good or bad for?" "If any young man should take arms to-day," said Cathbad, "his name will be greater than any other name in Ireland. But his span of life will be short," he said.

Cuchulain was outside at play, but he heard what Cathbad said, and there and then he put off his playing suit, and he went straight to Conchubar's sleeping-room and said : "All good be with you, King!"   "What is it you are wanting?" said Conchubar.   "What I want is to take arms to-day."   "Who put that into your head?" "Cathbad the Druid," said Cuchulain.   "If that is so, I will not deny you," said Conchubar.   Then he gave him his choice of arms, and the boy tried his strength on them, and there were none that pleased him or that were strong enough for him but Conchubar's own.   So he gave him his own two spears, and his sword and his shield.

Just then Cathbad the Druid came in, and there was wonder on him, and he said : "Is it taking arms this young boy is?"   "He is indeed," said the king.   "It is sorry I would be to see his mother's son take arms on this day," said Cathbad.   "Was it not yourself bade him do it?" said the king.   "I did not surely," he said. "Then you have lied to me, boy," said Conchubar.   "I told no lie, King," said Cuchulain, "for it was he indeed put it in my mind when he was teaching the others, for when one of them asked him if there was any special virtue in this day, he said that whoever would for the first time take arms to-day, his name would be greater than any other in Ireland, and he did not say any harm would come on him, but that his life would be short." "And what I said is true," said Cathbad, "there will be fame on you and a great name, but your lifetime will not be long."   "It is little I would care," said Cuchulain, "if my life were to last one day and one night only, so long as my name and the story of what I had done would live after me."   Then Cathbad said : "Well, get into a chariot now, and let us see if it was the truth I spoke."

Then Cuchulain got into a chariot and tried its strength, and broke it to pieces, and he broke in the same way the seventeen chariots that Conchubar kept for the boy troop at Emain, and he said : "These chariots

are no use, Conchubar, they are not worthy of me."
"Where is Ibar, son of Riangabra?" said Conchubar.
"Here I am," he answered. "Make ready my own
chariot, and yoke my own horses to it for this boy to
try," said Conchubar. So he tried the king's chariot
and shook it and strained it, and it bore him. "This is
the chariot that suits me," he said. "Now, little one,"
said Ibar, "let us take out the horses and turn them
out to graze." "It is too early for that, Ibar; let us
drive on to where the boy troop are, that they may
wish me good luck on the day of my taking arms." So
they drove on, and all the lads shouted when they saw
him—"Have you taken arms?" "I have indeed," said
Cuchulain. "That you may do well in wounding and
in first killing and in spoil-winning," they said; "but
it is a pity for us, you to have left playing."

"Let the horses go graze now," said Ibar. "It is too
soon yet," said Cuchulain, "and tell me where does that
great road that goes by Emain lead to?" "It leads to
Ath-an-Foraire, the watchers' ford in Slieve Fuad," said
Ibar. "Why is it called the watchers' ford?" "It is
easy to tell that; it is because some choice champion of
the men of Ulster keeps watch there every day to do
battle for the province with any stranger that might
come to the boundary with a challenge." "Do you
know who is in it to-day?" said Cuchulain. "I know
well it is Conall Cearnach, the Victorious, the chief
champion of the young men of Ulster and of all
Ireland." "We will go on then to the ford," said
Cuchulain. So they went on across the plain, and at the
water's edge they found Conall, and he said: "And are
those arms you have taken to-day, little boy?" "They
are indeed," Ibar said for him. "May they bring him
triumph and victory and shedding of first blood," said
Conall. "But I think, little Hound," he said, "that you
are too ready to take them; for you are not fit as yet

to do a champion's work." "What is it you are doing here, Conall?" said the boy. "I am keeping watch and guard for the province." "Rise out of it, Conall," he said, "and for this one day let me keep the watch." "Do not ask that, little one," said Conall; "for you are not able yet to stand against trained fighting men." "Then I will go down to the shallows of Lough Echtra and see if I can redden my arms on either friend or enemy." "Then I will go with you myself," said Conall, "to take care of you and to protect you, that no harm may happen you." "Do not," said Cuchulain. "I will indeed," said Conall, "for if I let you go into a strange country alone, all Ulster would avenge it on me."

So Conall's horses were yoked to his chariot, and he set out to follow Cuchulain, for he had waited for no leave, but had set out by himself. When Cuchulain saw Conall coming up with him he thought to himself, "If I get a chance of doing some great thing, Conall will never let me do it." So he picked up a stone, the size of his fist, from the ground, and made a good cast at the yoke of Conall's chariot, so that he broke it, and the chariot came down, and Conall himself was thrown to the ground sideways. "What did you do that for?" he said. "It was to see could I throw straight, and if there was the making of a good champion in me." "Bad luck on your throwing and on yourself," said Conall. "And any one that likes may strike your head off now, for I will go with you no farther." "That is just what I wanted," said Cuchulain. And with that, Conall went back to his place at the ford.

As for the lad, he went on towards Lough Echtra in the south. Then Ibar said: "If you will listen to me, little one, I would like that we would go back now to Emain; for at this time the carving of the food is beginning there, and it is all very well for you that have your place kept for you between Conchubar's knees.

But as to myself," he said, "it is among the chariot-drivers and the jesters and the messengers I am, and I must find a place and fight for myself where I can." "What is that mountain before us?" said Cuchulain. "That is Slieve Mourne, and that is Finncairn, the white cairn, on its top." "Let us go to it," said Cuchulain. "We would be too long going there," said Ibar. "You are a lazy fellow," said Cuchulain; "and this my first adventure, and the first journey you have made with me." "And that it may be my last," said Ibar, "if ever I get back to Emain again." They went on then to the cairn. "Good Ibar," said the boy, "show me now all that we can see of Ulster, for I do not know my way about the country yet." So Ibar showed him from the cairn all there was to see of Ulster, the hills and the plains and the duns on every side. "What is that sloping square plain before us to the south?" "That is Magh Breagh, the fine meadow." "Show me the duns and strong places of that plain." So Ibar showed him Teamhair and Tailte, Cleathra and Cnobhach and the Brugh of Angus on the Boyne, and the dun of Nechtan Sceine's sons. "Are those the sons of Nechtan that say in their boasting they have killed as many Ulstermen as there are living in Ulster to-day?" "They are the same," said Ibar. "On with us then to that dun," said Cuchulain. "No good will come to you through saying that," said Ibar; "and whoever may go there I will not go," he said. "Alive or dead, you must go there for all that," said Cuchulain. "Then if so, it is alive I will go there," said Ibar, "and it is dead I will be before I leave it."

They went on then to the dun of Nechtan's sons, and when they came to the green lawn, Cuchulain got out of the chariot, and there was a pillar-stone on the lawn, and an iron collar about it, and there was Ogham writing on it that said no man that came there, and he carrying arms, should leave the place without giving a challenge to some one of the people of the dun. When Cuchulain had read the Ogham, he put his arms around the stone and threw it into the water that was there at hand. "I don't see it is any better there than where it was before," said Ibar; "and it is likely this time you will get what you are looking for, and that is a quick death." "Good Ibar," said the boy, "spread out the coverings of the chariot now for me, until I sleep for a while." "It is no good thing you are going to do," said Ibar, "to be going to sleep in an enemy's country." He put out the coverings then, and Cuchulain lay down and fell asleep.

It was just at that time, Foill, son of Nechtan Sceine, came out, and when he saw the chariot, he called out to Ibar, "Let you not unyoke those horses." "I was not going to unyoke them," said Ibar; "the reins are in my hands yet." "What horses are they?" "They are Conchubar's two speckled horses." "So I thought when I saw them," said Foill. "And who is it has brought them across our boundaries?" "A young little lad," said Ibar, "that has taken arms to-day for luck, and it is to show himself off he has come across Magh Breagh." "May he never have good luck," said Foill, "and if he were a fighting man, it is not alive but dead he would go back to Emain to-day." "Indeed he is not able to fight, or it could not be expected of him," said Ibar, "and he but a child that should be in his father's house." At that the boy lifted his head from the ground, and it is red his face was, and his whole body, at hearing so great an insult put on him, and he said: "I am indeed well able to fight." But Foill said: "I am more inclined to think you are not." "You will soon know what to think," said the boy, "and let us go down now to the ford. But go first and get your armour," he said, "for I would not like to kill an un-

armed man." There was anger on Foill then, and he
went running to get his arms. "You must have a care
now," said Ibar, "for that is Foill, son of Nechtan, and
neither point of spear or edge of sword can harm him."
"That suits me very well," said the boy. With that
out came Foill again, and Cuchulain stood up to him,
and took his iron ball in his hand, and hurled it at his
head, and it went through the forehead and out at the
back of his head, and his brains along with it, so that
the air could pass through the hole it made. And
then Cuchulain struck off his head.

Then Tuachel, the second son of Nechtan, came out
on the lawn. "It is likely you are making a great
boast of what you are after doing," he said. "I see
nothing to boast of in that," said Cuchulain, "a single
man to have fallen by me." "You will not have long to
boast of it," said Tuachel, "for I myself am going to
make an end of you on the moment." "Then go back
and bring your arms," said Cuchulain, "for it is only a
coward would come out without arms." He went back
into the house then, and Ibar said: "You must have a
care now, for that is Tuachel, son of Nechtan, and if he
is not killed by the first stroke, or the first cast, or the
first thrust, he cannot be killed at all, for there is no way
of getting at him after that." "You need not be telling
me that, Ibar," said Cuchulain, "for it is Conchubar's
great spear, the Venomous, I will take in my hand, and
that is the last thrust that will be made at him, for after
that, there is no physician will heal his wounds for ever."

Then Tuachel came out on the lawn, and Cuchulain
took hold of the great spear, and made a cast at him,
that went through his shield and broke three of his ribs,
and made a hole through his heart. And then he struck
his head off, before the body reached the ground.

Then Fainnle, the youngest of the three sons of
Nechtan, came out. "Those were foolish fellows," he

said, "to come at you the way they did. But come out
now, after me," he said, "into the water where your
feet will not touch the bottom," and with that he made a
plunge into the water. "Mind yourself well now," said
Ibar, "for that is Fainnle, the Swallow, and it is why
that name was put on him, he travels across water with
the swiftness of a swallow, and there is not one of the
swimmers of the whole world can come near him." "It
is not to me you should be saying that," said Cuchulain,
"for you know the river Callan that runs through
Emain, and it is what I used to do," he said, "when the
boy troop would break off from their games and plunge
into the river to swim, I used to take a boy of them on
each shoulder and a boy on each hand, and I would
bring them through the river without so much as to wet
my back." With that he made a leap into the water,
where it was very deep, and himself and Fainnle
wrestled together, and then he got a grip of him, and
gave him a blow of Conchubar's sword, and struck his
head off, and he let his body go away down the stream.

Then he and Ibar went into the house and destroyed
what was in it, and they set fire to it, and left it burning,
and turned back towards Slieve Fuad, and they brought
the heads of the three sons of Nechtan along with them.

Presently they saw a herd of wild deer before them.
"What sort of cattle are those?" said the boy. "They
are not cattle, but the wild deer of the dark places of
Slieve Fuad." "Make the horses go faster," said Cuchulain, "until we can see them better." But with all their
galloping the horses could not come up with the wild
deer. Then Cuchulain got down from the chariot and
raced and ran after them until two stags lay moaning
and panting from the hardness of their run through the
wet bog, and he bound them to the back of the chariot
with the thongs of it. Then they went on till they came
to the plain of Emain, and there they saw a flock of white

swans that were whiter than the swans of Conchubar's lake, and Cuchulain asked where they came from. "They are wild swans," said Ibar, "that are come from the rocks and the islands of the great sea to feed on the low levels of the country." "Would it be best to take them alive or to kill them?" "It would be best to take them alive," said Ibar, "for many a one kills them, and many a one makes casts at them, but you would hardly find any one at all would bring them in alive." With that, Cuchulain put a little stone in his sling and made a cast, and brought down eight birds of them, and then he put a bigger stone in, and with it he brought down sixteen more. "Get out now, Ibar," he said, "and bring me the birds here." "I will not," said Ibar, "for it would not be easy to stop the horses the way they are going now, and if I leap out, the iron wheels of the chariot will cut through me, or the horns of the stags will make a hole in me." "You are no good of a warrior, Ibar; but give me the reins and I will quiet the horses and the stags." So then Ibar went and brought in the swans, and tied them, and they alive, to the chariot and to the harness. And it is like that they went on till they came to Emain.

It was Levarcham, daughter of Aedh, the conversation woman and messenger to the king, that was there at that time, and was sometimes away in the hills, was the first to see them coming. "There is a chariot-fighter coming, Conchubar," she said, "and he is coming in anger. He has the bleeding heads of his enemies with him in the chariot, and wild stags are bound to it, and white birds are bearing him company. By the oath of my people!" she said, "if he comes on us with his anger still upon him, the best of the men of Ulster will fall by his hand." "I know that chariot-fighter," said Conchubar. "It is the young lad, the son of Dechtire, that went over the boundaries this very day. He has surely reddened his hand, and if his anger cannot be cooled, the young men of Emain will be in danger from him," he said.

Then they all consulted together, and it is what they agreed, to send out three fifties of the women of Emain red-naked to meet him. When the boy saw the women coming, there was shame on him, and he leaned down his head into the cushions of the chariot, and hid his face from them. And the wildness went out of him, and his feasting clothes were brought, and water for washing; and there was a great welcome before him.

This is the story of the boy deeds of Cuchulain, as it was told by Fergus to Ailell and to Maeve at the time of the war for the Brown Bull of Cuailgne.

III

THE COURTING OF EMER

WHEN Cuchulain was growing out of his boyhood at Emain Macha, all the women of Ulster loved him for his skill in feats, for the lightness of his leap, for the weight of his wisdom, for the sweetness of his speech, for the beauty of his face, for the loveliness of his looks, for all his gifts. He had the gift of caution in fighting, until such time as his anger would come on him, and the hero light would shine about his head; the gift of feats, the gift of chess-playing, the gift of draught-playing, the gift of counting, the gift of divining, the gift of right judgment, the gift of beauty. And all the faults they could find in him were three, that he was too young and smooth-faced, so that young men who did not know him would be laughing at him, that he was too daring, and that he was too beautiful.

The men of Ulster took counsel together then about Cuchulain, for their women and their maidens loved him greatly, and it is what they settled among themselves, that they would seek out a young girl that would be a fitting wife for him, the way that their own wives and their daughters would not be making so much of him. And besides that they were afraid he might die young, and leave no heir after him.

So Conchubar sent out nine men into each of the provinces of Ireland to look for a wife for Cuchulain, to see if in any dun or in any chief place, they could find the

daughter of a king or of an owner of land or a house-
holder, who would be pleasing to him, that he might
ask her in marriage.

All the messengers came back at the end of a year,
but not one of them had found a young girl that would
please Cuchulain.   And then he himself went out to
court a young girl he knew in Luglochta Loga, the
Garden of Lugh, Emer, the daughter of Forgall Manach,
the Wily.

He set out in his chariot, that all the chariots of
Ulster could not follow by reason of its swiftness, and of
the chariot chief who sat in it.   And he found the
young girl on her playing field, with her companions
about her, daughters of the landowners that lived
near Forgall's dun, and they learning needlework and
fine embroidery from Emer.   And of all the young
girls of Ireland, she was the one Cuchulain thought
worth courting; for she had the six gifts—the gift of
beauty, the gift of voice, the gift of sweet speech, the
gift of needlework, the gift of wisdom, the gift of
chastity.   And Cuchulain had said that no woman
should marry him but one that was his equal in age, in
appearance, and in race, in skill and handiness; and one
who was the best worker with her needle of the young
girls of Ireland, for that would be the only one would
be a fitting wife for him.   And that is why it was Emer
he went to ask above all others.

And it was in his rich clothes he went out that day, his
crimson five-folded tunic, and his brooch of inlaid gold,
and his white hooded shirt, that was embroidered with
red gold.   And as the young girls were sitting together
on their bench on the lawn, they heard coming towards
them the clatter of hoofs, the creaking of a chariot, the
cracking of straps, the grating of wheels, the rushing
of horses, the clanking of arms.   "Let one of you see,"
said Emer, "what is it that is coming towards us."   And

Fiall, daughter of Forgall, went out and met him, and he came with her to the place where Emer and her companions were, and he wished a blessing to them. Then Emer lifted up her lovely face and saw Cuchulain, and she said, "May the gods make smooth the path before you." "And you," he said, "may you be safe from every harm." "Where are you come from?" she asked him. And he answered her in riddles, that her companions might not understand him, and he said, "From Intide Emna." "Where did you sleep?" "We slept," he said, "in the house of the man that tends the cattle of the plain of Tethra." "What was your food there?" "The ruin of a chariot was cooked for us," he said. "Which way did you come?" "Between the two mountains of the wood." "Which way did you take after that?" "That is not hard to tell," he said. "From the Cover of the Sea, over the Great Secret of the Tuatha De Danaan, and the Foam of the horses of Emain, over the Morrigu's Garden, and the Great Sow's back; over the Valley of the Great Dam, between the God and his Druid; over the Marrow of the Woman, between the Boar and his Dam; over the Washing-place of the horses of Dea; between the King of Ana and his servant, to Mandchuile of the Four Corners of the World; over Great Crime and the Remnants of the Great Feast; between the Vat and the Little Vat, to the Gardens of Lugh, to the daughters of Tethra, the nephew of the King of the Fomor." "And what account have you to give of yourself?" said Emer. "I am the nephew of the man that disappears in another in the wood of Badb," said Cuchulain.

"And now, maiden," he said, "what account have you to give of yourself?" "That is not hard to tell," said Emer, "for what should a maiden be but Teamhair upon the hills, a watcher that sees no one, an eel hiding in the water, a rush out of reach. The daughter of a king should be a flame of hospitality, a road that cannot be entered. And I have champions that follow me," she said, "to keep me from whoever would bring me away against their will, and against the will and the knowledge of Forgall, the dark king."

"Who are the champions that follow you, maiden?" said Cuchulain.

"It is not hard to tell you that," said Emer. "Two of the name of Lui; two Luaths; Luath and Lath Goible, sons of Tethra; Triath and Trescath; Brion and Bolor; Bas, son of Omnach; the eight Condla, and Cond, son of Forgall. Every man of them has the strength of a hundred and the feats of nine. And it would be hard for me," she said, "to tell of all the many powers Forgall has himself. He is stronger than any labouring man, more learned than any Druid, more quick of mind than any poet. You will have more than your games to do when you fight against Forgall, for many have told of his power and of the strength of his doings."

"Why do you not count me as a strong man as good as those others?" said Cuchulain. "Why would I not indeed, if your doings had been spoken of like theirs?" she said. "I swear by the oath of my people," said Cuchulain, "I will make my doings be spoken of among the great doings of heroes in their strength." "What is your strength, then?" said Emer. "That is easily told; when my strength in fighting is weakest I defend twenty; a third part of my strength is enough for thirty; in my full strength I fight alone against forty; and a hundred are safe under my protection. For dread of me, fighting men avoid fords and battles; armies and armed men go backward from the fear of my face."

"That is a good account for a young boy," said Emer, "but you have not reached yet to the strength of chariot chiefs." "But, indeed," said Cuchulain, "it is well I have been reared by Conchubar, my dear foster-father. It is not as a countryman strives to bring up his children, between the flags and the kneading trough, between the fire and the wall, on the floor of the one room, that Conchubar has brought me up; but it is among chariot chiefs and heroes, among jesters and Druids, among poets and learned men, among landowners and farmers of Ulster I have been reared, so that I have all their manners and their gifts."

"Who are these men, then, that have brought you up to do the things you are boasting of?" said Emer.

"That is easily told," he said. "Fair-speaking Sencha taught me wisdom and right judgment; Blai, lord of lands, my kinsman, took me to his house, so that I have entertained the men of Conchubar's province; Fergus brought me up to fights and to battles, so that I am able to use my strength. I stood by the knee of Amergin the poet, he was my tutor, so that I can stand up to any man, I can make praises for the doings of a king. Finchoem helped to rear me, so that Conall Cearnach is my foster-brother. Cathbad of the Gentle Face taught me, for the sake of Dechtire, so that I understand the arts of the Druids, and I have learned all the goodness of knowledge. All the men of Ulster have had a hand in bringing me up, chariot-drivers and chiefs of chariots, kings and chief poets, so that I am the darling of the whole army, so that I fight for the honour of all alike. And as to yourself, Emer," he said, "what way have you been reared in the Garden of Lugh?"

"It is easy to tell you that," said Emer. "I was brought up," she said, "in ancient virtues, in lawful behaviour, in the keeping of chastity, in stateliness of form, in the rank of a queen, in all noble ways among the women of Ireland." "These are good virtues indeed," said Cuchulain. "And why, then, would it not be right for us two to become one? For up to this time," he said, "I have never found a young girl

able to hold talk with me the way you have done."
"Have you no wife already?" said Emer. "I have
not, indeed." "I may not marry before my sister
is married," she said then, "for she is older than
myself." "Truly, it is not with your sister, but with
yourself, I have fallen in love," said Cuchulain.

While they were talking like this, Cuchulain saw
the breasts of the maiden over the bosom of her dress,
and he said: "Fair is this plain, the plain of the noble
yoke." And Emer said, "No one comes to this plain
who does not overcome as many as a hundred on each
ford, from the ford at Ailbine to Banchuig Arcait."

"Fair is the plain, the plain of the noble yoke," said
Cuchulain. "No one comes to this plain," said she,
"who does not go out in safety from Samhain to Oilmell,
and from Oilmell to Beltaine, and again from Beltaine
to Bron Trogain."

"Everything you have commanded, so it will be done
by me," said Cuchulain.

"And the offer you have made me, it is accepted, it
is taken, it is granted," said Emer.

With that Cuchulain left the place, and they talked
no more with one another on that day.

When he was driving across the plain of Bregia, Laeg,
his chariot-driver, asked him, "What, now, was the
meaning of the words you and the maiden Emer were
speaking together?" "Do you not know," said Cuchulain, "that I came to court Emer? And it is for this
reason we put a cloak on our words, that the young girls
with her might not understand what I had come for.
For if Forgall knew it, he would not consent to it, but to
you, Laeg," he said, "I will tell the meaning of our talk.

"'Where did you come from,' said she. 'From Intide
Emna,' said I, and I meant by that, from Emain Macha.
For it took its name from Macha, daughter of Aed the
Red, one of the three kings of Ireland. When he died

Macha asked for the kingship, but the sons of Dithorba said they would not give kingship to a woman. So she fought against them and routed them, and they went as exiles to the wild places of Connaught. And after a while she went in search of them, and she took them by treachery, and brought them all in one chain to Ulster. The men of Ulster wanted to kill them, but she said, ' No, for that would be a disgrace on my good government. But let them be my servants,' she said, ' and let them dig a rath for me, that shall be the chief seat of Ulster for ever.' Then she marked out the rath for them with the gold pin on her neck, and its name came from that; a brooch in the neck of Macha.

" The man, in whose house we slept, is Ronca, the fisherman of Conchubar. ' A man that tends cattle,' I said. For he catches fish on his line under the sea, and the fish are the cattle of the sea, and the sea is the plain of Tethra, a king of the kings of the Fomor.

" ' Our food was the ruin of a chariot,' I said. For a foal was cooked for us on the hearth, and it is the horse that holds up the chariot.

" ' Between the two mountains of the wood,' I said. These are the two mountains between which we came, Slieve Fuad to the west, and Slieve Cuilinn to the east of us, and we were in Oircil between them, the wood that is between the two.

" ' The road,' I said, ' from the Cover of the Sea.' That is from the plain of Muirthemne. And it is from this it got its name; there was at one time a magic sea on it, with a sea turtle in it that was used to suck men down, until the Dagda came with his club of anger and sang these words, so that it ebbed away on the moment :—

> ' Silence on your hollow head ;
> Silence on your dark body ;
> Silence on your dark brow.'

" ' Over the Great Secret of the men of Dea,' I said. That

is a wonderful secret and a wonderful whisper, because
it was there that the gathering to the battle of Magh
Tuireadh was first whispered of by the Tuatha De Danaan.

"'Over the horses of Emain,' I said. When Ema
Nemed, son of Nama, reigned over the Gael, he had his
two horses reared for him in Sidhe Ercman of the Tuatha
De Danaan, and when those horses were let loose from
the Sidhe, a bright stream burst out after them, and the
foam spread over the land for a great length of time,
and was there to the end of a year, so that the water
was called Uanib, that is, foam on the water, and it is
Uanib to-day.

"'The Back of the Great Sow,' I said. That is
Drimne Breg, the Ridge of Bregin. For the shape of
a sow appeared to the sons of Milid on every hill and on
every height in Ireland, when they came over the sea,
and wanted to land by force, after a spell had been cast
on it by the Tuatha De Danaan.

"'The Valley of the Great Dam,' I said, 'between the
God and his Druid.' That is, between Angus Og of the
Sidhe of the Brugh and his Druid, to the west of the
Brugh, and between them was the one woman, the wife
of the Smith. That is the way I went, between the hill
of the Sidhe of the Brugh where Angus is, and the Sidhe
of Bresal, the Druid.

"'Over the Marrow of the Woman,' I said. That
is the Boinne, and it gets its name from Boann, the
wife of Nechtan, son of Labraid. She went down
to the hidden well at the bottom of the dun with the
three cup-bearers of Nechtan, Flex and Lex and Luam.
No one came back from that well without blemish unless the three cup-bearers went with him. But the
queen went out of pride and overbearing to the well,
and it is what she said, that nothing would spoil her
shape or put a blemish on her. She passed left-hand-
wise round the well, to mock at its powers. Then three

waves broke over her and bruised her two knees and her right hand and one of her eyes, and she ran out of the dun to escape until she came to the sea, and wherever she ran, the water followed after her. Segain was its name on the dun; the River Segsa from the dun to the Pool of Mochua; the hand of the wife of Nechtan and the knee of the wife of Nechtan after that; the Boinne in Meath; Arcait it is called from the Finda to the Troma; the Marrow of the Woman from the Troma to the sea.

"'The Boar,' I said, 'and his Dam.' That is, between Cleitech and Fessi. For Cleitech is the name for a boar, but it is also the name for a king, the leader of great hosts, and Fessi is the name for the great sow of a farmer's house.

"'The King of Ana,' I said, 'and his servant.' That is Cerna, through which we passed, and that is its name since Enna Aignech put Cerna, king of Ana, to death on that hill, and he put his steward to death in the east of that place.

"'The Washing of the Horses of Dea,' I said. That is Ange, for in it the men of Dea washed their horses when they came from the battle of Magh Tuireadh. And it was called Ange, because the Tuatha De Danaan washed their horses in it.

"'The Four-cornered Mandchuile,' I said. That is Muincille. It is there Mann, the farmer, was, and there he made spells in his great four-cornered chambers underground, to keep off the plague from the cattle of Ireland in the time of Bresel Brec, king of Leinster.

"'Great Crime,' I said. That is Ailbine. There was a king here in Ireland, Ruad, son of Rigdond of Munster. He had an appointment of meeting with foreigners, and he set out for the meeting round the south of Alban with three ships, and thirty men were in each ship. But the ships were stopped, and were held from below in the middle of the sea, and throwing jewels and precious

things into the sea did not get them off.   Then lots
were cast among them who should go into the sea
and find out what was holding them.   The lot fell on
the king himself, Ruad, son of Rigdond, and he leaped
into the sea, and it closed over him.   He lit upon a
large plain, where nine beautiful women met him, and
they confessed that it was they themselves had stopped
the ships, the way that he might come to them.   And
he stopped with them nine days, and they gave him
nine vessels of gold; and through the length of that
time his men were not able to go on, through the
power of the women.   When he was going away, a
woman of them said she would bear him a son, and
that he must come back to them and bring away his
son, when he would be coming from the east.

"Then he joined his men, and they went on their
voyage, and they stopped away seven years, and then
they came back by a different way, and they did not
go near the same spot.   They landed in the bay, and
the sea-women came up to them there, and the men
heard them playing music in their brazen ship.   And
then the women came to the shore, and they put the
boy out of the ship on the land where the men were.
And the harbour was stony and rocky, and the boy
slipped and fell on one of the rocks, so that he died
there.   And the women saw it, and they cried all together, 'Olbine, Olbine,' that is 'Great Crime.'   And
it is from that it is called Ailbine.

"'The Remnants of the Great Feast,' I said.   That is
Tailne.   It was there the great feast was given to Lugh,
son of Ethlenn, to comfort him after the battle of Magh
Tuireadh, for that was his wedding feast of kingship.

"'In the Garden of Lugh, to the daughters of Tethra's
nephew,' I said; for Forgall Manach is sister's son of
Tethra, king of the Fomor.

"As to the account of myself I gave her, there are

two rivers in the land of Ross; Conchubar is the name
of one of them, and it mixes with the other; and I am
the nephew of Conchubar; and as to the plague that
comes on dogs, it is wild fierceness, and truly I am a
strong fighter of that plague, for I am wild and fierce in
battles and in fights. And the Wood of Badb, that is
the land of Ross, the Wood of the Morrigu, the Battle
Crow, the Goddess of Battle.

"And when she said that no man should come to the
plain of her breasts until he had killed three times nine
men with one blow, and yet had saved one man from
each nine, it is what she meant, that three brothers of
her own will be guarding her, Ibur and Seibur and Catt,
and a company of nine with each of them. And it is
what I must do, I must strike a blow on each nine, from
which eight will die, but no stroke will reach any of her
brothers among them; and I must carry her and her
foster-sister, with their share of gold and silver, out of
the dun of Forgall.

"'Go out from Samhain to Oimell,' she said. That
is, that I shall fight without harm to myself from
Samhain, the end of summer, to Oimell, the beginning
of spring; and from the beginning of spring to Beltaine,
and from that to Bron Trogain. For Oi, in the
language of poetry, is a name for sheep, and Oimell is
the time when the sheep come out and are milked, and
Suain is a gentle sound, and it is at Samhain that gentle
voices sound; and Beltaine is a favouring fire; for it is
at that time the Druids used to make fires with spells
and to drive the cattle between them against the plagues
every year. And Bron Trogain, that is the beginning
of autumn, for it is then the earth is in labour, that is, the
earth under fruit, Bron Trogain, the trouble of the earth."

Then Cuchulain went on his way, and he slept that
night in Emain Macha.

When Forgall came back to his dun, and his lords of land with him, their daughters were telling them of the young man that had come in a splendid chariot, and how himself and Emer had been talking together, and they could not understand their talk with one another. The lords of land told this to Forgall, and it is what he said, "You may be sure it is the mad boy from Emain Macha has been here, and he and the girl have fallen in love with one another. But they will gain nothing by that," he said; "for it is I will hinder them."

With that Forgall went out to Emain, with the appearance of a foreigner on him, and he gave out that he was sent by the king of the Gall, to speak with Conchubar, and to bring him a present of golden treasures, and wine of the Gall, and many other things. And he brought some of his men with him, and there was a great welcome before them.

And on the third day, Cuchulain and Conall and other chariot chiefs of Ulster were praised before him, and he said it was right for them to be praised, and that they did wonderful feats, and Cuchulain above them all. But he said that if Cuchulain would go to Scathach, the woman-warrior that lived in the east of Alban, his skill would be more wonderful still, for he could not have perfect knowledge of the feats of a warrior without that.

But his reason for saying this was that he thought if Cuchulain set out, he would never come back again, through the dangers he would put around him on the journey, and through the wildness and the fierceness of the people about Scathach.

So then Forgall went home, and Cuchulain rose up in the morning, and made ready to set out for Alban, and Laegaire Buadach, the Battle Winner, and Conall Cearnach said they would go with him. But first Cuchulain went across the plain of Bregia to visit Emer, and to talk with her before going in the ship. And she told him how it was Forgall had gone to Emain, and had advised him to go and learn warriors' feats, the way they two might not meet again. Then each of them promised to be true to the other till they would meet again, unless death should come between them, and they said farewell to one another, and Cuchulain turned towards Alban.

When they came there, they stopped for a while at the forge of Donall, the smith, and then they set out to go to the east of Alban. But before they had gone far, a vision came before their eyes of Emain Macha, and Laegaire and Conall were not able to pass by it, and they turned back. It was Forgall raised that vision, to draw them away from Cuchulain, that he might be in the more danger, being alone. Then Cuchulain went on by himself on a strange road, and he was sad and tired and down-hearted for the loss of his comrades, but he held to his word that he would not go back to Emain without finding Scathach, even if he should die in the attempt.

But now he was astray and ignorant, and not knowing which way to take, and he saw a terrible great beast like a lion coming towards him, and it watching him, but it did not try to harm him. Whatever way he went, the beast went before him, and then it stopped and turned its side to him. So he made a leap and was on its back, and he did not guide it, but went whatever way it chose. They travelled like that through four days, till they came to the end of the bounds of men, and to an island where lads were rowing in a small loch; and the lads began to laugh when they saw a beast of that sort, and a man riding it. And then Cuchulain leaped off, and the beast left him, and he bade it farewell.

He passed on till he came to a large house in a deep

valley, and a comely young girl in it, and she spoke to
him, and bade him welcome. "A welcome before you,
Cuchulain," she said. He asked her how did she know
him, and she said, "I was a foster-child of Wulfkin, the
Saxon, the time you came there to learn sweet speech
from him." And she gave him meat and drink, and he
went away from her. Then he met with a young man,
and he gave him the same welcome, and he said his
name was Eochu, and they talked together, and
Cuchulain asked him what was the way to Scathach's
dun. The young man told him the way, across the
Plain of Ill-Luck, that lay before him, and he said that
on the near side of the plain the feet of men would stick
fast, and on the far side every blade of grass would rise
and hold them fast on its points. And he gave him a
wheel, and bade him to follow its track across the one
half of the plain. And he gave him an apple along
with that, and bade him to throw it, and to follow the
way it went, till he would reach the end of the plain.
And he told him many other things that would happen
him, and how he would win a great name at the last.
And then each of them wished a blessing to the other,
and Cuchulain did as he bade him, and so he got across
the plain and went on his journey. And then, as the
young man had told him, he came to a valley, and it
full of monsters, sent there by Forgall to destroy him,
and only one narrow path through it, but he went
through it safely. And after that his road led through
a terrible, wild mountain. Then he came to the place
where Scathach's scholars were, and among them he
saw Ferdiad, son of Daman, and Naoise, Ainnle, and
Ardan, the three sons of Usnach, and when they knew
that he was from Ireland they welcomed him with
kisses, and asked for news of their own country. He
asked them where was Scathach. "In that island
beyond," they said. "What way must I take to reach

her ?" he asked.   "By the bridge of the cliff," they said,
"and no man can cross it till he has proved himself a
champion, and many a king's son has got his death
there."

And this is the way the bridge was : the two ends of
it were low, and the middle was high, and whenever
any one would leap on it, the first time it would narrow
till it was as narrow as the hair of a man's head, and the
second time it would shorten till it was as short as an
inch, and the third time it would get slippery till it was
as slippery as an eel of the river, and the fourth time
it would rise up on high against you till it was as tall as
the mast of a ship.

All the warriors and people on the lawn came down
to see Cuchulain making his attempt to cross the bridge,
and he tried three times to do it, and he could not, and
the others were laughing at him, that he should think
he could cross it, and he so young.   Then his anger
came on him, and the hero light shone round his head,
and it was not the appearance of a man that was on
him, but the appearance of a god ; and he leaped upon
the end of the bridge and made the hero's salmon leap,
so that he landed on the middle of it, and he reached the
other end of the bridge before it could raise itself fully
up, and threw himself from it, and was on the ground of
the island where Scathach's sunny house was, and it
having seven great doors, and seven great windows
between every two doors, and three times fifty couches
between every two windows, and three times fifty young
girls, with scarlet cloaks and beautiful blue clothing on
them, waiting on Scathach.

And Scathach's daughter, Uacthach, was sitting by a
window, and when she saw the young man, and he a
stranger, and comeliest of the men of Ireland, making
his attempt to cross the bridge, she loved him, and her
face and her colour began to change continually, so

that now she would be as white as a little flower, and
then again she would grow crimson red. And in her
needlework that she was doing, she would put the gold
thread where the silver thread should be, and the silver
thread in the place where the gold thread should be.
And when Scathach saw that, she said : " I think this
young man has pleased you." And Uacthach said:
" There would be great grief on me indeed, were he not
to return alive to his own people, in whatever part of the
world they may be, for I know there is surely some one
to whom it would be great anguish to know the way he
is now."

Then, when Cuchulain had crossed the bridge, he
went up to the house, and struck the door with the
shaft of his spear, so that it went through it. And
when Scathach was told that, she said, " Truly this
must be some one who has finished his training in some
other place." Then Uacthach opened the door for
him, and he asked for Scathach, and Uacthach told
him where she was, and what he had best do when he
found her. So he went out to the place where she was
teaching her two sons, Cuar and Cett, under the great
yew-tree; and he took his sword and put its point
between her breasts, and he threatened her with a
dreadful death if she would not take him as her pupil,
and if she would not teach him all her own skill in
arms. So she promised him she would do that.

Now it was while Cuchulain was with Scathach that
a great king in Munster, Lugaid, son of Ros, went
northward with twelve chariot chiefs to look for a wife
among the daughters of the men of Mac Rossa, but
they had all been promised before.

And when Forgall Manach heard this, he went to
Emain, and he told Lugaid that the best of the maidens
of Ireland, both as to form and behaviour and handiwork, was in his house unwed. Lugaid said he was

well pleased to hear that, and Forgall promised him his daughter Emer in marriage. And to the twelve chariot chiefs that were with him, he promised twelve daughters of twelve lords of land in Bregia, and Lugaid went back with him to his dun for the wedding.

But whem Emer was brought to Lugaid to sit by his side, she laid one of her hands on each side of his face, and she said on the truth of her good name and of her life, that it was Cuchulain she loved, although her father was against him, and that no one that was an honourable man should force her to be his wife.

Then Lugaid did not dare take her, for he was in dread of Cuchulain, and so he returned home again.

As to Cuchulain, after he had been a good time with Scathach, a war began between herself and Aoife, queen of the tribes that were round about. The armies were going out to fight, but Cuchulain was not with them, for Scathach had given him a sleeping-drink that would keep him safe and quiet till the fight would be over, for she was afraid some harm would come to him if he met Aoife, for she was the greatest woman-warrior in the world, and she understood enchantments and witchcraft. But after one hour, Cuchulain started up out of his sleep, for the sleeping-drink that would have held any other man for a day and a night, held him for only that length of time. And he followed after the army, and he met with the two sons of Scathach, and they three went against the three sons of Ilsuanach, three of the best warriors of Aoife, and it was by Cuchulain they were killed, one after the other.

On the morning of the morrow the fight was begun again, and the two sons of Scathach were going up the path of feats to fight against three others of the best champions of Aoife, Cire, Bire, and Blaicne, sons of Ess Enchenn. When Scathach saw them going up she gave a sigh, for she was afraid for her two sons, but just then Cuchulain came up with them, and he leaped before them on to the path of feats, and met the three champions, and all three fell by him.

When Aoife saw that her best champions were after being killed, she challenged Scathach to fight against herself, but Cuchulain went out in her place. And before he went, he asked Scathach, "What things does Aoife think most of in all the world?" "Her two horses and her chariot and her chariot-driver," said Scathach.

So then Cuchulain and Aoife attacked one another and began a fierce fight, and she broke Cuchulain's spear in pieces, and his sword she broke off at the hilt. Then Cuchulain called out, "Look, the chariot and the horses and the driver of Aoife are fallen down into the valley and are lost!" At that Aoife looked about her, and Cuchulain took a sudden hold of her, and lifted her on his shoulders, and brought her down to where the army was, and laid her on the ground, and held his sword to her breast, and she begged for her life, and he gave it to her. And after that she made peace with Scathach, and bound herself by sureties not to go against her again. And she gave her love to Cuchulain; and out of that love great sorrow came afterwards.

And as Cuchulain was going home by the narrow path, he met an old hag, and she blind of the left eye. She asked him to leave room for her to pass by, but he said there was no room on that path, unless he would throw himself down the great sea-cliff that was on the one side of it. But she asked him again to leave the road to her, and he would not refuse, and he dropped down the cliff, with only his one hand keeping a hold of the path. Then she came up, and as she passed him, she gave a hit of her foot at his hand, the way he would leave his hold and drop into the sea. But at that, he gave a leap up again on the path, and struck off the hag's head. For she was Ess Enchenn, the mother of the last three warriors that had fallen by him, and it was to destroy him she had come out to meet him, for she knew that under his rules of championship, he would make way for her when she asked it.

After that, he stayed for another while with Scathach, until he had learned all the arts of war and all the feats of a champion; and then a message came to him to come back to his own country, and he bade her farewell. And Scathach told him what would happen him in the time to come, for she had the Druid gift; and she told him there were great dangers before him, and that he would have to fight against great armies, and he alone; and that he would scatter his enemies, so that his name would come again to Alban; but that his life would not be long, for he would die in his full strength.

Then Cuchulain went on board his ship to set out for Ireland, and in the same ship with him were Lugaid and Luan, the two sons of Loch, and Ferbaeth and Larin and Ferdiad, and Durst, son of Derb.

On the night of Samhain they came to the island of Rechrainn, and Cuchulain left his ship and came to the strand. And there he heard a sound of crying, and he saw a beautiful young girl, and she sitting there alone. He asked her who was she, and what ailed her, and she said she was Devorgill, daughter of the king of Rechrainn, and that every year he was forced to pay a heavy tax to the Fomor, and this year, when he could not pay it, they made him leave her there near the sea, till they would come and bring her away in place of it.

"Where do these men come from?" said Cuchulain. "From that far country over there," she said, "and let you not stop here or they will see you when they come." But Cuchulain would not leave her, and presently three

fierce men of the Fomor landed in the bay, and made
straight for the spot where the girl was.   But before they
had time to lay a hand on her, Cuchulain leaped on them
and he killed the three of them, one after the other.
The last man wounded him in the arm, and the girl tore
a strip from her dress, and gave it to him to bind round
the wound.   And then she ran to her father's house and
told him all that had happened.   After that Cuchulain
came to the king's house, like any other guest, and his
companions with him, and Conall Cearnach and Laegaire
Buadach were there before them, where they had been
sent from Emain Macha to collect tribute.   For at that
time a tribute was paid to Ulster from the islands of
the Gall.

And they were all talking about the escape Devorgill
had, and some were boasting that it was they themselves
had saved her, for she could not be sure who it was had
come to her, because of the dusk of the evening.   Then
there was water brought for them all to wash before they
would go to the feast; and when it came to Cuchulain's
turn to bare his arms, she knew by the strip of her dress
that was bound about it, that it was he had saved her.
" I will give the girl to you as your wife," said the king,
" and I myself will pay her wedding portion."   " Not so,"
said Cuchulain, " for I must make no delay in going back
to Ireland."

So then he made his way back to Emain Macha, and
he told his whole story and all that had happened him.
And as soon as he had rested from the journey, he set
out to look for Emer at her father's house.   But Forgall
and his sons had heard he was come home again, and
they had made the place so strong, and they kept so
good a watch round it, that for the whole length of a
year he could not get so much as a sight of her.

It was one day at that time he went down to the
shore of Lough Cuan with Laeg, his chariot-driver, and

with Lugaid.   And when they were there, they saw two
birds coming over the sea.   Cuchulain put a stone in his
sling, and made a cast at the birds, and hit one of them.
And when they came to where the birds were, they
found in their place two women, and one of them the
most beautiful in the world, and they were Devorgill,
daughter of the king of Rechrainn, that had come from
her own country to find Cuchulain, and her serving-maid
along with her ; and it was Devorgill that Cuchulain had
hit with the stone.   " It is a bad thing you have done,
Cuchulain," she said, " for it was to find you I came,
and now you have wounded me."   Then Cuchulain put
his mouth to the wound and sucked out the stone and
the blood along with it.   And he said, " You cannot be
my wife, for I have drunk your blood.   But I will give
you to my comrade," he said, " to Lugaid of the Red
Stripes."   And so it was done, and Lugaid gave her
his love all through her life, and when she died he died
of the grief that was on him after her.

    After that, Cuchulain got his scythe chariot made
ready, and he set out again for Forgall's dun.   And
when he got there, he leaped with his hero leap over the
three walls, so that he was inside the court, and there he
made three attacks, so that eight men fell from each
attack, but one escaped in every troop of nine ; that is the
three brothers of Emer, Seibur and Ibur and Catt.   And
Forgall made a leap from the wall of the court to escape
Cuchulain, and he fell in the leap and got his death from
the fall.

    And then Cuchulain went out again, and brought
Emer with him and her foster-sister, and their two
loads of gold and silver.

    And then they heard cries all around them, and
Scenmend, Forgall's sister, came following them with
her men, and came up with them at the ford ; and
Cuchulain killed her in the fight, and it is from that

it is called the Ford of Scenmend. And her men came up with them again at the next ford, and he killed a hundred of them there. "It is a great thing you have done," said Emer. "You have killed a hundred strong armed men ; and Glondath, the Ford of Deeds, is the name that shall be on it for ever." Then they came to Raeban, the white field, and he gave three great angry blows to his enemies there, so that streams of blood went over it on every side. "This white hill is a hill of red sods to-day, through your work, Cuchulain," said Emer. And from that time it has been called the Ford of the Sods.

Then they were overtaken again at another ford on the Boinne, and Emer quitted the chariot, and Cuchulain followed his enemies along the banks, so that the sods were flying from the feet of the horses across the ford northward ; and then he turned and followed them northward, so that the sods flew over the ford southward. And from that it is called Ath na Imfuait, the Ford of the Two Clods. And at each of these fords Cuchulain killed a hundred, and so he kept his word to Emer, and he came safely out of it all, and they came to Emain Macha, toward the fall of night.

And then Cuchulain was given the headship of the young men of Ulster, of the warriors, the poets, the trumpeters, the musicians, the three pipers, the three jesters to say sharp words ; the three distributers of fame. It is of them the poet spoke, and set out their names, and it is what he said :—" The young men of Ireland, when they were in the Red Branch, it is they were the fairest of all hosts." And of Cuchulain he said, " He is as hard as steel and as bright, Cuchulain, the victorious son of Dechtire."

And then Cuchulain took Emer for his wife, after that long courting, and all the hardships he had gone through. And he brought her into the House of the Red Branch, and Conchubar and all the chief men of Ulster gave her a great welcome.

It was at Emain Macha, that was sometimes called Macha of the Spears, Conchubar, the High King, had the Eachrais Uladh, the Assembly House of Ulster, and it was there he had his chief palace.

A fine palace it was, having three houses in it, the Royal House, and the Speckled House, and the House of the Red Branch.

In the Royal House there were three times fifty rooms, and the walls were made of red yew, with copper rivets. And Conchubar's own room was on the ground, and the walls of it faced with bronze, and silver up above, with gold birds on it, and their heads set with shining carbuncles; and there were nine partitions from the fire to the wall, and thirty feet the height of each partition. And there was a silver rod before Conchubar with three golden apples on it, and when he shook the rod or struck it, all in the house would be silent.

It was in the House of the Red Branch were kept the heads and the weapons of beaten enemies, and in the Speckled House were kept the swords and the shields and the spears of the heroes of Ulster. And it was called the Speckled House because of the brightness and the colours of the hilts of the swords, and the bright spears, green or grey, with rings and bands of silver and gold about them, and the gold and silver that were on the rims and the bosses of the shields, and the brightness of the drinking-cups and the horns.

It was the custom with the men of the Red Branch, if one of them heard a word of insult, to get satisfaction for it on the moment. He would get up in the feasting hall itself, and make his attack; and it was to prevent that, the arms were kept together in one place. Conchubar's shield, the Ochain, that is the Moaning One, was hanging there; whenever Conchubar would be in

danger, it would moan, and all the shields of Ulster
would moan in answer to it. And Conall Cearnach's
Lam-tapaid, the Quick Hand, was in it. And Fergus's
Leochain, and Dubthach's Uathach, and Laegaire's
Nithach; and Sencha's Sciath-arglan and Celthair's
Comla Catha, the Gate of Battle, and a great many
others along with these.

And Cuchulain's shield was there, and the way he
got it was this.

There was a law made by the men of the Red Branch
that the carved device on every shield should be different
from every other. And the name of the man that used
to make the shields was Mac Enge. Cuchulain went
to him after coming back from Scathach, and bade him
make him a shield, and put some new device on it. "I
cannot do that," said Mac Enge, "for all I can do I have
done already on the shields of the men of Ulster."
There was anger on Cuchulain then, and he threatened
Mac Enge with death, was he, or was he not, under
Conchubar's protection.

Mac Enge was greatly put out at what had happened,
and he was thinking what was best for him to do, when
he saw a man coming towards him. "There is some
trouble on you," he said. "There is, indeed," said the
shield-maker, "for I am in danger of death unless I
make a shield for Cuchulain." "Clear out your work-
shop," said the strange man, "and spread ashes a foot
deep on the floor."

And when this was done, Mac Enge saw the man
coming over the outer wall to him again, and a fork
in his hand, and it having two prongs. And he put one
of the prongs in the ashes, and with the other he made
the pattern that was to be cut on Cuchulain's shield.
And so Cuchulain got it, and the name it had was
Dubhan, the Black One.

And as to Cuchulain's sword that was hanging along

with the shield, its name was the Cruaidin Cailid-
cheann; that is, the Hard, Hard Headed. And it had
a hilt of gold with ornaments of silver, and if the point
of the sword would be bent back to its hilt, it would
come as straight as a rod back again. It would cut
a hair on the water, or it would cut a hair off the head
without touching the skin, or it would cut a man in
two, and the one half of him would not miss the other
for some time after.

And as to Cuchulain's spear, the Gae Bulg, whether
it was or was not kept in the Speckled House, this is
the way he came by it. There were two monsters
fighting in the sea one time, the Curruid and the
Coinchenn their names were, and at the last the
Coinchenn made for the strand to escape, but the
other followed him and killed him there.

Then Bolg, son of Buan, a champion of the eastern
part of the world, found the bones of the Coinchenn
on the strand, and he made a spear with them. And
he gave it to a great fighting man, the son of Jubar,
and it went from one to another till it came to the
woman - champion, Aoife. And Aoife gave it to
Cuchulain, and he brought it to Ireland. And it
was with it he killed his own son, and his friend
Ferdiad afterwards.

There were three hundred and sixty-five men belonging to Conchubar's household; and one among them
served the supper every night, and when the year came
round, he would take his turn again. And it is not a
small thing that supper was: beef and pork and beer
for every man. But the three days before and the three
days after Samhain, the chief men of Ulster used to
come together, and to eat together in Conchubar's
palace, and Conchubar himself took charge of the
supper at that feast; for every man that did not
come on Samhain night, his wits would go from

him, and it was as well to make his grave and to put
his memorial stone over him the next day.

And there were a great many poets and learned men
used to come to Conchubar's court, for they were made
welcome there when they were driven out of other
places. Cathbad, the Druid, was among them, and his
son, bright-faced Geanann, and Sencha, and Ferceirtne,
that was very learned, and Morann, that could not give
a wrong judgment, for if he did, the collar round his
neck would tighten ; and many others.

Adhna was the chief poet there at one time, and
after he died Athairne was made chief poet of Ulster
in his place. But Neidhe, Adhna's son, came back from
Alban, expecting to be made chief poet. And it was
the waves of the sea, breaking on the strand where
he was, that told him of his father's death. And when
he got to Emain, he went into the palace and sat down
in the chief poet's chair, that he found empty, and put
the chief poet's cloak about him, that was lying there,
and that was ornamented with beautiful birds' feathers.
And then Athairne came in and found him there, and
they began an argument with one another in the
language of poetry, and Conchubar and all the chief
men of Ulster came in to listen to them, and some
of the other poets joined in the argument.

And Neidhe proved himself to be the best, but if he
did, as soon as it was given in his favour, he came
down from the chair, and took off the cloak and put
it about Athairne, and said that, his father being dead,
he would take him for his master.

So Athairne was chief poet, but no one had any
great liking for him, for he was too fond of riches,
and was no way hospitable or open-handed. It was
he went to Midhir, and brought away secretly his
three cranes of churlishness and denial, the way none
of the men of Ireland would get a good reception if

they would come to ask anything at his house. "Do not come, do not come," the first crane would say. "Get away, get away," the second would say. "Go past the house, past the house," the third would say to any one that came near it.

It was after that argument between Athairne and Neidhe, king Conchubar made a change in the laws. For it had been a law that no one that was not a poet could be a judge. But the language of the poets was hard to understand, and the king was vexed when he could understand but a small part of their argument. So he said that from that time out, any fitting man might be made judge, was he or was he not a poet. And all the people agreed to that, and the new law turned out very well in the end.

And the twelve chief heroes of Conchubar's Red Branch were these: Fergus, son of Rogh; Conall Cearnach, the Victorious; Laegaire Buadach, the Battle-Winner; Cuchulain, son of Sualtim; Eoghan, son of Durthact, chief of Fernmaige; Celthair, son of Uthecar; Dubthach Doel Uladh, the Beetle of Ulster; Muinremar, son of Geirgind; Cethern, son of Findtain; and Naoise, Ainnle, and Ardan, the three sons of Usnach.

IV

BRICRIU'S FEAST, AND THE WAR OF WORDS
OF THE WOMEN OF ULSTER

BRICRIU of the Bitter Tongue made a great feast one
time for Conchubar, son of Ness, and for all the
chief men of Ulster. He was the length of a year
getting the feast ready, and he built a great house to
hold it in at Dun-Rudraige. He built it in the likeness
of the House of the Red Branch in Emain, but it was
entirely beyond all the buildings of that time in shape
and in substance, in plan and in ornament, in pillars and
in facings, in doors and in carvings, so that it was spoken
of in all parts. It was on the plan of the drinking-hall
at Emain it was made inside, and it having nine divisions
from hearth to wall, and every division faced with bronze
that was overlaid with gold, thirty feet high. In the
front part of the hall there was a royal seat made for
Conchubar, high above all the other seats of the house.
It was set with carbuncles and other precious stones of
all colours, that shone like gold and silver, so that they
made the night the same as the day; and round about
it were the twelve seats of the twelve heroes of Ulster.

Good as the material was, the work done on it was as
good. It took six horses to bring home every beam,
and the strength of six men to fix every pole, and
thirty of the best skilled men in Ireland were ordering
it and directing it.

Then Bricriu made a sunny parlour for himself, on a
level with Conchubar's seat and the seats of the heroes
of valour, and it had every sort of ornament, and windows
of glass were put on every side of it, the way he could
see the hall from his seat, for he knew the men of Ulster
would not let him stop inside.

When he had finished building the hall and the sunny
parlour, and had furnished them with quilts and coverings,
beds and pillows, and with a full supply of meat and
drink, so that nothing was wanting, he set out for Emain
Macha to see Conchubar and the chief men of Ulster.

It happened that day they were all gathered together
at Emain Macha, and they made him welcome, and they
put him to sit beside Conchubar, and he said to Conchubar and to them all, "Come with me to a feast I have
made ready." "I am willing to go," said Conchubar,
"if the men of Ulster are willing."

But Fergus, son of Rogh, and the others, said: "We
will not go, for if we do, our dead will be more than
our living, after Bricriu has set us to quarrel with one
another." "It will be worse for you if you do not
come," said Bricriu. "What will you do if they do
not go with you?" said Conchubar. "I will stir up
strife," said Bricriu, "between the kings and the leaders,
and the heroes of valour, and the swordsmen, till every
one makes an end of the other, if they will not come
with me to use my feast." "We will not go for the sake
of pleasing you," said Conchubar. "I will stir up anger
between father and son, so that they will be the death
of one another," said Bricriu; "if I fail in doing that, I
will make a quarrel between mother and daughter; if
that fails, I will put the two breasts of every woman of
Ulster striking one against the other, and destroying
one another." "It is better for us to go," said Fergus.
"Let us consult with the chief men of Ulster," said
Sencha, son of Ailell. "Some harm will come of it,"

said Conchubar, "if we do not consult together against
this man."

On that, all the chief men met together in council, and
it is what Sencha advised: "It is best for you to get
securities from Bricriu, as you have to go along with
him; and put eight swordsmen around him, to make
him leave the house as soon as he has laid out the feast
for you." So Ferbenn Ferbeson, son of Conchubar,
brought the answer to Bricriu. "I am satisfied to do
that," said Bricriu. With that the men of Ulster set
out from Emain, host, troop, and company under king,
chief, and leader, and it was a good march they all made
together to Dun-Rudraige.

Then Bricriu set himself to think how with the securities that were given for him, he could best manage to set
the men of Ulster one against the other. After he had
been thinking a while, he went over to Laegaire Buadach,
son of Connad, son of Iliath. "All good be with you,
Laegaire, Winner of Battles, you mighty mallet of
Bregia, you hot hammer of Meath, you flame-red
thunderbolt, what hinders you from getting the
championship of Ireland for ever?" "If I want it
I can get it," said Laegaire. "You will be head of
all the champions of Ireland," said Bricriu, "if you
do as I advise." "I will do that, indeed," said
Laegaire.

"Well," said Bricriu, "if you can get the Champion's
Portion at the feast in my house, the championship of
Ireland will be yours for ever. And the Champion's
Portion of my house is worth fighting for," he said, "for
it is not the portion of a fool's house. There goes with it
a vat of good wine, with room enough in it to hold three
of the brave men of Ulster; with that a seven-year-old
boar, that has been fed since it was born on no other
thing but fresh milk, and fine meal in spring-time, curds
and sweet milk in summer, the kernel of nuts and wheat

in harvest, beef and broth in the winter; with that a seven-year-old bullock that never had in its mouth, since it was a sucking calf, either heather or twig tops, but only sweet milk and herbs, meadow hay and corn; along with that, five-score wheaten cakes made with honey. That is the Champion's Portion of my house. And since you are yourself the best hero among the men of Ulster," he said, "it is but right to give it to you; and that is my wish, you to get it. And at the end of the day, when the feast is spread out, let your chariot-driver rise up, and it is to him the Champion's Portion will be given." "There will be dead men if that is not done," said Laegaire. Then Bricriu laughed, for he liked to hear that.

When he had done stirring up Laegaire Buadach, he went on till he met with Conall Cearnach. "May good be with you, Conall," he said. "It is you are the hero of fights and of battles; it is many victories you have won up to this over the heroes of Ulster. By the time the men of Ulster cross the boundary of a strange country, it is three days and three nights in advance of them you are, over many a ford and river; it is you who protect their rear coming back again, so that no enemy can get past you or through you, or over you. What would hinder you from being given the Champion's Portion of Emain to hold for ever?" Great as was his treachery with Laegaire, he showed twice as much in what he said to Conall Cearnach.

When he had satisfied himself that Conall was stirred up to a quarrel, he went on to Cuchulain. "May all good be with you, Cuchulain, conqueror of Bregia, bright banner of the Lifé, darling of Emain, beloved by wives and by maidens, Cuchulain is no nickname for you to-day, for you are the champion of the men of Ulster; it is you keep off their great quarrels and disputes; it is you get justice for every man of them; it is you have what all the men of Ulster are wanting in; all the men of Ulster acknowledge that your bravery, your valour, and your deeds are beyond their own. Why, then, would you leave the Champion's Portion for some other one of the men of Ulster, when not one of them would be able to keep it from you?"

"By the god of my people," said Cuchulain, "whoever comes to try and keep it from me will lose his head." With that Bricriu left them and followed after the army, as if he had done nothing to stir up a quarrel at all.

After that they came to the feasting-houses and went in, and every one took his place, king, prince, landowner, swordsman, and young fighting man. One half of the house was set apart for Conchubar and his following, and the other half was kept for the wives of the heroes of Ulster.

And there were attending on Conchubar in the front part of the house Fergus, son of Rogh; Celthair, son of Uthecar; Eoghan, son of Durthact; the two sons of the king, Fiacha and Fiachaig; Fergus, son of Leti; Cuscraid, the Stutterer of Macha; Sencha, son of Ailell; the three sons of Fiachach, that is Rus and Dare and Imchad; Muinremar, son of Geirgind; Errge Echbel; Amergin, son of Ecit; Mend, son of Salchah; Dubthach Doel Uladh, the Beetle of Ulster; Feradach Find Fectnach; Fedelmid, son of Ilair Cheting; Furbaide Ferbend; Rochad, son of Fathemon; Laegaire Buadach; Conall Cearnach; Cuchulain; Conrad, son of Mornai; Erc, son of Fedelmid; Iollan, son of Fergus; Fintan, son of Nial; Cethern, son of Fintan; Factna, son of Sencad; Conla the False; Ailell the Honey-Tongued; the chief men of Ulster, with the young men and the song-makers.

While the feast was being spread out, the musicians and players made music for them. As soon as Bricriu had spread the feast with its well-tasting, savoury meats, he was ordered by his sureties to leave the hall on the moment; and they rose up with their drawn swords in their hands to put him out. So he and his followers went out, and when he was on the threshold of the house he turned and called out: "The Champion's Portion of my house is not the portion of a fool's house; let it be given to whoever you think the best hero of Ulster." And with that he left them.

Then the distributers rose up to divide the food, and the chariot-driver of Laegaire Buadach, Sedlang, son of Riangabra, rose up and said to them, "Let you give the Champion's Portion to Laegaire, for he has the best right to it of all the young heroes of Ulster."

Then Id, son of Riangabra, chariot-driver to Conall Cearnach, rose up, and bade them to give it to his master. But Laeg, son of Riangabra, said, "It is to Cuchulain it must be brought; and it is no disgrace for all the men of Ulster to give it to him, for it is he is the bravest of you all." "That is not true," said Conall, and Laegaire said the same.

With that they got up upon the floor, and put on their shields and took hold of their swords, and they attacked and struck at one another till the one half of the hall was as if on fire with the clashing of swords and spears, and the other half was as white as chalk with the whiteness of the shields. There was fear on the whole gathering; all the men were put from their places, and there was great anger on Conchubar himself and on Fergus, son of Rogh, to see the injustice and the hardship of two men fighting against one, Conall and Laegaire both together attacking Cuchulain; but there was no one among the men of Ulster dared part them till Sencha spoke to Conchubar. "It is time for you to part these men," he said.

With that, Conchubar and Fergus came between them, and the fighters let their hands drop to their sides. "Will you do as I advise?" said Sencha

"We will do it," they said. "Then my advice is," said Sencha, "for this night to divide the Champion's Portion among the whole gathering, and after that to let it be settled according to the judgment of Ailell, king of Connaught, for it will be better for the men of Ulster, this business to be settled in Cruachan."

So with that they sat down to the feast again, and gathered round the fire and drank and made merry.

All this time Bricriu and his wife were in their upper room, and from there he had seen how things were going on in the great hall. And he began to search his mind how he could best stir up the women to quarrel with one another as he had stirred up the men. When he had done searching his mind, it just chanced as he could have wished, that Fedelm of the Fresh Heart came from the hall with fifty women after her, laughing and merry. Bricriu went to meet her. "All good be with you to-night, wife of Laegaire Buadach. Fedelm of the Fresh Heart is no nickname for you, with respect to your appearance and your wisdom and your family. Conchubar, king of Ulster, is of your kindred; Laegaire Buadach is your husband. I would not think well of it that any of the women of Ulster should go before you into the hall, for it is at your heel that all the other women of Ulster should walk. If you go first into the hall to-night, you will be queen over them all for ever and ever."

Fedelm went on after that, the length of three ridges from the hall.

After that there came out Lendabair, the Favourite, daughter of Eoghan, son of Durthact, wife of Conall Cearnach.

Bricriu came over to her, and he said, "Good be with you, Lendabair; and that is no nickname, for you are the favourite and the darling of the men of the

whole world, because of the brightness of your beauty.
As far as your husband is beyond the whole world
in bravery and in comeliness, so far are you before
the women of Ulster." Great as his deceit was in
what he said to Fedelm, it was twice as great in what
he said to Lendabair.

Then Emer came out and fifty women after her.
"Health be with you, Emer, daughter of Forgall
Manach, wife of the best man in Ireland! Emer of the
Beautiful Hair is no nickname for you; the kings and
princes of Ireland are quarrelling with one another
about you. So far as the sun outshines the stars
of heaven, so far do you outshine the women of the
whole world in form, and shape, and birth, in youth,
and beauty, and nicety, in good name, and wisdom,
and speech." However great his deceit was towards
the other women, it was twice as much towards Emer.

The three women went on then till they met at one
spot, three ridges from the house, but none of them knew
that Bricriu had been speaking to the other. They set
out then to go back to the house. Their walk was even
and quiet and easy on the first ridge; hardly did one
of them put her foot before the other. But on the next
ridge their steps were closer and quicker; and when
they came to the ridge next the house, it was hardly
one of them could keep up with the other, so that
they took up their skirts nearly to their knees, each
one trying to get first into the hall, because of what
Bricriu had said to them, that whoever would be
first to enter the house, would be queen of the whole
province. And such was the noise they made in
their race, that it was like the noise of forty chariots
coming. The whole palace shook, and all the men
started up for their arms, striking against one another.

"Stop," said Sencha, "it is not enemies that are
coming, it is Bricriu has set the women quarrelling

By the god of my people!" he said, "unless the hall
is shut against them, those that are dead among us
will be more than those that are living." With that
the doorkeepers shut the doors. But Emer was quicker
than the other women, and outran them, and put her
back against the door, and called to the doorkeepers
before the other women came up, so that the men
rose up, each of them to open the door before his
own wife, so that she might be the first to come
within.

"It is a bad night this will be," said Conchubar; and
he struck the silver rod he had in his hand against the
bronze post of the hall, and they all sat down. "Quiet
yourselves," said Sencha; "it is not a war of arms we
are going to have here, it is a war of words." Each
woman then put herself under the protection of her
husband outside, and then there followed the war of
words of the women of Ulster.

Fedelm of the Fresh Heart was the first to speak, and
it is what she said :

"The mother who bore me was free, noble, equal to
my father in rank and in race; the blood that is in me
is royal; I was brought up like one of royal blood. I
am counted beautiful in form and in shape and in
appearance; I was brought up to good behaviour, to
courage, to mannerly ways. Look at Laegaire, my
husband, and what his red hand does for Ulster. It
was by himself alone its boundaries were kept from
the enemies that were as strong as all Ulster put
together; he is a defence and a protection against
wounds; he is beyond all the heroes; his victories
are greater than their victories. Why should not I,
Fedelm, the beautiful, the lovely, the joyful, be the
first to step into the drinking-hall to-night?"

Then Lendabair spoke, and it is what she said :

"I myself have beauty too, and good sense and good

carriage; it is I should walk into the hall with free, even steps before all the women of Ulster.

"For my husband is pleasant Conall of the great shield, the Victorious; he is proud, going with brave steps up to the spears of the fight; he is proud coming back to me after it, with the heads of his enemies in his hands.

"He brings his hard sword into the battle for Ulster; he defends every ford or he destroys it to keep out the enemy; he is a hero will have a stone raised over him.

"The son of noble Amergin, who can speak against his courage or his deeds? It is Conall who leads the heroes.

"All eyes look on the glory of Lendabair; why would she not go first into the hall of the king?"

Then Emer spoke, and it is what she said:

"There is no woman comes up to me in appearance, in shape, in wisdom; there is no one comes up to me for goodness of form, or brightness of eye, or good sense, or kindness, or good behaviour.

"No one has the joy of loving or the strength of loving that I have; all Ulster desires me; surely I am a nut of the heart. If I were a light woman, there would not be a husband left to any of you to-morrow.

"And my husband is Cuchulain. It is he is not a hound that is weak; there is blood on his spear, there is blood on his sword, his white body is black with blood, his soft skin is furrowed with sword cuts, there are many wounds on his thigh.

"But the flame of his eyes is turned westward; he is the strong protector; his chariot is red, its cushions are red; he fights from over the ears of horses, from over the breath of men; he leaps in the air like a salmon when he makes his hero leap; he does strange feats, the dark feat, the blind feat, the feat of nine; he breaks

down armies in the hard fight; he saves the life of
proud armies; he finds joy in the terror of the
ignorant.

"Your fine heroes of Ulster are not worth a stalk of
grass compared with my husband, Cuchulain, letting
on to have a woman's sickness on them; he is like
the clear red blood, they are like the scum and the
leavings, worth no more than a stalk of grass.

"Your fine women of Ulster, they are shaped like
cows and led like cows, when they are put beside the
wife of Cuchulain."

"When the men in the hall heard what the women
said, Laegaire and Conall made a rush at the wall,
and broke a plank out of it at their own height, to
let their own wives in. But Cuchulain raised up that
part of the house that was opposite to his place, so
that the stars and the sky could be seen through the
wall. By that opening Emer came in with the fifty
women that waited on her, and with them the women
that waited on the other two. None of the other
women could be compared at all with Emer, and no
one at all could be compared with her husband. And
then Cuchulain let the wall he had lifted fall suddenly
again, so that seven feet of it went into the ground,
and the whole house shook, and Bricriu's upper room
was laid flat in such a way that Bricriu himself and
his wife were thrown into the dirt among the dogs.
"My grief," cried Bricriu, "enemies are come in!"
And he got up quickly and took a turn round, and
he saw that the hall was now crooked and leaning
entirely to one side. He clapped his hands together
and went inside, but he was so covered with dirt that
none of the Ulster people could know him, it was
only by his way of speaking they made out who he was.

Then he said, from the middle of the floor, "It is
a pity I ever made a feast for you, men of Ulster.

My house is more to me than everything else I have. I put *geasa*, that is, bonds, on you, not to drink or to eat or to sleep till you leave my house the same way as you found it." At that, all the men of Ulster went out and tried to pull the house straight, but they did not raise it by so much as a hand's breadth.

"What are we to do?" they said. "There is nothing for you to do," said Sencha, "but to ask the man that pulled it crooked to set it straight again."

Upon that they bid Cuchulain to put the wall up straight again, and Bricriu said, "O king of the heroes of Ireland, unless you can set it up straight, there is no man in the world can do it." And all the men of Ulster begged and prayed of Cuchulain to settle the matter. And that they might not have to go without food or drink, Cuchulain rose up and tried to lift the house with a tug, and he failed. Anger came on him then, and the hero light shone about him, and he put out all his strength, and strained himself till a man's foot could find place between each of his ribs, and he lifted the house up till it was as straight as it was before. After that they enjoyed the feast, with the chief men on the one side round about Conchubar, High King of Ulster, and their wives on the other side—Fedelm of the Nine Shapes (nine shapes she could take on, and each shape more beautiful than the other), and Findchoem, daughter of Cathbad, wife of Amergin of the Iron Jaw, and Devorgill, wife of Lugaid of the Red Stripes, besides Emer, and Fedelm of the Fresh Heart, and Lendabair; and it would be too long to count and to tell of all the other noble women besides.

There was soon a buzzing of words in the hall again, with the women praising their men, as if to stir up another quarrel between them. Then Sencha, son of

Ailell, got up and shook his bell branch, and they all stopped to listen to him, and then to quiet the women he said:

"Have done with this word-fighting, lest you drive the men of Ulster to grow white-faced in the anger and the pride of battle with one another.

"It is through the fault of women the shields of men are broken, heroes go out to fight and struggle with one another in their anger.

"It is the folly of women brings men to do these things, to bruise what they cannot bind up again, to strike down what they cannot raise up again. Wives of heroes, keep yourself from this."

But Emer answered him, and it is what she said:

"It is right for me to speak, Sencha, and I the wife of the comely, pleasant hero, who is beyond all others in beauty, in wisdom, in speaking, since the learning that was easy to him is done with.

"No one can do his feats, the over-breath feat, the apple feat, the ghost feat, the screw feat, the cat feat, the red-whirling feat, the barbed-spear feat, the quick stroke, the fire of the mouth, the hero's cry, the wheel feat, the sword-edge feat; no one can throw himself against hard-spiked places the way he does.

"There is no one is his equal in youth, in form, in brightness, in birth, in mind, in voice, in bravery, in boldness, in fire, in skill; no one is his equal in hunting, in running, in strength, in victories, in greatness. There is no man to be found who can be put beside Cuchulain."

"If it is truth you are speaking, Emer," said Conall Cearnach, "let this lad of feats stand up, that we may see them."

"I will not," said Cuchulain. "I am tired and broken to-day, I will do no more till after I have had food and sleep." It was true what he said, for it was on that morning he had met with the Grey of Macha by the side of the grey lake at Slieve Fuad. When it came out of the lake, Cuchulain slipped his hands round the neck of the horse, and the two of them struggled and wrestled with one another, and in that way they went all round Ireland, till late in the day he brought the horse home to Emain. It was in the same way he got the Black Sainglain from the black lake of Sainglen.

And Cuchulain said: "To-day myself and the Grey of Macha have gone through the great plains of Ireland, Bregia of Meath, the seashore marsh of Muirthemne Macha, through Moy Medba, Currech Cleitech Cerna, Lia of Linn Locharn, Fer Femen Fergna, Curros Domnand, Ros Roigne, and Eo. And now I would sooner eat and sleep than do any other thing. But I swear by the gods my people swear by," he said, "I would be ready to fight with any man of you if I had but my fill of food and of sleep." "Well," said Bricriu, "this has gone on long enough. Let food and drink be brought, and let the women's war be put a stop to till the feast is done."

They did so, and it was a pleasant time they had till the end of three days and three nights.

V

THE CHAMPIONSHIP OF ULSTER

AFTER they were gone back to Emain after Bricriu's feast, a quarrel began between Conall and Laegaire and Cuchulain about the Champion's Portion, and Conchubar and the chief men of Ulster came between them to settle it. And Conchubar bade them to go to Cruachan in Connaught, to have the matter judged by Ailell and by Maeve. "And if that fails you," he said, "what you have to do is to go to Curoi, son of Daire, at Slieve Mis, in Munster. And it is a true judgment he will give, for he is just and fair-minded, his house is open to guests, his hand is good in battle, in leading he is a king. He will give you a right judgment, but it is only a brave man will ask it from him, for he is wise in all sorts of enchantments, and can do things that no other man can do."

"We will go first to Cruachan," said Cuchulain. "I agree to that," said Laegaire. "Let us go then," said Conall Cearnach. "Let horses be brought, and your chariot yoked, Conall," said Cuchulain; "and go on the first." "I would not like that," said Conall. "That is no wonder," said Cuchulain, "for every one knows the awkwardness of your horses, and the unsteadiness of your chariot; it is so heavy that each of the wheels raises the sod on each side wherever it goes, the way that for the length of a year it is easy for the men of Ulster to know the track it has left after it."

"Do you hear that, Laegaire?" said Conall. "It is for you to go first." "Do not begin to mock at me," said Laegaire, "for I am good at crossing fords, and I am ready to go up and face a storm of spears before any man. But do not put me beside chariot kings till I practise going through hard and narrow places, and racing against single chariots, till the champion of a single chariot will be afraid to pass me."

With that Laegaire had his chariot yoked, and leaped into it. He drove over Magh da Gabal, the Plain of the Two Forks, over Bernaid na Foraire, the Gap of the Watch, over the Ford of Carpat Fergus, over the Ford of the Morrigu, to Caerthund Cluana da Dam, the Rowan Meadow of the Two Oxen, in the Fews of Firbuide; by the four ways, past Dundealgan, across Magh Slicech, the Peeled Plain, westward by Bregia. And it was not long till Conall Cearnach followed after him, and many of the chief men of Ulster with them.

But Cuchulain stayed behind the others, amusing the women of Ulster with his feats. He did nine feats with apples, nine with spears, and nine with knives, without ever letting one touch the other. And he took three times fifty needles from the women, and threw them up, one after the other, so that each needle went into the eye of the other, and in that way they were all joined together. Then he gave every woman her needle back into her own hand.

But Laeg, son of Riangabra, went to look for him, and reproached him, and said: "You pitiful squinter, your courage has gone from you! The Champion's Portion is lost to you, the men of Ulster have got to Cruachan before this." "I never thought of it, my Laeg," said Cuchulain; "but yoke the chariot for me now." So Laeg yoked it, and they set out on their journey. By that time the men of Ulster were come to Magh Breagh, the Fine Meadow; but Cuchulain, after he was roused up by Laeg, travelled so fast, and the Grey of Macha and the Black Sainglain went racing in such a way with his chariot across the whole province of Conchubar, across Slieve Fuad and the plain of Bregia, that he came up with the others before they came to Cruachan.

The noise the whole troop made was so great, going at such speed as they did, that a great shaking came on Cruachan, and the arms fell from the racks to the ground, and the whole of the dun began to shake, so that every man was trembling like a rush in a stream. On that Maeve said: " Since the day I first came to Cruachan I never before heard thunder, there being no clouds in the sky." Then Findabair of the Fair Eyebrows, daughter of Ailell and of Maeve, went up, for she had a bird's sight, to her sunny parlour over the great door of the fort, to tell them what was coming. " Dear mother," she said, " I see a chariot coming over the plain." " Tell me what is its appearance," said Maeve, " and the colour of its horses, and the appearance of the man that sits in it." " I see well," said Findabair, " the two horses that are in the chariot. Two fiery dappled greys, of the one colour, shape, and goodness, having the one speed, keeping the one pace; their ears pricked, their heads high, their nostrils broad, foreheads broad, manes and tails curled, thin-sided, wide-chested, galloping together. The chariot is made of fine wood with wicker-work newly polished, the yoke curved, with silver ornaments on it; it has two black wheels, soft looped yellow reins. I see in the chariot a big stout man, with reddish yellow hair, with long forked beard. He has a soft purple coat about him, and it striped with bright gold. His bronze shield is edged with gold; there is a five-pronged javelin at his wrist, a cover of strange birds' feathers over his head."

"I know well who that man is," said Maeve, and it is what she said: "A companion of kings, an old bestower of victories, a storm of war, a flame of judgment a long knife of victory that will cut us to pieces, mighty Laegaire of the Red Hand. His sword cuts through men as a knife cuts through a leek; his stroke is the back stroke of the wave to the land. And I swear by the gods my people swear by," she said, "if it is in anger and for fighting Laegaire Buadach is coming at us, that as leeks are cut close to the ground with a sharp knife, the same way we will be cut down, as many of us as are in Cruachan, unless we smooth down his anger by giving in to everything he asks."

"Good mother," said Findabair, "I see another chariot as good as the first coming over the plain."
"Tell me what is its appearance," said Maeve.

"I see," she said, "yoked to the chariot, on the one side a red horse, taking strong, high strides across fords and splashes, over banks and gaps, over plains and hollows, with the quickness of birds that the quick eye loses in following. On the other side a bay horse of great strength; it is at full speed he races over the plain, between stones and hard places; he finds no hindrance in the land of oaks, hurrying on his way. A chariot of fine wood with wicker-work, on two wheels of bright bronze; its pole bright with silver, its frame very high and creaking, having a curved, firm yoke, with looped yellow reins.

"In the chariot a fair man, with wavy, hanging hair; his face white and red, his vest clean and white, his cloak blue and crimson, his shield brown with yellow bosses, its edge worked with bronze. In his hand a bright spear; a cover of the feathers of strange birds over the wicker frame of his chariot."

"I know who that man is," said Maeve, and she said then: "The growling of a lion; a flame that can cut

like a sharpened stone; he heaps head on head, battle on
battle. As a trout is cut upon red sandstone, so would
the son of Finchoem cut us if he came on us in anger.

"For, by the oath of my people," she said, "as a
speckled fish is beaten upon a shining red stone with
iron rods, so would we be broken by Conall Cearnach,
if he came against us."

"I see another chariot coming over the plain," said
Findabair. "Tell me what its appearance is," said
Maeve. "I see two horses of the one size and beauty,
the one fierceness and speed, with ears pricked, heads
high, spirited and powerful, with fine nostrils, wide foreheads, mane and tail curled, leaping together. The one
grey, handsome, with broad thighs, eager, leaping,
thundering, and trampling. As he goes, his fierce
hoofs throw up sods of earth like a flock of swift birds
after him. As he gallops on his way, he breathes out
a blast of hot breath, a fire comes from his curbed jaws.
The other, dark, small-headed, well-shaped, broad-
hoofed, thin-sided, high-couraged, broad-backed, sure-
footed, spirited; he takes long strides in the race;
he leaps over streams, he throws off heaviness, he
crosses the plains of the middle valley. They come
together with fast, joyful steps, moving over the plain
like a swift mountain mist, or like the speed of a hill
hind, or like a hare on level ground, or like the rushing
of a loud wind in winter.

"The chariot is of fine wood with wicker-work,
having two iron wheels, a bright silver pole with
bronze ornaments, a frame very high and creaking
strengthened with iron, a curved yoke overlaid with
gold, two soft looped yellow reins.

"I see in the chariot a dark, sad man, comeliest of
the men of Ireland. A pleated crimson tunic about
him, fastened at the breast with a brooch of inlaid gold;
a long-sleeved linen cloak on him with a white hood

embroidered with flame-red gold. His eyebrows as
black as the blackness of a spit, seven lights in his
eyes, seven colours about his head, love and fire in
his look. Across his knees there lies a gold-hilted
sword, there is a blood-red spear ready to his hand, a
sharp-tempered blade with a shaft of wood. Over his
shoulders a crimson shield with a rim of silver, overlaid
with shapes of beasts in gold.

"There is before him in the chariot a driver, a very
thin, tall, freckled man; very bright red hair, kept
back from his face with a golden thread, a cup of gold
at each side of his head. A short cloak about him with
sleeves opening at the two elbows; in his hand a goad
of red gold to guide his horses."

"That is truly a drop before a downpour," said Maeve.
"I know well who that man is." And it is what she
said: "Like the sound of an angry sea, like a great
moving wave, with the madness of a wild beast that is
vexed, he leaps through his enemies in the crash of
battle, they hear their death in his shout. He heaps
deed upon deed, head upon head; his is a name to be
put in songs. As fresh malt is ground in the mill, so
shall we be ground by Cuchulain.

"For I swear by the oath of my people," she said,
"that as a mill of ten spokes grinds very hard malt, so
he, with only himself, would grind us to dust and to
gravel, if we had the whole province with us, unless his
anger and his heat go down.

"And what way are the rest of the men of Ulster
coming?" she said. And Findabair answered her, and
it is what she said: "Hand to hand, arm to arm, side
to side, shoulder to shoulder, wheel to wheel, axle to
axle, that is the way they are coming. Their horses are
coming on us like thunder on the roof, like heavy waves
stirred by the storm; the trampling of their feet makes
the earth shake under them."

And Maeve said, "Let our women be ready before them with vats of cold water; let the beds be made ready, bring the best of food, the best of ale. Open the courtyard, have a welcome before them, and surely they will not harm us."

Then Maeve went out by the high door of the dun into the courtyard, and three times fifty young girls attending her, with three vats of cold water to cool the heat of the three heroes in front of the rest. And she gave them their choice, would each man have a house for himself, or would they have one house for the three? "A house for each to himself," said Cuchulain. And when the rest of the men of Ulster came, Ailell and Maeve with their whole household went out and bade them welcome. "We are well pleased with the welcome," said Sencha for them.

After that, they all came into the fort and into the palace. They went round from one door to the other, and there was room for them all, and the musicians were playing music while everything was being made ready. And Conchubar, and Fergus, son of Rogh, were in Ailell's division, with nine others along with them, and there was a great feast made ready then, and they stopped there the length of three days and three nights.

At the end of that time Ailell asked Conchubar what was the business that had brought them there. And Sencha told him the whole story, about the quarrel of the women as to who should walk first, and the quarrel of their husbands for the Champion's Portion. "And they were not satisfied to be judged by any one but yourself," he said. Ailell did not seem to be well pleased at that. "Indeed, it was no friend of mine that left this judgment on me," he said. "There is no better judge than yourself," said Sencha. "Well," said Ailell, "you must give me time to think upon it." "Do not make too much delay," said Sencha, "for we cannot spare our heroes long from us." "Three days and three nights will be enough for me," said Ailell. "That much will not break friendship," said Sencha.

With that the men of Ulster went home to Emain, leaving Laegaire and Conall and Cuchulain to be judged by Ailell, and they left their blessing with Ailell and with Maeve, and their curse with Bricriu, because it was he had first started the quarrel.

That night the three heroes were given as good a feast as before, but they were put to eat it in a room by themselves. When night came on, three enchanted monsters, with the shape of cats, were let out from the cave that was in the hill of the Sidhe at Cruachan, to attack them. When Conall and Laegaire saw them, they got up into the rafters, leaving their food after them, and there they stayed till morning. Cuchulain did not leave his place, but when one of the monsters came to attack him, he gave a blow of his sword at its head; but the sword slipped off as if from a stone. Then the monster stayed quiet, and Cuchulain sat there through the night watching it. With the break of day the cats were gone, and Ailell came in and saw what way the three heroes were. "Are you not satisfied to give the Championship to Cuchulain, after this?" he said. "We are not," said Conall and Laegaire; "it is not against beasts we are used to fight, but against men."

Then Maeve said to them, "Go and spend the night with my foster-father, Ercol, and his wife Garmna." So they went, but first they were given their choice of food for their horses. Conall and Laegaire chose oats two years old for theirs, but Cuchulain chose barley grain for his. Then they set out, racing all the way, and Cuchulain winning the race.

Ercol and Garmna bade them welcome, and they knew it was to try them they had been sent there, so they sent them out that night, one after the other, to fight with the witches of the valley.

Laegaire went first, but he could not stand against them, and he came back, and left his arms and his clothes with them.

Then Conall went, and he was driven back, and left his spear with them, but he brought his sword that was his best weapon away with him.

Then Cuchulain went down into the valley and the witches screamed at him and attacked him, and he and they fought together till his spear was in splinters, his shield broken and his clothes torn off him. The witches were beating him and getting the better of him, but Laeg saw it, and he called out. "O Cuchulain," he said, "you poor coward, you squinting clown! Your courage is gone from you, witches to be beating you!" Then great anger came on Cuchulain, and he turned on the witches and cut and gashed them till the valley was filled with their blood, and he brought away their cloaks of battle with him, and went back to the house where his comrades were. And Garmna and her daughter Buan made much of him and bade him welcome.

They slept there that night, and the next day Ercol challenged them to come one by one, each man with his horse, to fight against himself and his horse. Laegaire was the first to go against him, and his horse was killed by Ercol's horse, and he himself was overcome by Ercol, so that he took to flight, and did not stop till he got back to Cruachan, and he brought the story there that both his companions had been killed by Ercol. Conall was the next to run away, after his horse being killed by Ercol's horse; and his servant Rathand was drowned in the river as he ran, and it takes its name after him, Snam Rathand, from that day.

But the Grey of Macha killed Ercol's horse, and Cuchulain put down Ercol and tied him behind his chariot and set out for Cruachan. And Buan, Garmna's daughter, ran out after the chariot for love of Cuchulain to follow him. And she knew the track of his chariot, for it was no roundabout track it used to take, but to be breaking through gaps or going over them; and in following it at last she gave a great leap and fell, and her forehead struck against a rock, and she died; and it is from this the place was given the name of Buan's Grave.

And when Conall and Cuchulain got back to Cruachan, they found the people of the dun keening them, for by the report Laegaire brought, they were sure they had been killed.

Then Ailell went to his inner room, and leaned his back against the wall, for he was not quiet in his mind, and he knew there was danger in whatever judgment he might give; and he had not eaten or slept for three days and three nights. Then Maeve said to him, "It is a coward you are, and if you do not settle this matter I will settle it myself." "It is hard for me to give judgment," said Ailell, "it is a misfortune for any one to have to do it." "It is easy enough," said Maeve, "for Laegaire and Conall Cearnach are as different as bronze and silver, and Conall Cearnach and Cuchulain are as different as silver and red gold."

After a while, when Maeve had searched her mind, Laegaire Buadach was called to her. "Welcome, Laegaire Buadach," she said, "it is right for you to have the Champion's Portion. We give you the headship of the heroes of Ireland from this out, and the Champion's Portion, and along with that this cup of bronze, having a bird in raised silver on the bottom. Take it with you as a token of the judgment, but let no one see it till you come to Conchubar and his Red Branch at the end of the day. When the Champion's Portion is set out, then bring out your cup in the presence of all the great men of Ulster, and not one of them will dispute it with you any more, for they will know by this token that the Championship has been given to you." With that, the cup was given to him with its full of rich wine, and he drank it off at a draught. " Now you have the Championship," said Maeve; "and I wish you may enjoy it a hundred years at the head of all Ulster."

So Laegaire left her, and Conall Cearnach was called up to the queen. " Welcome, Conall Cearnach," she said ; "it is right for us to give you the Champion's Portion, and a silver cup along with it, having a bird on the bottom in raised gold." And she said the same to him as she had said to Laegaire before.

Then Conall went away, and a messenger was sent to bring Cuchulain. " Come up to speak with the king and queen," said the messenger.

Cuchulain was playing chess at the time with Laeg, his chariot-driver. " I am not a fool to be mocked at," he said, and he hurled one of the chessmen at the messenger, and hit him between the eyes, so that it is hardly he could get back to Ailell and Maeve.

"By my word," said Maeve, "this Cuchulain is hard to deal with." And then she came down herself to Cuchulain, and put her two arms round his neck. "Give your flattery to some other one," said Cuchulain.

But Maeve said, "Great son of Ulster, flame of the heroes of Ireland, there is no flattery in our mind when it is you we have to do with. For if all the heroes of Ireland should come here, it is to you we would give the Champion's Portion, for as to bravery and a great name, and as to youth and great deeds, it is well-known that you are far beyond all the men of Ireland."

Cuchulain rose up then, and went with Maeve into the palace, and Ailell gave him a great welcome. And he was given a gold cup full of wine, and it having on the bottom of it a bird in precious stones. " Now, you

have the Championship," said Maeve, "and it is my wish
you may enjoy it a hundred years at the head of all the
heroes of Ulster." "And besides that," Ailell and
Maeve said, "it is our judgment, that as much as you
are beyond the heroes of Ulster, so far is your wife
beyond their wives. And we think it right that she
should walk before all the women of Ulster when they
go together into the drinking-hall."

Then Cuchulain drank at one draught the full of the
cup, and bade farewell to the king and the queen and
the whole household. And he went till he came to
Emain Macha at the end of the day. And there was
no one among the men of Ulster would venture to ask
news of any of the three until the time came to eat and
to drink in the great hall.

When the feast was laid out, they all stopped their
arguing and their talking, and gave themselves up to
eating and to enjoyment. It was Sualtim, son of Roig,
father of Cuchulain, was attending the feast that night,
and Conchubar's great vat had been filled for it. The
distributers began serving out the meat, but at first they
kept back the Champion's Portion. Then Dubthach
of the Chafer Tongue said, "Why is not the Champion's
Portion given to one of these three heroes that are come
back from Cruachan? They must surely have brought
some token with them, that we may know which one
is to have it."

Upon that, Laegaire Buadach rose up and held out the
bronze cup with the silver bird on it. "The Champion's
Portion is mine," he said, "and no one can dispute it
with me."

"That is not so," said Conall Cearnach; "here is my
token. Yours is a bronze cup but mine is a silver cup.
You see by the difference in them it is to me the
Champion's Portion belongs."

"It belongs to neither of you," said Cuchulain, and

he rose up and he said, " It was only to deceive you
and to keep up the quarrel between us, the king and
queen we went to gave you those. It is to me the
Champion's Portion belongs, for you see my token, that
it is far above the others."

With that he lifted high up the cup of red gold, with
the bird on it of precious stones, and all the men in the
feasting-hall saw it. " It is I myself that will get the
Championship," he said, "if I get fair play." " It is yours
indeed," said Conchubar, and Fergus, and all the chief
men. " It is yours by the judgment of Ailell and
Maeve." " I swear by the oath of my people," said
Laegaire, "that the cup you have with you was not
given to you, but bought. You gave riches and
treasures for it to Ailell and Maeve, the way the
Championship would not go to any other person; but
by my hand of valour," he said, "that judgment shall
not stand."

Then, with their swords drawn, they sprang at one
another, but Conchubar went between them, and then
they let down their hands and sheathed their swords.
" It is best," said Sencha, "for you to go to Curoi for
judgment." " We agree to that," said they.

So on the morning of the morrow, the three—Cuchulain, Conall, and Laegaire—set out for Curoi's dun. At
the gate of the dun they unyoked their chariots, and
they went into the courtyard, and Blanad, daughter of
Mind, Curoi's wife, gave them a good welcome. Curoi
was not at home that night, but knowing, by his enchantments, they would come, he had left instructions
with his wife how to entertain them; and she did according to his wish, giving them water for washing, and
drinks for refreshing, and beds of the best, so that they
were well satisfied.

When bedtime came, Blanad told them they were
each to take a night to watch the fort, till Curoi would

come back. "And it is what he said, that you should take your turn according to age."

Now in whatever part of the world Curoi was, he made a spell every night over the dun, so that it went round like a mill, and no entrance could be found in it after the setting of the sun.

The first night Laegaire Buadach took the watch, for he was the oldest of the three. As he was keeping watch, towards the end of the night he saw a great shadow coming towards him from the sea westward. Very huge and ugly and terrible he thought it, and it took the shape of a giant and reached up to the sky, and the shining of the sea could be seen between its legs. It is how it came, its hands full of what had the appearance of stripped oaks, and each of them enough for a load for six horses ; and he hurled one of them at Laegaire, but it went past him. He did this two or three times, but the beam did not reach either the skin or the shield of Laegaire. Then Laegaire hurled a spear at him, and it did not hit him.

He stretched out his hand then to Laegaire, and the length of it reached across the three ridges that were between them while they were throwing at one another, and he gripped hold of him. Big and strong as Laegaire was, he fitted like a child of a year old into his hand. The giant turned him round between his two palms as a chessman is turned in a groove, and then he threw him half dead over the wall of the fort, into a heap of mud. There was no opening there, and the people inside the dun thought he had leaped over from outside, as a challenge to the others to do the same.

There they stayed until the end of the day, and at the fall of night Conall went out to take the watch, as he was older than Cuchulain. Everything happened as it did to Laegaire the first night. And when the third night came, Cuchulain went into the seat of the watch.

When midnight was come he heard a noise, and by the light of the cold moon he saw nine grey shapes coming towards him over the marsh. "Stop," said Cuchulain, "who is there? If they are friends, let them not stir; if they are enemies, let them come on." Then they raised a great shout at him, and Cuchulain rushed at them and attacked them, so that the nine fell dead to the ground, and he cut their heads off and made a heap of them, and sat down again to keep the watch. Another nine and then another shouted at him, but he made an end of the three nines, and made one heap of their heads and their arms.

While he was watching on through the night, tired and down-hearted, he heard a sound rising from the lake, like the sound of a very heavy sea. However tired he was, his mind would not let him keep quiet, without going to see what was the cause of that great noise he heard. Then he saw a great worm coming up from the lake, and it raised itself into the air over him and made for the dun, and opened its mouth, and it seemed to him that one of the houses would fit into its gullet.

Then Cuchulain with one leap reached its head and put his arm round its neck, and stretched his hand across its gullet, and tore the monster's heart out and threw it to the ground. Then the beast fell down, and Cuchulain hacked it with his sword, and made little bits of it, and brought the head along with him to the heap of skulls.

He was sitting there, towards the break of day, worn out and discouraged, and he saw the great shadow shaped like a giant coming to him westward from the sea. "This is a bad night," he said. "It will be worse for you yet," said Cuchulain. Then he threw one of the beams at Cuchulain, but it passed by him, and he did that two or three times, but it did not reach either his shield or his skin. Then he stretched out his hand to grip Cuchulain as he did the others, but Cuchulain

leaped his salmon leap at the head of the monster, with
his drawn sword, and brought him down. "Life for
life, Cuchulain," he said, and with that he vanished and
was no more seen.

Then Cuchulain wondered to himself how his fellows
had made their leap over the fort, for the wall was big
and broad and high, and twice he tried it and failed.
Then anger came on him, and he went a good way back
and made a run, and with the dint of the anger that was
on him, and the courage of his heart and of his mind, he
hardly took the dew off the tips of the grass in the run,
and he made one leap over the wall, and lit in the
middle, at the door of the house. Then he went in
through the door and gave a sigh. And Blanad, wife of
Curoi, said, "That is not the sigh of a beaten man, but a
conqueror's sigh of triumph." For the daughter of the
King of the Isle of the Men of Falga knew well all
Cuchulain had gone through that night.

"The Champion's Portion must go now to Cuchulain,"
she said to the others; "for you see by this that you
are not equal to him." "We do not agree to that," said
they; "for we know it was one of his friends among
the Sidhe came to put us down and to put us out of the
Championship. We will not give up for that," they
said.

Then she gave them a message she had from Curoi,
that the three champions were to go back to Emain,
until he would bring his judgment there himself. So
they bade her farewell, and went back to the Red
Branch.

It was a good while after this, as the men of Ulster
were in Emain, tired after the gathering and the games,
Conchubar and Fergus, son of Rogh, with the chief men,
went from the field of sports outside, and sat down in
the house of the Red Branch; but Cuchulain was not

there that night, or Conall Cearnach, but all the rest of
the chief heroes were in it.

As they were sitting there towards evening, and the
day wearing to its close, they saw a big awkward
fellow, very ugly, coming to them into the hall. It
seemed to them as if none of the men of Ulster could
reach to half his height. He was frightful to look at ;
next his skin he had an old cow's hide, and a grey cloak
around him, and over him he had a great spreading
branch the size of a winter shed under which thirty
cattle could find shelter. Ravenous yellow eyes he had,
and in his right hand an axe weighing fifty cauldrons of
melted metal, its sharpness such that it would cut
through hairs, if the wind would blow them against its
edge.

He went over and leaned against the branched beam
that was beside the fire.

" Who are you at all ? " said Dubthach of the Chafer
Tongue. " Is there no other place for you in the hall
that you come up here ? Is it to be candlestick to the
house you want, or is it to set the house on fire you
want ? "

" Uath, the Stranger, is my name," said he ; " and
neither of those things is the thing I want. The thing
I want is the thing I cannot find, and I after going
through the world of Ireland and the whole world looking for it, and that is a man that will keep his word and
will hold to his agreement with me."

" What agreement is that ? " said Fergus. " Here is
this axe," he said, " and the man into whose hands it is
put is to cut off my head to-day, I to cut his head off
to-morrow. And as you men of Ulster have a name
beyond the men of all other countries for strength and
skill, for courage, for greatness, for highmindedness,
for behaviour, for truth and generosity, for worthiness,
let you find one among you that will hold to his word

and keep to his bargain. Conchubar I put aside because of his kingship, and Fergus, son of Rogh, for the same reason. But outside these two, come, which-ever of you will venture, he to cut off my head to-night, I to cut off his head to-morrow night."

"It is not right for dishonour to be put on a whole province," said Fergus, "for the want of one man that will keep his word." "Sure there is no champion here after these two are left out," said Dubthach. "By my word, there will be one this moment," said Laegaire, and he leaped out on the floor of the hall. "Stoop down, clown, that I may cut off your head to-night, you to cut off mine to-morrow night." "By the oath of my people," said Dubthach, "it is no good prospect you have if the man killed to-night comes to kill you to-morrow."

Then Uath put spells on the edge of the axe and laid his neck down on a block, and Laegaire struck a blow across it with the axe, till it went into the block underneath, and the head fell on the floor and the house was filled with the blood. But presently Uath rose up and gathered his head and his axe to his breast and went out from the hall, his neck streaming with blood, so that there was terror on all the people in the house.

"I swear," said Dubthach, "if this stranger, being killed, comes back to-morrow night, he will not leave a man alive in Ulster."

Back he came the next night to have his agreement kept. But Laegaire's heart failed him, and he was nowhere to be found. But Conall Cearnach was in the hall, and he said he would make a new agreement with him. So all happened the same as the night before, but when Uath came the next day, it was the same with Conall as with Laegaire, his heart failed him when it came to the keeping of his bargain.

Cuchulain was there that night when Uath came in and began to reproach and to mock at them all. "As for you, men of Ulster," he said, "all your courage and your daring is gone from you; you covet a great name, but you are not able to earn it. Where is that poor squinting fellow that is called Cuchulain," he said, "till I see if his word is any better than the word of the others?" "I will keep my word without any agreement," said Cuchulain. "That is likely, you miserable fly, it is in great fear of death you are."

On that, Cuchulain made a leap towards him and gave him a blow with the axe, and hurled his head to the top rafter of the hall, so that the whole house shook.

On the morrow the men of Ulster were watching Cuchulain to see if he would break his word to the stranger, as the others had done. As Cuchulain sat there waiting for him, they saw that he was very down-hearted, and they made sure his life was at its end, and that they might as well begin keening him. And then Cuchulain said to Conchubar, and there was hanging of the head on him, "Do not go from this till my agreement is fulfilled, for death is coming to me, but I would sooner meet with death than break my word."

They were there till the close of day, and then they saw Uath coming. "Where is Cuchulain?" he said. "Here I am," he answered. "It is dull your speech is to-night," said the stranger; "it is in great fear of death you are. But however great your fear, you have not failed me."

Then Cuchulain went to him and laid his head on the block. "Stretch out your head better," said he. "You are keeping me in torment," said Cuchulain; "put an end to me quickly. For last night," he said, "by my oath, I made no delay with you." Then he stretched out his neck, and Uath raised his axe till it reached the rafters of the hall, and the creaking of the old hide that was about him, and the crashing of the axe through the rafters, was like the loud noise of a wood in a stormy night. But when the axe came down, it was with its blunt side, and it was the floor it struck, so that Cuchulain was not touched at all. And all the chief men of Ulster were standing around looking on, and they saw on the moment that it was no strange clown was in it, but Curoi, son of Daire, that had come to try the heroes through his enchantments.

"Rise up, Cuchulain," he said. "Of all the heroes of Ulster, whatever may be their daring, there is not one to compare with you in courage and in bravery and in truth. The Championship of the heroes of Ireland is yours from this out, and the Champion's Portion with it, and to your wife the first place among all the women of Ulster. And whoever tries to put himself before you after this," he said, "I swear by the oath my people swear by, his own life will be in danger."

With that he left them. And this was the end of the Women's War of Words, and of the quarrel among the heroes for the Championship of Ulster.

VI

THE HIGH KING OF IRELAND

THERE was a king over Ireland before this time whose name was Eochaid Feidlech, and it is he was grandfather to Conaire the Great.

He was going one time over the fair green of Bri Leith, and he saw at the side of a well a woman, with a bright comb of silver and gold, and she washing in a silver basin, having four golden birds on it, and little bright purple stones set in the rim of the basin. A beautiful purple cloak she had, and silver fringes to it, and a gold brooch; and she had on her a dress of green silk with a long hood embroidered in red gold, and wonderful clasps of gold and silver on her breasts and on her shoulders. The sunlight was falling on her, so that the gold and the green silk were shining out. Two plaits of hair she had, four locks in each plait, and a bead at the point of every lock, and the colour of her hair was like yellow flags in summer, or like red gold after it is rubbed.

There she was, letting down her hair to wash it, and her arms out through the sleeve-holes of her shift. Her soft hands were as white as the snow of a single night, and her eyes as blue as any blue flower, and her lips as red as the berries of the rowan-tree, and her body as white as the foam of a wave. The bright light of the moon was in her face, the highness of pride in her eyebrows, a dimple of delight in each of her cheeks, the light of wooing in her eyes, and when she walked she had a step that was steady and even, like the walk of a queen.

Of all the women of the world she was the best and the nicest and the most beautiful that had ever been seen, and it is what King Eochaid and his people thought, that she was from the hills of the Sidhe. It is of her it was said, "All are dear and all are shapely till they are put beside Etain."

Then Eochaid sent his people to bring her to him, and when she came, he said, "Who are you yourself, and where do you come from?" "It is easy to say that," she said; "I am Etain, daughter of Etar, king of the Riders of the Sidhe. And I have been in this place ever since I was born, twenty years ago, in a hill of the Sidhe, and kings and great men among them have been asking my love, but they got nothing from me, for since the time I could first speak I have loved yourself, and given you a child's love, because of the great talk I heard of your grandeur. And when I saw you now I knew you by all I had heard of you; and so I have reached to you at last."

"It is no bad friend you have been looking for," said Eochaid, "but there will be a welcome before you, and I will leave every other woman for you, and it is with yourself I will live from this out, so long as you keep good behaviour."

Then he gave her the bride price, and she lived with him till he died. But one time she was brought away from him by Midhir, and Eochaid brought her back by force, and the Sidhe had no good will towards him after that, but brought a revenge on his house, and on his grandson, Conaire.

They had one daughter, that was called by the same name as her mother, Etain, and that was married to

Cormac, king of Ulster. And, like her mother, she had but the one daughter, and there was vexation on Cormac when she had no son, and he bade two of his serving-men to bring the child away out of his sight, and to do away with her. So they brought her to a pit, but when they were putting her in, she smiled a laughing smile at them, and they had not the heart to harm her. So they brought her to a calf-shed belonging to the herds that minded the cattle of Eterscel, great-grandson of Iar, king of Teamhair; and they cared her well there, and there was not a king's daughter in Ireland was nicer than herself. And they made a little house of wicker-work for her, with no door, but only a window high up in it.

King Eterscel's people thought it was provisions the herds used to keep in that house. But one day a man of them got up and looked in through the window, and what he saw was the nicest and the most beautiful young girl of the whole world.

When King Eterscel heard that, he sent his people to break into the house and to bring her away, and ask no leave of the cowherds. For he had no child, and it is what his Druids had foretold, that it was a woman of unknown race would bear him a son; and he was sure this was the woman that had been foretold for him.

But before the king's messengers reached the house in the morning, Etain saw a bird coming in at the window. And when it came in, it left its birdskin on the floor, and what she saw was a man before her. And he said, "The king is sending messengers to bring you to him, that he may have a son. But it is to me you will bear a son, and no bird must ever be killed by him. And his name will be Conaire, son of Mess Buachall, that is, son of the cowherd's foster-child."

Then she was brought away to the king, and the herds

that had fostered her went with her, and they all got good treatment. And it is what she asked, when her son Conaire was born, that he might be brought up between three households, the household of her own fosterers, and of the two honey-worded Maines, and her own. And she said that if any of the men of Ireland had a mind to give help in his bringing up, they should give it to those three households.

So it was like that the boy was reared, and there were five other boys reared along with him, Ferger, Fergel, Ferogain, Ferobain, and Lomna Druth the Fool, of the house of Dond Dessa, the champion of the army from Muclesi. And they all used the same food, and their clothing and their armour and the colour of their horses were the same.

And after a while King Eterscel died, and there was a bull feast made ready at Teamhair, as the custom was, to find out by it the best man for the kingship.

It is this way the bull feast was made. A white bull was killed, and one man would eat his fill of the meat and of the broth, and in his sleep after that meal, a charm of truth would be said over him by four Druids. And whoever he would see in his sleep would be king, and he would tell them his appearance; and if he told what was not true, his lips would perish. And what the dreamer saw in his sleep this time was a young man, and he naked, and having a stone in his sling, passing the road to Teamhair.

Now just at that time Conaire was out playing games near the Lifé River with his foster-brothers, and the cowherds that had reared him came and bid him go up to Teamhair to attend the bull feast that was going on there.

So he left his foster-brothers at their games, and turned his chariot and went on till he came to Ath Cliath. And there he saw great white speckled birds, the best in size and appearance he had ever seen, and he followed after them till his horses were tired, but he could not come up with them, for they always kept just out of his reach. Then he got down from his chariot and took his sling and followed them to the strand, and they went into the sea and were swimming on the waves, and he went after them to take hold of them. Then they left their birdskins, and it was men he saw before him, and they turning to face him with spears and swords.

But one of them took him under his protection and said, "I am Nemglan, king of your father's birds, and there was a command put on you never to make a cast at birds, for there is not one here but should be dear to you." "I never knew of that command till this day," said Conaire. Then Nemglan said, "What you have to do is to go to Teamhair to-night, to the bull feast, and it is through it you will be made king, for it is a man that will go naked, and having a sling and a stone in his hand, along one of the roads to Teamhair, towards the end of the night, that will be king.

"And your bird reign will be great," he said. "But there is *geasa*, that is a bond, on you not to do these things:

"Do not go righthandwise round Teamhair, and lefthandwise round Bregia; do not hunt the evil beasts of Cerna; do not go out beyond Teamhair every ninth night; do not settle the quarrel of two of your own people; let no robbery be done in your reign; do not sleep in a house you can see the firelight shining from after sunset; do not let one woman or one man come into the house where you are after sunset; do not let three Reds go before you to the House of Red."

Then Conaire set out for Teamhair, naked, and having a stone in his sling. And on every one of the four roads to Teamhair there were three kings waiting, and having clothing with them, for the king that was foretold.   And when the three kings on Conaire's road saw him coming, they met him, and put royal clothes on him, and brought him in a chariot to Teamhair.   But the people of Teamhair said when they saw him: "Our bull feast and our charm of truth were not worth much, when it is only a young, beardless lad they have brought us!"

"That is no matter," said Conaire, "for it is no disgrace for you to have a young king, when my father and my grandfather held the same place."   "That is true," they all said then, and they gave him the kingship, and he said, "I will learn of wise men, that I myself may be wise."

Now there was great plenty in Ireland through his reign; seven ships coming at the one time to Inver Colptha, and corn and nuts up to the knees in every harvest, and the trees bending from the weight of fruit, and the Buais and the Boinne full of fish every summer, and that much law and peace and good-will among the people, that each one thought the other's voice as sweet as the strings of harps.   And the wolves themselves were held by hostages not to kill more than one calf in every pen. There was no thunder or storm in his reign, and from spring to harvest there was not as much wind as would stir a cow's tail, and the cattle were without keepers because of the greatness of peace.   And in his reign there were the three crowns in Ireland, the crown of flowers, the crown of acorns, and the crown of wheatears.

But after a while there began to be discontent on the sons of Donn Dessa, because they were hindered from the robbery and killing there used to be in the old time.   And to vex the king, and to see what would he do, they stole three things, a pig and a bullock and a cow, from the same man every year for three years. And every year the countryman would come to the king to make his complaint, and every year the king would say, "It is to the sons of Donn Dessa you should go, for it is they took the beasts." But whenever he would go and speak to them, they would go near to kill him, and he would not go back to the king for fear he might be vexed.

So the sons of Donn Dessa went on with their robbery, and three times fifty other young men joined with them, sons of the great men of Ireland.

But one time they went doing their bad work in Connaught, and they followed a swineherd that ran from them, and he called out for help, and the people gathered to him, and the robbers were taken and brought back to Teamhair.

King Conaire was asked to give judgment then, and it is what he said, "Let every father of a robber put his own son to death, but let my foster-brothers be spared." "Give us leave," said all the people, "and we will put them to death for you." "I will not consent to that, indeed," said Conaire. "Their life must be spared. But if they must do robbery," he said, "let them go across the sea, and do it on the men of Alban."

So the sons of Donn Dessa and their men were driven out of the country, and some of the Maines went with them, the sons of Ailell and Maeve, and three great fighting men of Leinster, that were called the Three Red Hounds of Cualu, and they brought a troop of wild restless men with them.

They set out then in their ships, and when they were out on the rough sea, they met with the ship of Ingcel, the One-Eyed, grandson of Cormac of Britain. They were going to make an attack on him, but Ingcel said, "It would be best for us to come to an agreement together, for you have been driven out of Ireland, and I myself have been driven out from Britain. Let us make this agreement," he said. "Let you come and spoil the people of my country, and then I will go back with you and spoil the people of your country."

So they agreed to that, and they cast lots as to where they would go first, and it is how the lot fell, that they should go first to Britain with Ingcel. And when they got there it chanced that the father and mother and the seven brothers of Ingcel had been sent for to the house of the king of the district, and Ingcel and his comrades made an attack on them, and killed them all in the one night.

Then they made for Alban, and there they did every sort of destruction and robbery. And at last they turned back again to Ireland, that Ingcel might spoil their people the same way as they had spoiled his.

Now just at that time peace was after being broken in Ireland by the two Carbres that were at war with one another in Tuathmumain of Munster, and no one was able to put an end to their quarrel till Conaire himself went there to make peace. And he did that, although by doing it he broke two of the bonds put on him by the Man of the Waves. And on his way back to Teamhair, when he was passing Usnach in Meath, he and his people thought they saw fighting from east to west, and from north to south, and armies of naked men, and the country of the Ua Neills like a cloud of fire around them.

"What is that?" said Conaire. "It is easy to know that," said his people. "The king's law has broken down, and the country is on fire." "What way had we best go?" said Conaire. "To the north-west," said his people.

So then they went righthandways round Teamhair, and lefthandways round Bregia, and that was another breaking of his bonds, and they met with beasts and hunted them, and he did not know till afterwards that they were the evil beasts of Cerna.

And it was the Sidhe had made that Druid mist of smoke about him, because he had begun to break his bonds.

Great fear came on Conaire then, and he did not know what way would be best to go, and they went on by the sea-coast, towards the south by the road of Cualu. And then Conaire said, "Where shall we go to spend the night?"

"I can say this truly," said Mac Cecht, one of his fighting men, he that kept three of the Fomor as hostages at the king's court, the way their people would not spoil corn or milk in Ireland through his reign; "it is oftener the men of Ireland have been quarrelling to have you in the house, than you have been straying about, looking for a lodging." "I have a friend not far from this," said Conaire, "if we but knew the way to his house." "What is his name?" said Mac Cecht. "Da Derga of Leinster, that keeps the great Inn," said Conaire. "He came to ask a gift of me, and it is not a refusal he met with. I gave him a hundred head of cattle, I gave him a hundred fat swine, I gave him a hundred cloaks of fine cloth, I gave him a hundred swords and spears, I gave him a hundred red-gilded brooches, I gave him ten vats of good brown ale, I gave him three times nine white hounds in silver chains, I gave him a hundred swift horses. I would give him the same if he would come again. He will make a return to me to-night, for it would be a strange thing, he to begrudge me anything when I come to his house."

"When I knew his house," said Mac Cecht, "the road we are in now led straight to it. Seven doorways there are in it, and seven sleeping-rooms between every two doorways." "We will go to the house with all our people," said Conaire. "If that is so," said Mac Cecht,

"I will go on first till I light a fire in the house before you."

They went on then towards Ath Cliath, and presently a man with hair cut short, with a dreadful appearance, with but one hand and one foot and one eye, overtook them. A forked pole of black iron he had in his hand, and on his back a black-bristled singed pig, and it squealing; and there was a woman coming after him, ugly and big-mouthed. "Welcome to you, my master, Conaire," he said. "It is long we have known of your coming." "Who gives that welcome?" said Conaire. "Fer Coille, the Man of the Wood," he said, "and his black pig with him, that you may not be fasting to-night, for you are the best king that ever came into the world." "Leave me for to-night," said Conaire, "and I will go to you any other night that pleases you." "We will not," said he; "but we will go to the place you will be in to-night, O fair little master, Conaire."

So he went on towards the Inn, and his wife behind him, and his black pig squealing on his back.

After that Conaire saw before him three horsemen going towards the Inn. Red cloaks they had, and red shields, and red spears in their hands, and they riding on red horses.

"What men are these before me?" said Conaire. "It is in my bonds not to let them go before me; three Reds to the House of Red, that is, of Derga. Who will follow them and bid them to come back and to follow after me?" "I will follow them," said Lefriflaith, Conaire's son.

So he struck his horse and went after them, but he could not come up with them. So he called to them to turn back, and not to go on before the king. And he did this three times, and the third time one of the three men turned his head and said, "There is great news before us, my son; wetting of swords, destroying of life, shields with broken bosses, after the fall of night. Our horses are tired; we are riding the horses of the Sidhe; although we are alive we are dead." And with that they went from him, and he went back to his father.

"You did not keep back the men," said Conaire. "It was not my fault, indeed," said Lefriflaith. Then he told the answer they had given him, and Conaire and his people were not well pleased to hear that, and uneasiness came on them. "All my bonds are ended to-night," said Conaire, "and those three Reds before me are sent by the Sidhe."

Now while he and his people were in the road of Cualu going towards the Inn, Ingcel and the outlaws of Ireland were come in their ships to the coast of Bregia against Etair. And the sons of Donn Dessa said, "Strike the sails now, and let some light-footed messenger go on shore and see can we keep our bargain with Ingcel, and give him a spoil for the spoil he gave us." "Let some man go," said Ingcel, "that has the gift of hearing and of far sight and of judgment."

"I have the gift of hearing," said Maine Milscothach. "I have the gift of far sight and of judgment," said Maine Andoe. "It is as well for you to go, so," said the others.

So they landed and went on till they came to Beinn Etair, and they stopped there to try what they might see and hear. "Be quiet now," said Maine Milscothach, "and listen." "What do you hear?" said Maine Andoe. "I hear the coming of a king," he said, "and look now and tell me what you see." "I see," he said, "a great company of men, travelling over hills and rivers. Clothes of every colour they have, and grey spears over their chariots, and swords with

ivory hilts beside them, and silver shields; and I swear
by the oath my people swear by," he said, "the horses
they have with them are the horses of some good lord.
And it is my opinion that it is Conaire, son of Eterscel,
and a good share of the men of Ireland with him, that
is travelling the road."

With that they went back and told their comrades
what they had heard and seen. And when they
heard it they brought the boats to shore and landed
on the strand of Furbuithe. And it was just at the
same moment Mac Cecht was striking a spark to kindle
a fire at the Inn before the High King.

Then Conaire came to the lawn of the Inn, and he
went in, and his people, and they took their seats,
and the three Red Men sat down along with them, and
the Man of the Wood that was a swineherd of the Sidhe
with his squealing pig.

And Da Derga came to them with three times fifty
fighting men, every one of them having a long head
of hair and a short cloak and a great blackthorn stick
with bands of iron in his hand. "Welcome, my master,
Conaire," said Da Derga, "and if you were to bring
the whole of the men of Ireland with you, there would
be a welcome before them all."

After the fall of evening they saw a lone woman
coming to the door of the Inn; long hair she had, and
a grey woollen cloak, and her mouth was drawn to
one side of her head. She came and leaned up against
the doorpost, and she threw an evil eye on the king
and the young men about him. "Well, woman," said
Conaire, "if you have the Druid sight, what is it you
see for us?" "It is what I see for you," she said,
"that nothing of your skin or of your flesh will escape
from the place you are in, except what the birds will
bring away in their claws. And let me come into the
house now," she said. "There are bonds on me," said

Conaire, "not to let one woman come by herself into the house after the setting of the sun. And bring her out," he said, "a good share of food from my own table, but let her stop for the night in some other place."

"If the king's hospitality is gone from him," she said, "and if it is the way with him not to have room in his house for one lone woman to be fed and lodged, I will go and get food and lodging from some better man." "Let her in, in spite of my bonds," said Conaire, when he heard that. So they let her in, but none of them felt easy in their minds after what she had said.

Now all this time the outlaws were on their way to the Inn, and they stopped at Leccaibcend Slebe. And when they saw the great light that was shining from the Inn through the wheels of the chariots that were outside the doors, Ingcel said to Ferogain, "What is that great light beyond?" "It is what I think," said Ferogain, "that it is the fire of Conaire, the High King. And I would be glad he not to be there to-night, for it would be a pity if harm would come on him, or his life be shortened, for he is a branch in its blossom."

"It is good luck for me," said Ingcel, "it he is there. Spoil for spoil. It is no worse for you than it was for me when I gave up my father and mother and my seven brothers and the king of my country into your hands." "That is true, that is true," said all the others.

Then every man of them brought up a stone from the strand to make a cairn, as they were used to do before they would make an attack on any place, to know by it afterwards how many men they had lost. For every man that would come from the fight would take his stone from the cairn, and the stones of all that would be killed would be left there.

After that they held a council, and it is what they agreed, that one man should go and spy out what way things were at the Inn. And it was Ingcel himself went to do that, and he was a good while looking in by the seven doors of the house, but at last some one of the men inside caught sight of him, and he made his way back to his comrades, where they were all sitting down, and their leaders in the middle, waiting to hear his news.

"Did you see the house, Ingcel?" said Ferogain. "I did see it," said Ingcel; "and whether or not there is a king in it, it is a royal house, and I will take it as my share when the time comes." "You may do that," said Conaire's foster-brothers. "But we will not go against it before we know who is in it."

"The first I saw," said Ingcel, "was a large man, of good race, with bright eyes, with hair like flax; his face open, wide above and narrow below; with modest looks, and having no beard. A five-barbed spear in his hand, and a shield with five gold circles on it. Nine men he had about him, all beautiful and all alike, so that you would think they had the one father and mother. Who were those men, Ferogain?" he said.

"It is easy to say that," said Ferogain. "That was Cormac Conloingeas, son of Conchubar, the best fighter behind a shield in all Ireland, but he is modest with all that. And those were his nine comrades about him; they have never put men to death because of their poverty, or spared them because of their riches. He is a good leader they have with them. I swear by the gods my people swear by, it is no small slaughter they will make before the Inn to-night."

"It is a pity for him that will make the attack," said Lomna Druth, the Fool, "because of that man only, Cormac Conloingeas. And if I had my way," he said, "the attack would not be made, for the sake of that man alone and his beauty and his goodness."

"You will not be able to hinder it, Lomna," said

Ingcel. "You are no good of a fighter; I know you well, there are clouds of weakness coming on you. No one, whether old man or story-teller, will be able to say I drew back from this fight before I had gone through with it."

"It is well enough for you, Ingcel," said Lomna; "you will escape after the fight, and you will bring away the head of a strange king with you, but as for myself," he said, "it is my head will be the first to be tossed to and fro to-night."

"What did you see after that?" said Ferogain.

"I saw a room with three soft young boys in it and they wearing cloaks of silk with gold brooches. Long yellow hair they had, as curly as a ram's head; a golden shield and a candle of a king's house over each of them, and every one in the house humours them. Who were those, Ferogain?" he said.

But Ferogain was crying tears down, so that the front of his cloak was wet, and it was a long time before he could bring out his voice. "O little ones," he said then, "I have good reason for crying. Those are the three sons of the king, Oball and Obline and Corpre Findmor."

"There is grief on us if that story is true," said the other sons of Donn Dessa; "for it is good those three are. They are as mannerly as young girls, and they have the hearts of brothers, and the courage of lions. Whoever has been with them and parts from them, it is little he sleeps or eats till the end of nine days, fretting after their company. It is a pity for him that will destroy them."

"I saw after that," said Ingcel, "a very fair man, having a golden bush of hair, the size of a reaping basket. A long, heavy three-edged sword in his hand, a red shield speckled with rivets of white bronze between plates of gold."

"That man is known to all the men of Ireland," said Ferogain. "It is Conall Cearnach, son of Amergin, and he is the man Conaire thinks most of in the world; and that shield in his hand is the Lam-tapaid. There are seven doorways in that inn, and when the attack is made, Conall Cearnach will be at every one of them. What did you see after that, Ingcel?" he said.

"I saw," he said, "a brown big man, with short brown hair and a red speckled cloak, and a black shield with clasps of gold; and with him two chief men, in their first greyness, and black swords at their sides. And one of them had in his hand a great spear, with fifty rivets through it, and he shook it over his head, and struck the haft against the palm of his hand three times, and then he plunged it into a great pot that stood before them, with some black thing in it, and when he was putting it in there were flames on the shaft. Who were those men, Ferogain?"

"That brown man is Muinremar, son of Geirgind, one of the champions of the Red Branch. And another is Sencha, the beautiful son of Ailell; and the man with the spear is Dubthach, the Beetle of Ulster, and the spear in his hand is Celthair's Luin, that was in the battle of Magh Tuireadh, and that was brought from the east by the three children of Tuireann, and when a battle is coming near, it flames up of itself, and it must be kept quenched in a vessel, or it will go through whoever has it in his hand."

"I saw after that," said Ingcel, "a room with nine men in it, fair-haired and beautiful, with speckled cloaks, and above them were nine bagpipes, and light was shining from the ornaments that were on them."

"Those are the nine pipers that came to Conaire out of the hill of the Sidhe at Bregia," said Ferogain, "because of the great stories about him. The best pipers they are in the whole world. And they are good fighters, but to fight with them is to fight with a shadow, for they kill but cannot be killed, because they are from the Sidhe."

"I saw after that," said Ingcel, "three very big men, with terrible looks. A dress of rough hair they had, and a club of iron with chains on it in every man's hand. There was sadness on them, and they standing alone, and every one in the house avoiding them. Who were those, Ferogain?"

Ferogain was silent for a while, and he said then, "I do not know of any such men in the world, unless they might be the three giants Cuchulain spared, the time he took them from the men of Falga, he would not let them be killed because of their strangeness; Conaire bought them from Cuchulain after that, so it is along with him they are."

"I saw nine men in the north side of the house," said Ingcel, "having very yellow manes of hair, and short linen dresses, and purple cloaks without brooches; broad spears, and red curved shields."

"I know those men," said Ferogain; "three royal princes of Britain that are with the king, Oswald and his two foster-brothers, Osbrit of the Long Hand and his two foster-brothers, Lindas and his two foster-brothers."

"Three red men I saw after that," said Ingcel; "red shields above them, red spears in their hands, their three red horses in their bridles in front of the Inn."

"Those are the three champions that did deceit and falsehood among the Sidhe," said Ferogain, "and it is the punishment was put on them by the king of the Sidhe, to be three times destroyed by the King of Teamhair; and Conaire is the last king through whom they will be destroyed; yet they will not be killed, nor will they kill any one. It is to work out their own destruction they are come."

"I saw after that," said Ingcel, "a big man, and his

hair white, and the shame of baldness on him, and gold earrings in his ears. Nine swords he had in his hand, and nine silver shields, and nine golden apples. He was throwing each of them upwards, and not one would fall on the ground, but each of them rising and falling past each other like bees on a sunny day. But as I looked at him, he let all fall to the ground, and the people about him cried out, and the king that was sitting there said to him, 'We have been together since I was a little boy, and your tricks never failed till to-night.'

"'My grief!' he said. 'Fair master, Conaire, I have good cause for it; an unfriendly eye looked at me; there is some bad thing in front of the Inn.'

"And when the king heard that, it is what he said: 'I had a dream in my sleep a while ago, of the howling of my dog Ossar, of wounded men, of a wind of terror, of keening that overcame laughter.'"

"That was Taulchinne, Conaire's juggler," said Ferogain. "And tell me now," he said, "what was the appearance of the king?"

"Of all the men I ever saw in the world," said Ingcel, "he is the best in shape, and the most beautiful; young he is, and wise and kinglike. The colour of his hair was like the shining of purified gold; the cloak about him was like the mist of a May morning, changing from colour to colour, every colour more beautiful than another; a wheel brooch of gold reaching from his chin to his waist; his golden-hilted sword within his reach."

"That was Conaire, the High King, indeed," said Ferogain; "and it is he is the greatest and the best and the comeliest of the kings of the whole world, and there is no fault in him, either as to wisdom or bravery or knowledge or words or worthiness. Tender he is, a sleepy, simple man, till he chances on some brave thing to do, but when his anger is awaked, the champions of Ireland and of Scotland will not win their battle so long as he is against them. And I swear by the oath my people swear by, unless drink should fail him, or the like, that man alone would hold the Inn till help would gather to him from the Wave of Cliodna in the south, to the Wave of Essruadh in the north."

"It is time for us to rise up," said Ingcel then, "and to get on to the house."

So with that the outlaws rose up and went on to the Inn, and the noise of their voices was heard about it.

"Be quiet now and listen," said Conaire. "What is that we hear?"

"Fighting men about the house," said Conall Cearnach. "There are fighting men to meet them here," said Conaire. "They will be wanted to-night," said Conall.

Then Lomna Druth, the Fool, broke in first to the house, and the doorkeepers struck off his head, and it was tossed three times in and out of the Inn, just as he himself had foretold.

Then they all attacked one another, and Conaire himself went out with his people and killed a great many of the outlaws outside. And three times the Inn was set on fire, and three times it was put out again. And Conaire got to his arms then, for he had not got them in the first attack, and he went out again and made a great slaughter, so that the outlaws were driven back. "I told you," said Ferogain, "that all the men of Ireland and of Alban could not take the house till Conaire's rage would be quenched." "It is short his time will be," said the Druids that were along with the outlaws. And what they put on him by their enchantments was a great thirst, so that he went back to the house and called for a drink. "A drink to me, Mac Cecht," he said. "That is not the order you are used to give me," said

Mac Cecht. "What I have to do is to keep you from the men that are attacking you all round the house; ask a drink of your steward and of your cup-bearers," he said.

Then Conaire called to his cup-bearers for a drink. "There is none," they said, "for every drop in the house was thrown on the fire to put it out." "Get me a drink, Mac Cecht," he said again then; "for if I am to die, it is all the same to me by what death I die."

Then Mac Cecht gave a choice to the champions of Ireland that were in the house, would they go out and look for a drink for Conaire, or would they stop in the house and defend him.   And Conall Cearnach called out: "Leave the defence of the king to us, and go you and look for the drink, for it was of you it was asked."   And he was vexed with Mac Cecht for putting the choice to them, and there was never a very friendly feeling between them afterwards.

Then Mac Cecht went to look for a drink, and he brought Conaire's great golden cup with him, and an iron spit, the cauldron spit, in his other hand.

He burst out on the outlaws, and attacked them with blows of the spit, so that many got their death; and then he took his shield and made a round with his sword above his head, and cut down all before him, and got through the whole band.

And it would be too long to tell, and it would tire the hearers, all that happened after that; the people of the Inn coming out and making attacks, and some of them getting their death, and the most part making their escape.   And at last there were none left in the Inn with Conaire but Conall, and Sencha, and Dubthach.

Now from the rage that was on Conaire, and the greatness of the fight he had fought, a great drouth came on him again, and such a fever of thirst, and no drink to get, that he died of it in the end.

Then the other three, when they saw the High King was dead, went out and cut their way through their enemies, and got away with their lives, but if they did, they were wounded, and hurt, and broken.

And Conall Cearnach, after he got away, went on to his father's house, and but half his shield left in his hand, and a few bits left of his two spears. And he found Amergin, his father, out before his dun in Tailltin.

"Those are fierce wolves that have hunted you, my son," said he. "It was not wolves that wounded me, but a sharp fight with fighting-men," said Conall. "Have you news from Da Derga's Inn?" said Amergin. "Is your lord living?" "He is not living," said Conall. "I swear by the gods the great tribes of Ulster swear by, the man is a coward that came out alive, leaving his lord dead among his enemies," said Amergin. "My own wounds are not white, old hero," said Conall. And with that he showed him his right arm, that was full of wounds. "That arm fought there, my son," said Amergin. "That is true," said Conall. "There are many in front of the Inn now it gave drinks of death to last night."

Now, as to Mac Cecht, after he got away from the Inn, he went on to the well of Casair, that was near him in Crith Cualann, but he could not find so much as the full of the cup of water in it. Then he went on through the night, from lake to lake, and from river to river, but he could not find the full of the cup of water in any one of them. But at last he came to Uaran Garad on Magh Ai, and it could not hide itself from him, and he filled the cup, and went back again, and reached Da Derga's Inn before morning. And when he got there, he saw two men, and they striking off Conaire's head; and Mac Cecht struck off the head of one of them, and then the other man was going away with the king's head, and he took up a stone and threw it at him, that it broke his back.

Then Mac Cecht stooped down and poured the water into Conaire's mouth and his throat. And when the water was poured in, the head spoke and it said: "A good man Mac Cecht is, a good man, a good champion without and within. He gives drink, he saves a king, he does a deed ; it is well he fought at the door, it is well he made an end of fighting men. It is good I would be, and I alive, to Mac Cecht of the great name."

And it was after that, Mac Cecht brought the body of the High King on his back to Teamhair, and buried him there as some say. And he himself went to his own country, into Connaught. And the place he stopped in was called, from his sharp grief, Magh Bron-gear.

And there was no High King chosen to rule over Ireland for a good many years after that.

VII

FATE OF THE SONS OF USNACH

NOW it was one Fedlimid, son of Doll, was harper to King Conchubar, and he had but one child, and this is the story of her birth.

Cathbad, the Druid, was at Fedlimid's house one day. "Have you got knowledge of the future?" said Fedlimid. "I have a little," said Cathbad. "What is it you are wanting to know?" "I was not asking to know anything," said Fedlimid, "but if you know of anything that may be going to happen me, it is as well for you to tell me."

Cathbad went out of the house for a while, and when he came back he said: "Had you ever any children?" "I never had," said Fedlimid, "and the wife I have had none, and we have no hope ever to have any; there is no one with us but only myself and my wife." "That puts wonder on me," said Cathbad, "for I see by Druid signs that it is on account of a daughter belonging to you, that more blood will be shed than ever was shed in Ireland since time and race began. And great heroes and bright candles of the Gael will lose their lives because of her." "Is that the foretelling you have made for me?" said Fedlimid, and there was anger on him, for he thought the Druid was mocking him; "if that is all you can say, you can keep it for yourself; it is little I think of your share of knowledge." "For all that," said Cathbad, "I am certain of its truth, for I can see it all clearly in my own mind."

The Druid went away, but he was not long gone when Fedlimid's wife was found to be with child. And as her time went on, his vexation went on growing, that he had not asked more questions of Cathbad, at the time he was talking to him, and he was under a smouldering care by day and by night, for it is what he was thinking, that neither his own sense and understanding, or the share of friends he had, would be able to save him, or to make a back against the world, if this misfortune should come upon him, that would bring such great shedding of blood upon the earth; and it is the thought that came, that if this child should be born, what he had to do was to put her far away, where no eye would see her, and no ear hear word of her.

The time of the delivery of Fedlimid's wife came on, and it was a girl-child she gave birth to. Fedlimid did not allow any living person to come to the house or to see his wife, but himself alone.

But just after the child was born, Cathbad, the Druid, came in again, and there was shame on Fedlimid when he saw him, and when he remembered how he would not believe his words. But the Druid looked at the child and he said: "Let Deirdre be her name; harm will come through her.

"She will be fair, comely, bright-haired; heroes will fight for her, and kings go seeking for her."

And then he took the child in his arms, and it is what he said: "O Deirdre, on whose account many shall weep, on whose account many women shall be envious, there will be trouble on Ulster for your sake, O fair daughter of Fedlimid.

"Many will be jealous of your face, O flame of beauty; for your sake heroes shall go to exile. For your sake deeds of anger shall be done in Emain; there is harm in your face, for it will bring banishment and death on the sons of kings.

"In your fate, O beautiful child, are wounds, and ill-doings, and shedding of blood.

"You will have a little grave apart to yourself; you will be a tale of wonder for ever, Deirdre."

Cathbad went away then, and he sent Levarcham, daughter of Aedh, to the house; and Fedlimid asked her would she take the venture of bringing up the child, far away where no eye would see her, and no ear hear of her. Levarcham said she would do that, and that she would do her best to keep her the way he wished.

So Fedlimid got his men, and brought them away with him to a mountain, wide and waste, and there he bade them to make a little house, by the side of a round green hillock, and to make a garden of apple-trees behind it, with a wall about it. And he bade them put a roof of green sods over the house, the way a little company might live in it, without notice being taken of them.

Then he sent Levarcham and the child there, that no eye might see, and no ear hear of Deirdre. He put all in good order before them, and he gave them provisions, and he told Levarcham that food and all she wanted would be sent from year to year as long as she lived.

And so Deirdre and her foster-mother lived in the lonely place among the hills without the knowledge or the notice of any strange person, until Deirdre was fourteen years of age. And Deirdre grew straight and clean like a rush on the bog, and she was comely beyond comparison of all the women of the world, and her movements were like the swan on the wave, or the deer on the hill. She was the young girl of the greatest beauty and of the gentlest nature of all the women of Ireland.

Levarcham, that had charge of her, used to be giving Deirdre every knowledge and skill that she had herself. There was not a blade of grass growing from root, or a bird singing in the wood, or a star shining from heaven, but Deirdre had the name of it. But there was one thing she would not have her know, she would not let her have friendship with any living person of the rest of the world outside their own house.

But one dark night of winter, with black clouds overhead, a hunter came walking the hills, and it is what happened, he missed the track of the hunt, and lost his way and his comrades.

And a heaviness came upon him, and he lay down on the side of the green hillock by Deirdre's house. He was weak with hunger and going, and perished with cold, and a deep sleep came upon him. While he was lying there a dream came to the hunter, and he thought that he was near the warmth of a house of the Sidhe, and the Sidhe inside making music, and he called out in his dream, " If there is any one inside, let them bring me in, in the name of the Sun and the Moon." Deirdre heard the voice, and she said to Levarcham, " Mother, mother, what is that ? " But Levarcham said, " It is nothing that matters ; it is the birds of the air gone astray, and trying to find one another. But let them go back to the branches of the wood." Another troubled dream came on the hunter, and he cried out a second time. " What is that ? " asked Deirdre again. " It is nothing that matters," said Levarcham. " The birds of the air are looking for one another ; let them go past to the branches of the wood." Then a third dream came to the hunter, and he cried out a third time, if there was any one in the hill to let him in for the sake of the Elements, for he was perished with cold and overcome with hunger. " Oh !

what is that, Levarcham?" said Deirdre. "There is nothing there for you to see, my child, but only the birds of the air, and they lost to one another, but let them go past us to the branches of the wood. There is no place or shelter for them here to-night." "Oh, mother," said Deirdre, "the bird asked to come in for the sake of the Sun and the Moon, and it is what you yourself told me, that anything that is asked like that, it is right for us to give it. If you will not let in the bird that is perished with cold and overcome with hunger, I myself will let it in." So Deirdre rose up and drew the bolt from the leaf of the door, and let in the hunter. She put a seat in the place for sitting, food in the place for eating, and drink in the place for drinking, for the man who had come into the house. "Come now and eat food, for you are in want of it," said Deirdre. "Indeed it is I was in want of food and drink and warmth when I came into this house; but by my word, I have forgotten that since I saw yourself," said the hunter. "How little you are able to curb your tongue," said Levarcham. "It is not a great thing for you to keep your tongue quiet when you get the shelter of a house and the warmth of a hearth on a dark winter night." "That is so," said the hunter, "I may do that much, to keep my mouth shut; but I swear by the oath my people swear by, if some others of the people of the world saw this great beauty that is hidden away here, they would not leave her long with you." "What people are those?" said Deirdre. "I will tell you that," said the hunter; "they are Naoise, son of Usnach, and Ainnle and Ardan, his two brothers." "What is the appearance of these men, if we should ever see them?" said Deirdre. "This is the appearance that is on those three men," said the hunter: "the colour of the raven is on their hair, their skin is like the swan on the wave, their cheeks like the blood of the speckled red calf, and their swiftness and their leap are like the

salmon of the stream and like the deer of the grey
mountain; and the head and shoulders of Naoise are
above all the other men of Ireland." "However they
may be," said Levarcham, "get you out from here, and
take another road; and by my word, little is my thank-
fulness to yourself, or to her that let you in." "You need
not send him out for telling me that," said Deirdre,
"for as to those three men, I myself saw them last night
in a dream, and they hunting upon a hill."

The hunter went away, but in a little time after he
began to think to himself how Conchubar, High King of
Ulster, was used to lie down at night and to rise up in
the morning by himself, without a wife or any one to
speak to; and that if he could see this great beauty it
was likely he would bring her home to Emain, and that
he himself would get the good-will of the king for
telling him there was such a queen to be found on the
face of the world.

So he went straight to King Conchubar at Emain
Macha, and he sent word in to the king that he had
news for him, if he would hear it. The king sent for
him to come in. "What is the reason of your journey?"
he said. "It is what I have to tell you, King," said the
hunter, "that I have seen the greatest beauty that ever
was born in Ireland, and I am come to tell you of it."

"Who is this great beauty, and in what place is she to
be seen, when she was never seen before you saw her,
if you did see her?" "I did see her, indeed," said the
hunter, "but no other man can see her, unless he knows
from me the place where she is living." "Will you
bring me to the place where she is, and you will have
a good reward?" said the king. "I will bring you
there," said the hunter. "Let you stay with my household to-night," said Conchubar, "and I myself and my
people will go with you early on the morning of to-
morrow." "I will stay," said the hunter, and he

stayed that night in the household of King Conchubar.

Then Conchubar sent to Fergus and to the other chief men of Ulster, and he told them of what he was about to do. Though it was early when the songs and the music of the birds began in the woods, it was earlier yet when Conchubar, king of Ulster, rose up with his little company of near friends, in the fresh spring morning of the fresh and pleasant month of May, and the dew was heavy on every bush and flower as they went out towards the green hill where Deirdre was living

But many a young man of them that had a light glad, leaping step when they set out, had but a tired, slow, failing step before the end, because of the length and the roughness of the way. "It is down there below," said the hunter, "in the house in that valley, the woman is living, but I myself will not go nearer it than this.

Conchubar and his troop went down then to the green hillock where Deirdre was, and they knocked at the door of the house. Levarcham called out that neither answer nor opening would be given to any one at all, and that she did not want disturbance put on herself or her house. "Open," said Conchubar, "in the name of the High King of Ulster." When Levarcham heard Conchubar's voice, she knew there was no use trying to keep Deirdre out of sight any longer, and she rose up in haste and let in the king, and as many of his people as could follow him.

When the king saw Deirdre before him, he thought in himself that he never saw in the course of the day, or in the dreams of the night, a creature so beautiful, and he gave her his full heart's weight of love there and then. It is what he did; he put Deirdre up on the shoulders of his men, and she herself and Levarcham were brought away to Emain Macha.

With the love that Conchubar had for Deirdre, he wanted to marry her with no delay, but when her leave was asked, she would not give it, for she was young yet, and she had no knowledge of the duties of a wife, or the ways of a king's house. And when Conchubar was pressing her hard, she asked him to give her a delay of a year and a day. He said he would give her that, though it was hard for him, if she would give him her certain promise to marry him at the year's end. She did that, and Conchubar got a woman teacher for her, and nice, fine, pleasant, modest maidens to be with her at her lying down and at her rising up, to be companions to her. And Deirdre grew wise in the works of a young girl, and in the understanding of a woman; and if any one at all looked at her face, whatever colour she was before that, she would blush crimson red. And it is what Conchubar thought, that he never saw with the eyes of his body a creature that pleased him so well.

One day Deirdre and her companions were out on a hill near Emain Macha, looking around them in the pleasant sunshine, and they saw three men walking together. Deirdre was looking at the men and wondering at them, and when they came near, she remembered the talk of the hunter, and the three men she saw in her dream, and she thought to herself that these were the three sons of Usnach, and that this was Naoise, that had his head and shoulders above all the men of Ireland. The three brothers went by without turning their eyes at all upon the young girls on the hillside, and they were singing as they went, and whoever heard the low singing of the sons of Usnach, it was enchantment and music to them, and every cow that was being milked and heard it, gave two-thirds more of milk. And it is what happened, that love for Naoise came into the heart of Deirdre, so that she could not but follow him. She gathered up her skirt and went after the three men that had gone past the foot of the hill, leaving her companions there after her.

But Ainnle and Ardan had heard talk of the young girl that was at Conchubar's Court, and it is what they thought, that if Naoise their brother would see her, it is for himself he would have her, for she was not yet married to the king. So when they saw Deirdre coming after them, they said to one another to hasten their steps, for they had a long road to travel, and the dusk of night coming on. They did so, and Deirdre saw it, and she cried out after them, "Naoise, son of Usnach, are you going to leave me?" "What cry was that came to my ears, that it is not well for me to answer, and not easy for me to refuse?" said Naoise. "It was nothing but the cry of Conchubar's wild ducks," said his brothers; "but let us quicken our steps and hasten our feet, for we have a long road to travel, and the dusk of the evening coming on." They did so, and they were widening the distance between themselves and her. Then Deirdre cried, "Naoise! Naoise! son of Usnach, are you going to leave me?" "What cry was it that came to my ears and struck my heart, that it is not well for me to answer, or easy for me to refuse?" said Naoise. "Nothing but the cry of Conchubar's wild geese," said his brothers; "but let us quicken our steps and hasten our feet, the darkness of night is coming on." They did so, and were widening the distance between themselves and her. Then Deirdre cried the third time, "Naoise! Naoise! Naoise! son of Usnach, are you going to leave me?" "What sharp, clear cry was that, the sweetest that ever came to my ears, and the sharpest that ever struck my heart, of all the cries I ever heard," said Naoise. "What is it but the scream of Conchubar's lake swans," said his brothers. "That was the third cry of some person beyond there," said Naoise, "and I swear by my hand of valour," he said, " I will go no further until I see where the cry comes from." So Naoise turned back and met Deirdre, and Deirdre and Naoise kissed one another three times, and she gave a kiss to each of his brothers. And with the confusion that was on her, a blaze of red fire came upon her, and her colour came and went as quickly as the aspen by the stream. And it is what Naoise thought to himself, that he never saw a woman so beautiful in his life; and he gave Deirdre, there and then, the love that he never gave to living thing, to vision, or to creature, but to herself alone.

Then he lifted her high on his shoulder, and he said to his brothers to hasten their steps; and they hastened them.

" Harm will come of this," said the young men. " Although there should harm come," said Naoise, " I am willing to be in disgrace while I live. We will go with her to another province, and there is not in Ireland a king who will not give us a welcome." So they called their people, and that night they set out with three times fifty men, and three times fifty women, and three times fifty greyhounds, and Deirdre in their midst.

They were a long time after that shifting from one place to another all around Ireland, from Essruadh in the south, to Beinn Etair in the east again, and it is often they were in danger of being destroyed by Conchubar's devices. And one time the Druids raised a wood before them, but Naoise and his brothers cut their way through it. But at last they got out of Ulster and sailed to the country of Alban, and settled in a lonely place; and when hunting on the mountains failed them, they fell upon the cattle of the men of Alban, so that these gathered together to make an end of them. But the sons of Usnach called to the king of Scotland, and he took them into his friendship, and they gave him their help when he went out into battles or to war.

But all this time they had never spoken to the king of Deirdre, and they kept her with themselves, not to let any one see her, for they were afraid they might get their death on account of her, she being so beautiful.

But it chanced very early one morning, the king's steward came to visit them, and he found his way into the house where Naoise and Deirdre were, and there he saw them asleep beside one another. He went back then to the king, and he said: "Up to this time there has never been found a woman that would be a fitting wife for you; but there is a woman on the shore of Loch Ness now, is well worthy of you, king of the East. And what you have to do is to make an end of Naoise, for it is of his wife I am speaking." "I will not do that," said the king; "but go to her," he said, "and bid her to come and see me secretly." The steward brought her that message, but Deirdre sent him away, and all that he had said to her, she told it to Naoise afterwards. Then when she would not come to him, the king sent the sons of Usnach into every hard fight, hoping they would get their death, but they won every battle, and came back safe again. And after a while they went to Loch Eitche, near the sea, and they were left to themselves there for a while in peace and quietness. And they settled and made a dwelling house for themselves by the side of Loch Ness, and they could kill the salmon of the stream from out their own door, and the deer of the grey hills from out their window. But when Naoise went to the court of the king, his clothes were splendid among the great men of the army of Scotland, a cloak of bright purple, rightly shaped, with a fringe of bright gold; a coat of satin with fifty hooks of silver; a brooch on which were a hundred polished gems; a gold-hilted sword in

his hand, two blue-green spears of bright points, a
dagger with the colour of yellow gold on it, and a hilt
of silver. But the two children they had, Gaiar and
Aebgreine, they gave into the care of Manannan, Son of
the Sea. And he cared them well in Emhain of the
Apple Trees, and he brought Bobaras the poet to give
learning to Gaiar. And Aebgreine of the Sunny Face
he gave in marriage afterwards to Rinn, son of Eochaidh
Juil of the Land of Promise.

Now it happened after a time that a very great
feast was made by Conchubar, in Emain Macha, for
all the great among his nobles, so that the whole
company were easy and pleasant together. The
musicians stood up to play their songs and to give
poems, and they gave out the branches of relationship
and of kindred. These are the names of the poets
that were in Emain at the time, Cathbad, the Druid,
son of Conall, son of Rudraige; Geanann of the
Bright Face, son of Cathbad; Ferceirtne, and Geanann
Black-Knee, and many others, and Sencha, son of
Ailell.

They were all drinking and making merry until
Conchubar, the king, raised his voice and spoke aloud,
and it is what he said : " I desire to know from you, did
you ever see a better house than this house of Emain,
or a hearth better than my hearth in any place you
were ever in ? " " We did not," they said. " If that is
so," said Conchubar, " do you know of anything at all
that is wanting to you ? " " We know of nothing," said
they. " That is not so with me," said Conchubar. " I
know of a great want that is on you, the want of the
three best candles of the Gael, the three noble sons
of Usnach, that ought not to be away from us for the
sake of any woman in the world, Naoise, Ainnle, and
Ardan ; for surely they are the sons of a king, and

they would defend the High Kingship against the best men of Ireland." "If we had dared," said they, "it is long ago we would have said it, and more than that, the province of Ulster would be equal to any other province in Ireland, if there was no Ulsterman in it but those three alone, for it is lions they are in hardness and in bravery." "If that is so," said Conchubar, "let us send word by a messenger to Alban, and to the dwelling-place of the sons of Usnach, to ask them back again." "Who will go there with the message?" said they all. "I cannot know that," said Conchubar, "for there is *geasa*, that is bonds, on Naoise not to come back with any man only one of the three, Conall Cearnach, or Fergus, or Cuchulain, and I will know now," said he, "which one of those three loves me best." Then he called Conall to one side, and he asked him, "What would you do with me if I should send you for the sons of Usnach, and if they were destroyed through me—a thing I do not mean to do?" "As I am not going to undertake it," said Conall, "I will say that it is not one alone I would kill, but any Ulsterman I would lay hold of that had harmed them would get shortening of life from me and the sorrow of death." "I see well," said Conchubar, "you are no friend of mine," and he put Conall away from him. Then he called Cuchulain to him, and asked him the same as he did the other. "I give my word, as I am not going," said Cuchulain, "if you want that of me, and that you think to kill them when they come, it is not one person alone that would die for it, but every Ulsterman I could lay hold of would get shortening of life from me and the sorrow of death." "I see well," said Conchubar, "that you are no friend of mine." And he put Cuchulain from him. And then he called Fergus to him, and asked him the same question, and Fergus said, "Whatever may happen, I promise your blood will be safe from me, but besides yourself there is no Ulsterman that would try to harm them, and that I would lay hold of, but I would give him shortening of life and the sorrow of death." "I see well," said Conchubar, "it is yourself must go for them, and it is to-morrow you must set out, for it is with you they will come, and when you are coming back to us westward, I put you under bonds to go first to the fort of Borach, son of Cainte, and give me your word now that as soon as you get there, you will send on the sons of Usnach to Emain, whether it be day or night at the time." After that the two of them went in together, and Fergus told all the company how it was under his charge they were to be put.

Then Conchubar went to Borach and asked had he a feast ready prepared for him. "I have," said Borach, "but although I was able to make it ready, I was not able to bring it to Emain." "If that is so," said Conchubar, "give it to Fergus when he comes back to Ireland, for it is *geasa* on him not to refuse your feast." Borach promised he would do that, and so they wore away that night.

So Fergus set out in the morning, and he brought no guard nor helpers with him, but himself and his two sons, Fair-Haired Iollan, and Rough-Red Buinne, and Cuillean, the shield-bearer, and the shield itself. They went on till they got to the dwelling-place of the sons of Usnach, and to Loch Eitche in Alba. It is how the sons of Usnach lived; they had three houses, and the house where they made ready the food, it is not there they would eat it, and the house where they would eat it, it is not there they would sleep.

When Fergus came to the harbour he let a great shout out of him. And it is how Naoise and Deirdre were, they had a chessboard between them, and they playing on it. Naoise heard the shout, and he said,

"That is the shout of a man of Ireland." "It is not, but the cry of a man of Alban," said Deirdre. She knew at the first it was Fergus gave the shout, but she denied it. Then Fergus let another shout out of him. "That is an Irish shout," said Naoise again. "It is not, indeed," said Deirdre, "let us go on playing." Then Fergus gave the third shout, and the sons of Usnach knew this time it was the shout of Fergus, and Naoise said to Ardan to go out and meet him. Then Deirdre told him that she herself knew at the first shout that it was Fergus. "Why did you deny it, then, Queen?" said Naoise. "Because of a vision I saw last night," said Deirdre. "Three birds I saw coming to us from Emain Macha, and three drops of honey in their mouths, and they left them with us, and three drops of our blood they brought away with them." "What meaning do you put on that, Queen?" said Naoise. "It is," said Deirdre, "Fergus that is coming to us with a message of peace from Conchubar, for honey is not sweeter than a message of peace sent by a lying man." "Let that pass," said Naoise. "Is there anything in it but troubled sleep and the melancholy of woman? And it is a long time Fergus is in the harbour. Rise up, Ardan, to be before him, and bring him with you here." And Ardan went down to meet him, and gave a fond kiss to himself and to his two sons. And it is what he said: "My love to you, dear comrades." After that he asked news of Ireland, and they gave it to him, and then they came to where Naoise and Ainnle and Deirdre were, and they kissed Fergus and his two sons, and they asked news of Ireland from them. "It is the best news I have for you," said Fergus, "that Conchubar, king of Ulster, has sworn by the earth beneath him, by the high heaven above him, and by the sun that travels to the west, that he will have no rest by day nor sleep by night, if the sons of Usnach, his own foster-brothers, will not come back to the land of their home and the country of their birth; and he has sent us to ask you there." "It is better for them to stop here," said Deirdre, "for they have a greater sway in Scotland than Conchubar himself has in Ireland." "One's own country is better than any other thing," said Fergus, "for no man can have any pleasure, however great his good luck and his way of living, if he does not see his own country every day." "That is true," said Naoise, "for Ireland is dearer to myself than Alban, though I would get more in Alban than in Ireland." "It will be safe for you to come with me," said Fergus. "It will be safe indeed," said Naoise, "and we will go with you to Ireland; and though there were no trouble beneath the sun, but a man to be far from his own land, there is little delight in peace and a long sleep to a man that is an exile. It is a pity for the man that is an exile; it is little his honour, it is great his grief, for it is he will have his share of wandering."

It was not with Deirdre's will Naoise said that, and she was greatly against going with Fergus. And she said: "I had a dream last night of the three sons of Usnach, and they bound and put in the grave by Conchubar of the Red Branch." But Naoise said: "Lay down your dream, Deirdre, on the heights of the hills, lay down your dream on the sailors of the sea, lay down your dream on the rough grey stones, for we will give peace and we will get it from the king of the world and from Conchubar." But Deirdre spoke again, and it is what she said: "There is the howling of dogs in my ears; a vision of the night is before my eyes, I see Fergus away from us, I see Conchubar without mercy in his dun; I see Naoise without strength in battle; I see Ainnle without his loud-sounding shield; I see Ardan without shield or breastplate, and the Hill of Atha without delight. I see Conchubar asking for blood; I see Fergus caught with hidden lies; I see Deirdre crying with tears, I see Deirdre crying with tears."

"A thing that is unpleasing to me, and that I would never give in to," said Fergus, "is to listen to the howling of dogs, and to the dreams of women; and since Conchubar, the High King, has sent a message of friendship, it would not be right for you to refuse it." "It would not be right, indeed," said Naoise, "and we will go with you to-morrow." And Fergus gave his word, and he said, "If all the men of Ireland were against you, it would not profit them, for neither shield nor sword or a helmet itself would be any help or protection to them against you, and I myself to be with you." "That is true," said Naoise, "and we will go with you to Ireland."

They spent the night there until morning, and then they went where the ships were, and they went on the sea, and a good many of their people with them, and Deirdre looked back on the land of Alban, and it is what she said: "My love to you, O land to the east, and it goes ill with me to leave you; for it is pleasant are your bays and your harbours and your wide flowery plains and your green-sided hills; and little need was there for us to leave you." And she made this complaint: "Dear to me is that land, that land to the east, Alban, with its wonders; I would not have come from it hither but that I came with Naoise.

"Dear to me, Dun Fiodhaigh and Dun Fionn; dear is the dun above them; dear to me Inis Droignach, dear to me Dun Suibhne.

"O Coill Cuan! Ochone! Coil Cuan! where Ainnle used to come. My grief! it was short I thought his stay there with Naoise in Western Alban. Glen Laoi, O Glen Laoi, where I used to sleep under soft coverings;

fish and venison and badger's flesh, that was my portion in Glen Laoi.

"Glen Masan, my grief! Glen Masan! high its hart's-tongue, bright its stalks; we were rocked to pleasant sleep over the wooded harbour of Masan.

"Glen Archan, my grief! Glen Archan, the straight valley of the pleasant ridge; never was there a young man more light-hearted than my Naoise used to be in Glen Archan.

"Glen Eitche, my grief! Glen Eitche, it was there I built my first house; beautiful were the woods on our rising; the home of the sun is Glen Eitche.

"Glen-da-Rua, my grief! Glen-da-Rua, my love to every man that belongs to it; sweet is the voice of the cuckoo on the bending branch on the hill above Glen-da-Rua.

"Dear to me is Droighin over the fierce strand, dear are its waters over the clean sand; I would never have come out from it at all but that I came with my beloved!"

After she had made that complaint they came to Dun Borach, and Borach gave three fond kisses to Fergus and to the sons of Usnach along with him. It was then Borach said he had a feast laid out for Fergus, and that it was *geasa* for him to leave it until he would have eaten it. But Fergus reddened with anger from head to foot, and it is what he said: "It is a bad thing you have done, Borach, laying out a feast for me, and Conchubar to have made me give my word that as soon as I would come to Ireland, whether it would be by day or in the night-time, I would send on the sons of Usnach to Emain Macha." "I hold you under bonds," said Borach, "to stop and use the feast."

Then Fergus asked Naoise what should he do about the feast. "You must choose," said Deirdre, "whether you will forsake the children of Usnach or the feast, and it would be better for you to refuse the feast than to forsake the sons of Usnach." "I will not forsake them," said he, "for I will send my two sons, Fair-Haired Iollan and Rough-Red Buinne, with them, to Emain Macha." "On my word," said Naoise, "that is a great deal to do for us; for up to this no other person ever protected us but ourselves." And he went out of the place in great anger; and Ainnle, and Ardan, and Deirdre, and the two sons of Fergus followed him, and they left Fergus dark and sorrowful after them. But for all that, Fergus was full sure that if all the provinces of Ireland would go into one council, they would not consent to break the pledge he had given.

As for the sons of Usnach, they went on their way by every short road, and Deirdre said to them, "I will give you a good advice, Sons of Usnach, though you may not follow it." "What is that advice, Queen?" said Naoise. "It is," said she, "to go to Rechrainn, between Ireland and Scotland, and to wait there until Fergus has done with the feast; and that will be the keeping of his word to Fergus, and it will be the lengthening of your lives to you." "We will not follow that advice," said Naoise; and the children of Fergus said it was little trust she had in them, when she thought they would not protect her, though their hands might not be so strong as the hands of the sons of Usnach; and besides that, Fergus had given them his word. "Alas! it is sorrow came on us with the word of Fergus," said Deirdre, "and he to forsake us for a feast," and she made this complaint: "It is grief to me that ever I came from the east on the word of the unthinking son of Rogh. It is only lamentations I will make. Och! it is very sorrowful my heart is!

"My heart is heaped up with sorrow; it is to-night my great hurt is. My grief! my dear companions, the end of your days is come."

And it is what Naoise answered her : "Do not say that in your haste, Deirdre, more beautiful than the sun. Fergus would never have come for us eastward to bring us back to be destroyed."

And Deirdre said, "My grief! I think it too far for you, beautiful sons of Usnach, to have come from Alban of the rough grass ; it is lasting will be its life-long sorrow."

After that they went forward to Finncairn of the watch-tower on sharp-peaked Slieve Fuad, and Deirdre stayed after them in the valley, and sleep fell on her there.

When Naoise saw that Deirdre was left after them, he turned back as she was rising out of her sleep, and he said, "What made you wait after us, Queen?" "Sleep that was on me," said Deirdre ; "and I saw a vision in it." "What vision was that?" said Naoise. "It was," she said, "Fair-Haired Iollan that I saw without his head on him, and Rough-Red Buinne with his head on him ; and it is without help of Rough-Red Buinne you were, and it is with the help of Fair-Haired Iollan you were." And she made this complaint :

"It is a sad vision has been shown to me, of my four tall, fair, bright companions ; the head of each has been taken from him, and no help to be had one from another."

But when Naoise heard this he reproached her, and said, "O fair, beautiful woman, nothing does your mouth speak but evil. Do not let the sharpness and the great misfortune that come from it fall on your friends." And Deirdre answered him with kind, gentle words, and it is what she said : "It would be better to me to see harm come on any other person than upon any one of you three, with whom I have travelled over the seas and over the wide plains ; but when I look on you, it is only Buinne I can see safe and whole, and

I know by that his life will be longest among you; and indeed it is I that am sorrowful to-night."

After that they came forward to the high willows, and it was then Deirdre said, "I see a cloud in the air, and it is a cloud of blood; and I would give you a good advice, sons of Usnach," she said. "What is that advice?" said Naoise. "To go to Dundealgan where Cuchulain is, until Fergus has done with the feast, and to be under the protection of Cuchulain, for fear of the treachery of Conchubar." "Since there is no fear on us, we will not follow that advice," said Naoise. And Deirdre complained, and it is what she said: "O Naoise, look at the cloud I see above us in the air; I see a cloud over green Macha, cold and deep red like blood. I am startled by the cloud that I see here in the air; a thin, dreadful cloud that is like a clot of blood. I give a right advice to the beautiful sons of Usnach not to go to Emain to-night, because of the danger that is over them.

"We will go to Dundealgan, where the Hound of the Smith is; we will come to-morrow from the south along with the Hound, Cuchulain."

But Naoise said in his anger to Deirdre, "Since there is no fear on us, we will not follow your advice." And Deirdre turned to the grandsons of Rogh, and it is what she said: "It is seldom until now, Naoise, that yourself and myself were not of the one mind. And I say to you, Naoise, that you would not have gone against me like this, the day Manannan gave me the cup in the time of his great victory."

After that they went on to Emain Macha. "Sons of Usnach," said Deirdre, "I have a sign by which you will know if Conchubar is going to do treachery on you." "What sign is that?" said Naoise. "If you are let come into the house where Conchubar is, and the nobles of Ulster, then Conchubar is not going to do treachery on you.   But if it is in the House of the Red Branch you are put, then he is going to do treachery on you."

After that they came to Emain Macha, and they took the handwood and struck the door, and the doorkeeper asked who was there. They told him that it was the sons of Usnach, and Deirdre, and the two sons of Fergus were there.

When Conchubar heard that, he called his stewards and serving men to him, and he asked them how was the House of the Red Branch for food and for drink. They said that if all the seven armies of Ulster would come there, they would find what would satisfy them. "If that is so," said Conchubar, "bring the sons of Usnach into it."

It was then Deirdre said, "It would have been better for you to follow my advice, and never to have come to Emain, and it would be right for you to leave it, even at this time."   "We will not," said Fair-Haired Iollan, "for it is not fear or cowardliness was ever seen on us, but we will go to the house." So they went on to the House of the Red Branch, and the stewards and the serving-men with them, and well-tasting food was served to them, and pleasant drinks, till they were all glad and merry, except only Deirdre and the sons of Usnach ; for they did not use much food or drink, because of the length and the greatness of their journey from Dun Borach to Emain Macha. Then Naoise said, "Give the chessboard to us till we go playing." So they gave them the chessboard and they began to play.

It was just at that time Conchubar was asking, "Who will I send that will bring me word of Deirdre, and that will tell me if she has the same appearance and the same shape she had before, for if she has, there is not a woman in the world has a more beautiful shape or appearance than she has, and I will bring her out with edge of blade and point of sword in spite of the sons of Usnach, good though they be. But if not, let Naoise have her for himself." " I myself will go there," said Levarcham, " and I will bring you word of that." And it is how it was, Deirdre was dearer to her than any other person in the world; for it was often she went through the world looking for Deirdre and bringing news to her and from her. So Levarcham went over to the House of the Red Branch, and near it she saw a great troop of armed men, and she spoke to them, but they made her no answer, and she knew by that it was none of the men of Ulster were in it, but men from some strange country that Conchubar's messengers had brought to Emain.

And then she went in where Naoise and Deirdre were, and it is how she found them, the polished chessboard between them, and they playing on it; and she gave them fond kisses, and she said: "You are not doing well to be playing; and it is to bring Conchubar word if Deirdre has the same shape and appearance she used to have that he sent me here now; and there is grief on me for the deed that will be done in Emain to-night, treachery that will be done, and the killing of kindred, and the three bright candles of the Gael to be quenched, and Emain will not be the better of it to the end of life and time," and she made this complaint sadly and wearily:

"My heart is heavy for the treachery that is being done in Emain this night; on account of this treachery, Emain will never be at peace from this out.

"The three that are most king-like to-day under the sun; the three best of all that live on the earth, it is grief to me to-night they to die for the sake of any woman. Naoise and Ainnle whose deeds are known, and Ardan, their brother; treachery is to be done on the young, bright-faced three; it is not I that am not sorrowful to-night."

When she had made this complaint, Levarcham said
to the sons of Usnach and to the children of Fergus to
shut close the doors and the windows of the house and
to do bravery. "And oh, sons of Fergus," she said,
"defend your charge and your care bravely till Fergus
comes, and you will have praise and a blessing for it."
And she cried with many tears, and she went back to
where Conchubar was, and he asked news of Deirdre
of her. And Levarcham said, "It is good news and
bad news I have for you." "What news is that?"
said Conchubar. "It is the good news," she said, "the
three sons of Usnach to have come to you and to be
over there, and they are the three that are bravest and
mightiest in form and in looks and in countenance, of
all in the world; and Ireland will be yours from this
out, since the sons of Usnach are with you; and the
news that is worst with me is, the woman that was best
of the women of the world in form and in looks, going
out of Emain, is without the form and without the
appearance she used to have."

When Conchubar heard that, much of his jealousy
went backward, and he was drinking and making merry
for a while, until he thought on Deirdre again the
second time, and on that he asked, "Who will I get
to bring me word of Deirdre?" But he did not find
any one would go there. And then he said to Gelban,
the merry, pleasant son of the king of Lochlann: "Go
over and bring me word if Deirdre has the same shape
and the same appearance she used to have, for if she has,
there is not on the ridge of the world or on the waves
of the earth, a woman more beautiful than herself."

So Gelban went to the House of the Red Branch,
and he found the doors and the windows of the fort
shut, and fear came on him. And it is what he said:
"It is not an easy road for any one that would get to
the sons of Usnach, for I think there is very great

anger on them." And after that he found a window that was left open by forgetfulness in the house, and he was looking in. Then Deirdre saw him through the window, and when she saw him looking at her, she went into a red blaze of blushes, and Naoise knew that some one was looking at her from the window, and she told him that she saw a young man looking in at them. It is how Naoise was at that time, with a man of the chessmen in his hand, and he made a fair throw over his shoulder at the young man, that put the eye out of his head. The young man went back to where Conchubar was. "You were merry and pleasant going out," said Conchubar, "but you are sad and cheerless coming back." And then Gelban told him the story from beginning to end. "I see well," said Conchubar, "the man that made that throw will be king of the world, unless he has his life shortened. And what appearance is there on Deirdre?" he said. "It is this," said Gelban, "although Naoise put out my eye, I would have wished to stay there looking at her with the other eye, but for the haste you put on me; for there is not in the world a woman is better of shape or of form than herself."

When Conchubar heard that, he was filled with jealousy and with envy, and he bade the men of his army that were with him, and that had been drinking at the feast, to go and attack the place were the sons of Usnach were. So they went forward to the House of the Red Branch, and they gave three great shouts around it, and they put fires and red flames to it. When the sons of Usnach heard the shouts, they asked who those men were that were about the house. "Conchubar and the men of Ulster," they all said together. "Is it the pledge of Fergus you would break?" said Fair-Haired Iollan. "On my word," said Conchubar, "there will be sorrow on the sons of Usnach, Deirdre to be with them." "That is true," said Deirdre, "Fergus had deceived you." "By my oath," said Rough-Red Buinne, "if he betrayed, we will not betray." It was then Buinne went out and killed three-fifths of the fighting men outside, and put great disturbance on the rest; and Conchubar asked who was there, and who was doing destruction on his men like that. "It is I, myself, Rough-Red Buinne, son of Fergus," said he. "I will give you a good gift if you will leave off," said Conchubar. "What gift is that?" said Rough-Red Buinne. "A hundred of land," said Conchubar. "What besides?" said Rough-Red Buinne. "My own friendship and my counsel," said Conchubar. "I will take that," said Rough-Red Buinne. It was a good mountain that was given him as a reward, but it turned barren in the same night, and no green grew on it again for ever, and it used to be called the Mountain of the Share of Buinne.

Deirdre heard what they were saying. "By my word," she said, "Rough-Red Buinne has forsaken you, and in my opinion, it is like the father the son is." "I give my word," says Fair-Haired Iollan, "that is not so with me; as long as this narrow, straight sword stays in my hand, I will not forsake the sons of Usnach."

After that, Fair-Haired Iollan went out, and made three courses around the house, and killed three-fifths of heroes outside, and he came in again where Naoise was, and he playing chess, and Ainnle with him. So Iollan went out the second time, and made three other courses round the fort, and he brought a lighted torch with him on the lawn, and he went destroying the hosts, so that they dared not come to attack the house. And he was a good son, Fair-Haired Iollan, for he never refused any person on the ridge of the world anything that he had, and he never took wages from any person but only Fergus.

It was then Conchubar said : " What place is my own
son, Fiacra the Fair ? " " I am here, High Prince,"
said Fiacra. "By my word," said Conchubar, "it is
on the one night yourself and Iollan were born, and
as it is the arms of his father he has with him, let
you take my arms with you, that is, my shield, the
Ochain, my two spears, and my great sword, the Gorm
Glas, the Blue Green—and do bravery and great deeds
with them."

Then Fiacra took Conchubar's arms, and he and
Fair-Haired Iollan attacked one another, and they
made a stout fight, one against the other. But
however it was, Fair-Haired Iollan put down Fiacra,
so that he made him lie under the shelter of his shield,
till it roared for the greatness of the strait he was in ;
for it was the way with the Ochain, the shield of Conchubar, to roar when the person on whom it would be
was in danger ; and the three chief waves of Ireland,
the Wave of Tuagh, the Wave of Cliodna, and the Wave
of Rudraige, roared in answer to it.

It was at that time Conall Cearnach was at Dun
Sobairce, and he heard the Wave of Tuagh. "True it
is," said Conall, "Conchubar is in some danger, and it
is not right for me to be here listening to him."

Conall rose up on that, and he put his arms and his
armour on him, and came forward to where Conchubar
was at Emain Macha, and he found the fight going on
on the lawn, and Fiacra, the son of Conchubar, greatly
pressed by Fair-Haired Iollan, and neither the king of
Ulster nor any other person dared to go between
them. But Conall went aside, behind Fair-Haired Iollan
and thrust his sword through him. "Who is it has
wounded me behind my back ? " said Fair-Haired Iollan.
"Whoever did it, by my hand of valour, he would have
got a fair fight, face to face, from myself." "Who are
you yourself?" said Conall. "I am Iollan, son of

Fergus, and are you yourself Conall?" "It is I," said
Conall. "It is evil and it is heavy the work you have
done," said Iollan, "and the sons of Usnach under my
protection." "Is that true?" said Conall. "It is true,
indeed," said Iollan. "By my hand of valour," said
Conall, "Conchubar will not get his own son alive
from me to avenge it," and he gave a stroke of the
sword to Fiacra, so that he struck his head off, and he
left them so. The clouds of death came upon Fair-
Haired Iollan then, and he threw his arms towards
the fortress, and called out to Naoise to do bravery,
and after that he died.

It is then Conchubar himself came out and nineteen
hundred men with him, and Conall said to him: "Go
up now to the doorway of the fort, and see where your
sister's children are lying on a bed of trouble." And
when Conchubar saw them he said: "You are not
sister's children to me; it is not the deed of sister's
children you have done me, but you have done harm
to me with treachery in the sight of all the men of
Ireland." And it is what Ainnle said to him: "Although
we took well-shaped, soft-handed Deirdre from you, yet
we did a little kindness to you at another time, and
this is the time to remember it. That day your ship
was breaking up on the sea, and it full of gold and
silver, we gave you up our own ship, and ourselves
went swimming to the harbour." But Conchubar said:
"If you did fifty good deeds to me, surely this would
be my thanks; I would not give you peace, and you in
distress, but every great want I could put on you."

And then Ardan said: "We did another little kindness to you, and this is the time to remember it; the
day the speckled horse failed you on the green of
Dundealgan, it was we gave you the grey horse that
would bring you fast on your road."

But Conchubar said: "If you had done fifty good

deeds to me, surely this would be my thanks; I would not give you peace, and you in distress, but every great want I could put on you."

And then Naoise said: "We did you another good deed, and this is the time to remember it; we have put you under many benefits; it is strong our right is to your protection.

"The time when Murcael, son of Brian, fought the seven battles at Beinn Etair, we brought you, without fail, the heads of the sons of the king of the South-East."

But Conchubar said: "If you had done me fifty good deeds, surely this is my thanks; I would not give you peace in your distress, but every great want I could put upon you.

"Your death is not a death to me now, young sons of Usnach, since he that was innocent fell by you, the third best of the horsemen of Ireland."

Then Deirdre said: "Rise up, Naoise, take your sword, good son of a king, mind yourself well, for it is not long that life will be left in your fair body."

It is then all Conchubar's men came about the house, and they put fires and burning to it. Ardan went out then, and his men, and put out the fires and killed three hundred men. And Ainnle went out in the third part of the night, and he killed three hundred, and did slaughter and destruction on them.

And Naoise went out in the last quarter of the night, and drove away all the army from the house.

He came into the house after that, and it is then Deirdre rose up and said to him: "By my word, it is well you won your way; and do bravery and valour from this out, and it was bad advice you took when you ever trusted Conchubar."

As for the sons of Usnach, after that they made a good protection with their shields, and they put Deirdre in the middle and linked the shields around her, and they gave three leaps out over the walls of Emain, and they killed three hundred men in that sally.

When Conchubar saw that, he went to Cathbad, the Druid, and said to him : " Go, Cathbad, to the sons of Usnach, and work enchantment on them ; for unless they are hindered they will destroy the men of Ulster for ever if they go away in spite of them ; and I give the word of a true hero, they will get no harm from me, but let them only make agreement with me." When Cathbad heard that, he agreed, believing him, and he went to the end of his arts and his knowledge to hinder the sons of Usnach, and he worked enchantment on them, so that he put the likeness of a dark sea about them, with hindering waves. And when Naoise saw the waves rising he put up Deirdre on his shoulder, and it is how the sons of Usnach were, swimming on the ground as they were going out of Emain ; yet the men of Ulster did not dare to come near them until their swords had fallen from their hands. But after their swords fell from their hands, the sons of Usnach were taken. And when they were taken, Conchubar asked of the children of Durthacht to kill them. But the children of Durthacht said they would not do that. There was a young man with Conchubar whose name was Maine, and his surname Rough-Hand, son of the king of the fair Norwegians, and it is Naoise had killed his father and his two brothers ; Athrac and Triathrach were their names And he said he himself would kill the sons of Usnach. " If that is so," said Ardan, " kill me the first, for I am younger than my brothers, so that I will not see my brothers killed." " Let him not be killed but myself," said Ainnle. "Let that not be done," said Naoise, "for I have a sword that Manannan, son of Lir, gave me, and the stroke of it leaves nothing after it, track nor trace ; and strike the three of us together, and we will die at the one time." " That is well," said they all, "and let you lay down your heads," they said. They did that, and Maine gave a strong quick blow of the sword on the three necks together on the block, and struck the three heads off them with one stroke ; and the men of Ulster gave three loud sorrowful shouts, and cried aloud about them there.

As for Deirdre, she cried pitifully, wearily, and tore her fair hair, and she was talking on the sons of Usnach and on Alban, and it is what she said :

" A blessing eastward to Alban from me ; good is the sight of her bays and valleys, pleasant was it to sit on the slopes of her hills, where the sons of Usnach used to be hunting.

" One day, when the nobles of Scotland were drinking with the sons of Usnach, to whom they owed their affection, Naoise gave a kiss secretly to the daughter of the lord of Duntreon. He sent her a frightened deer, wild, and a fawn at its foot; and he went to visit her coming home from the host of Inverness. When myself heard that, my head filled full of jealousy ; I put my boat on the waves, it was the same to me to live or to die. They followed me swimming, Ainnle and Ardan, that never said a lie ; they turned me back again, two that would give battle to a hundred ; Naoise gave me his true word, he swore three times with his arms as witness, he would never put vexation on me again, until he would go from me to the hosts of the dead.

" Och ! if she knew to-night, Naoise to be under a covering of clay, it is she would cry her fill, and it is I would cry along with her."

After she had made this complaint, seeing they were all taken up with one another, Deirdre came forward on the lawn, and she was running round and round, up and down, from one to another, and Cuchulain met her, and she told him the story from first to last, how it had happened to the sons of Usnach. It is sorrowful Cuchulain was for that, for there was not in the world a man was dearer to him than Naoise. And he asked who killed him. "Maine Rough-Hand," said Deirdre. Then Cuchulain went away, sad and sorrowful, to Dundealgan.

After that Deirdre lay down by the grave, and they were digging earth from it, and she made this lament after the sons of Usnach :

"Long is the day without the sons of Usnach; it was never wearisome to be in their company; sons of a king that entertained exiles; three lions of the Hill of the Cave.

"Three darlings of the women of Britain; three hawks of Slieve Cuilenn; sons of a king served by valour, to whom warriors did obedience. The three mighty bears; three lions of the fort of Conrach; three sons of a king who thought well of their praise; three nurslings of the men of Ulster.

"Three heroes not good at homage; their fall is a cause of sorrow; three sons of the sister of a king; three props of the army of Cuailgne.

"Three dragons of Dun Monad, the three valiant men from the Red Branch; I myself will not be living after them, the three that broke hard battles.

"Three that were brought up by Aoife, to whom lands were under tribute; three pillars in the breach of battle; three pupils that were with Scathach.

"Three pupils that were with Uathach; three champions that were lasting in might; three shining sons of Usnach; it is weariness to be without them.

"The High King of Ulster, my first betrothed, I forsook for love of Naoise; short my life will be after him; I will make keening at their burial.

"That I would live after Naoise let no one think on the earth; I will not go on living after Ainnle and after Ardan.

"After them I myself will not live; three that would leap through the midst of battle; since my beloved is gone from me I will cry my fill over his grave.

"O young man, digging the new grave, do not make the grave narrow; I will be along with them in the grave, making lamentation and ochones!

"Many the hardship I met with along with the three heroes; I suffered want of house, want of fire, it is myself that used not to be troubled.

"Their three shields and their spears made a bed for me often. O young man, put their three swords close over their grave.

"Their three hounds, their three hawks, will be from this time without huntsmen; three helpers of every battle; three pupils of Conall Cearnach.

"The three leashes of those three hounds have brought a sigh from my heart; it is I had the care of them, the sight of them is a cause of grief.

"I was never one day alone to the day of the making of this grave, though it is often that myself and yourselves were in loneliness.

"My sight is gone from me with looking at the grave of Naoise; it is short till my life will leave me, and those who would have keened me do not live.

"Since it is through me they were betrayed I will be tired out with sorrow; it is a pity I was not in the earth before the sons of Usnach were killed.

"Sorrowful was my journey with Fergus, betraying me to the Red Branch; we were deceived all together with his sweet, flowery words. I left the delights of Ulster for the three heroes that were bravest; my life will not be long, I myself am alone after them.

" I am Deirdre without gladness, and I at the end of my life; since it is grief to be without them, I myself will not be long after them."

After that complaint Deirdre loosed out her hair, and threw herself on the body of Naoise before it was put in the grave and gave three kisses to him, and when her mouth touched his blood, the colour of burning sods came into her cheeks, and she rose up like one that had lost her wits, and she went on through the night till she came to where the waves were breaking on the strand. And a fisherman was there and his wife, and they brought her into their cabin and sheltered her, and she neither smiled nor laughed, nor took food, drink, or sleep, nor raised her head from her knees, but crying always after the sons of Usnach.

But when she could not be found at Emain, Conchubar sent Levarcham to look for her, and to bring her back to his palace, that he might make her his wife. And Levarcham found her in the fisherman's cabin, and she bade her come back to Emain, where she would have protection and riches and all that she would ask. And she gave her this message she brought from Conchubar : "Come up to my house, O branch with the dark eye-lashes, and there need be no fear on your fair face, of hatred or of jealousy or of reproach." And Deirdre said : "I will not go up to his house, for it is not land or earth or food I am wanting, or gold or silver or horses, but leave to go to the grave where the sons of Usnach are lying, till I give the three honey kisses to their three white, beautiful bodies." And she made this complaint :

"Make keening for the heroes that were killed on their coming to Ireland ; stately they used to be, coming to the house, the three great sons of Usnach.

"The sons of Usnach fell in the fight like three branches that were growing straight and nice, and they destroyed in a heavy storm that left neither bud nor twig of them.

"Naoise, my gentle, well-learned comrade, make no delay in crying him with me; cry for Ardan that killed the wild boars, cry for Ainnle whose stength was great.

"It was Naoise that would kiss my lips, my first man and my first sweetheart; it was Ainnle would pour out my drink, and it was Ardan would lay my pillow.

"Though sweet to you is the mead that is drunk by the soft-living son of Ness, the food of the sons of Usnach was sweeter to me all through my lifetime.

"Whenever Naoise would go out to hunt through the woods or the wide plains, all the meat he would bring back was better to me than honey.

"Though sweet to you are the sounds of pipes and of trumpets, it is truly I say to the king, I have heard music that is sweeter.

"Delightful to Conchubar, the king, are pipes and trumpets; but the singing of the sons of Usnach was more delightful to me.

"It was Naoise had the deep sound of the waves in his voice; it was the song of Ardan that was good, and the voice of Ainnle towards their green dwelling-place.

"Their birth was beautiful and their blossoming, as they grew to the strength of manhood; sad is the end to-day, the sons of Usnach to be cut down.

"Dear were their pleasant words, dear their young, high strength; in their going through the plains of Ireland there was a welcome before the coming of their strength.

"Dear their grey eyes that were loved by women, many looked on them as they went; when they went freely searching through the woods, their steps were pleasant on the dark mountain.

"I do not sleep at any time, and the colour is gone from my face; there is no sound can give me delight since the sons of Usnach do not come.

"I do not sleep through the night; my senses are scattered away from me, I do not care for food or drink. I have no welcome to-day for the pleasant drink of nobles, or ease, or comfort, or delight, or a great house, or the palace of a king.

"Do not break the strings of my heart as you took hold of my young youth, Conchubar; though my darling is dead, my love is strong to live. What is country to me, or land, or lordship? What are swift horses? What are jewels and gold? Och! it is I will be lying to-night on the strand like the beautiful sons of Usnach."

So Levarcham went back to Conchubar to tell him what way Deirdre was, and that she would not come with her to Emain Macha.

And when she was gone, Deirdre went out on the strand, and she found a carpenter making an oar for a boat, and making a mast for it, clean and straight, to put up a sail to the wind. And when she saw him making it, she said: "It is a sharp knife you have, to cut the oar so clean and so straight, and if you will give it to me," she said, "I will give you a ring of the best gold in Ireland for it, the ring that belonged to Naoise, and that was with him through the battle and through the fight; he thought much of it in his lifetime; it is pure gold, through and through." So the carpenter took the ring in his hand, and the knife in the other hand, and he looked at them together, and he gave her the knife for the ring, and for her asking and her tears. Then Deirdre went close to the waves, and she said: "Since the other is not with me now, I will spend no more of my lifetime without him." And with that she drove the black knife into her side, but she drew it out again and threw it in the sea to her right hand, the way no one would be blamed for her death.

Then Conchubar came down to the strand and five hundred men along with him, to bring Deirdre away to Emain Macha, but all he found before him was her white body on the ground, and it without life. And it is what he said:

" A thousand deaths on the time I brought death on my sister's children ; now I am myself without Deirdre, and they themselves are without life.

" They were my sister's children, the three brothers I vexed with blows, Naoise, and Ainnle, and Ardan ; they have died along with Deirdre."

And they took her white, beautiful body, and laid it in a grave, and a flagstone was raised over her grave, and over the grave of the sons of Usnach, and their names were written in Ogham, and keening was made for their burial.

And as to Fergus, son of Rogh, he came on the day after the children of Usnach were killed, to Emain Macha. And when he found they had been killed and his pledge to them broken, he himself, and Cormac Conloingeas, Conchubar's own son, and Dubthach, the Beetle of Ulster, with their men, made an attack on Conchubar's house and men, and a great many were killed by them, and Emain Macha was burned and destroyed.

And after doing that, they went into Connaught, to Ailell and to Maeve at Cruachan, and they were made welcome there, and they took service with them and fought with them against Ulster because of the treachery that was done by Conchubar. And that is the way Fergus and the others came to be on the side of the men of Connaught in the war for the Brown Bull of Cuailgne.

And Cathbad laid a curse on Emain Macha, on account of that great wrong. And it is what he said, that none of the race of Conchubar should have the kingdom, to the end of life and time.

And that came true, for the most of Conchubar's sons died in his own lifetime, and when he was near his death, he bade the men of Ulster bring back Cormac Conloingeas out of Cruachan, and give him the kingdom.

So they sent messengers to Cormac, and he set out and his three troops of men with him, and he left his blessing with Ailell and with Maeve, and he promised them a good return for all the kind treatment they had given him. And they crossed the river at Athluain, and there they saw a red woman at the edge of the ford, and she washing her chariot and her harness. And after that they met a young girl coming towards them, and a light green cloak about her, and a brooch of precious stones at her breast. And Cormac asked her was she coming with them, and she said she was not, and it would be better for himself to turn back, for the ruin of his life was come.

And he stopped for the night at the House of the Two Smiths on the hill of Bruighean Mor, the great dwelling-place.

But a troop of the men of Connaught came about the house in the night, for they were on the way home after destroying and robbing a district of Ulster, and they thought to make an end of Cormac before he would get to Emain.

And it chanced there was a great harper, Craiftine, living close by, and his wife, Sceanb, daughter of Scethern, a Druid of Connaught, loved Cormac Conloingeas, and three times she had gone to meet him at Athluain, and she planted three trees there—Grief, and Dark, and Dumbness.

And there was great hatred and jealousy of Cormac on Craiftine, so when he knew the men of Connaught were going to make an attack on him, he went outside the house with his harp, and played a soft sleepy tune to him, the way he had not the strength to rouse himself up, and himself and the most of his people were killed. And Amergin, that had gone with the message to him, made his grave and his mound, and the place is called Cluain Duma, the Lawn of the Mound.

VIII

THE DREAM OF ANGUS OG

ANGUS, son of the Dagda, was asleep in his bed one night, and he saw what he thought was a young girl standing near him at the top of the bed, and she the most beautiful he had ever seen in Ireland. He put out his hand to take her hand, but she vanished on the moment, and in the morning when he awoke there were no trace or tidings of her.

He got no rest that day thinking of her, and that she had gone away before he could speak to her. And the next night he saw her again, and this time she brought a little harp in her hand, the sweetest he ever heard, and she played a song to him, so that he fell asleep and slept till morning. And the same thing happened every night for a year. She would come to his bedside and be playing on the harp to him, but she would be gone before he could speak with her. And at the end of the year she came no more, and Angus began to pine away with love of her and with fretting after her; and he would take no food, but lay upon the bed, and no one knew what it was ailed him. And all the physicians of Ireland came together, but they could not put a name on his sickness or find any cure for him.

But at last Fergne, the physician of Conn, was brought to him, and as soon as he looked at him he knew it was not on his body the sickness was, but on his mind. And

143

he sent every one away out of the room, and he said : " I think it is for the love of some woman that you are wasting away like this." " That is true, indeed," said Angus ; " and it is my sickness has betrayed me." And then he told him how the woman with the most beautiful appearance of any woman in Ireland, used to come and to be playing the harp to him through the night, and how she had vanished away.

Then Fergne went and spoke with Boann, Angus's mother, and he told her all that happened, and he bade her to send and search all through Ireland if she could find a young girl of the same appearance as the one Angus had seen in his sleep. And then he left him in his mother's care, and she had all Ireland searched for a year, but no young girl of that appearance could be found.

At the end of the year, Boann sent for Fergne to come again, and she said : " We have not got any help from our search up to this." And Fergne said : " Send for the Dagda, that he may come and speak to his son." So they sent for the Dagda, and when he came, he said : " What have I been called for?" " To give an advice to your son," said Fergne, "and to help him, for he is lying sick on account of a young girl that appeared to him in his sleep, and that cannot be found ; and it would be a pity for him to die." " What use will it be, I to speak to him?" said the Dagda, " for my knowledge is no higher than your own." " By my word," said Fergne, "you are the king of all the Sidhe of Ireland, and what you have to do is to go to Bodb, the king of the Sidhe of Munster, for he has a name for knowledge all through Ireland." So messengers were sent to Bodb, at his house in Sidhe Femain, and he bade them welcome. " A welcome before you, messenger of the Dagda," he said, "and what is the message you have brought?" " This is the message," they said, " Angus

Og, son of the Dagda, is wasting away these two years with love of a woman he saw in his dreams, and we have not been able to find her in any place. And this is an order to you," they said, "from the Dagda, to search out through Ireland a young girl of the same form and appearance as the one he saw." "The search will be made," said Bodb, "if it lasts me a year."

And at the end of a year he sent messengers to the Dagda. "Is it a good message you have brought?" said the Dagda. "It is, indeed," they said; "and this is the message Bodb bade us give you, 'I have searched all Ireland until I found the young girl with the same form and appearance that you said, at Loch Beul Draguin, at the Harp of Cliach.' And now," they said, "he bids Angus to come with us, till he sees if it is the same woman that appeared to him in his dream."

So Angus set out in his chariot to Sidhe Femain, and Bodb bade him welcome, and made a great feast for him, that lasted three days and three nights. And at the end of that time he said: "Come out now with me, and see if this is the same woman that came to you."

So they set out together till they came to the sea, and there they saw three times fifty young girls, and the one they were looking for among them; and she was far beyond them all. And there was a silver chain between every two of them, but about her own neck there was a necklace of shining gold. And Bodb said "Do you see that woman you were looking for?" "I see her, indeed," said Angus. "But tell me who is she, and what her name is." "Her name is Caer Ormaith, daughter of Ethal Anbual, from Sidhe Uaman, in the province of Connaught. But you cannot bring her away with you this time," said Bodb.

Then Angus went to visit his father, the Dagda, and his mother, Boann, at Brugh na Boinne; and Bodb went with him, and they told how they had seen the girl, and they had heard her own name, and her father's name. "What had we best do now?" said the Dagda. "The best thing for you to do," said Bodb, "is to go to Ailell and Maeve, for it is in their district she lives, and you had best ask their help."

So the Dagda set out until he came into the province of Connaught, and sixty chariots with him; and Ailell and Maeve made a great feast for him. And after they had been feasting and drinking for the length of a week, Ailell asked the reason of their journey. And the Dagda said: "It is by reason of a young girl in your district, for my son has sickness upon him on account of her, and I am come to ask if you will give her to him." "Who is she?" said Ailell. "She is Caer Ormaith, daughter of Ethal Anbual." "We have no power over her that we could give her to him," said Ailell and Maeve. "The best thing for you to do," said the Dagda, "would be to call her father here to you."

So Ailell sent his steward to Ethal Anbual, and he said: "I am come to bid you to go and speak with Ailell and with Maeve." "I will not go," he said; "I will not give my daughter to the son of the Dagda." So the steward went back and told this to Ailell. "He will not come," he said, "and he knows the reason you want him for."

Then there was anger an Ailell and on the Dagda, and they went out, and their armed men with them, and they destroyed the whole place of Ethal Anbual, and he was brought before them. And Ailell said to him: "Give your daughter now to the son of the Dagda." "That is what I cannot do," he said, "for there is a power over her that is greater than mine." "What power is that?" said Ailell. "It is an enchantment," he said, "that is on her, she to be in the shape of a bird for one year, and in her own shape the next year," "Which shape is on her at this time?" said Ailell. "I would not like to say that," said her father. "Your head from you if you will not tell it," said Ailell.

"Well," said he, "I will tell you this much; she will be in the shape of a swan next month at Loch Beul Draguin, and three fifties of beautiful birds will be along with her, and if you will go there, you will see her."

So then Ethal was set free, and he made friends again with Ailell and Maeve; and the Dagda went home and told Angus all that had happened, and he said: "Go next summer to Loch Beul Draguin, and call her to you there."

So when the time came, Angus Og went to the loch, and he saw the three times fifty white birds there, with their silver chains about their necks. And Angus stood in a man's shape at the edge of the loch, and he called to the girl: "Come and speak with me, O Caer!" "Who is calling me?" said Caer. "Angus calls you," he said, "and if you come, I swear by my word, I will not hinder you from going into the loch again." "I will come," she said. So she came to him, and he laid his two hands on her, and then, to hold to his word, he took the shape of a swan on himself, and they went into the loch together, and they went around it three times. And then they spread their wings and rose up from the loch, and went in that shape till they were at Brugh na Boinne. And as they were going, the music they made was so sweet that all the people that heard it fell asleep for three days and three nights.

And Caer stopped there with him ever afterwards, and from that time there was friendship between Angus Og and Ailell and Maeve. And it was on account of that friendship, Angus gave them his help at the time of the war for the Brown Bull of Cuailgne.

IX

CRUACHAN

NOW as to Cruachan, the home of Ailell and of Maeve, it is on the plain of Magh Ai it was, in the province of Connaught.

And this is the way the plain came by its name. In the time long ago, there was a king whose name was Conn, that had the Druid power, so that when the Sidhe themselves came against him, he was able to defend himself with enchantments as good as their own. And one time he went out against them, and broke up their houses, and carried away their cattle, and then, to hinder them from following after him, he covered the whole province with a deep snow.

The Sidhe went then to consult with Dalach, the king's brother, that had the Druid knowledge even better than himself; and it is what he told them to do, to kill three hundred white cows with red ears, and to spread out their livers on a certain plain. And when they had done this, he made spells on them, and the heat the livers gave out melted the snow over the whole plain and the whole province, and after that the plain was given the name of Magh Ai, the Plain of the Livers.

Ailell was son of Ross Ruadh, king of Leinster, and Maeve was daughter of Eochaid, king of Ireland, and her brothers were the Three Fair Twins that rose up against

their father, and fought against him at Druim Criadh.
And they were beaten in the fight, and went back over
the Sionnan, and they were overtaken and their heads
were cut off, and brought back to their father, and he
fretted after them to the end of his life.

Seven sons Ailell and Maeve had, and the name of
every one of them was Maine. There was Maine
Mathremail, like his mother, and Maine Athremail,
like his father, and Maine Mo Epert, the Talker, and
Maine Milscothach, the Honey-Worded, and Maine
Andoe the Quick, and Maine Mingor, the Gently
Dutiful, and Maine Morgor, the Very Dutiful. Their
own people they had, and their own place of living.

This now was the appearance of Cruachan, the Royal
house of Ailell and of Maeve, that some called Cruachan
of the poets; there were seven divisions in the house,
with couches in them, from the hearth to the wall; a
front of bronze to every division, and of red yew with
carvings on it; and there were seven strips of bronze
from the foundation to the roof of the house. The
house was made of oak, and the roof was covered with
oak shingles; sixteen windows with glass there were,
and shutters of bronze on them, and a bar of bronze across
every shutter. There was a raised place in the middle
of the house for Ailell and Maeve, with silver fronts
and strips of bronze around it, and four bronze pillars
on it, and a silver rod beside it, the way Ailell and
Maeve could strike the middle beam and check their
people.

And outside the royal house was the dun, with the
walls about it that were built by Brocc, son of Blar, and
the great gate; and it is there the houses were for
strangers to be lodged.

And besides this, there was at Cruachan the Hill of
the Sidhe, or, as some called it, the Cave of Cruachan. It
was there Midhir brought Etain one time, and it is there

the people of the Sidhe lived; but it is seldom any living person had the power to see them.

It is out of that hill a flock of white birds came one time, and everything they touched in all Ireland withered up, until at last the men of Ulster killed them with their slings. And another time enchanted pigs came out of the hill, and in every place they trod, neither corn nor grass nor leaf would sprout before the end of seven years, and no sort of weapon would wound them. But if they were counted in any place, or if the people so much as tried to count them, they would not stop in that place, but they would go on to another. But however often the people of the country tried to count them, no two people could ever make out the one number, and one man would call out, " There are three pigs in it," and another, " No, but there are seven," and another that it was eleven were in it, or thirteen, and so the count would be lost. One time Maeve and Ailell themselves tried to count them on the plain, but while they were doing it, one of the pigs made a leap over Maeve's chariot, and she in it. Every one called out, " A pig has gone over you, Maeve!" " It has not," she said, and with that she caught hold of the pig by the shank, but if she did, its skin opened at the head, and it made its escape. And it is from that the place was called Magh-mucrimha, the Plain of Swine-counting.

Another time Fraech, son of Idath, of the men of Connaught, that was son of Boann's sister, Befind, from the Sidhe, came to Cruachan. He was the most beautiful of the men of Ireland or of Alban, but his life was not long. It was to ask Findabair for his wife he came, and before he set out his people said : " Send a message to your mother's people, the way they will send you clothing of the Sidhe." So he went to Boann, that was at Magh Breagh, and he brought away fifty blue cloaks with four black ears on each cloak, and a brooch of red gold with each, and pale white shirts with looped beasts of gold around them; and fifty silver shields with edges, and a candle of a king's house in the hand of each of the men, knobs of carbuncle under them, and their points of precious stones. They used to light up the night as if they were sun's rays.

And he had with him seven trumpeters with gold and silver trumpets, with many coloured clothing, with golden, silken, heads of hair, with coloured cloaks; and three harpers with the appearance of a king on each of them, every harper having the white skin of a deer about him and a cloak of white linen, and a harp-bag of the skins of water-dogs.

The watchman saw them from the dun when they had come into the Plain of Cruachan. "I see a great crowd," he said, "coming towards us. Since Ailell was king and Maeve was queen, there never came and there never will come a grander or more beautiful crowd than this one. It is like as if I had my head in a vat of wine, with the breeze that goes over them."

Then Fraech's people let out their hounds, and the hounds found seven deer and seven foxes and seven hares and seven wild boars, and hunted them to Rath Cruachan, and there they were killed on the lawn of the dun.

Then Ailell and Maeve gave them a welcome, and they were brought into the house, and while food was being made ready, Maeve sat down to play a game of chess with Fraech. It was a beautiful chess-board they had, all of white bronze, and the chessmen of gold and silver, and a candle of precious stones lighting them.

Then Ailell said: "Let your harpers play for us while the feast is being made ready." "Let them play, indeed," said Fraech.

So the harpers began to play, and it was much that the people of the house did not die with crying and with sadness. And the music they played was the Three Cries of Uaithne. It was Uaithne, the harp of the Dagda, that first played those cries the time Boann's sons were born. The first was a song of sorrow for the hardness of her pains, and the second was a song of smiling and joy for the birth of her sons, and the third was a sleeping song after the birth.

And with the music of the harpers, and with the light that shone from the precious stones in the house, they did not know the night was on them, till at last Maeve started up, and she said: "We have done a great deed to keep these young men without food." "It is more you think of chess-playing than of providing for them," said Ailell; "and now, let them stop from the music," he said, "till the food is given out."

Then the food was divided. It was Lothar used to be sitting on the floor of the house, dividing the food with his cleaver, and he not eating himself, and from the time he began dividing, food never failed under his hand.

After that, Fraech was brought into the conversation-house, and they asked him what was it he wanted.

"A visit to yourselves," he said, but he said nothing of Findabair. So they told him he was welcome, and he stopped with them for a while, and every day they went out hunting, and all the people of Connaught used to come and to be looking at them.

But all this time Fraech got no chance of speaking with Findabair, until one morning at daybreak, he went down to the river for washing, and Findabair and her young girls had gone there before him. And he took her hand, and he said: "Stay here and talk with me, for it is for your sake I am come, and would you go away with me secretly?" "I will not go secretly," she said, "for I am the daughter of a king and of a queen."

So she went from him then, but she left him a ring to remember her by. It was a ring her mother had given her.

Then Fraech went to the conversation-house to Ailell and to Maeve. "Will you give your daughter to me?" he said. "We will give her if you will give the marriage portion we ask," said Ailell, "and that is, sixty black-grey horses with golden bits, and twelve milch cows, and a white red-eared calf with each of them; and you to come with us with all your strength and all your musicians at whatever time we go to war in Ulster." "I swear by my shield and my sword, I would not give that for Maeve herself," he said; and he went away out of the house.

But Ailell had taken notice of Findabair's ring with Fraech, and he said to Maeve: "If he brings our daughter away with him, we will lose the help of many of the kings of Ireland. Let us go after him and make an end of him before he has time to harm us." "That would be a pity," said Maeve, "and it would be a reproach on us." "It will be no reproach on us, the way I will manage it," said he. And Maeve agreed to it, for there was vexation on her that it was Findabair that Fraech wanted, and not herself. So they went into the palace, and Ailell said: "Let us go and see the hounds hunting until mid-day." So they did so, and at mid-day they were tired, and they all went to bathe in the river. And Fraech was swimming in the river, and Ailell said to him: "Do not come back till you bring me a branch of the rowan-tree there beyond, with the beautiful berries." For he knew there was a prophecy that it was in a river Fraech would get his death.

So he went and broke a branch off the tree and brought it back over the water, and it is beautiful he looked over the black water, his body without fault, and his face so nice, and his eyes very grey, and the branch with the red berries between the throat and the white face. And then he threw the branch to them out of the water. "It is ripe and beautiful the berries are," said Ailell; "bring us more of them."

So he went off again to the tree, and the water-worm that guarded the tree caught a hold of him. "Let me have a sword," he called out, but there was not a man on the land would dare to give it to him, through fear of Ailell and of Maeve. But Findabair made a leap to go into the water with a gold knife she had in her hand, but Ailell threw a sharp-pointed spear from above, through her plaited hair, that held her; but she threw the knife to Fraech, and he cut off the head of the monster, and brought it with him to the land, but he himself had got a deep wound. Then Ailell and Maeve went back to the house. "It is a great deed we have done," said Maeve. "It is a pity, indeed, what we have done to the man," said Ailell. "And let a healing-bath be made for him now," he said, "of the marrow of pigs and of a heifer." Fraech was put in the bath then, and pleasant music was played by the trumpeters, and a bed was made for him.

Then a sorrowful crying was heard on Cruachan, and they saw three times fifty women with purple gowns, with green head-dresses, and pins of silver on their wrists, and a messenger went and asked them who was it they were crying for. "For Fraech, son of Idath," they said, "boy darling of the king of the Sidhe of Ireland."

Then Fraech heard their crying, and he said: "Lift me out of this, for that is the cry of my mother, and of the women of Boann." So they lifted him out, and the women came round him and brought him away into the Hill of Cruachan.

And the next day he came out, and he whole and

sound, and fifty women with him, and they with the appearance of women of the Sidhe. And at the door of the dun they left him, and they gave out their cry again, so that all the people that heard it could not but feel sorrowful. It is from this the musicians of Ireland learned the sorrowful cry of the women of the Sidhe.

And when he went into the house, the whole household rose up before him and bade him welcome, as if it was from another world he was come. And there was shame and repentance on Ailell and on Maeve for trying to harm him, and peace was made, and he went away to his own place.

And it was after that he came to help Ailell and Maeve, and that he got his death in a river as was foretold, at the beginning of the war for the Brown Bull of Cuailgne.

And one time the Hill was robbed by the men of Cruachan, and this is the way it happened.

One night at Samhain, Ailell and Maeve were in Cruachan with their whole household, and the food was being made ready.

Two prisoners had been hanged by them the day before, and Ailell said: "Whoever will put a gad round the foot of either of the two men on the gallows, will get a prize from me."

It was a very dark night, and bad things would always appear on that night of Samhain, and every man that went out to try came back very quickly into the house. "I will go if I will get a prize," said Nera, then. "I will give you this gold-hilted sword," said Ailell.

So Nera went out and he put a gad round the foot of one of the men that had been hanged. Then the man spoke to him. "It is good courage you have," he said, "and bring me with you where I can get a drink, for I was very thirsty when I was hanged." So Nera brought him where he would get a drink, and then he put him on the gallows again, and went back to Cruachan.

But what he saw was the whole of the palace as if on fire before him, and the heads of the people of it lying on the ground, and then he thought he saw an army going into the Hill of Cruachan, and he followed after the army. "There is a man on our track," the last man said. "The track is the heavier," said the next to him, and each said that word to the other from the last to the first. Then they went into the Hill of Cruachan. And they said to their king: "What shall be done to the man that is come in?" "Let him come here till I speak with him," said the king. So Nera came, and the king asked him who it was had brought him in. "I came in with your army," said Nera. "Go to that house beyond," said the king: "there is a woman there will make you welcome. Tell her it is I myself sent you to her. And come every day," he said, "to this house with a load of firing."

So Nera went where he was told, and the woman said: "A welcome before you, if it is the king sent you." So he stopped there, and took the woman for his wife. And every day for three days he brought a load of firing to the king's house, and on each day he saw a blind man, and a lame man on his back, coming out of the house before him. They would go on till they were at the brink of a well before the Hill. "Is it there?" the blind man would say. "It is, indeed," the lame man would say. "Let us go away," the lame man would say then.

And at the end of three days, as he thought, Nera asked the woman about this. "Why do the blind man and the lame man go every day to the well?" he said. "They go to know is the crown safe that is in the well. It is there the king's crown is kept." "Why do these two go?" said Nera. "It is easy to tell that," she said; "they are trusted by the king to visit the crown, and one of them was blinded by him, and the other was lamed. And another thing," she said, "go now and give a warning to your people to mind themselves next Samhain night, unless they will come to attack the hill, for it is only at Samhain," she said, "the army of the Sidhe can go out, for it is at that time all the hills of the Sidhe of Ireland are opened. But if they will come, I will promise them this, the crown of Briun to be carried off by Ailell and by Maeve."

"How can I give them that message," said Nera, "when I saw the whole dun of Cruachan burned and destroyed, and all the people destroyed with it?" "You did not see that, indeed," she said. "It was the host of the Sidhe came and put that appearance before your eyes. And go back to them now," she said, "and you will find them sitting round the same great pot, and the meat has not yet been taken off the fire."

"How will it be believed that I have gone into the Hill?" said Nera. "Bring flowers of summer with you," said the woman. So he brought wild garlic with him, and primroses and golden fern.

So he went back to the palace, and he found his people round the same great pot, and he told them all that had happened him, and the sword was given to him, and he stopped with his people to the end of a year.

At the end of the year Ailell said to Nera: "We are going now against the Hill of the Sidhe, and let you go back," he said, "if you have anything to bring out of it." So he went back to see the woman, and she bade him welcome. "Go now," she said, "and bring in a load of firing to the king, for I went in myself every day for the last year with the load on my back, and I said there was sickness on you." So he did that.

Then the men of Connaught and the black host of the exiles of Ulster went into the Hill and robbed it and brought away the crown of Briun, son of Smetra, that

was made by the smith of Angus, son of Umor, and that
was kept in the well at Cruachan, to save it from the
Morrigu. And Nera was left with his people in the
hill, and he has not come out till now, and he will not
come out till the end of life and time.

Now one time the Morrigu brought away a cow from
the Hill of Cruachan to the Brown Bull of Cuailgne,
and after she brought it back again its calf was born.
And one day it went out of the Hill, and it bellowed three
times. At that time Ailell and Fergus were playing
draughts, for it was after Fergus had come as an exile
from Ulster, because of the death of the sons of Usnach,
and they heard the bellowing of the bull-calf in the plain.
Then Fergus said : " I do not like the sound of the calf
bellowing. There will be calves without cows," he said,
" when the king goes on his march."

But now Ailell's bull, Finbanach, the White-Horned,
met the calf in the plain of Cruachan, and they fought
together, and the calf was beaten and it bellowed.
" What did the calf bellow ? " Maeve asked her cow-herd
Buaigle. " I know that, my master, Fergus," said Bricriu.
" It is the song that you were singing a while ago." On
that Fergus turned and struck with his fist at his head,
so that the five men of the chessmen that were in his
hand went into Bricriu's head, and it was a lasting hurt
to him. " Tell me now, Buaigle, what did the calf
bellow ? " said Maeve. " It said indeed," said Buaigle,
" that if its father the Brown of Cuailgne would come to
fight with the White-Horned, he would not be seen any
more in Ai, he would be beaten through the whole plain
of Ai on every side." And it is what Maeve said : " I
swear by the gods my people swear by, I will not lie
down on feathers, or drink red or white ale, till I see
those two bulls fighting before my face."

X

THE WEDDING OF MAINE MORGOR

WHEN Maine Morgor, the Very Dutiful, the son of Ailell and of Maeve, set out for his wedding with Ferb, daughter of Gerg of Rath Ini, in Ulster, he brought three troops of young men with him, and fifty men in each troop, and this is the appearance that was on the first two troops. Shining white shirts they had, striped with purple down the sides; gold shields on their backs with borders of white silver, with figures engraved on them, and with edges of white bronze as sharp as knives. Great two-edged swords with silver hilts at their belts; chains of white silver round their necks. And there were neither helmets on their heads, or shoes on their feet.

And as to the third troop, the one Maine himself was in, there were fifty reddish-brown horses in it, and fifty white horses with red ears, with long manes and tails coloured purple, and bridles on them, with a ball of red gold on the one side, and a ball of white silver on the other side, and a gold or a silver bit to every one of them. A collar of gold with bells from it on the neck of every horse, and when the horses would be moving, the sound of these bells would be as sweet as the strings of a harp when the player strikes it with his hand. There was a chariot of white bronze ribbed with gold and silver to every two of the horses;

purple cushions sewed with gold bound to every chariot;
fifty fair slender young men in these fifty chariots, and
not one among them but was the son of a king and
a queen, and was a hero and a brave man of Connaught,
and they wearing purple cloaks about them, that had
borders ornamented with gold and silver, and a clasp
of pure red gold to every cloak ; fine silk coats fastened
with hooks of gold close to their white bodies; fifty
silver shields on their backs with gold rims studded
with carbuncles and other precious stones of every
colour; two candles of valour were the two shining
spears on the hand of every man of them ; fifty rivets
of bronze and of gold in every spear, and if any man
of them had a debt of a bushel of silver or gold, one
rivet from his spear would pay it. And there were
precious stones on their spears that would flame in
the night like the rays of the sun. At their belts they
had long, gold-hilted swords with silver sheaths ; goads
in their hands of white bronze with silver crooks. And
as to the young men themselves, they were very handsome and stately, and large and shining ; curled yellow
hair on them, hanging down on their shoulders ; proud,
clear, blue eyes; their cheeks like the flowers of the
woods in May, or like the foxglove of the mountains.
There were seven greyhounds following Maine's chariot
in chains of silver, and apples of gold on every chain.
There were seven trumpeters with gold and silver
trumpets, wearing clothes of many colours, and having
all of them light yellow hair. And three Druids went
in front of them, and they having bands of silver on
their heads, and speckled cloaks on them, and carrying
shields of bronze with ornaments of red copper. And
there were three harpers with them, that had the appearance of kings.

It is like that they gathered at the royal house of
Cruachan, and they went three times round the lawn

before the house. And they said farewell to Maeve and to Ailell, and then they set out for Rath Ini.

"It is a fine setting out you are having," said Bricriu; "but maybe the coming back will not be so fine." "It is a journey that will be heard of in every place," said Maine. "I suppose," said Bricriu, "it is but a day visit you will make there, for you will hardly stop to feast through the night in a district that is under Conchubar." "I give my word," said Maine, "we will not turn back to Cruachan till we have feasted three days and three nights in Gerg's house." He did not waste any more time talking, but set out on the journey.

When the messengers they sent before them came to Gerg's house at Rath Ini, the people there began to make all ready before them, and they laid down green-leaved birch branches and fresh green rushes in the house. Then Ferb sent her foster-sister, Findchoem, daughter of Erg, and bade her go a part of the way with the messengers, and bring her back word what appearance was on Maine and on his companions. She was not long away, and as soon as she came back she went with her report to the sunny parlour where Ferb was, and it is what she said: "I never saw since Conchubar was in Emain, and I never will see till the end of life and time, a finer, or grander, or a more beautiful troop, than the troop that is coming now over the plain. It was the same as if I was in a sweet apple-garden, from the sweetness that came to me when the light wind passed over them and stirred their clothes."

With that, the men of Connaught came to the dun, and the people within pressed upon one another to look at them. And the gates were set open, and their chariots unyoked, and baths of pure water were made ready for them. And then they were brought into the hall of heroes in the middle of the house, and they were given every sort of food and of drink that is to be found on the whole ridge of the world.

But as they were using the feast and making merry, there came a sudden blast of wind that shook the whole place, so that the hall they were in trembled, and the shields fell from their hooks, and the spears from their places, and the tables fell like leaves in an oak wood. All the young men were astonished, and Gerg asked Maine's Druids what meaning they could put on that blast. And Ollgaeth, Maine's chief Druid, said : " I think it is no good sign for those who are come to-night to this wedding. A blast of wind," he said ; " a sorrowful sound ; it is the man that will conquer.

" A shield struck out of a white hand ; the bodies of dead men laid under stones ; a high stone over stiff bodies ; the story is sorrowful !

" And if you will take my advice," he said, " you will quit this feast this very night."

But he got a sharp rebuke from Maine for saying that, and Gerg said : " There is no cause for any uneasiness, for the men of Ulster are not gathered at Emain at this time. And if they were itself," he said, " I and my two sons would be ready to go out and fight against Conchubar along with you."

They hung up their arms then again, and gave no more heed to what the Druid had said.

Now on the mornihg of this very day, when Conchubar was lying in his sleep at Emain, he saw in a dream a beautiful woman coming to his bedside, and she having the appearance of a queen. Yellow plaited hair she had, and folds of silk over her white skin, and a cloak of green silk from her shoulders, and two sandals of white bronze between her soft feet and the ground. " All good be with you, Conchubar," she said. " What is the reason of your coming ? " said Conchubar. " It is not long from this time," she said, "that Ulster will be attacked and will be robbed, and the Brown Bull of Cuailgne will be driven away. And the son of the man that will do this thing," she said, "Maine Morgor, son of Ailell and of Maeve, is coming this very night to his wedding with Ferb, daughter of Gerg of Rath Ini, and three times fifty young men with him. Rise up now," she said, "there are but three times fifty men against you, and the victory will be with you."

Then Conchubar sprang up, and sent for Cathbad, the Druid, and told him his vision. "It is likely enough," he said, "that it is meant to warn us against the men of Connaught. And you may be sure," he said, "that if we stop here quietly, they will be doing their robbery. And let me have the truth from you now, and tell me what is best to do, for there is not the like of you among the Druids."

And Cathbad said: "It is what your vision means, that many men will get their death, and Maine of Connaught, he that is above all disgrace, along with them; and he and his companions will never go back again to beautiful Cruachan. But you yourself will come back safe," he said, "with fame and victory."

Then Conchubar set out, and there went with him Cathrach Catuchenn, a queen with a great name, that had come to Emain from the country of Spain for love of Cuchulain; and she went out now with Conchubar's army. And there went with him as well, the three outlaws of the race of the Fomor, Siabarcha, son of Suilremar, and Berngal Brec, and Buri of the Rough Word. And Facen, son of Dublongsech of the old stock of Ulster came, and Fabric Fiacail from Great Asia, and Forais Fingalach from the Isle of Man. So Conchubar set out, and three times fifty men with him, but he brought none of the men of Ulster with him, but himself and his chariot-driver Brod, and

Imrinn the Druid, Cathbad's son. And none of them brought a servant with him, except only Conchubar, but their shields on their backs, and their bright green spears in their hands, and their heavy swords in their belts. And if they were not many in number, the pride of their minds was great.

When they were come within sight of Rath Ini, they saw a great heavy cloud over it, the one end of it black and the middle red, and the other end green. And Conchubar asked Imrinn the Druid, "What is this cloud over the house a token of?" "I know well," said Imrinn, "it is a sign there will be fighting to-night, and the sorrow of death will be on the house like a cloud, and it is for a young man the death darkness is made ready."

Then Conchubar went on towards the dun, and just at that time the great vat that belonged to the house, and that got afterwards the name of the Ol Guala, was brought into the feasting hall, and it full of wine. But whoever went to draw it let the silver vessel fall into the vat, so that the wine flowed over the edges in three waves. "My grief!" said Ollgaeth the Druid, "it is not long before these vessels will be with strangers. He is not a happy son born of a mother that is in this house to-night."

Then Conchubar came to the door, and the strangers that were with him gave their shout of attack around the dun, as their custom was. At that Gerg rose up, and his two sons with him, Conn Coscorach and Cobthach Cnesgel, and they took hold of their arms. And Gerg said to Maine: "Let this be fought out now between us men of Ulster till you see which of us are the bravest. And we are all answerable for you, and it is best for you that we should fight together. But if we fall, then let you hold the place if you can."

And then Gerg went out and his two sons along with him and their people. And they held the place, and

fought Conchubar outside; and for a long time they did
not let any one go past them.   And Gerg stood outside
the door, and a hewing and cutting was aimed at him on
every side, and five men of the Fomor fell by him, and
Imrinn the Druid, along with them, and he cut his head
off and brought it to the door with him.

Then Cathrach Catuchenn came between him and the
door, and she made a sharp attack on him, and Gerg
struck her head off, and brought it back with him into
the house, for he had got a hard wound.   And he threw
the heads down before Maine, and he sat down on a
bed, and gave a heavy sigh and asked for a drink.   And
then Conchubar and his people came up to the wall, and
they were holding their shields over their heads with
their left hands, and tearing down the wall with their
right hands, till they were able to make their way
through it.

Then Brod, Conchubar's chariot-driver, threw one of
the spears he had in his hand into the house, and it went
through Gerg's body, and through the body of Airisdech
his servant that was behind him, so that the two of them
fell together.   And Conchubar attacked Gerg's people
in the house, so that thirty of them fell, and he killed
Conn, Gerg's son, by his own hand, and many of his own
people got their death as well.

Then Nuagal, Gerg's wife, rose up, and she gave three
great angry cries of grief, and she took the head of her
husband into her bosom.   " By my word," she said, " it
is a fine servant's deed, Brod to have killed Gerg in his
own house.   But there are many," she said, "that will
keen you, and as you have fallen on account of your
daughter, many women shall have sorrow on account of
you."   And she made this complaint:

" It is a good fight Gerg made, that is lying here now,
the fair-haired champion with the red sword; he that
was proud, open-handed, brave, wise, beautiful.

"Where is there a better hero than Gerg? Where is the man that has not anger on him. Where is the army that does not keen for your death?

"It is grief to me to see you on your bed of death, O beautiful fair-haired Gerg! It is a pity for me, you to be dead.

"Before you here in Rath Ini, and at Loch Ane and at Irard, and in the valleys of the south, there were many women that gave you their love.

"You were the friend of every army; every one gave you full obedience; your friendly word was dear to every one; surely it is you were the good adviser.

"It is great indeed your deeds were, it is stately your assemblies were; you were a king among great lords.

"Your house was great, it was well-known, the house within which harm came to you; it was there Brod killed you in the hall of kings.

"It was a great harm and a great curse Brod put on us, he to kill a king of Ireland before his time; he has killed him; he has killed all of us along with him."

Then Gerg's two sons said they would hold the place, and they were not without killing many in the fight. Then Maine could not hold in his strength any longer, and he went out to avenge his father-in-law. And his three times fifty companions rose up along with him, and it was not easy to stand against them. There was great pride in the mind, and great courage in the heart of every one of them, and there was great desire and longing on them to do high deeds.

And as to Maine, the king's son, he was stately, kind, mannerly, and although he was hardly out of his boyhood, he was braver in the fight than any other. He was gentle in the drinking-house, and he was hard in battle, and he was mindful of his enemies, and he was pitiful in wounding, and a spender of treasure, and a stone of anger, and a wave of justice; and he was the head in the gatherings of the three Connaughts, and their hand in spending, and their fitting king.

He thought it would be dishonour on him, ever to be overcome in equal fight by any men in the world, or the place to be taken that he was defending. And he went out and drove the Fomor away from the house, and it is not a hand of healing Maine had that time; and nine of the Fomor fell by his first attack. Then the outlaw of Great Asia, Fabric Fiacail, came up to the threshold, and began destroying the men before him, and no one stood against him till he came to the place where Maine was. And then they two set their shields one against the other, and they were fighting together till after midnight; and Fabric gave Maine three deep wounds, and when they were tired out with the fight, Maine struck off his head. Then Conchubar came, and thirty of Gerg's men were killed by him, and the two armies fell upon one another, and it is much that even the toes of their feet did not make an attack of their own. And the blood that was in the dun was as high as a man's knees, and in all the district round nothing could be heard but the striking of blows on shields, and the clinking of spears, and the clash of swords against one another, and the roar of beaten men.

And Maine, when he had overcome the Fomor, came where Facen, son of Dublongsech was, and they fought together a good while, and then Facen was killed. Then Maine and Cobthach were driven up into the house after their people were put down, and they held it bravely till morning, and no one was able to make a way in.

In this same night, the same woman that had brought news to Conchubar, went to where Maeve was lying in her sleep at Cruachan, and said to her: "If you had the Druid sight, Maeve," she said, "you would not be in your sleep now." "What has happened?" said Maeve. "Conchubar is at this very moment," said the strange woman, "getting the upper hand of Maine, and he is on the point of putting him to death. Rise up now, and gather your men together," she said, "and go out and avenge him."

With that Maeve wakened out of her sleep, and she called to Ailell and told him the vision, and told it to her people as well. "There is no truth in it," said Bricriu.

But when Fiannamail, the innkeeper's son at Cruachan, heard it, he waited for no one and made no delay, but set out for the place where Maine was, for Maine was his foster-brother. And Maeve chose out seven hundred armed men, the best that were to be found in Cruachan at that time. And then Donall Dearg came, that was the best fighter in the province, and that was another of Maine's foster-brothers. And he set out in the same way, before the others, and thirty fighting men with him, and the name of every one of them was Donall. And then Maeve set out after them on her journey.

But as to Maine, he held the house till the bright rising of the sun on the morrow, and it was not pleasant rest this night brought to either side. When they could see each other by the light of day, each remembered the other to his hurt, and Conchubar began to rouse up his people. "If it was the men of Ulster I had with me now," he said, "they would not be dragging on with this battle, the way the Fomor are doing." When the Fomor heard that sharp reproach, their courage rose up in them, and they pressed on hard in the fight, and never left off till they were through the door of the house. The house they came into had a great name for grandeur, but it was bad work that was done in it now. There were a hundred tables of white silver in it, and three hundred of brass, and three hundred of white bronze. And there were thirty vessels with pure silver from Spain on their rims, and two hundred cowhorns ornamented with gold or silver, and thirty silver cups, and thirty brass cups, and on the walls there were hangings of white linen with wonderful figures worked on them.

Then the two armies met one another in the middle of the house, and a great many were killed there. And Cobthach, Gerg's son, after he had killed many of the Fomor, came to where Berngal Brec was hewing the heads off the men of Connaught, and they fought together, and Berngal was worsted in the end.

And as to Maine, he killed Buri of the Rough Word, and after that he went mad and raging through the house, and thirty other men fell by him. But when Conchubar saw the madness that was on Maine, he turned to him, and Maine waited for him, and they fought a long while, and Maine threw his casting spear so strong and straight, that it went through Conchubar's body; and while Conchubar was striving to draw out that spear, Maine wounded him with the long spear that was in his hand. Then Brod came to help Conchubar, and Maine gave him three heavy wounds, so that he was able to fight no more. But then Conchubar attacked him with blows on every side, until he laid him dead before him.

And after he had killed Maine, he began to attack the crowd about him, so that they fell, foot to foot, and neck to neck, all through the house. And at the end, there was not one of Maine's people left living; and of the three times fifty men that came with Conchubar, there was not one left living but himself and Brod, and if they were itself, they did not come whole out of it.

Then Conchubar drove Cobthach, Gerg's son, out of the house; and while he was following him over the plain, Ferb came with her foster-sister to the place where Maine was lying, and she cried and lamented over him, and she said: "My grief! you are alone now, you that spent so many nights in company." And she made this complaint:—

"O young man, it is red your bed is! It is bad the signs were, and you coming into the house, a foretelling of tears to all your people.

"O son of Maeve! O branch of high honour! O son of Ailell who is not weak! It is a pity it is for my heart and my body, you to be lying there for ever!

"O young man, the best I ever saw; a rod of gold and you lying on the pillow; whenever you and an enemy met together, that was the last meeting there was between you.

"There is grief on me, you to be lying there, young man, son of Maeve; your face was ruddy, your hand was rough in battle; it is grief has been put into my heart that was waiting for you.

"It is seldom you were without arms up to this, until you were struck down, lying dead. The shining spear pierced you, the hard sword wounded you, till blood was dropping down on your cheeks.

"Och! What were you to me, and I not to have seen your death; my darling, my choice among men, he that was worth good treasure.

"He is my husband for all my days, great Maine, Ailell's son; I will die for the want of him, and he not able to come and care me.

"His purple cloak is grief to me, and himself lying there on the floor of the house, and his hand that was struck off after he fell, and his head in the hand of Conchubar;

"And his sword that was strong, heavy in striking, Conchubar has carried it far away; and his shield there where he fell, and he defending his people

"He himself a hero, and no lie in it; it is he divided

much riches; it is not a little thing he did to die like that, and he defending his people.

"The fair young man of Connaught to be lying there cold, and the best of his troop along with him; it is a pity for his people that died defending him; it is a pity for me, his unmarried wife.

"There is nothing I can do for you, Maine; it is on myself the hurt is come; my heart is broken with it, and I looking at you, Maine."

Then Fiannamail, the innkeeper's son from Cruachan, came to the house, and Ferb saw him, and she said: "Here is Fiannamail come to visit us, but whatever companions he has left at home, he will find none before him here." "That is rough news you are giving me, Ferb," said Fiannamail; "and indeed I am parted from my companions if it is they that are lying here," he said. "They are your companions indeed," said Ferb; "they overcame others, and now they are overcome themselves."

And Fiannamail said: "And Maine, is he living? my comrade, my dear friend, my prince at home!" And Ferb said: "It is bitter to me, you to ask this, for I know you did not think it was Maine's last bed you would find here."

And then she told Fiannamail all that had happened. And Fiannamail said; "When this news of the thing the people of Ulster have done goes out, they will be attacked in the west and in the east as long as there is a man living in Connaught." But Ferb said: "There are not left of the army of Ulster but Conchubar himself and Brod his chariot-driver, and the both of them were wounded by Maine before Conchubar killed him at the last."

Then Fiannamail went out to follow after Conchubar, to get satisfaction for Maine's death. And he met with Niall of the Fair Head, Conchubar's son, and a hundred men with him, and they looking for Conchubar; and

for all they were so many, he fought a hot battle with
them, till he fell dead.

And after he left Ferb, she was looking at the young
men of Connaught, and she made this complaint:

"A pity it is, young men of Connaught, that there is
not soft down in your pillows under you; you that took
the defence and would not give it up. What troop was
there better than yourselves, and now you are lying like
a loosened thread.

"It is a heavy hand was laid on your eyes; you were
given the sour drink of beaten men; your story is hard,
it will be a cause of battles; it will be a foretelling of
many tears.

"It is a pity there is no help for me to bring you, but
only to be keening and crying over you; it would be
better for me to go with you, and my ashes to be
scattered abroad.

"You were the best of the armies of Ireland, young
men of Connaught, and I keening you; many women
will cry Och! Och! after your proud ways.

"It is proud you were coming into the house; it is not
common men you had for your fathers. O beautiful
young men of Connaught, it is a pity it is the way
you are now!"

Then Donall Dearg came to the lawn before the dun.
And Ferb's foster-sister saw him, and she said: "It is a
pity he was not here and Maine living, for he would have
given him good help." And when Ferb heard he was there,
she went out to him and she said: "Well, Donall, hawk
of valour, here is a thing for you to do, to avenge your
foster-brother that has got his death." And it is what
Donall said: "If Maine has fallen, the man has fallen
that was above all his companions, in courage, in wisdom,
and in gentleness." And Ferb said: "It is not the
work of a hero, you to be sighing and keening and
crying Ochone! But since Maine will not come back for

that, it is better for you to go out against his enemies."
And Donall said : " I will go ; I will destroy Conchubar,
I will destroy his two sons in revenge for Maine."   And
Ferb said : " If it had been yourself, Donall Dearg, that
had got your death from the men of Ulster on account of
me, the story of the great vengeance Maine did for it
would be told in every place."   Then Donall said :
" And as it is Maine Morgor himself has got his death,
I will never go home westward so long as there is a man
left living in Ulster.

So Donall went out, and he had not long to wait till
he saw a great troop coming towards him, and Feradach
of the Long Hand, Conchubar's son, with them.   And
Donall and his men attacked them, but they were out-
numbered, and all his men fell.   And he himself
wounded Feradach twice, but then his men came at him,
and Feradach struck his head off, and let out his shout
of victory, and his people shouted along with him.

And Ferb was gone into the house again, and she was
looking at Maine.   "There is no good appearance on
you now, the way you are, Maine," she said ; "and my
father got his death through you, and my father's son ;
but even so, I will die with the fret of losing you."   And
it is what she said : " There are many women and many
young girls will be lonely after you, you to be the only
one to fail them.

" It is beautiful you were up to this, proud and tall,
going out with your young hounds to the hunting ; it
is spoiled your body is now, it is pale your hands are.

" It is bad the news is that will travel westward to
Findabair of the Fair Eyebrows ; the story of her
brother that failed Ferb ; it is not I that have not my
fill of sorrow."

Then Maeve and her men came up to where
Conchubar was, and his two sons that had joined him,
and they faced one another, and the fight began ; and

Maeve broke through the army of Ulster to get satisfaction for her son and for her people, and she killed Conchubar's two sons. But Conchubar stood out and faced her in spite of his wounds, and in spite of being tired out; for his hurts were healed by the greatness of his anger after his two sons being kiiled.

Then Maeve was driven back and lost the battle; and the Druids brought her away as was their custom; and Conchubar followed after them till they had passed Magh Ini. And then he turned back to spoil Gerg's dun, and he carried away with him all he could find of treasures; and he took away the great brass vat that was in the house, and brought it to Emain. And when it was filled with beer, all the province of Ulster used to drink from it; and it got the name of the Champion's Drinking Vat.

And Ferb died with grief for Maine, and Nuagal died with grief for her husband and for her two sons. And a grave was made for them, and a stone put over it, and their names were written in Ogham; and Rath Ini got the name of Duma Ferb, Ferb's Mound, after that.

And this was the first blood shed in Ulster on the account of the Brown Bull of Cuailgne.

XI

THE WAR FOR THE BULL OF CUAILGNE

IT happened one time before Maeve and Ailell rose up from their royal bed in Cruachan, they began to talk with one another. " It is what I am thinking," said Ailell, " it is a true saying, 'Good is the wife of a good man.'" "A true saying, indeed," said Maeve, "but why do you bring it to mind at this time?" "I bring it to mind now because you are better to-day than the day I married you." "I was good before I ever had to do with you," said Maeve. "How well we never heard of that and never knew it until now," said Ailell, "but only that you stopped at home like any other woman, while the enemies at your boundaries were slaughtering and destroying and driving all before them, and you not able to hinder them." "That is not the way it was at all," said Maeve, "but of the six daughters of my father Eochaid, King of Ireland, I was the best and the one that was thought most of. As to dividing gifts and giving counsel, I was the best of them, and as to battle feats and arms and fighting, I was the best of them. It was I had fifteen hundred soldiers sons of exiles, and fifteen hundred sons of chief men. And I had these," she said, "for my own household; and along with that my father gave me one of the provinces of Ireland, the province of Cruachan; so that Maeve of Cruachan is the name that was given to me.

"And as to being asked in marriage," she said,
"messengers came to me from your own brother, Finn,
son of Ross Ruadh, king of Leinster, and I gave him
a refusal; and after that there came messengers from
Cairbre Niafer, son of Rossa, king of Teamhair; and
from Conchubar, son of Ness, king of Ulster; and after
that again from Eochu Beag, son of Luchta, and I refused
them all. For it is not a common marriage portion would
have satisfied me, the same as is asked by the other
women of Ireland," she said; "but it is what I asked as
a marriage portion, a man without stinginess, without
jealousy, without fear. For it would not be fitting for
me to be with a man that would be close-handed, for
my own hand is open in wage-paying and in free-giving;
and it would be a reproach on my husband, I to be a
better wage-payer than himself. And it would not be
fitting for me to be with a man that would be cowardly,
for I myself go into struggles and fights and battles and
gain the victory; and it would be a reproach to my
husband, his wife to be braver than himself. And it
would not be fitting for me to be with a husband that
would be jealous, for I was never without one man
being with me in the shadow of another. Now I have
got such a husband as I looked for in yourself, Ailell,
for you are not close-handed or jealous or cowardly.
And I gave you good wedding gifts," she said, "suits
of clothing enough for twelve men; a chariot that
was worth three times seven serving-maids; the width
of your face in red gold, the round of your arm in a
bracelet of white bronze. And the fine or the tribute
you can ask of your enemies is no more than the fine
or the tribute I have a right to ask, for you are nothing
of yourself, but it is in the pay of a woman you are,"
she said. "That is not so," said Ailell, "for I am a
king's son, and I have two brothers that are kings, Finn,
king of Leinster, and Cairbre, king of Teamhair, and I

would have been king in their places but that they are
older than myself. And as to giving of wages and
dividing of gifts," he said, "you are no better than myself; and if this province is under the rule of a woman,
it is the only province in Ireland that is so; and it is
not through your right I took the kingship of it, but
through the right of my mother, Mata of Murrisk,
daughter of Magach. And if I took the daughter of the
chief king of Ireland for my wife, it was because I
thought she was a fitting wife for me." "You know
well," said Maeve, "the riches that belong to me are
greater than the riches that belong to you." "That is
a wonder to me," said Ailell, "for there is no one in
Ireland has a better store of jewels and riches and
treasure than myself, and you know well there is not."

"Let our goods and our riches be put beside one
another, and let a value be put on them," said Maeve,
"and you will know which of us owns most." "I am
content to do that," said Ailell.

With that, orders were given to their people to bring
out their goods and to count them, and to put a value on
them. They did so, and the first things they brought
out were their drinking vessels, their vats, their iron
vessels, and all the things belonging to their households,
and they were found to be equal. Then their rings were
brought out, and their bracelets and chains and brooches,
their clothing of crimson and blue and black and green
and yellow and saffron and speckled silks, and these
were found to be equal. Then their great flocks of
sheep were driven from the green plains of the open
country and were counted, and they were found to be
equal; and if there was a ram among Maeve's flocks
that was the equal of a serving-maid in value, Ailell had
one that was as good. And their horses were brought
in from the meadows, and their herds of swine out of the
woods and the valleys, and they were equal one to

another. And the last thing that was done was to bring in the herds of cattle from the forest and the wild places of the province, and when they were put beside one another they were found to be equal, but for one thing only. It happened a bull had been calved in Maeve's herd, and his name was Fionnbanach, the White-horned. But he would not stop in Maeve's herds, for he did not think it fitting to be under the rule of a woman, and he had gone into Ailell's herds and stopped there ; and now he was the best bull in the whole province of Connaught. And when Maeve saw him, and knew he was better than any bull of her own, there was great vexation on her, and it was as bad to her as if she did not own one head of cattle at all. So she called Mac Roth, the herald, to her, and bade him to find out where there was a bull as good as the White-horned to be got in any province of the provinces of Ireland.

"I myself know that well," said Mac Roth, "for there is a bull that is twice as good as himself at the house of Daire, son of Fachtna, in the district of Cuailgne, and that is Donn Cuailgne, the Brown Bull of Cuailgne." "Rise up, then," said Maeve, "and make no delay, but go to Daire from me, and ask the loan of that bull for a year, and I will return him at the end of the year, and fifty heifers along with him, as fee for the loan. And there is another thing for you to say, Mac Roth ; if the people of Daire's district and country think bad of him for sending away that wonderful jewel the Donn of Cuailgne, let Daire himself come along with him, and I will give him the equal of his own lands on the smooth plain of Ai, and a chariot that is worth three times seven serving-maids, and my own close friendship along with that."

So Mac Roth set out on his journey, and nine men along with him, and when they came to Daire's house there was a good welcome before them, as there

should be, for Mac Roth was the chief herald of all
Ireland.

Daire asked him then what was the reason of his
journey, and Mac Roth told him the whole story of the
quarrel between Maeve and Ailell and of the counting
of their herds, and of the great rewards Maeve offered
him if he would give her the loan for one year of the
Brown Bull of Cuailgne. Daire was so well pleased
when he heard this, that he wagged himself till the
stitches of the feathers under him burst, and he said:
"I will send him to Maeve into Connaught, whether
the men of Ulster like it or do not like it." Mac Roth
was well content with that; and he and his men were
attended to, and fresh rushes were spread, and a feast
was put before them, with every sort of food and of
drink, so that after a while they were not so clear in
their wits as they were before.

Two of them began talking to one another then, and
one said: "This is a good man in whose house we are."
"He is good indeed," said the other. "Is there any man
in Ulster better than himself?" said the first. "There is,
surely," said the other, "for Conchubar the High King is
a better man, and it is no shame for all the men of
Ulster to gather to him." "It is a wonder," said the
first, "Daire to have given up to us what it would have
taken the strength of the four provinces of Ireland to
bring away by force." "That I may see the mouth that
spoke those words filled with blood," said another of the
men; "for if Daire had refused to give it willingly, the
strength of Ailell and of Maeve, and the knowledge of
Fergus, son of Rogh, would have brought it from him
against his will."

Just as they were talking, the chief steward of Daire's
house came in, and servants along with him bringing
meat and drink; and he heard what the men of
Connaught said and great anger came on him, and he

bade the servants put down the food for them, but he never told them to use it or not to use it, but he went to where Daire was and said : " Was it you, Daire, promised the Brown Bull of Cuailgne to these messengers ? " " It was myself indeed," said Daire. " Then what they have said is true ? " " What is that ? " said Daire. " They say that you knew if you did not give him willingly you would have had to give him against your will by the strength of Ailell and Maeve and by the guidance of Fergus, son of Rogh." " If they say that," said Daire, " I swear by the gods my people swear by, that they will not take him away till they take him by force."

On the morning of the morrow the messengers rose up and went into the house where Daire was. " Show us now," they said, " the place where the bull is." " I will not indeed," said Daire ; " but if it was a habit with me," he said, " to do treachery to messengers or to travellers or to men on their road, not one of you would go back alive to Cruachan." " What reason have you for this change ? " said Mac Roth. " I have a good reason for it, for you were saying last night that if I did not give the bull willingly, I would be forced to give it against my will by Ailell and by Maeve and by Fergus." " If that was said, it was the talk of common messengers, and they after eating and drinking," said Mac Roth, " and it is not fitting for you to take notice of a thing like that."

" It may be so " said Daire ; " but for all that," he said " I will not give the bull this time."

They went back then to Cruachan, and Maeve asked news of them, and Mac Roth told her the whole story, how Daire gave them the promise of the bull at first, and refused it afterwards. " What was the reason of that ? " she asked. And when it was told her she said : " This riddle is not hard to guess ; they did not intend to let us get the bull at all; but now we will take him from them by force," she said.

And this was the cause of the great war for the Brown Bull of Cuailgne.

Then Maeve sent messengers to the six Maines, her sons, to come to Cruachan, the brothers of Maine Morgor that got his death at Dun Gerg. And she sent messengers to the sons of Magach; and they came, with thirty hundred armed men, and to Cormac Conloingeas, son of King Conchubar, and to Fergus, son of Rogh; and they came, and thirty hundred armed men with them.

This is the appearance that was on the first troop. Black heads of hair they had, and green cloaks about them, held with silver brooches, and on their bodies shirts of gold thread, embroidered with red gold, and they had swords with white sheaths and hilts of silver.

As to the second troop, they had short-cut hair, and grey cloaks about them, and on their bodies pure white shirts; and they had swords with knobbed hilts of gold, and sheaths of silver. Every one asked: "Is that Cormac among them?" "It is not indeed," said Maeve.

As to the last troop, they had gold-yellow hair, falling loose like manes, and crimson cloaks, well ornamented, about them, and gold brooches with jewels at their breasts, and long silk shirts coming down to their ankles. And as they walked they lifted up their feet and put them down again all together. "Is that Cormac among them?" every one asked. "It is, surely," said Maeve.

So they made their camp there, and between the four fords of Ai, Athmaga, Athslisen, Athberena, and Athcoltna, there were red fires blazing through the night.

And they stopped a fortnight there at Cruachan, eating
drinking, and resting themselves, that they might be
the better able for the journey and the marching.

Then Maeve bade her chariot-driver to yoke her
horses, that she might go and consult with her Druid
and ask a prophecy from him, to foretell for her if the
army she was bringing out would get the victory, and
would come back safely. And she said to the Druid:
"There are many that will part here to-day from their
companions and their friends, from their country and
their lands, from their father and their mother. And if
it happens that the whole of them do not come back
again safe and sound, it is on me the complaints and
the curses will fall. And besides that," she said, "there
is no one that goes out or that stops behind, that is
dearer to us than we are to ourselves. So find out for
us now whether we shall return, or not return." And
the Druid said: "Whoever returns or does not return,
you yourself will return."

Her chariot was turned then, and she went back again
homeward. But presently she saw a thing she wondered
at, a woman sitting on the shaft of the chariot, facing
her, and this is how she was: a sword of white bronze
in her hand, with seven rings of red gold on it and she
seemed to be weaving a web with it; a speckled green
cloak about her, fastened at the breast with a brooch
of red gold; a ruddy, pleasant face she had, her eyes
grey, and her mouth like red berries, and when she
spoke her voice was sweeter than the strings of a curved
harp, and her skin showed through her clothes like the
snow of a single night. Long feet she had, very white,
and the nails on them pink and even; her hair gold-
yellow, three locks of it wound about her head, and
another that fell down loose below her knee.

Maeve looked at her, and she said: "What are you
doing here, young girl?" "It is looking into the future

for you I am," she said, "to see what will be your
chances and your fortunes, now you are gathering the
provinces of Ireland to the war for the Brown Bull of
Cuailgne." "And why would you be doing this for me?"
said Maeve. "There is good reason for it," she said,
"for I am a serving-maid of your own people." "Which
of my people do you belong to?" said Maeve. "I am
Fedelm of the Sidhe, of Rath Cruachan." "It is well,
Fedelm of the Sidhe; tell me what way you see our
hosts." "I see crimson on them, I see red." "Yet
Conchubar is lying in his weakness at Emain; my
messengers are come back from there, and we need not
be in dread of anything from Ulster," said Maeve. "But
look again, Fedelm of the Sidhe, and tell me the truth
of the matter." "I see crimson on them, I see red,"
said the girl. "Yet Eoghan, son of Durthacht, is in his
weakness at Rathairthir; my messengers are come back
from him; we need not be afraid of anything from Ulster.
Look again, Fedelm of the Sidhe; how do you see our
hosts?" "I see them all crimson, I see them all red."
"Celtchair, son of Uthecar, is lying in his weakness
within his fort; my messengers are come back from him.
Tell me again, Fedelm of the Sidhe, how do you see our
hosts?" "I see crimson on them, I see red." "There
may be no harm in what you see," said Maeve, "for
when all the men of Ireland are gathered together in one
place, there will surely be quarrels and fights among
them, about going first or last over fords and rivers, or
about the first wounding of some stag or boar, or such
like. Tell me truly now, Fedelm of the Sidhe, what
way do you see our hosts?" "I see crimson on them,
I see red. And I see," she said, "a low-sized man doing
many deeds of arms; there are many wounds on his
smooth skin; there is a light about his head, there is
victory on his forehead; he is young and beautiful, and
modest towards women; but he is like a dragon in the

battle. His appearance and his courage are like the appearance and the courage of Cuchulain of Muirthemne; and who that Hound from Muirthemne may be I do not know; but I know this much well, that all this host will be reddened by him. He is setting out for the battle; he will make your dead lie thickly, the memory of the blood shed by him will be lasting; women will be keening over the bodies brought low by the Hound of the Forge that I see before me."

This is the foretelling that was made for Maeve by Fedelm of the Sidhe, before the setting out of the hosts at Cruachan for Ulster.

Now, when Maeve told Fedelm of the Sidhe that there need be no fear of the men of Ulster coming out to attack the army, for they were lying in their weakness, she meant that they were under the curse and the enchantment that was put on them one time by a woman they had ill-treated. And the story of it is this:—

There was a man of the name of Crunden, son of Agnoman, that lived in a lonely part of Ulster, among the mountains, and he had a good way of living; but his wife had died, and he had the care of all his children on him. One day he was sitting in the house, and he saw a woman come in at the door, tall and handsome, and with good clothes on her, and she did not say a word, but she sat down by the hearth and began to make up the fire. And then she went to where the meal was, and took it out and mixed it, and baked a cake. And when the evening was drawing on, she took a vessel and went out and milked the cows, but all the time she never spoke a word. Then she came back into the house, and took a turn to the right, and was the last to stop up and to cover over the fire.

She stayed on there, and Crunden, the man of the

house, married her, and she tended him and his sons, and everything he had prospered.

It happened, one day, there was to be a great gathering of the men of Ulster, for games and races and all sorts of amusements, and all that could go, both of men and women, used to go to that gathering. "I will go there to-day," said Crunden, "the same as every other man is going." "Do not," said his wife, "for if you so much as say my name there at the fair," she said, "I will be lost to you for ever." "Then indeed I will not speak of you at all," said Crunden. So he set out with the others to the fair, and there was every sort of amusement there, and all the people of the country were at it.

At the ninth hour, the royal chariot was brought on the ground, and the king's horses won the day. Then the bards and poets, and the Druids, and the servants of the king, and the whole gathering, began to praise the king and the queen and their horses, and they cried out: "There were never seen such horses as these; there are no better runners in all Ireland." "My wife is a better runner than those two horses," said Crunden. When the king was told of that he said: "Take hold of the man, and keep him until his wife can be brought to try her chance and to run against the horses."

So they took hold of him, and kept him, and messengers were sent from the king to the woman. She bade the messengers welcome, and asked what brought them. "We are come by the king's order," they said, "to bring you to the fair, to see if you will run faster than the king's horses; for your husband boasted that you would, and he is kept prisoner now until you will come and release him." "It is foolish my husband was to speak like that," she said; "and as for myself, I am not fit to go, for I am soon going to give birth to a child." "That is a pity," said the messengers, "for if you do not come, your husband will be put to death." "If that is so, I must go, whatever happens," she said.

So with that she set out for the gathering, and when she got there all the people were crowding about her to see her. "It is not fitting to be looking at me, and I the way I am," she said; "and what have I been brought here for?" "To run against the two horses of the king," the people called out. "Ochone!" she said, "do not ask me, for I am close upon my hour." "Take out your swords and put the man to death," said the king. "Give me your help," she said to the people, "for every one of you has been born of a mother." And then she said to the king: "Give me even a delay until my child is born." "I will give no delay," said the king. "Then the shame that is on you will be greater than the shame that is on me," she said. "And because you have showed no pity and no respect to me," she said, "it is a heavier punishment will fall on you than has fallen upon me. And bring out the horses beside me now." Then they started, and the woman outran the horses and gained the race; and at the goal the pains of childbirth came on her, and she bore two children, a boy and a girl, and she gave a great cry in her pain.

And a weakness came suddenly on all that heard the cry, so that they had no more strength than the woman as she lay there. And it is what she said: "From this out, and till the ninth generation, the shame that you have put on me will fall on you; and at whatever time you most want your strength, at the time your enemies are closing on you, that is the time the weakness of a woman in childbirth will come upon all the men of the province of Ulster."

And so it happened; and of all the men of Ulster that were born after that day, there was no one escaped that curse and that enchantment but only Cuchulain.

When the men of Connaught set out from Cruachan for the north they stopped towards evening at Cuilsilinne, and there they made their encampment for the night. Ailell took his place in the middle of the camp, and on his right was Fergus, son of Rogh, and Cormac Conloingeas next to him again, and their people on the same side; and on Ailell's left there was a place made for Maeve and Findabair her daughter. But Maeve stopped behind until the whole of the army had come up, and then she went in her chariot to see if all was in order, and after that she came and took her seat at Ailell's right hand. "Which of the troops do you think the best?" said Ailell. "None of them are any good at all," said Maeve, "compared with the men of Leinster, the Gailiana." "What have they done beyond all the others that you praise them so much?" said Ailell. "There is reason for praising them," said Maeve; "for while the others were choosing a place for themselves, the Gailiana had their huts and their shelters made, and while the others were making their shelters, they had their share of food and drink cooked and set out, and while the others were making ready their food they had theirs eaten, and while the others were eating, they were laid down and sleeping. And as their servants have been better than the servants of the men of Ireland," she said, "so will their young men and their fighting men be better than the young men of Ireland on this march." "I am well pleased to hear that," said Ailell, "for it was with me they came, and they are of my own province." "Then you need not be so well pleased," said Maeve, "for they shall march no further with you, for I will not have them boasted of, before me or to me." "Let them stop in this camp, then," said Ailell. "They shall not do that either," said Maeve. "What must they do, then?" said Findabair, "if they are neither to go on nor to stop in the camp?" "They will get death and destruction from myself," said Maeve. "It is a pity you to say that," said Ailell, "and they only just after joining us." "If you think to harm them," said Fergus, "you will have to fight with me as well as with them; for by the oath of my people," he said, "it is only over my body and the bodies of the men of Ulster that are with me, you can come at their death." "Do not speak that way, Fergus," said Maeve; "for if you were to join with these strangers against me, I would have the six Maines and their men on my side, and the sons of Magach and their men, and my own troops along with them. And I think we would be well able for you," she said. "It is not right for you to say that," said Fergus, "for there are no men in Ireland better than the young men of Ulster that came to Connaught with me, and they have been a good help to you up to this. But I will tell you another thing to do," he said: "let the men of Leinster be divided through all the other troops of the men of Ireland, the way there will not be more than five of them together in any one place." "I will agree to that," said Maeve, "for I know there would be nothing but fighting and jealousy if they were left together the way they are now."

On the morning of the morrow, they made ready to set out again, but the chief men among them consulted together first, what way they could best keep the peace between so many troops and tribes and families; and it is what they settled, to put every troop under its own leader, and to let it, great or small, take a road of its own. And besides that, they consulted who would be the best man to put over the whole army, to lead them and to show them the way. And they all said Fergus would be the best, for he had been king of Ulster seventeen years, until Conchubar put him out of the kingship, and he had stopped on in Ulster after that until the time Conchubar killed the sons of Usnach in spite of the guarantee he had given them.

So Fergus was made leader of the whole army; but as they went on, a great love for his own province and his home came on him, and instead of going on northwards he turned to the south. And while he was delaying the army like that, he sent messsengers into Ulster to give warning and news of their coming. But Maeve was keeping a watch on him, and when she saw what had happened, she went to him and said: "Why is it, Fergus, that we have turned again to the south?" Then Fergus knew it was no use to try and deceive her, and they turned again, but they did not go far, but only to the place they had left in the morning, Cuilsilinne.

Then Fergus called to mind that they were coming near the borders of Ulster, and that it was likely it would not be long before they would meet with Cuchulain; and he gave a warning to the army to mind themselves well, lest the Hound of Muirthemne should fall on them, angry and beautiful, and destroy them.

And then the men of Connaught set out again eastward, and when they came to Monecolthan, they saw before them eight-score deer, in the one herd, and the whole army surrounded them, and all the deer were killed; but if they were, it was the Gailiana, scattered as they were, that killed all the deer but five, and those five were all that were killed by the rest of the men of Ireland.

It was on that same day Cuchulain and his father, Sualtim, came to the pillar-stone at Ardcullin, for they had got the warning Fergus had sent, and there they let their horses graze, and Sualtim's horses cropped the grass to the north of the pillar-stone to the earth, but Cuchulain's horses, at the south side, cropped it to the bare flags.

"It is in my mind, Sualtim," said Cuchulain, "that the army of Connaught is not far away from us now. Go now, then," he said, "and bring a warning to the men of Ulster, and tell them not to stop in the open plains, but to go into the woods and the valleys of the province, that the men of Ireland may not come upon them." "And you yourself, little son, what will you do?" said Sualtim. "I must go," said Cuchulain, "southward to Teamhair, for I promised to go there to-day, to see a young girl of the household of Fedelm of the Fair Shape, Laegaire's wife." "It is a pity for you to go for a thing like that," said Sualtim, "and you leaving Ulster under the feet of enemies and strangers." "I must go, indeed," said Cuchulain, "for if I break my word to a woman, it will be said from this out that a woman's word is better than a man's."

So Sualtim set out then, to give a warning to the men of Ulster, and Cuchulain went into the oak woods and cut down an oak sapling, and twisted it into a ring, and cut a message on it in Ogham. And then he forced the ring over the top of the pillar-stone, and down to the thick part of it. And then he went on to keep his appointment at Teamhair.

As to the men of Ireland, they went on till they came to Ardcullin, and the whole country of Ulster lay there before them. And then they saw the pillar-stone and the oak ring that was on it; and Ailell took it off, and gave it to Fergus, and bade him read the Ogham. And what he read on it was Cuchulain's name, and the warning on it that the men of Ulster should not pass the pillar-stone that night, for if they did, he would do a great revenge on them at the sunrise of the morrow.

"It would be a pity," said Maeve, "that the first blood to be shed after going into the province should be the blood of our own people: it would be best for us to draw blood first on the people of Ulster." "I agree to that," said Ailell, "for I am loth to go against this ring or the man that twisted it; but let us go into the wood and make our camp there for the night." So they went into the wood, and cut a way for the chariots with their swords as they went, and it is from that the place is called Sleact na Gearbat, the Cut Way of the Chariots, until this time. And a great snow fell that night, so that it made one plain of the five provinces of Ireland, and they could make no shelter or prepare food, and none of the men in the camp knew through the whole night was it friend or enemy was near him, until the clear light of the sun fell on the snow in the morning. And then they left that place, and went on into Ulster.

As to Cuchulain, he did not rise very early that morning, and when he did, there was food made ready for him, and a bath of pure water. Then he bade Laeg to make his chariot ready, and they set out; and after a while they came to the track of the army of Ireland where it had gone over the border into Ulster. "Well, Laeg," said Cuchulain, "I have not much luck out of my appointment that I kept last night; for it is expected of one that is watching the borders that the least he should do is to raise a cry or give a warning of the enemy that is coming, and I have missed doing this, so that the men of Ireland have slipped by without news or notice into Ulster." "I told you, Cuchulain," said Laeg, "that if you kept to your meeting last night, some vexation like this would fall on you." "Well, Laeg," said Cuchulain, "let you follow their track now, and count them, and see what number of the men of Ireland are come over the border." Laeg did this, and he came back and told their number, as he had counted them. "There is a mistake in your counting," said Cuchulain. "I will count them myself this time." Then he told their number. "It is with yourself the mistake is, Cuchulain," said Laeg. "It is not," he said, "but there are eighteen divisions have passed the border, but the eighteenth is broken up and distributed among the others, so that no sure reckoning can be made of it."

This, now, was one of the three best estimates ever made in Ireland, and the other two were made by Lugh of the Long Hand, and by Angus at Brugh na Boinne.

"But now, Laeg," he said, "turn the chariot towards the army, and hurry on the horses; for unless I can make an end of some of them to-day," he said, "I will not live through the night myself."

So they went on to the place that is called now Athgowla, northward from Knowth.

There they met with the two young men, the sons of Neara, that were sent out in front of Maeve's army, to see was there any hindrance before it, and Cuchulain struck off their heads and the heads of their chariot-drivers.

And he cut down a tree with his sword, and it having four branches, and he lopped them short, and cleared the tree; and he stood up in his chariot, and with one cast he drove the tree into the ground that it stood deep and firm, and he set the four heads he had struck off on the four lopped branches of it. And then he turned back their horses in their chariots towards the army.

Now it is the way Maeve used to be going, she in a chariot by herself, and two chariots on each side of her, and behind her and before her, the way no sod from the feet of the horses of the army, or foam from their mouths, would touch her clothing. And when she saw the two chariots coming back, and the bodies in them without heads, she stopped to see what had happened. "What are these?" she said. "They are the chariots and the bodies of the two sons of Neara that went on before us," said her chariot-driver.

Then she held a council with her chief men, and it is what they agreed, that it must be some part of the army of Ulster was there before them at the ford they were drawing near, and that it was best to send out

Cormac Conloingeas and his men to see who was in it, for the men of Ulster would not be willing to harm the son of their High King.

So Cormac and his troop went on to the ford, but when he got there all he saw was a lopped tree and four heads on it, and the blood dripping down from them, and the track of one chariot only, going eastward out of the ford. Then the rest of the army came with the other chief men. "There is wonder on me," said Ailell; "our four men to have been made an end of so easily as this." "You may wonder as well," said Fergus, "at the way this pole was driven into the ground by one man, and it will be hard for you to find a man of your army will drag it out again." "Do it yourself, Fergus," said Maeve, "for you are of my army." So Fergus called for a chariot, and stood up in it, and gave such a strong pull at the pole, that the chariot broke under him. "Give me another chariot," he said. And when he had broken seventeen of the war-chariots of Connaught one after another, and had not so much as loosened the pole, Maeve said: "Leave off now, Fergus, from breaking my people's chariots; and if you yourself had not been with us on this march," she said, "we would have been up with the men of Ulster before now, and we would have taken men and cattle. And I know well why you did this; it was to give the men of Ulster time to get over their weakness and their pains, and to come out against us to defend their bull and their cattle." "Give me my own chariot, then," said Fergus. So they gave him his own chariot, and he got up in it and gave a great pull at the pole; and neither the frame nor the wheels of his chariot started or strained like the others, and he pulled up the pole and gave it into Ailell's hand, and Ailell looked at it and said: "There is dread on me, of the man that set that pole there; do you think, Fergus," he said, "was it Conchubar the High King that did it?" "It was not," said Fergus, "for if Conchubar had come here, his army would have come along with him, and all the men of Ulster, and he would not have been so near to you without offering you battle, and by this time whichever got the better would be boasting of it." "Do you think was it Cuscraid, Conchubar's son?" said Ailell; "or Eoghan, son of Durthacht, king of Fernmaighe; or Celthair, son of Uthecar?" "I do not," said Fergus, "but it is what I think, that it was my own foster-son and Conchubar's that was here, Cuchulain, son of Sualtim." "We heard you often talking at Cruachan about that young man, and what is his age at this time?" "His age is of no great matter," said Fergus, "for he did great deeds, when he was but a soft child." "He is young enough yet," said Maeve, "and I think it will not be hard to find some one of our own men that will get the better of this wild Hound, for he has but the one body to wound or to put to flight." "You will get no one," said Fergus, "among your fighting men and your young men and your champions that will be able to put down Cuchulain."

They stopped there then and made their camp, and rested that night, with food and with music.

And it was in that night Fergus gave Maeve and Ailell the whole story of the boy deeds of Cuchulain, and how he used to have a stone for a pillow, and no one dared wake him, lest he might chance to give them a blow of the stone in his anger. And he told of one night when he was asleep, and Conchubar was attacked and was beaten by Eoghan, son of Durthacht. And Cuchulain was awakened by the cries of the beaten men that were running away, and he went out in the darkness of the night to look for Conchubar; and where the battle had been, he saw a man with the half of a man's body on his back, and he called to

Cuchulain to help him, and threw the half-body to him, and Cuchulain threw it back again, and they fought, and he struck off the man's head. And then he found Conchubar lying in a grave, and he dug him out of that, and as they went home, they met Cuscraid that was wounded, and Cuchulain brought him home to Emain on his back. And another time he went into a wood and saw a terrible-looking man having a wild boar in one hand, and his weapon in the other hand, and he killed him, and brought home the boar. And another time when the men of Ulster were in their weakness, three times nine sea-robbers came to Emain, and the women ran shrieking to the palace when they saw them, and when the boys that were at play on the lawn knew what they were running from, they ran along with them. But Cuchulain went out and killed nine of the sea-robbers and wounded the rest of them, so that he drove them all back. And he told them many other stories of his doings beside these.

The next day, the army marched on eastward beyond the mountain. But there was a narrow place they had to pass through, and Cuchulain cut down a great oak tree, and laid it across the gap, and wrote an Ogham on it; and when the men of Ireland came up to it, it hindered them, and they could not move it, and they made their camp there that night. And early in the morning they sent the young man Fraech, son of Idath, to get the hindrance cleared away. But Fraech went on beyond it, till he came to a river, and there he found Cuchulain bathing. And they attacked one another in the water, and Fraech was beaten, and Cuchulain went away and left his body on the bank.

And when the men of Ireland found his body they began to keen him. And then they saw a great band of women of the Sidhe, with green dresses on them, coming for his body, and they gave out a great cry over him and brought him away to a hill of the Sidhe. And Findabair cried after him, and went to see the green bank where he was lying.

And they knew that Cuchulain was not far from them, for presently Maeve's little dog, Baiscne, got his death by a stone from a sling. There was anger on Maeve then, and she urged her men to follow after Cuchulain, so that they broke the poles of their chariots in their hurry.

The next day Cuchulain was going through the wood, and he heard the sound of blows on the trees.

"It is too bold the men of Ulster are, Laeg," he said, "to be cutting down trees like this, with the men of Ireland coming on them; and stop here," he said, "till I find out who is it that is in the wood."

He went on till he met with a young man of Connaught, that was chariot-driver to Orlam, son of Maeve and Ailell. "What is it you are doing there, young man?" he asked. "I am cutting holly poles," said the young man, "for we have broken our chariots hunting that notable deer, Cuchulain. And now, good friend," he said, "lend me a hand with these poles, lest that same notable Cuchulain should come upon me here." "Your choice, boy; shall I cut the holly poles, or shall I trim them for you?" "Let you do the trimming," said he. So Cuchulain took them and trimmed them straight and smooth, that a fly could not have kept his footing on them. The chariot-driver looked at the poles, and he said: "I am thinking this is not the work you have a right to be put to. And who are you at all?" he said. "I am that notable Cuchulain you were speaking of just now." "That is bad news for me," said the driver, "for surely I am a dead man." "There need be no fear on you," said Cuchulain, "for I do not fight against drivers or messengers or unarmed men. But

where is your master?" he said. "He is out before
you on the plain." "Go to him, then, and give him
this warning, that I am here, and that if we meet, he
will surely get his death from me." With that the
young man went to look for his master, but quick as he
went, Cuchulain was quicker, and as soon as he came
up with Orlam he struck off his head, and held it up
and shook it before the men of Ireland.

After that, the three sons of Garach came out and
made an attack on him, but he overcame them, and
struck off their heads, and he killed their chariot-
drivers as well, that they had armed against him.
And Lethan and his chariot-driver came against him,
and he killed them in the same way.

At that time the harpers of Cainbile came to Maeve's
camp, and played on their magic harps; but the men of
Ireland thought it might be as spies they came, and they
drove them out of the camp, and followed after them
till they came to the great stone of Lecmore. But when
they thought to overtake them there, the harpers took
on themselves the shape of wild deer, and went away.
And it was on the same day that Cuchulain, with two
casts of a sling stone, killed the marten and the pet bird
that were sitting on Maeve's two shoulders.

Then the men of Ireland came into Magh Breagh and
Muirthemne, and carried off and destroyed all before
them. And Fergus warned them that Cuchulain was
not far off, and that he would do a great vengeance on
them, since they had spoiled Muirthemne. And it was
at that time Lugaid, son of Nois, that had gone into
Connaught with Fergus, went secretly to Cuchulain and
told him of all that was going on in the camp, and of the
dread of him that was on all the men of Ireland, so that
they did not dare to stir out alone, and that he himself
was true to him yet.

And now that the army was coming so near to

Cuailgne, the War-goddess, the Battle Crow, the Morrigu, came and sat on a pillar-stone at Teamhair, and gave a warning to the Brown Bull of Cuailgne, and it is what she said : " Have a care, and keep a good watch, my poor bull, or the men of Ireland will come on you and will drive you away to their camp." And when the bull heard the warning, he brought fifty of his heifers with him, and went away to a valley of Slieve Cuilinn.

And the men of Ireland came on, bringing the herds of cattle they took on the way, where there was no one to defend them. And they stopped for the night at Conaille Muirthemne, and there Maeve bade one of her women go down to the stream for water. And the woman was wearing Maeve's golden covering on her head, and Cuchulain saw her, and he thought it was Maeve herself that was in it, and he made a cast of a stone that killed her, and the gold covering was broken in pieces.

And they were delayed there for a while, for the river was in flood, and when they tried to cross it, the chariots that went in were swept away to the sea ; and one of Maeve's best men, Uala, that she sent to try the depth of it, was swept away along with them. And while they were stopping there, Cuchulain killed Raen and Rae, that were come to tell the story of the war, and a hundred men along with them.

Then Maeve said : " Some man of you must go out and stand against Cuchulain to save the army." " It is not I that will go," said one of them. " It is not I," said all the others, " for Cuchulain is no easy man to stand against." And they were for going round by the head of the river, but Maeve made them cut a way through the mountain before them, that it might be left as a lasting disgrace to Ulster. So they did this, and it is called Berna Ulaid, the Gap of Ulster, to this day.

Now, when they were setting out to cross the moun-

tain, Maeve gave orders that the army was to be
divided in two parts, each with its own share of cattle,
and of all other things, and she said that she herself
and Fergus would go with the one part, by the Gap of
Ulster, and that Ailell should go with the other part,
by the road of Midluachair.

So Ailell set out, and his chariot-driver, Ferloga, with
him, and that was the same Ferloga that made a bargain
with Conchubar, the High King, one time; and this is
the way it happened. It was at the time Mac Datho of
Leinster had stirred up a fight between the men of
Ulster and the men of Connaught, about the dividing
of a pig at a feast he made, the same way Bricriu had
stirred up a fight about the Championship, and
Conchubar was following after the men of Connaught
over the plain of Fearbile; and all of a sudden Ferloga,
that had been left behind by Ailell, and that was
hiding himself, made a leap to the back of Conchubar's
chariot, and took a hold of his neck between his two
hands. "What will you give me to let you loose, king?"
he said. "What is it you are asking?" said Conchubar.
"Indeed it is no great gift I am asking," said Ferloga,
"but only you to bring me along with you to Emain
Macha, and the young women and the young girls of
Ulster to sing a song around me every evening, and
every one of them to say, 'Ferloga is my favourite.'"
Conchubar agreed to that, and Ferloga went with him
to Emain; but at the end of a year they sent him back,
and presents with him, to Ailell and to Maeve.

At that time, a suspicion came on Ailell, that there
was some understanding between Maeve and Fergus,
and he bade Ferloga to keep a watch on them. After a
while, Ferloga saw that Maeve and Fergus had stopped
in a wood behind the rest of the army, and he followed
after them quietly, the way they would not hear him,
and there he found Fergus's sword lying on the ground.

So he took the sword out of the sheath, and he cut a wooden sword and shaped it, and put it into the sheath in its place, and he brought Fergus's sword back to Ailell, and told him how he had found it, and Ailell bade him hide it in his chariot. When Fergus saw that his sword was gone and a wooden sword was put in its place, there was great confusion on him; but Ailell said nothing of it when they met, but asked him to come and play a game of chess with him. And at the game they quarrelled, and Ailell said sharp words of blame to Fergus and to Maeve, and they answered him back, and Fergus bade him give him up his sword. But Ailell said he would never give it to him until the day of the great battle would come, between the men of Ireland and the men of Ulster.

Then Cuchulain came there and stood on a height and shook his spears and his sword before them, so that great dread came on them.

After that, Maeve sent Fiacha, son of Firaba, to talk with Cuchulain, and to try could he win him over. "What will you offer him?" said Fiacha. "I will give him full payment for all that has been spoiled of his goods, and a good place for himself in Cruachan Ai, and my own protection and Ailell's, if he will give up Conchubar's service and come into ours. And indeed that would be better for him," she said, "than to stop under a little king like Conchubar."

So Fiacha went to speak with Cuchulain, and he gave him a good welcome. And Fiacha told him the message he had brought from Maeve, and the offer she had made if he would quit Conchubar's service. "I will not do that," said Cuchulain; "I will not betray my mother's brother for the sake of any strange king. But I will consent to go myself to-morrow," he said, "to speak with Maeve and Ailell and with Fergus." So Fiacha bade him farewell, and went back to the army.

On the morning of the morrow Cuchulain went to
Glen Ochain, and Maeve and Fergus came to meet him;
and Maeve looked at him and she said: "Is this the same
Cuchulain you put such a great name on, Fergus? I see
that he has not yet grown out of his boyhood." Then she
spoke with Cuchulain and made her offer again, and he
refused it, and they left the place with great anger on
them one against the other. And that night, and the
two nights after it, the men of Ireland were afraid either
to eat or to sleep or to make music; for Cuchulain killed
so many of their men before the clear light of every
morning, that it was as if the whole army was melting
away. "Some one must go and make him another offer,"
said Maeve, and this time she sent Mac Roth, the herald.
"Where will I find him?" said Mac Roth. "Ask
Fergus for news of him," said Maeve. "It is likely,"
said Fergus, "he will be between Ochain and the sea,
letting the sun shine and the wind blow upon him after
so many nights spent without sleep."

It was there he found him sure enough, and Laeg
keeping a watch a good way off. "There is an armed
man coming towards us, Cuchulain," said Laeg. "What
sort of a man is he?" said Cuchulain. "A brown-haired,
broad-faced, handsome young man; a fine brown cloak on
him; a bright bronze spear-like brooch fastening his
cloak; a well-fitting shirt next his skin; two strong shoes
between his feet and the ground. There is a white hazel
rod in one hand, and a sword with a sea-horse tooth for a
hilt in the other." "Well, Laeg," said Cuchulain, "let
him come, for these are the tokens of a herald."

Mac Roth came up to him then and asked: "Who
are you serving under, young man?" "We are serving
under Conchubar, High King of Ulster." "Can you tell
me where can I find Cuchulain, that has killed so many
of the men of Ireland?" "Whatever you would say to
him, you may say it to me," said Cuchulain. Then Mac
Roth told him all the new offers he had brought from

Maeve, and Cuchulain said: "I am Cuchulain that you are looking for, and I refuse all your offers." So Mac Roth went back to the camp. "Did you find Cuchulain?" said Maeve. "I found," he said, "an angry boy between Ochain and the sea, and I do not know if it was Cuchulain." "Did he take your offer?" said Maeve. "He did not," said Mac Roth. "It is Cuchulain he was talking to," said Fergus. "You must go to him again," said Maeve, "and make new offers." So Mac Roth went out again to make some terms with Cuchulain, but he refused all his offers. "And another thing," he said, "I would never consent to give in to a woman, or to be under a woman's rule." "Is there any bargain you would make?" said Mac Roth. "If there is," said Cuchulain, "you must find it out for yourselves, and there is one in the camp can tell you of it," he said; "and if he himself comes to me, I will speak with him, but if any other man comes to me again with offers, that will be the last day of his life."

So Mac Roth went back again and told all this to Maeve. "And I will not go near him again, myself," he said, "for all that any king in Ireland could give me." Then Maeve said to Fergus: "Have you any knowledge of the terms Cuchulain would take?" "I have not," said Fergus. But after she had questioned him a while, he said: "It is what he wants, that one man of the men of Ireland should meet him and fight alone with him every day. And while that fight is going on, he will put no hindrance on the rest of the army, but it may march on. But so soon as he has killed the man set against him, the army must stop, and make its camp until the morning of the morrow." "I will agree to that," said Maeve, "for it is better to lose one man every day than a hundred every night. And who will go and make this agreement with him?" "Fergus must go," they all said. "I will not go,"

said Fergus. "Why so?" said Ailell. "I will not go,"
he said, "unless you bind yourselves on your oath to
keep to your agreement with him." "We will do that,"
they said; and so Fergus bound them on their oath, and
his horses were yoked to his chariot.

Then a young lad, Etarcomal by name, of the people
of Maeve and of Ailell, made ready his own chariot.
"What side are you going, Etarcomal?" said Fergus.
"I am going with you," he said, "the way I will get a
sight of Cuchulain." "If you take my advice, you will
not make that journey," said Fergus. "Why so?"
"Because if your pride and his pride meet together, some
misfortune will surely happen." "I give my word not
to anger him in any way," said Etarcomal.

They went on then to where Cuchulain was, between
Ochain and the sea, and himself and Laeg were playing a game with their casting spears. "There is an
armed man coming to us," said Laeg. "What sort of
man is he?" said Cuchulain. "He is large and proud,
and he standing in a high chariot, and the waving
yellow hair about his head gives him the appearance
of the top of a tall tree that stands on a green lawn,"
said Laeg. "He has a crimson cloak about him with a
deep border of gold thread, and an inlaid gold brooch in
the cloak; a broad green spear in his hand; a shield
with a boss of red gold over him; a long sword in a
toothed sheath across his knees." "It is Fergus that is
in it," said Cuchulain. Then Fergus came where he was
and got out of his chariot, and Cuchulain gave him
a great welcome. "Do you welcome me indeed?"
said Fergus. "I do surely," said Cuchulain; "but if
it is to look for a feast from me you are come, when
a flock of birds passes over the plain a wild goose will
fall to your share, and when fish rise in the invers a
salmon will fall to your share; a handful of seaweed
and a handful of water-cress." "We know well your
hospitality is straitened in this war," said Fergus.

But I am come for the men of Ireland, to agree to your
conditions. And from this out they will send one of
their best men to fight with you alone every day." "I
agree to keep to my part of the bargain," said Cuchulain,
"and let us not stop talking here any more," he said,
"or the men of Ireland will be thinking you are doing
some treachery on them."

So Fergus went back to the camp, but Etarcomal
stopped for a while looking at Cuchulain. "What are you
looking at?" said Cuchulain. "I am looking at yourself," he said. "Then take your eyes off me, and go after
Fergus; and maybe you think yourself a better fighting
man than the one you are looking at," said Cuchulain.
"You look to me as good a fighter as I ever saw for one
of your age," said Etarcomal, "but you would not be
thought much of among trained fighters and grown
men." "It is well for you," said Cuchulain, "it is under
Fergus's protection you came, or I swear, by the gods
my people swear by, you would not go back safe and
sound to the camp." "You have no right to say that,"
said Etarcomal; "and what you want of the men of
Ireland, I will give it to you," he said, "for you ask for
one champion at a time to fight with, and I myself will
be the first to come to you to-morrow." "Come, then,"
said Cuchulain, "and however early you may come in
the morning, you will find me here before you."

So Etarcomal set out, and he began to tell his chariot-
driver all he had said, and how he had promised to go
out and fight with Cuchulain on the morrow. "Did you
make that promise?" said his driver. "I did," said
Etarcomal, "and I have given my word I will go; and I
do not know," he said, "would it be better for me to wait
till to-morrow, or to go back and fight with him to-day."
"You will not get the better of him to-morrow," said his
driver, "and it would be just as well for you to be beaten
to-night." "Turn the chariot and let us go back," said

Etarcomal, "for I swear by the oath of my people, I will not go back to the camp without bringing Cuchulain's head in my hand." So they turned back again towards the sea.

Then Laeg said: "That chariot that was here a while ago has turned back again to us, Cuchulain." "It is Etarcomal coming back to challenge me, and it is not I that will fall in this fight," said Cuchulain. "But bring me my arms," he said, "for it would not be right for me not to be ready to meet him." So he went to meet him, and took his sword out of the sheath, and said: "What are you come back for?" "I am come to fight with you." "I am loth to fight with you," said Cuchulain, "for it was under the protection of Fergus you came here."

And with that he gave a blow of his sword that cut the sod clean away from under the soles of Etarcomal's feet, so that he fell on his back. "Go back now," he said, "for you have had a warning." "I will not go back until I have fought with you." Then Cuchulain gave another stroke with the edge of his sword that cut the hair close off his head, but drew no blood. "You may go back now, at least," he said. "I will not go," said Etarcomal, "until I have made an end of you, or you have made an end of me." "Well," said Cuchulain, "if you are set upon that, it is I must make an end of you." With that he made a cross blow at him that cut him through and through, so that he fell dead.

Fergus, now, had seen nothing of all this, for it was his custom, when he was travelling, never to look back, but always to be looking before him; and presently, Etarcomal's chariot-driver came up with him, and he said: "Where have you left your master?" "Cuchulain is after attacking and making an end of him on the plain," said the man. "It was not right of him to do that," said Fergus, "to any one that came under my protection. Turn my chariot about now," he said, "until I go back and talk with him." And when he came to where Cuchulain was, he said: "It was not right of you, my own foster-son, to kill one that came under my protection." "Ask his chariot-driver," said Cuchulain, "on which of us the blame should be laid." Then the chariot-driver told the whole story, and when Fergus heard it, he said: "There is no blame on you, Cuchulain." Then he bound the body of Etarcomal to his chariot, so that it was dragged after it along the road and through the camp to the door of Ailell and Maeve. "There is the young man you sent out," he said, "and this is the treatment Cuchulain will give to every other man that goes out against him." And Maeve came out of the door and spoke high, angry, loud words: "I had put great hopes in that young man," she said, "and I did not think it was under bad protection he was going, when he went under the protection of Fergus." And Fergus said: "What business had he going out at all, to meddle with Cuchulain? And if I went there myself," he said, "it is well pleased I was to get back again safely."

The next day, the men of Ireland consulted together as to who should go against Cuchulain, and they agreed that it was best to send Natchrantal, that was a great fighting man.

So he set out, but he would bring no arms with him but three times nine holly rods, and they having hardened points.

Cuchulain was at that time following after a flock of wild birds, to bring some of them down for the evening's food, and he took no notice of Natchrantal, but went on following after the birds. But Natchrantal thought it was afraid of him he was, and he went back to the door of Maeve's tent and gave a loud shout, and he said: "That great Cuchulain there is so much talk about, is running away now after the challenge I gave him." "I would hardly believe that," said Maeve, "for he has stood against many good fighting men before now, and why would he not stand against you?" Fergus heard what was said, and it vexed him, any man to say Cuchulain had run before him; and he sent Fiacha, son of Firaba, to reproach him, for letting such a thing be said, and Cuchulain bade him welcome. "I am come from Fergus," said Fiacha, "and it is what he says, that it would have been more fitting for you to spill the blood of the man that was sent against you, than to run from him." "Who did I run from?" said Cuchulain. "Tell me who makes that boast." "It is Natchrantal," said Fiacha. "What would Fergus have me do?" said Cuchulain; "would he have me kill an unarmed man? For he brought nothing with him but wooden rods, and it is not my custom to wound chariot-drivers or messengers or unarmed men. But let him come out armed to meet me," he said, "on the morning of to-morrow."

So Fiacha went back to the camp, and the day seemed long to Natchrantal till he could meet Cuchulain. But when he went out in the morning and came to the plain he said to Cormac Conloingeas: "Where is Cuchulain?" "He is there before you," said he. "That is not the appearance that was on him yesterday," said Natchrantal; for Cuchulain's anger had come on him so that the appearance he had was changed, and he was leaning against a pillar-stone, and in the strength of his anger, as he was throwing his cloak about him, he broke off the pillar-stone, and he never noticed that it was wrapped between the cloak and himself; and Natchrantal threw his sword at him, and it broke to pieces against the pillar-stone, and then Cuchulain gave him a blow over the top of his shield that struck off his head.

While this fight was going on, Maeve, having a third part of the army with her, set out Northward

to Dun-Sobairce, to look for the Brown Bull. And
Cuchulain followed after her for a while; but then he
turned back to defend his own country. And he saw
before him Buac, son of Bainblai, that was the man
Maeve trusted better than any other, and twenty-four
men along with him, and they driving the Brown Bull
before them and fifteen of his heifers, that they had
brought out of Glen-na-masc in Slieve Cuilinn. "Where
are you bringing these cattle from?" said Cuchulain.
"Out of that mountain beyond." "What is your name?"
he said. "If I tell it, it is not either through love of
you or through fear of you," he said. "I am Buac, son of
Bainblai, from Ailell's country and Maeve's." "Take
this from me, then," said Cuchulain, and with that he
threw his spear at him so that it went through his body,
and he fell dead. But while he was doing this, the rest
of the men drove away the Bull with great haste to the
camp of the men of Ireland; and this was the greatest
affront that was put on Cuchulain through the whole of
the war for the Brown Bull of Cuailgne.

Then the men of Ireland began saying to one another
that Cuchulain would not have the mastery over them
but for the bronze spear he had, and that there must be
enchantment on it, for none of them could stand against
it. And they said to Maeve that she should send Rae,
the satirist, to ask it of him, for he could not refuse a
satirist; so Rae went and asked it of him. "Give me
your spear," he said. "I will not give you that indeed,"
said Cuchulain, "but I will give you other things." "I
will not take any other thing," said Rae, "and I will
put a bad name on you, if you refuse me the spear."
"Take it, then," said Cuchulain, and with that he threw
it with all his force at his head. "That is a weighty
present," said the satirist, and he dropped dead.

Then Cur, son of Daltach, was sent out, for the men of
Ireland thought he would be able ro rid them of

Cuchulain. But it was hard to persuade Cur, because he thought it was not worth his while to go and fight with a young beardless boy. And when he went out in the morning, Cuchulain was practising all his feats that he had learned, and Cur was for a while trying to get near enough to come at him with his weapons, but he could not ; and Cuchulain was so taken up with doing his feats that he never noticed him at all. Then Laeg saw him and said : " Have a care, Cuchulain ; there is an armed man making ready to attack you." Cuchulain was doing his apple feat at that time, keeping nine apples, and his shield, and his sword in the air, that none of them fell to the ground. And when he saw Cur, he threw the apple that was in his hand straight at his forehead, and it went through, and brought out a share of his brains the size of itself, at the other side.

And after that, other fighting men were sent out every day through a week, and he killed them all. And one day he said : " Go, Laeg, to the camp, to my friends, Lugaid and Ferbaeth and Ferdiad, and say you are come from me, and ask him which of the men of Ireland is to be sent against me to-morrow." So Laeg went, and when he came back he said : " It is your own comrade and fellow-pupil with Scathach, Ferbaeth, your blood-friend, is coming against you ; for he has only lately joined the army, and he has brought four-fifths of his men with him, and Maeve has promised him her daughter Findabair, and he has drunk from her cup, and been fed by her hand. And it is not to every one Maeve gives the ale that she gave out for Ferbaeth." " I am sorry to hear that," said Cuchulain, " for I think worse of a comrade of my own coming against me, than of any other man." And when Ferbaeth came out to fight against him in the morning, Cuchulain did his best to make him give up the fight, for the sake of their old friendship, but Ferbaeth would not listen. Cuchulain turned from him then in anger, and he struck the sole of his own foot with a spear, that it drew blood, and then he threw his spear at Ferbaeth, but he did not look to see did it hit him or not. But the spear went through his head and out of his mouth, and this is the way Ferbaeth came to his death.

Then Ailell made up a plan by which he thought to make Cuchulain give up the stand he was making against the army, and his plan was to offer Findabair to him if he would give his word to leave off attacking the men of Ireland, and he sent Lugaid to make the offer to him. Cuchulain was not very well pleased with the message, and he thought there might be some treachery in it, but he agreed that he would meet Ailell and Findabair, and speak with them. But when the time came, Ailell made his fool put on his clothes, and wear his gold circle on his head, and go with Findabair; and he bade him stop as far back as he could, the way Cuchulain would not know it was not the king that was in it; and then Findabair was to bind him over to their side, not to fight any more against the men of Ireland, and when that was done, she herself and the fool were to hurry back to the camp together. But when Cuchulain saw them, he knew the fool, and he sent a stone out of his sling and killed him. And because Findabair had taken a share in the treachery, he cut off her two plaits of hair and took them away. And after a while Ailell and Maeve came to see what had happened them, and there they found Findabair beside the dead body of the fool. And they brought her home and said nothing of it, but all the same the story was talked of in the camp.

Then Cuchulain sent Laeg into the camp again to ask news of Lugaid. And it is what Lugaid told him that the next to be sent against him was his own brother Larine, that Maeve had persuaded with wine, and with the promise of Findabair, to go against him. "And it is what they think," said Lugaid, "that if Cuchulain should kill my brother, I myself would have to go and get satisfaction for his death; and tell Cuchulain," he said, "not to make an end of Larine, but only to give him some punishment he will not forget." So when Larine came out, at the breaking of the day, Cuchulain struck the weapons out of his hands as one might strike toys out of the hands of a child, and he took him in his two hands and shook him, and left him there with the life still in him. But he was never the better of the shaking he got to the end of his life.

As Cuchulain lay in his sleep one night a great cry from the North came to him, so that he started up and fell from his bed to the ground like a sack. He went out of his tent, and there he saw Laeg yoking the horses to the chariot. "Why are you doing that?" he said. "Because of a great cry I heard from the plain to the north-west," said Laeg. "Let us go there then," said Cuchulain. So they went on till they met with a chariot, and a red horse yoked to it, and a woman sitting in it, with red eyebrows, and a red dress on her, and a long red cloak that fell on to the ground between the two wheels of the chariot, and on her back she had a grey spear. "What is your name, and what is it you are wanting?" said Cuchulain. "I am the daughter of King Buan," she said, "and what I am come for is to find you and to offer you my love, for I have heard of all the great deeds you have done." "It is a bad time you have chosen for coming," said Cuchulain, "for I am wasted and worn out with the hardship of the war, and I have no mind to be speaking with women." "You will have my help in everything you do," she said, "and it is protecting you I was up to this, and I will protect you from this out." "It is not trusting to a woman's protection I am in this work I have in my hands," said Cuchulain. "Then if you will not take my help." she said, "I will turn it against you; and at the time when you will be fighting with some man as good as yourself, I will come against you in all shapes, by water and by land, till you are beaten." There was anger on Cuchulain then, and he took his sword, and made a leap at the chariot. But on the moment, the chariot and the horse and the woman had disappeared, and all he saw was a black crow, and it sitting on a branch; and by that he knew it was the Morrigu had been talking with him.

After that, Loch, son of Mofebis, was sent for to Maeve, and she asked him would he go out to the next day's fight. "I will not go," he said, "for it would not be fitting for me to go out against a young boy, whose beard is not grown; but I have one to meet him," he said, "and that is my brother Long, son of Emonis, and you can make an agreement with him." So then Long was sent for, and Maeve promised him a great reward, suits of armour for twelve men, and a chariot, and Findabair for a wife, and the right of coming to every feast at Cruachan. Then Long went out to the fight, but Cuchulain killed him.

Then Maeve said to her women: "Go now to Cuchulain, and tell him to put some likeness of a beard on himself, and say to him there is no good warrior in the camp thinks it fitting to go out and fight him, he being young and beardless."

When Cuchulain heard what Maeve had said, he smeared his face, the way he would have the appearance of a beard, and then he came out on the hill and showed himself to the men of Ireland. When Loch, son of Mofebis, saw him, he said: "Is that a beard on Cuchulain?" "That is certainly what I see," said Maeve. "Then I will go out and meet him," said Loch. So they met beside the ford, where Long had got his death. "Come to the ford that is higher up," said Loch, for he would not fight at the ford where his brother died. So they fought at the upper ford, and while they were fighting, the Morrigu came against

Cuchulain with the appearance of a white, red-eared heifer, and fifty other heifers along with her, and a chain of white bronze between every two of them, and they made a rush into the ford. But Cuchulain made a cast at her, and wounded one of her eyes. Then she came down the stream in the shape of a black eel, and wound herself about Cuchulain's legs in the water; and while he was getting himself free of her, and bruising her against a green stone of the ford, Loch wounded his body. Then she took the appearance of a grey wolf, and took hold of his right arm, and while he was getting free of her, Loch wounded him again. Then great anger came on him, and he took the spear Aoife had given him, the Gae Bulg, and gave him a deadly wound. "I ask one thing for the sake of your great name, Cuchulain," he called out. "What thing is that?" "It is not to spare my life I am asking you," said Loch, "but let me rise up, the way I may fall on my face, and not backwards towards the men of Ireland, so that none of them can say it was in running away or in going backward I fell." "I will surely give that leave," said Cuchulain, "for the thing you ask is a right gift for a fighting man." And after that he went back to his own camping-place.

Now, on that day above any other, a very downhearted feeling came on Cuchulain, he to be fighting alone against the four provinces of Ireland. And he bade Laeg to go to Conchubar and to the men of Ulster, and to say to them that he, the son of Dechtire, was tired with fighting every day, and with the wounds he had got, and not one of his people or his friends coming to help him.

After that Maeve sent out six all together against him, three men and three women that understood enchantments; but he destroyed them all. And now that Maeve had broken her agreement with him, not to send more than one against him at a time, he did not spare

her men any longer, but from where he was he used his
sling so well that in the whole army there was neither
dog, horse, or man, that dared turn his face towards
Cuchulain.

It was one day at that time the Morrigu came to try
and get healing of her wounds from him, for it was only
by his own hand the wounds he gave could be healed.
She took the appearance of an old woman on her, and
she milking a cow with three teats. Cuchulain was
passing by, and there was thirst on him, and he asked a
drink, and she gave him the milk of one teat. "May
this be to the good of the giver," he said, and with that
her eye that was wounded was healed. Then she gave
him milk from another teat, and he said the same words;
then she gave him the milk from the third teat. "The
full blessing of the gods, and of the people of the plough,
on you," he said. And with that, all the wounds of the
Great Queen were healed.

Then the men of the four great provinces of Ireland
made their camp, and put up walls at the place called
the Great Breach, on the plain of Muirthemne; but they
sent the cattle they had with them southward. And
Cuchulain took his place on a mound; and in the evening
Laeg made a fire for him there, and the flame flashed
on the bright shining weapons of the men of Ireland.
And when Cuchulain saw so many of them, and they so
near him, great anger came on him, and he took his
spears and his shield and his sword and shook them, and
he gave out his loud hero cry, and it was such a great
cry he gave that the Bocanachs and Bananachs and the
witches of the valley answered it from all parts.

And when the men in the camp heard these great
cries, they thought it was an attack that was being made
upon them, and they ran against one another, and fought
one another in their fright, so that a hundred of them
were killed in that night.

Then Laeg saw a man coming through the camp from the north-east. "There is a man coming towards us, little Hound," he said. "What is the appearance on him?" said Cuchulain. "He is very tall and handsome and shining, and he has a green cloak about him, fastened with a silver brooch; a shirt of silk that is embroidered with red gold, falling to his knees; a black shield in his hand, with a border of white bronze, and a spear with five prongs. And it is a strange thing," he said, "that no one in the whole camp seems to see him or to take any heed of him." "That is so," said Cuchulain; "and the men of Ireland take no heed of him because they cannot see him; and I know well it is one of my friends among the Sidhe that is coming to give me help and relief; for they know it is hard for me to be standing alone against the four provinces of Ireland."

Then the man of the Sidhe, that was Lugh of the Long Hand, came and spoke with Cuchulain, and it is what he said, that he knew he was tired out and in want of sleep. "And sleep now, Cuchulain," he said, "by the grave in the Lerga, and I myself will keep watch over you till the end of three days and three nights. So Cuchulain fell asleep there and then by the grave that is in the Lerga, and no wonder in that, for he had been fighting since before the feast of Samhain without sleep, but all the while killing and attacking and destroying the men of Ireland—unless he might sleep a little while beside his spear in the middle of the day, his head on his hand, and his hand on his spear, and his spear on his knee. And while he was lying in his heavy sleep, the man of the Sidhe put Druid herbs on his wounds, so that they were all healed. So he slept for three days and three nights, and at the end of that time he rose up and passed his hand over his face, and he blushed red from head to foot with the strengthening of his courage that he felt in him, and he would have been ready to go there and then

into any great gathering or feasting hall in all Ireland.
"How long have I been in my sleep?" he asked the
man. "Three days and three nights." "Then you have
done me a bad turn indeed," he said, "for the men of
Ireland have been left in quiet all that time." "They
were not indeed," said the man. "Who was it stood up to
them then?" said Cuchulain. "It was the boy troop
came from the North, from Emain Macha," he said;
"three times fifty sons of the chief men of Ulster, and
they attacked the army three times, and they killed three
times their own number, but they themselves were all
killed in the end. And Follaman, son of Conchubar, was
leading them, and he had made a boast that he would
never go home again unless he could bring Ailell's head
along with him, and the gold crown that was on it. But
two foster-sons of Ailell, the two sons of Betchach, son of
Baen, fell on him and wounded him, so that he got his
death." "My grief, and oh! my grief that I was not
there," said Cuchulain; "for if I had been in it, the boy
troop would never have been destroyed, and Conchubar's
son would not have come to his death." "Do not be
fretting, little Hound," said the strange man; "there is no
reproach on your name by it." "Stop here with me
to-night," said Cuchulain, "and the two of us together
will avenge the boy troop." "I will not indeed," said he;
"but let you yourself play the game out now with the
men of Ireland, for it is not they that have power over
your life at this time."

With that he went away, and Cuchulain said to Laeg,
"Yoke the scythed chariot for me now, if you have the
things belonging to it." Then Laeg rose up and got
ready the chariot, and he put on his light dress of deer-
skins, that was spotted and striped and close-fitting, so
that his arms were left free. And over that he put his
raven-black cloak, and his shining helmet on his head;
and on his forehead he put the narrow band of gold that

chariot-drivers were used to wear. And then he threw
over the horses the cloths that covered them all over,
and that were studded with little blades, and spikes,
and points, so that every time the chariot moved, it
brought some sharp point against those that were near
it, the way every point and every head of the chariot
would cut its sure path; and he gathered the reins in
his hand, and the goad, and the long whip.

And then Cuchulain put on his armour, and took his
spears, and his sword, and his shield that had a rim so
sharp it would cut a hair against the stream, and his
cloak that was made of the precious fleeces of the land
of the Sidhe, that had been brought to him by Manannan
from the King of Sorcha. He went out then against
the men of Ireland, and attacked them, and his anger
came on him, so that it was not his own appearance he
had on him, but the appearance of a god. And after that
he turned back and left them, and there was no wound
on himself, or on the horses, or on Laeg that day. And
he made a round of the whole army, mowing men down
on every side, in revenge for the boy troop of Emain.

But the next day he was standing on the hill, young,
and comely, and shining, and the cloud of his anger had
gone from him. Then the women and the young girls
in the camp, and the poets and the singers, came out to
look at him; but Maeve hid her face behind a shelter of
shields, thinking he might make a cast at her with his
sling. And there was wonder on these women to see
him so quiet and so gentle to-day, and he such a terror
to the whole army yesterday; and they bade the men
lift them up on their shields to the height of their
shoulders, the way they could have a good sight of him.

But Dubthach, the Beetle of Ulster, saw his own wife
climbing up with the other women to look at Cuchulain,
and great anger and jealousy came on him; and he said
to the chief men of the army that it would be best for

them to surround Cuchulain secretly on all sides, and
then to let on to be fighting among themselves, so as to
lead him down where he could not escape them. But
when Fergus was told this, he gave a great kick of his
foot to Dubthach, that sent him from where he was.
And he spoke angry words against Dubthach, and he
told him he would be well paid for the harm he had
planned, whenever the men of Ulster would get up from
their weakness, and come out to help Cuchulain.

And that night the army of Ireland made their camp
at the great stone in the country of Ross; and then
Maeve asked which of them would go out and fight with
Cuchulain on the morrow. But every one of the men of
Ireland said: "It is not I that will go." "It is not one
of my family that should be sent to his death." Then
Maeve asked Fergus to go out and fight him. "It is
not right for you," said Fergus, "to ask me to go against
a young boy, and he my own pupil and my foster-son."
But Maeve pressed him so hard that he could not but
take the work in hand ; and early in the morning he went
out to the ford of fighting where Cuchulain was. When
Cuchulain saw him coming he said: "Truly, my master,
it is not safe for you to come and fight, and you without
a sword," for Ailell had not given him back his own
sword yet. "It is no matter," he said, "for if I had a
sword in my sheath, it is not on you I would use it.
And now, Cuchulain," he said, "for the sake of all I did
for you, and all Conchubar and the whole of Ulster did
for you in your bringing-up, let you give way before me
to-day, in the sight of the men of Ireland." "Indeed I
am loth to give way before any man in this war," said
Cuchulain. "You need not mind that," said Fergus,
"for I will do the same for you when the great last
battle of this war is fought; it is then I will turn and run
before you, when you are covered with wounds and with
blood. And if I run then," he said, "all the men of

Ireland will run along with me. So Cuchulain agreed
to do that, because it would be for the profit of Ulster.
And he bade Laeg make ready his chariot; and
presently, as if he had been beaten by Fergus, he gave
way to him in the sight of the men of Ireland. When
they saw it, they called out: "He is running before you,
Fergus." And Maeve called out: "Follow him, Fergus—
make haste, the way he will not escape you." "I will
not indeed," said Fergus, "I will follow him no farther;
and if you think I did not make him run far enough,"
he said, "I did more than all the rest of the men that
went against him up to this; and I will make no other
attack on him," he said, "until all the men of Ireland
have fought with him, one by one."

So that was the end of the fight between Fergus and
Cuchulain.

There was a man of Connaught at that time whose
name was Ferchu, and he had been at war with Ailell
and Maeve from the time they got the kingdom, and
he used to be robbing the country and destroying it, so
that he was made an outlaw. And some of his men
heard that the whole army of Connaught was being
vexed and hindered by one man; and when they told it
to Ferchu, he said: "It would be a good chance for us
to go and attack that man, and to bring his head with
us to Ailell and Maeve, for if we do that," he said,
"they will forgive us all the harm we have done their
country."

So he himself and his twelve men went forward to
where Cuchulain was, and they attacked him all
together. But Cuchulain was not long in making an
end of them, and he struck off their heads, and put them
on twelve stones; and he put Ferchu's head on a stone
by itself.

Then the men of Ireland consulted together again
who they would send out to fight on the next day; and

it is what they all said, that it was Calatin and his twenty-seven sons and his sister's son, Glas, son of Delga, should go out. Now it is the way they were, every man of them had poison in himself and in his weapons; and there was not one of them ever made a cast of a spear or a stone that missed, and there was no one that would be wounded by them but he would die, either on the spot or within nine days. So great rewards were promised them, if they would go out against Cuchulain. And Fergus was there at the time the business was knotted. "And surely," every one said, "they are only one man, for they are all members of Calatin's body." After that, Fergus went into his tent, to his people, and he gave a deep groan of trouble, and he said: "My grief for the thing that is to be done to-morrow." "What thing is that?" said they all. "Cuchulain to be killed," he said. "Who would kill him?" said they. "Calatin and his sons," he said, "and if there is any one of you would go and watch the fight and bring me word what happens, I would give him a good reward, and my blessing." "I will go," said Fiacha, son of Firaba.

So in the morning Calatin, with his sons and his sister's son, rose up and went to where Cuchulain was, and Fiacha, son of Firaba, went along with them. And as soon as they came near him, they threw their twenty-nine spears at him all together, in one cast, and not one of them drew blood, for he caught them all on his shield. Then Cuchulain drew his sword from the sheath to hack off the spears and to lighten his shield; but while he was doing that, they all ran at him as one man and put their twenty-nine right hands on his head, and forced his face down to the gravel and the sand of the ford. And he gave out his great hero cry, and the cry of a man in unequal fight, and there was not a man in the camp, and he not dead or asleep, but heard it.

Then Fiacha, son of Firaba, came up, and when he saw what had happened, the love of his own countryman came over him, and he pulled out his sword and hit the nine-and-twenty hands off Calatin and his sons, with one blow. Cuchulain raised up his head then, and gave a deep sigh of relief, and he saw who it was had come to his help. "That was done quiet and easy, my good comrade," he said. "You may think it is quiet and easy I was," said Fiacha, "but if what I did is heard of in the camp, the reward that will fall on me will not be quiet and easy. For if the men of the children of Rudraige should hear of the stroke I made for you, it is with sword and spear my reward will be paid." "I give you my word," said Cuchulain, "that now I have lifted my head and got my breath again, unless you tell tales on yourself, none of these men will tell tales on you."

With that he made an attack on Calatin and his sons, and he began to hack and to cut at them till there was nothing left of them but limbs and little pieces eastward and westward over the whole face of the ford. Only one man of them, Glas, son of Delga, got away and ran, but Cuchulain rushed after him and gave him a great blow. But he got as far as Ailell and Maeve's tent, and all he could say was, "Fiacha! Fiacha!" before he fell dead.

Fergus and Maeve said: "What debts are those he called out about?"—for Fiacha is the word for a debt in Irish. "I do not know indeed," said Fergus, "unless it might be that some one in the camp owed him a debt, and that it was on his mind." "That must have been so," said Ailell. "By my word," said Fergus, "however it was, all his debts are paid now."

And at the ford where Calatin and his sons got their death, there is a stone with the marks of their sword-hilts, and the butt-ends of their spears on it to this day.

Then it was settled by the men of Ireland that it was

Ferdiad, son of Daire, the great champion of the men
of Domnand, should go out and meet Cuchulain the
next day. For they had the same way of fighting, and
it was with the same teachers they had learned the
knowledge of arms, with Scathach and with Uathach
and with Aoife; and neither of them had an advantage
over the other, except that Cuchulain had the feat of
the Gae Bulg. But Ferdiad had good armour to protect him against any man he would fight with.

So they sent messengers to bring Ferdiad, but he
refused and would not come, for he knew it was what
they wanted of him, to fight against his friend, his
companion and his fellow pupil, Cuchulain.

Then Maeve sent the Druids and the satirists to him,
that they might make three hurtful satires and three hill-
top satires on him, if he would not come with them, that
would raise three blisters on his face, Shame and Blemish
and Reproach, so that if he did not die on the moment,
he would be dead before the end of nine days.

Then Ferdiad came with them for the sake of his
good name, for he thought it better to fall by spears
than by satires. And when he came he was received
with honour and attendance, and he was served with
pleasant drinks, so that he grew merry, and his mind
was confused. And great rewards were offered him if
he would go out against Cuchulain; clothes of all
colours for his men, and speckled satins, and silver
and gold, and the equal of his own lands of the level
plains of Magh Ai, without rent or disturbance, secure
to his son and to his grandson and to their children to
the end of life and time.

And it is what Maeve said: "It is a great reward I am
giving you, Ferdiad, and why would you not accept it?"
And Ferdiad was making excuses. "I will not take
your reward without good pledges," he said, "for it is a
heavy fight is before me; he that has the name of

Cuchulain is surely a good Hound." "I will give you
a champion's pledge," said Maeve; "you will not be
bound to come to our gatherings, you will get horses
and bridles; I will call you my friend above all other
men." "I will not go to this fight," said Ferdiad,
"without some other securities, for this is a fight will
be heard of till the end of life and time." "Take all
you want," said Maeve. "There is no delay except with
yourself. Bind us till you are satisfied by the right
hand of kings and of princes; there is nothing I will
refuse you." "I must have six securities and no less,"
said Ferdiad, "before I will go out and be destroyed by
Cuchulain, and all the whole army looking on." "I will
give you whatever securities you want," said Maeve,
"however hard it may be to come at them; Domnall
in his chariot; Niaman of the Slaughter, both of them
protectors of bards; bind Morann if you want sure
payment; bind Carpre Min of Manand, he that has a
string of knowledge in his harp; bind our own two
sons." "O Maeve, it is a bitter woman you are," said
Ferdiad. "And it is not a gentle wife to a husband you
are, but it is a fit queen you are for Cruachan of the
Swords, with your high talk and your fierce strength.
But in spite of all the words you are stirring me up
with," he said, "if you would offer me the land and
the sea, I would not take them, without the sun and the
moon along with them." "You need not wait longer
than to-day and to-morrow," said Maeve, "before you
will get your fill of all sorts of the jewels of the
earth. And here is my brooch with its hooked pin,"
she said; "and more than all that, Ferdiad, so soon as
you have killed this Hound of feats, I will give you
Findabair of the champions, queen of the west of
Elga." Then every one was saying what great rewards
those were. "But however great they are," said
Ferdiad, "it is with Maeve herself they will stay and

not with myself; and I will not take them to go into battle with my fellow and my near friend, that is Cuchulain." And it is what he said:

"A pity indeed a woman to have come between myself and himself! The half of my heart is Cuchulain's without fault, and I am the half of his own heart.

"By my shield! If Cuchulain were killed from Ath Cliath, it is I would thrust my sword through my heart, through my side, through my breast.

"By my sword! If Cuchulain were killed from Glen Bolg, I would kill no man after him till I had leaped over the edge of the well.

"By my hand! If the Hound were killed from Glen an Scail, I would make an end of Maeve and her army and of no one else of the men of Ireland.

"By my spear! If it were from Ath Cro the Hound was killed, it is I would be buried in his grave; the one grave would be for the two of us.

"Say to him, the Hound without blemish, that Scathach without fear made a prophecy I would be put down by him at a ford.

"Misfortune on Maeve, misfortune on Maeve, that put her face between us! Sending us one against the other, myself and strong Cuchulain."

Then Maeve said to her people, the way she would stir him up: "It is a true word Cuchulain spoke." "What word was that?" said Ferdiad. "He said it would be no great wonder if you would fall by him in the first trial of arms in this country." "He had no right to say that," said Ferdiad; "for it is not fear or want of skill he learned of me up to this time. And I swear by my arms if it is true he said this thing, that I will be the first to fight with him to-morrow before the men of Ireland." "May good be with you for saying that," said Maeve; "and this is better to me than to see you show fear or weakness, for every man

cares for his own country, and why has he a right to
do more for the profit of Ulster than you would do
for the profit of Connaught?"

Ferdiad gave in to her then, and he bound her on the
sureties of the aforesaid six for the fulfilment of her
promises of the reward; and she bound him to fight
with Cuchulain on the morrow.

Then Fergus got his horses harnessed and his chariot
yoked, and he went out to where Cuchulain was, to tell
him of all that had happened. "My welcome before
you, my master Fergus," said Cuchulain. "I am glad
of that welcome, my pupil," said Fergus. "But what I
am come for is to tell you who it is that is coming to
fight at the early hour of the morning of to-morrow."
"I will listen to that," said Cuchulain. "Your own
friend and companion, and fellow-pupil, the man that
learned the use of arms with you, Ferdiad, son of Daire,
the hero of the men of Domnand." "I give my word,"
said Cuchulain, "it is not my wish, my friend to come
out against me." "And now," said Fergus, "you must
be careful and ready more than any other time, for there
was not the like of Ferdiad among any of the men
who have fought you up to this." "I am here," said
Cuchulain, "hindering and delaying the four great
provinces of Ireland, from the beginning of the winter
to the beginning of spring, and I have not drawn back
one foot before any man in that time, and I think it
likely I will not draw back before him." "Neither has
Ferdiad any fear on him before you, now his anger is
stirred up," said Fergus, "and besides that, he has good
armour to protect him." "Be quiet now, Fergus, and
do not let me hear any more of that story," said
Cuchulain. "I was always well able to stand against
him in any place, or on any ground." "It is not easy to
get the better of him," said Fergus, "for he is fierce in
fighting, and he has the strength of a hundred." "There

will be a sharp fight when myself and Ferdiad come to
the ford," said Cuchulain; "it will not be without being
told in stories." "O Cuchulain of the red sword," said
Fergus, "it would be better to me than a great reward,
you to carry proud Ferdiad's purple cloak eastward."
"I give my word and my oath," said Cuchulain, "it is I
myself will get the victory over Ferdiad." Then Fergus
went back to the encampment.

At the same time Ferdiad went to his tent and to his
people, and told them how he was bound by Maeve to
fight with Cuchulain on the morrow, and he told how he
had bound Maeve by six sureties for the fulfilment of
her promises, if Cuchulain should fall by him.

It is not happy in their minds the people of Ferdiad's
tent were that night, but gloomy and heavy-hearted; for
they were sure that wherever Cuchulain and Ferdiad
would meet, it was there one of them would get his
death, and they were sure that one would be their own
master; for no one at all had been able to stand against
Cuchulain since the beginning of the war.

Ferdiad slept through the early part of the night very
heavily, and when the latter end of the night came, his
sleep went from him, and his drunkenness had passed
away, and the thought of the fight was pressing on him.
And he bade his driver to harness the horses, and to
yoke his chariot. But the driver tried to turn him from it.
"It would be better for you to stop here than to go," he
said, "for my liking of it is not more than my disliking."

"Be silent, boy," said Ferdiad, "for I will not be
turned from this journey by any young lad; but I will
go to the ford, a ford the ravens will be croaking over;
I will fight with Cuchulain till I wound his strong body,
till I crush the courage out of him the way that he will
die."

"It would be better for you to stop here," said the
driver, "for it is not gentle your threats are; your parting

will be sorrowful; there is one to whom it will be a sickness; grief will come of that meeting with Cuchulain; it is long it will be remembered; it is a pity for him who goes that journey." "It is not right what you are saying," said Ferdiad; "it is not for a brave man to refuse—it is not in our race. I will delay no longer, courage is better than fear; let us set out now to the ford."

Then Ferdiad's horses were harnessed, and his chariot was yoked, and he went forward to the ford, and the day with its full light came upon him there. "Now, boy," he said, "spread out the skins and the cushions of my chariot under me here, until I get some sleep and rest, for I got no sleep at the end of the night, with the care of the fight upon me."

So his servant unharnessed the horses, and settled the skins and cushions of the chariot under him, and the heavy rest of sleep came upon him.

But as to Cuchulain, he did not rise up at all till the day had come with its full light, the way the men of Ireland would not say it was fear that was on him that made him rise. And when the day came: "It would be as well, Laeg," he said, "to yoke the chariot, for it is an early-rising man that is coming to meet us to-day."

"The horses are harnessed, and the chariot is yoked," said Laeg; "let you get into it, and there will be no hindrance to your courage."

With that the ready-handed, battle-winning son of Sualtim leaped into the chariot, and there shouted around him the Bocanachs and Bananachs, and witches of the valley. For the Tuatha de Danaan were used to set up their shouts around him, the way the fear and the wonder would be great before him in every fight he would go into.

And it was not long until Ferdiad's driver heard the noise coming near, the straining of the harness, the creaking of the chariot, the ringing of the armour and of the shield, the trampling of the horses, the joyful coming of Cuchulain to the ford.

The driver came and laid his hand on his master. "Good Ferdiad," he said, "rise up; here they are coming. For I hear," he said, "the creaking of a chariot; it has come over Breg Ross, over Braine; it has come over the highway by the foot of Baile-in-Bile; he is a mighty Hound that urges it; he is a good driver that yokes it; he is a free hawk that hurries his horses towards the south. It is not he that will be slow in the fight. It is a pity for him that is on the height waiting for the Hound of valour. It is a year ago I foretold there would come a Hound, the Hound of Emain, a Hound with all colours about him—the Hound of Ulster, the Hound of Battle; I hear him—I have heard him coming."

"Good servant," said Ferdiad, "why is it you have been praising that man ever since you came out from the house? It is likely you are not without wages for your great praise of him. Yet it has been foretold to me by Ailell and by Maeve, it is he that will fall by me. And it is a time to help me," he said; "and let you be silent, and give up praising him, that your foretelling may not come true. It is not for you to give up on the brink of the fight; surely I will soon have the reward."

And the driver said: "He is coming, not slowly, but quick as the wind, or as water from a high cliff, or like swift thunder." "Surely you have taken wages for these great praises you put upon him," said Ferdiad; "it is not against him you are, but praising him, and putting a great name on him."

It was not long then until Ferdiad saw Cuchulain coming towards him in his chariot, and it is how his two horses were going, like a hawk sweeping from a cliff on a day of hard wind, or like a sweeping gust of the spring wind on a March day over a smooth plain, or like the swift-

ness of a wild stag when he is first started by the hounds
in his first field ; as if they were on fiery flagstones, so that
the earth was shaking and trembling with the quickness
of their going.

So Cuchulain reached the ford, and Ferdiad came to
the south side, and Cuchulain drew up on the north side,
and Ferdiad bade Cuchulain welcome. " I am happy at
your coming, Cuchulain," he said. " I would have been
glad of that welcome up to this time," said Cuchulain,
" but to-day I do not take it as the welcome of a friend.
And, Ferdiad," he said, "it would be fitter for me to
welcome you than for you to welcome me, for it is you
have come to me in the country and province where I
am, and it is not right for you to come to fight with me,
but it is I should go to fight with you, for it is out before
you are the women and the children, the young men and
the horses, the flocks, the herds, and the cattle of the
province of Ulster."

" Good Cuchulain," said Ferdiad, " what has brought
you to fight with me at all ? For when we were with
Scathach and with Uathach and with Aoife, you were
my serving-boy, to tie up my spears and to make ready
my bed." " That is true indeed," said Cuchulain ; " but
it was as less in age than you I was used to do so ; but
that is not the story that will be told of us after this day,
for there is not a man in the whole world I would not
fight to-day."

And it is then each of them spoke sharp, unfriendly
words against the other ; and it is what Ferdiad said :
" What has brought you, O Hound, to fight with a strong
fighter ? It is red your blood will be, flowing over the
harness of your horses ; it is a pity for your journey ; it
is long it will be spoken of ; you will be in much want
of healing if you ever get back to your own house,"
he said.

" I have fought with heroes, with chiefs of armies, with

troops, with hundreds before now," said Cuchulain, "and
what I have to do to-day is to make an end of you, to
bring you down in our first path of battle."

"You have met now with a man that will put reproach on you," said Ferdiad, "for it is I myself will do
that. It is well the loss of the men of Ulster will be
remembered," he said, "their champion to be put down,
and they looking on."

"What way shall we meet one another?" said
Cuchulain. "Is it in our chariots we had best fight, or
is it with my sword and spear I am to overthrow you, if
the time has come?" And Ferdiad said: "Before the
setting of the sun to-night, you will be fighting as if with
a mountain, and it is not white that battle will be. The
men of Ulster will be shouting for you," he said, "till you
grow overbold; but it is sorrowful they will be, when your
ghost passes over them and through them." "You are
fallen into the gap of danger, Ferdiad," said Cuchulain;
"the end of your life has come, not by treachery, but by
sharp weapons. You may think much of yourself till
we meet one another, but you will never fight in a battle
again, from this day to the end of time." "Leave off
now from your boastings," said Ferdiad; "it is you are
the greatest boaster in the world. I know well you are
no fighter at all, you heart of a bird in a cage; you are
but a giggling fellow, without courage, without strength."
But Cuchulain said: "When we were together with
Scathach, we used to be practising together, we used to
go to every battle together, because of our bravery that
was equal. You were my heart companion, you were
my people, you were my family—I never found one was
dearer; it is sorrowful your death would be to me."

"Where is the use of all this talk?" said Ferdiad; "your
great name will be lost, your head will be on a stake
before the crowing of the cock. Madness and grief are
taking hold of you, Cuchulain," he said, "and it is bad

treatment you will get from me, because it is on yourself the fault is."

"Good Ferdiad," Cuchulain said then, "it was not right for you to come out against me, through the stirring up and the meddling of Ailell and of Maeve; and none of those who came before you got victory or success, but they all fell by me, and you will fall along with them. And, O Ferdiad, strong fighter," he said, "do not come against me; the meeting will bring sorrow to many, and what is worse than sorrow to you. Have you not been bought with many presents? A purple belt, a suit of armour? But, Ferdiad," he said, "the woman for whom you are come to this fight, Findabair, daughter of Maeve, however comely she may be, will never be given to you; for she has been offered to many before you," he said, "and many like you have been wounded for her sake." And he said, and Fergus began to listen to him:

"Do not break your oath not to fight with me; do not break friendship. Do not break the word you gave me, do not come against me.

"The woman has been promised to fifty others; it was a heavy gift for them; it is by me they were sent to their grave; it was by me they got the end that was fitting for them.

"'Though Ferbaeth was boastful, he who had a houseful of brave men, it is short the time was till I quieted his rage; I killed him by the one cast.

"The striking down of Srub Daire's courage was bitter to him; it is he held the secrets of a hundred women; he had a great name at one time; it is not silver thread but gold thread was in his clothes.

"If it were to me the woman was promised on whom the kings of the fair province smile, I would not bring the red blood on your body for it, south or north, east or west.

"And, good Ferdiad," he said, "this is why it is not right for you to come to this fight. When we were with Scathach, it is together we used to go to every battle, to every wild place, through every darkness and every hardship. We were heart companions; we were comrades in gatherings; we shared the one bed where we used to sleep sound sleep. We used to practise together, in many far countries; we used to go to hard fights; we used to go through every forest together."

"O Cuchulain of the wonderful feats," said Ferdiad, "although we learned knowledge together, and although I know the bonds friendship put upon us, it is I that will give you your first wounds; do not be remembering our companionship, for it will not protect you. And it is too long we are delaying like this," he said; "and what arms shall we use to-day, Cuchulain?"

"It is you have the choice of arms to-day," said Cuchulain, "for it is you were the first to reach the ford." "Do you remember at all," said Ferdiad, "the casting spears we used to practise with Scathach and with Uacthach and with Aoife?" "I remember them indeed," said Cuchulain. "If you remember, let us begin with them," said Ferdiad.

So they began with their casting weapons, and they took their protecting shields, and their round-handled spears, and their little quill spears, and their ivory-hilted knives, and their ivory-hafted spears, eight of each of them they had. And these were flying from them and to them like bees on the wing on a fine summer day; there was no cast that did not hit, and each one went on shooting at the other with those weapons from the twilight of the early morning to the full midday, until all their weapons were blunted against the faces and the bosses of the shields. And as good as the throwing was, the defence was so good that neither of them drew blood from the other through that time.

"Let us leave these weapons now, Cuchulain," said
Ferdiad, "for it is not by the like of them our fight will
be settled." "Let us leave them indeed if the time is
come," said Cuchulain.

They stopped then, and threw their darts into the
hands of their chariot-drivers. "What weapons shall
we use now, Cuchulain?" said Ferdiad. "The choice of
weapons is yours till night," said Cuchulain. "Let us,
then," said Ferdiad, "take to our straight spears, with
the flaxen strings in them." "Let us now indeed," said
Cuchulain. And then they took two stout shields, and
they took to their spears.

Each of them went on throwing at the other with
the spears from the middle of mid-day until the fall of
evening. And good as the defence was, yet the
throwing was so good that each of them wounded the
other in that time.

"Let us leave this now," said Ferdiad. "Let us leave
it indeed if the time has come," said Cuchulain.

So they left off, and they threw their spears away
from them into the hands of their chariot-drivers. Each
of them came to the other then, and each put his hands
round the neck of the other, and gave him three kisses.
Their horses were in the one enclosure that night, and
their chariot-drivers at the one fire; and their chariot-
drivers spread beds of green rushes for them, with
wounded men's pillows on them. The men that had
knowledge of healing came then, and put herbs of healing to their wounds. And of every herb and plant that
was put to Cuchulain's wounds, he would send an equal
share from him westward over the ford to Ferdiad, the
way the men of Ireland might not say if Ferdiad should
fall by him, that it was by better means of cure he was
able to overcome him.

And of every kind of food and of drink that was sent
by the men of Ireland to Ferdiad, he would send a fair

share over the ford northward to Cuchulain; because the
providers of Ferdiad were more than the providers of
Cuchulain. All the men of Ireland were providers to
Ferdiad for beating off Cuchulain from them, but only
the Bregians were providers to Cuchulain. They used
to come and to be talking with him at the dusk of every
night.

They rested there that night, and they rose up
early on the morrow, and came forward to the ford of
battle.

"What weapons shall we use to-day, Ferdiad?"
said Cuchulain. "It is you have the choice of weapons
until night," said Ferdiad, "because I had my choice
of them the last day." "Let us then," said Cuchulain,
"take to our great broad spears to-day; for we shall be
nearer to the end of our battle by the thrusting to-day
than we were by the throwing yesterday."

Each of them continued to cut, and to wound, and to
redden the other, from the twilight of the early morning
till the fall of the evening. If it were the custom for
birds in their flight to pass through the bodies of men,
they could have passed through their bodies on that
day, and they could have carried pieces of flesh and
blood through their stabs and cuts, into the clouds and
the sky all around. And when the fall of evening came,
their horses were tired, and their chariot-drivers were
down-hearted, and they were tired themselves as well.

"Let us stop from this now, Ferdiad," said Cuchulain,
"for our horses are tired, and our chariot-drivers are
down-hearted; and when they are tired, why would not
we be tired as well? And we are not bound to go on
for ever," he said, "as is the custom with the Fomor.
Let us put the quarrel away for a while, now the noise
of the fighting is over." "Let us leave off indeed if the
time is come," said Ferdiad.

They threw their spears from them then into the

hands of their chariot-drivers, and each of them came
towards the other. Each of them put his hand round
the neck of the other and gave him three kisses. Their
horses were in the one enclosure that night, and their
chariot-drivers at the one fire.

Their chariot-drivers made beds of green rushes for
them, with wounded men's pillows on them, and the men
that had knowledge of healing came to examine them
that night, but they could do nothing more for them,
because of the deepness of their many wounds, but to
use charms and spells on them, to staunch their blood.
Every charm and every spell that was used on the
wounds of Cuchulain, he sent a full share of them over
the ford westward to Ferdiad. And of every sort of
food and of drink that was sent to Ferdiad, he sent a
share of them over the ford northward to Cuchulain.

They rested there that night, and they rose up early
on the morrow, and they came forward to the ford of
battle. Cuchulain saw a sort of a dark look on Ferdiad
that day. "It is bad you are looking to-day, Ferdiad,"
he said; "there is a darkness on your face, and a heaviness on your eyes, and your own appearance is gone
from you." "It is not from fear or dread of you I am
like this to-day," said Ferdiad; "for there is not a
champion in Ireland to-day I could not put down."
And Cuchulain was fretted to see him that way, and
it is what he said: "O Ferdiad, if it is you yourself, I am
sure you are a miserable man, to have come at the
bidding of a woman to fight against your own companion." But Ferdiad said: "O Cuchulain, giver of
wounds, true hero, every man must come in the end to
the sod where his last grave shall be."

"As to Findabair, daughter of Maeve," said Cuchulain,
"whatever her beauty may be, it is not for love of you
she was given to you, but only for the sake of your great
strength." "O Hound of the gentle sway," said Ferdiad,

"it is long ago my strength was tried; but I never heard of any man braver in fight than yourself; I never met so brave a man until to-day." "It is your own fault what has happened," said Cuchulain; "you to have come at the bidding of a woman to try your sword against your fellow." "If I had gone back," said Ferdiad, "without doing battle with you, it is little my name and my word would be thought of by Ailell and by Maeve of Cruachan." "No one has ever put food to his lips," said Cuchulain, "and no one has ever been born in honour of a king or queen, for whose sake I would have harmed you." "O Cuchulain, winner of battles," said Ferdiad; "it was not you but Maeve that betrayed me; let you take the victory and the fame, for it is not on you the blame is."

And Cuchulain said: "My faithful heart is like a clot of blood; my life is nearly gone from me; I have no strength for high deeds, fighting with you, Ferdiad." "Much as you are complaining over me now," said Ferdiad, "what arms shall we use to-day?" "It is you have the choice to-day," said Cuchulain, "because it was I had it yesterday." "Let us then," said Ferdiad, "take to our swords to-day, for we will be nearer the end of our battle by the hewing to-day, than we were by the thrusting yesterday." "Let us do so indeed," said Cuchulain.

And then they put two long wide shields on them, and they took to their swords, and each of them continued to hack at the other, from the dawn of the early morning till the time of the fall of evening. "Let us leave off from this now," said Cuchulain. So they left off.

They threw their swords from them into the hands of their chariot-drivers, and it was the parting, mournful, sorrowful, downhearted, of two men that night.

Their horses were not in the one enclosure that night,

their chariot-drivers were not at the one fire. They rested that night there.

And Ferdiad rose up early next morning, and went forward by himself to the ford. For he knew that day would decide the fight, and he knew one of them would fall on that day there, or they would both fall.

And then he put on his battle suit, before the coming of Cuchulain to him. He put on his shirt of striped silk, with its border of speckled gold, next his white skin. He put on his coat of brown leather, well sewed, over the outside. He put on his apron of purified iron, through dread of the Gae Bulg that day. He put his crested helmet of battle on his head, on which were forty gems, carbuncles, in each division, and it was studded with crystal and with shining rubies of the eastern world. He took his strong spear into his right hand, and his curved sword upon his left side, with its golden hilt, and its knobs of red gold, and his great large, bossed shield on his back.

And then he began to show off many changing, wonderful feats, that he had never learned with any other person, neither with nurse or with tutor, or with Scathach or with Uacthach, or with Aoife, but that were made up that day by himself against Cuchulain.

Then Cuchulain came to the ford, and when he saw all Ferdiad was doing: " I see, my friend Laeg," he said, " all those feats will be tried on me one after another ; and because of that," he said, " if it is I that begin to give in to-day, it is for you to reproach me, and to speak hard words to me, the way that the strength of my anger may grow the more on me. But if I am getting the better of him, then you are to praise me, and make much of me, that my courage may be the greater." " I will do that indeed, my master Cuchulain," said Laeg.

And then Cuchulain put on his battle suit, and he said: "What arms shall we take to-day, Ferdiad?" "The choice is yours to-day," said Ferdiad. "Let us try the ford feat then," said Cuchulain. "Let us indeed," said Ferdiad. But though Ferdiad agreed to it, it is sorry he was to say those words, for he knew Cuchulain was used to put an end to every fighter that was against him in the feat of the ford.

It was great work, now, that was done on that day at the ford; the two champions of western Europe, the two gift-giving and wage-giving hands of the north-west of the world; the two pillars and the two keys of the courage of the Gael; to be brought from far off, to fight one against the other, through the stirring up and the meddling of Ailell and Maeve. Each of them began to throw his weapons at the other, from the dawn of early morning to the middle of mid-day. And when mid-day came, the anger of the men grew hotter, and each of them drew nearer to the other. And then it was that Cuchulain leaped on to the boss of Ferdiad's shield, to strike at his head over the rim of the shield. But Ferdiad gave the shield a blow of the left elbow, and threw Cuchulain from him like a bird on the brink of the ford. Cuchulain leaped up again to the boss of the shield, but Ferdiad gave it a stroke of his left knee, and threw Cuchulain from him like a little child.

Laeg saw that done. "My grief indeed," he said, "the fighter that is against you, Cuchulain, casts you away as a light woman would cast her child. He throws you as foam is thrown by the river; he grinds you as a mill would grind fresh malt; he cuts through you as the axe cuts through the oak; he binds you as the woodbine binds the tree; he darts on you as the hawk darts on little birds; and from this out, you have no call nor claim to courage or a brave name to the end of life and time, you little fairy fighter," said Laeg.

It is then Cuchulain leaped up with the quickness of the wind, and with the readiness of the swallow, and with the fierceness of the lion, towards the troubled clouds of the air the third time until he lit on the boss

oı Ferdiad's shield, to strike at his head from above.
And Ferdiad gave his shield a shake and cast Cuchulain
from him, the same as if he had never been cast off
before at all.

And it is then Cuchulain's anger came on him, and
the flames of the hero light began to shine about his
head, like a red-thorn bush in a gap, or like the sparks
of a fire, and he lost the appearance of a man, and what
was on him was the appearance of a god.

So close was the fight they made now, that their heads
met above and their feet below, and their hands in the
middle, over the rims and bosses of their shields. So
close was the fight, that they broke and loosened their
shields from the rim to the middle. So close was the
fight, that they turned and bent and shattered their
spears from the points to the hilts. So close was the
fight, that the Bocanachs and Bananachs and the witches
of the valley screamed from the rims of their shields and
from the hilts of their swords, and from the handles of
their spears. So close was the fight, that they drove the
river out of its bed and out of its course, so that it might
have been a place for a king or a queen to rest in, so
that there was not a drop of water in it, unless it dropped
into it by the trampling and the hewing the two
champions made in the middle of the ford.

So great was the fight, that the horses of the men of
Ireland broke away in fright and shyness, with fury and
madness, breaking their chains and their yokes, their
ropes and their traces; and the women and the young
lads and the children and the crazy and the followers of
the men of Ireland broke out of the camp to the
south-west.

They were using the edge of their swords through
that time; and it was then Ferdiad found a time when
Cuchulain was off his guard, and he gave him a stroke
of the sword, and hid it in his body, and the ford was
reddened with Cuchulain's blood and Ferdiad kept on

making great strokes at him. And Cuchulain could not
bear with this, and he called to Laeg for the Gae Bulg,
and it was sent down the stream to him, and he caught
it with his foot. And when Ferdiad heard the name of
the Gae Bulg, he made a stroke of his shield down to
protect his body. But Cuchulain made a straight cast of
the spear, the Gae Bulg, off the middle of his hand, over
the rim of the shield, and it passed through his armour
and went out through his body, so that its sharp end
could be seen.

Ferdiad gave a stroke of his shield up to protect the
upper part of his body, though it was "the relief after
danger," as the saying is. "That is enough," said
Ferdiad; "I die by that. And I may say, indeed, you
have left me sick after you, and it was not right that
I should fall by your hand. O Hound of the beautiful
feats, it was not right, you to kill me; the fault of my
death is yours, it is on you my blood is. A foolish man
does not escape when he goes into the gap of danger;
my grief! I am going away, my end is come. My ribs
will not hold my heart, my heart is all turned to blood.
I have not done well in the battle; you have killed me,
Cuchulain."

Cuchulain ran towards him after that, and put his
two arms about him, and lifted him across the ford
northwards, so that his body should be by the ford on
the north, and not on the west of the ford with the men
of Ireland.

He laid him down then, and a cloud and a weakness
came on him as he stood over Ferdiad. Laeg saw that,
and he saw that all the men of Ireland were rising up to
come towards him. "Good Cuchulain," said Laeg, "rise
up now, for the men of Ireland are coming towards us,
and it is not one man they will put to fight against us
now that Ferdiad has fallen by you." "What use is it
to me to rise up now, and he after falling by me?" said
Cuchulain. But Laeg said : "Rise up, O chained Hound

of Emain ; it is glad and shouting you have a right to
be now, since Ferdiad of the hosts has fallen by you."
"What are joy and shouting to me now?" said Cuchulain ;
"it is to madness and to grief I am driven after
the thing I have done, and the body I wounded so
hard." "It is not right for you to be lamenting him,"
said Laeg. "It is making rejoicings over him you
should be. It was at you he aimed his spears." But
Cuchulain said : "Even if he had cut one arm and one
leg from me, it is my grief Ferdiad not to be riding
his horses through the long days of his lifetime." And
Laeg said : "It is better pleased the women of the Red
Branch will be, he to have died and you to be living.
They know it is not few but many you have sent away
for ever ; for from the day you came out of Cuailgne to
meet Maeve of the great name, it is a grief to her all you
have killed of her people and of her fighting men. You
have not taken quiet sleep since the spoiling of your
country began ; though there were few along with you,
many were the mornings you rose up early."

Then Cuchulain began to keen and to lament for
Ferdiad there, and it is what he said : "Well, Ferdiad,
it is a pity for you it was not one of the men that knew
my courage you asked an advice of before you came to
meet me in the fight that was too hard for you. It is a
pity it was not Laeg, son of Riangabra, you asked how
we stood one to another. It is a pity you did not ask
a true advice of Fergus. It is a pity it was not pleasant
comely Conall you asked which of us would put down
the other.

"And these men know well," he said, "there will
never be born one among the men of Connaught who
will do deeds equal to yours, to the end of life and time.
And they know that if they looked among the places,
the gatherings, the swearings, the false promises of the
fair-haired women of Connaught, or in the playing with
targets and shields, the playing with shields and swords,

the playing backgammon and chess, the playing with horses and chariots, there will not be found the hand of a man that will wound like Ferdiad's hand, or a man to bring the red-mouthed birds croaking over the speckled battle, nor one that will fight for Cruachan, that will be your equal to the end of life and time, O red-cheeked son of Daman." And then he rose up and stood over Ferdiad. "Well, Ferdiad," he said, "it is great wrong and treachery was played on you by the men of Ireland, to bring you out to fight with me. For it has not been easy to stand against me in the war for the Bull of Cuailgne." And he made this complaint :—

"O Ferdiad, you were betrayed to your death ; your last end was sorrowful ; you to die, I to be living ; our parting for ever is a grief for ever.

"When we were far away, with Scathach the victorious, we gave our word that to the end of time we would never go against one another.

"Dear to me was your beautiful ruddiness; dear to me your comely form; dear to me your clear grey eye; dear to me your wisdom and your talk.

"There has not come to the battle, there has not been made angry in the fight, there has not held up shield on the field of spears, the like of you, O red son of Daman.

"Findabair, the daughter of Maeve, with all her great beauty, it was putting a gad on the sand, or on the sun, for you to think to get her, Ferdiad."

Then Cuchulain was still looking down on Ferdiad, "Well, my friend Laeg," he said, "strip Ferdiad now, and take his armour and his clothes off him, until I see the brooch for the sake of which he undertook the fight."

Laeg stripped Ferdiad then, and when Cuchulain saw the brooch, he began to lament and complain over him again, and it is what he said :

"My grief, O gold brooch ! O Ferdiad of the poets, O strong striker of many blows, it is brave your arm was.

"Your yellow hair, curled, well-loved; your soft, leaf-like belt about you until death.

"Dear was our fellowship, dear the brightness of your eyes; your shield with its rim of gold; your chessboard that was worth riches.

"It was not right, you to fall by my hand; it was not a friendly ending. My grief, O gold brooch, my grief!

"Well, my friend Laeg," he said then, "come now and take the Gae Bulg out of him, for I cannot afford to be without my spear." So Laeg took the Gae Bulg out of him, and when Cuchulain saw his reddened spear lying beside Ferdiad, he said: "O Ferdiad, it is a sorrowful story to me, that I should see you so red and so pale, I with my spear reddened, and you in a bed of blood.

"When we were over in the east with Scathach, there would not have been angry words between us, or destroying weapons.

"Scathach spoke fiery words to us, 'Go all of you to the battle that will be fought by Germain the terrible.'

"I said to Ferdiad and to Lugaid, the always generous, and to the son of Baetan the fair, 'Let us all go against Germain.'

"We all of us came to the battle-ground on the shore of the lake of Lind Formait; we brought four hundred out with us from the islands of the Athisech.

"As I and brave Ferdiad were together in the door of Germain's dun, I killed Rind, the son of Niul, I killed Ruad, son of Finnial.

"Ferdiad killed upon the shore Blath, son of Calba of the red swords. Lugaid killed Mugarne of the Torrian Sea, a surly, fierce man.

"We spoiled the dun of Germain the crafty; we brought him with us alive over the wide sea of speckled waters; we brought him to Scathach of the broad shield.

"She, our teacher, whose name was well known, bound us to friendship together, the way our anger would not turn against one another among the fair tribes of Elga.

"Sorrowful the morning when the strength was taken from the son of Daman. My grief! I loved the friend to whom I have given a drink of red blood.

"It is a sorrowful thing has happened to us the pupils of Scathach—I myself red and wounded; you yourself not driving your chariot.

"It is a sorrowful thing has happened to us the pupils of Scathach—I myself hard with blood; you yourself entirely dead.

"It is a sorrowful thing has happened to us the pupils of Scathach—yourself to have died, myself to be alive and strong; it is angry we were in the battle."

"Good Cuchulain," said Laeg, "let us leave this ford now; it is too long we are here." "Let us leave it now indeed, my friend Laeg," said Cuchulain. "But every other fight I ever made was as a game and a sport beside the fight with Ferdiad." And it is what he said:

"Each fight was a game, each one was a jest, until Ferdiad came to the ford; we got the same teaching, we got the same rewards; our teacher was kind to us both alike, setting us both above all the others.

"Each was as a game, each was as a jest, until Ferdiad came to the ford; we had the same ways, we used to do the same deeds; it was at the one time Scathach gave a shield to me, and a shield to Ferdiad.

"Each was a game, each was a jest, until Ferdiad came to the ford; dear to me was the pillar of gold that I broke down on the ford; he who, when he attacked the tribes, was braver than any other.

"Each was a game, each was a jest, until Ferdiad came to the ford, like a proud swelling wave, threatening to destroy all before him.

"Each was a game, each was a jest, until Ferdiad came to the ford; this thing will hang over me for ever. Yesterday he was larger than a mountain; to-day there is nothing of him but a shadow."

XII

THE AWAKENING OF ULSTER

THEN some of the men of Ulster came to comfort Cuchulain, and among them were Senoll Uathach and the two sons of Gege, Muredach and Cotreb. They brought him away to the five streams of Conaille Muirthemne, to wash his hurts in them. And the Sidhe threw all sorts of herbs and plants into the streams for his healing, so that they were all strewed over with green leaves.

Then when Ailell and Maeve heard there were men beginning to come from Ulster, they sent Mac Roth, the herald, to watch at Slieve Fuad, and to warn them if he could see any one coming. And after a while he came back, and Ailell asked news of him. "I saw," he said, "one chariot only, to the north of Slieve Fuad, and it coming straight on, and the man that was in it naked, and without armour or weapons, but only an iron spit in his hand, and he goading on the horses as if he would never get to the army alive." "Who do you think was that man, Fergus?" said Ailell. "I think," said Fergus, "it was Cethern, son of Fintan, from the North, and he will soon be upon us." With that, Cethern came bursting into the camp, and he attacked everyone he met with his spit, and he himself got many wounds back again, so that he had to hold up the board of the chariot to his body to keep his bowels from falling out; and at last he made his escape, and came to the place where Cuchulain was lying. Then Cuchulain said to Laeg: "Rise up now, and go into the camp, and bring some of Ailell's physicians to cure Cethern; for I give my word, if they do not come before this time to-morrow, I will bring death and destruction on them." So Laeg went, and he brought back the physicians with him, and it was only the dread of Cuchulain that made them come. Then Cethern showed the first one of them his wounds, and it is what he said, that he could not be cured. Then Cethern gave him a blow that sent him out of the house. And the same thing happened with all the rest, fifteen there were of them altogether. Then he asked Cuchulain would he get him another physician, for those of the men of Ireland had done him no good. "Rise up, Laeg," said Cuchulain; "go to Slieve Fuad, to Fingan, the Druid physician of Conchubar, and bid him to come here and to heal Cethern." Now, Fingan was the greatest physician in all Ireland, and it was said of him that he could tell what a person's sickness was by looking at the smoke of the house he was in; and he knew by looking at a wound what sort the person was that gave it. Then he came, and Cethern showed him his wounds. "Look at this wound for me, good Fingan," he said. "There came at me two young men, with clear noble looks, with strange foreign clothes on them, and each of them threw a spear into me, and I threw my spear into each of them. "I know those two very well," said Cuchulain; "they are two choice men of Norway, and they were sent against you by Ailell and Maeve." "Look at this wound for me, Fingan," said Cethern. Fingan looked at it. "That is the work of two brothers," he said. "That is true indeed," said Cethern. "Two young men came at me, and they were like one another; but one had curling brown hair, and the other had curling yellow hair. Two green cloaks about them, with brooches of bright silver; two soft shirts of yellow silk; bright swords in their belts they had, and shields with bright silver fastenings, and spears with veins of silver on their handles." "I know those two very well," said Cuchulain; "they are Maine Athremail and Maine Mathremail, two sons of Ailell and Maeve."

"Look at this wound for me, good Fingan," said Cethern. Fingan looked at the wound, and he said : " It was a father and a son made that together." " That is true," said Cethern ; "there came at me two large men with flaming eyes, and they having gold bands on their heads, and the dress of kings, and gold swords at their sides." "I know those two very well," said Cuchulain ; "it was Ailell and his son Maine Andoe that gave you that wound." "Look at this wound, good Fingan," said Cethern. Fingan looked at the wound. " That is the work of a proud woman," he said. " That is true," said Cethern ; "there came at me a beautiful, pale, long-faced woman, with long, flowing yellow hair on her, a crimson cloak with a brooch of gold over her breast, and a straight spear shining red in her hand. It was she gave me that wound, and she got a little wound from me." "I know that woman well," said Cuchulain. "She is Maeve, daughter of the High King of Ireland, and Queen of Connaught. She would have thought it a great victory and a great triumph, you to have fallen by her hand." "Good Fingan," said Cethern then, "tell me now, what do you think of the way I am, and what can you do for me ?" " It is what I think," said Fingan, "you will hardly see the calves that are following your cows at this time grow to be yearlings ; or if you do itself," he said, " it will not be much use your life will be to you." " That is what all the others said to me," said Cethern, " and it is not much profit or credit they got by it, and it is not much you yourself will get"; and with that he made a kick at him, to drive him out of the house. But in spite of that treatment, Fingan gave him his choice of two things : the first to be a long time on his bed, so that he would see the men of Ulster coming in the end to avenge him ; or to be made well enough at the end of three days to go out himself and spend what he had of strength on his enemies.

"I will choose that," he said, "for I would not like to leave my enemies after me; and I would sooner get satisfaction from them myself." So then Fingan bade Cuchulain to make a healing bath that would ease Cethern. So Cuchulain went down to the camp, and he brought away with him all that he met of the cattle of the men of Ireland. Then their flesh was cut up with their bones and their skins to make a Druid bath, and Cethern was put in it for the length of three days and three nights. And at the end of that time he rose up and got into his chariot, to do vengeance on the men of Ireland. And his wife Ionda, daughter of Eochaid, came to him from the North, and brought him his sword that he had forgotten in his hurry at his first setting out.

But it happened that one of the physicians he had driven out with a blow had fallen down outside the tent, and lay there, not able to stir from that. But when Cethern was making ready to set out, he rose up and made his way back to the camp, and he said to the men of Ireland : "Cethern is after being cured by Fingan, the Druid, and he is coming at you now, and do you lay some trap for him." So it is what they did : they took Ailell's cloak and his shirt, and they put them about the pillar-stone, at the boundary of Ross, and his crown on top of it, and left them there. Cethern came rushing on them, and when he saw the pillar-stone, he thought it was Ailell was standing there, and he made at it, and gave a great blow of his sword, that it broke in pieces against the stone.

Then he saw what it was, and he said: "This is some trick they have played on me. And by the oath of my people," he said, "I will not stop my hand from killing, until such time as I have killed some man having a dress like this."

When Maine Andoe heard that, he put on his father's armour, and came out to meet him. And Cethern saw him, and made for him, and threw his shield at him, so that he was cut through and through the body by the rim of the shield.

And when the men of Ireland saw that, they pressed on Cethern from all sides and made an end of him. And his wife Ionda, daughter of Eochaid, came and cried over him there. And it is what she said:

"It is all one to me, it is all one, since there will be no hand of a man under my head for ever; since a grave has been made in the earth for Cethern from the Dun of the Two Hills.

"Cethern, son of Fintan, he that was like a king, was in no need of arms for his work; with nothing in his hand but a two-headed spit, his anger did not spare the men of Connaught.

"I will not take a mate for ever from the flocks of the living world; I will not wed with a man; my husband is sleeping with no woman.

"Dear the little hill, dear the dun where our fighting men were used to gather; dear the sweet fair water, dear was Inis Ruadh.

"Pitiful the grief, pitiful the grief the War for the Bull has brought on me; I will be keening him until my death, I Ionda, daughter of Eochaid!"

And then Fintan, Cethern's father, came with three times fifty men to get satisfaction for his son, and he made three attacks on the army, and killed a great

many of Ailell's men; but Fintan lost a good many of
his own men, and his son Crimthan was made prisoner.
And the men of Ireland were afraid their army would
be too much weakened by little fights of this sort before
the great last battle that was foretold would come, and
they made an agreement with Fintan to give him back
his son, and to fall back themselves a day's march; and
he gave his word not to vex them again until the time
of the last battle. And they found, where the fight had
been, one of Fintan's men and one of Ailell's men lying
dead together, and they with their teeth fixed into one
another. And it is from this the fight was given the
name of Fintan's Tooth-fight.

Then Rochad, son of Fatheman, came to help
Cuchulain, and three times fifty men with him. Now
Findabair loved him, and when she heard he was coming,
she told her secret, and she said to her mother: "That is
my love and my choice out of all the men of Ireland."
And when Maeve heard that, she made a plan to draw
him off, and she said to Findabair: "If he is dear to
you, go and spend the night with him, and bid him to go
back with his men until the day of the great battle, and
I give you my leave to be his wife." So Findabair
went and did as Maeve bade her, and he went back to
the North. But this was heard of in the camp, and the
twelve kings of Munster that were in Maeve's army
began speaking with one another; and it is what they
all said, that Maeve had secretly promised Findabair as
a wife to each one of them as a reward, if he would join
in the war. "And the best thing we can do now," they
said, "is to go and avenge ourselves on Maeve's men,
and on Rochad, for the treachery that was done on us."

So they went out and made an attack on them, and
Ailell and Maeve's men and Rochad made ready to
defend themselves; but Fergus went out and tried to
make them leave off, and to make peace between them,

and before he could do that, seven hundred men had got their death.

And it was told to Findabair how these seven hundred men had got their death on account of her, and how Maeve had promised her in marriage to every one of the twelve kings of Munster. And when she heard that, her heart broke with the shame and the pity that came on her, and she fell dead there and then, and they buried her.

Now at that time Iliach, son of Cas, of the race of Rudraige, was living in the North with his son's son, Laegaire Buadach. And it was told him how the four provinces of Ireland were plundering and destroying the people of Ulster since the day before Samhain, and driving off their cattle and their goods, and all that they had. So he consulted with his people, and it is what he said, that he would go out himself and make an attack on the men of Ireland, and let loose his strength on them, and destroy what he could of them, and do what he could for Ulster. "For as to myself," he said, "if I come out of it, or do not come out of it, is all one to me." Then his two old spent horses, that had been let loose for life, were brought from where they were on the shore by the dun, and yoked to his old chariot, that had neither cushions nor skins in it. And he took his rough, dark, iron shield, with its hard rim of silver, over his shoulder, and his rough, grey, heavy sword at his left side. And he put in the chariot his two rusty, blunt spears, and his people gave him a store of stones and bits of rocks in a heap about him ; and that is the way he went out against the army, and no armour on him at all.

When the men of Ireland saw him coming that way, they began mocking and laughing at him, but it is what Maeve said: "I would be glad indeed all the men of Ulster to come and meet us like that." Then Doche, son of Magach, chanced to meet him, and bade him welcome. "Who is it bids me welcome?" said Iliach.

"The comrade and friend of Laegaire Buadach," said he; "Doche, son of Magach." "I am glad of that welcome," said Iliach, "and for the sake of it, let you come to me when I have spent my rage on the army, and when my strength is going, and when my hand is tired, and let you, and no other of the men of Ireland, make an end of me. And keep my sword," he said, "for your friend, Laegaire Buadach."

Then he made an attack on the men of Ireland, and when his spears were all broken in pieces, he began hitting and throwing with the stones he had. And when they were out, he attacked the men that were near him with the strength of his own hands, so that he made an end of some of them. And when all he could do was done, he saw Doche, son of Magach, near him, and he said: "Come to me now, Doche, and strike my head off, and take charge of my sword for Laegaire Buadach." And Doche did as he bade him, but he brought his head to Ailell and to Maeve.

At this time Sualtim, son of Roig, was told that Cuchulain had fought with Calatin and his sons, and with Ferdiad, and of the hard fight he had made, and the wounds he had got. And it is what Sualtim said: "Is it the sky bursting I hear, or is it the sea going backward, or the earth breaking up, or is it the groaning of my son in his weakness?" With that he set out to visit him, and he found him covered with hurts and wounds, and he began to cry over him. But that did not please Cuchulain, and he knew Sualtim would do no good by stopping there, for he was not the man to avenge him, for he was no great hero; not that he was a coward, but just like any other good fighting man. And Cuchulain said to him: "Well, Sualtim, stop your crying over me, and rise up and go to Emain, and tell the men of Ulster they must come themselves and follow on with the war from this out, for I am not able to defend them any more; for after all I went through, not one of them comes to help me or to comfort me. And tell them," he said, "what way you found me, that I cannot bear to have my clothing next my skin, but it is with crooks of hazel I have to hold it off me, and it is grass that is laid over my wounds; for there is not the place of the point of a needle on me from head to foot but has some hurt on it, except my left hand that was holding my shield; and tell them to make no delay in coming," he said.

Then Sualtim set out on the Grey of Macha to give his message; and when he got close to Emain he called out: "Men are being killed, women brought away, cattle driven off in Ulster," but he got no word of answer. Then he went up to the very wall, and he cried again: "Men are being killed, women brought away, cattle brought away in Ulster"; but the second time he got no answer. Then he went on to the Stone of the Hostages at Emain, and he called out the same words the third time. Then Cathbad, the Druid, asked: "Who are taken, and who is it is taking them?" "It is Ailell and Maeve that are robbing you and destroying you," said Sualtim; "they are bringing away your women, your little boys, your cattle and your horses, and there is only Cuchulain to delay and to hinder the four great provinces of Ireland in the gaps and the passes of Muirthemne; the lad is wounded and no one is coming to his help." But Cathbad was vexed at being waked out of his sleep, and he said: "Any man that comes to scold at the king this way has a right to be put to death." But Conchubar, the king, said: "It is true what Sualtim is saying." "It is true indeed," said all the men of Ulster.

Then anger came on Sualtim that he got no better answer than that, and he turned sharply, and the Grey of Macha reared up, the way the sharp edge of Sualtim's shield came against his own head, and cut it clean off.

Then the Grey turned again to Emain, and the shield dragged after him by its thongs, and Sualtim's head in the hollow of it, and the head said the same words as before: "Men are being killed, women brought away, cattle brought away in Ulster." Then Conchubar said: "The sky is over our heads, the earth is under our feet, the sea is round about us; and unless the sky with all its shower of stars comes down on earth, or the earth breaks open under our feet, or the blue sea goes over the whole face of the world, I swear that I will bring back every cow to its own shed, and every woman to her own dwelling-house."

Then he called to one of his messengers, Finnched, son of Troiglethan, that chanced to be there, and he bade him to go and to call out the men of Ulster. But with the sleep that was on him still, and the weakness, he bade him go and call those of his people that were dead, as well as those that were living. And one of the names he gave him to call to was Cuchulain, son of Sualtim.

It was easy work Finnched had to do now, for the men of Ulster were rising from out of their weakness, and they all made ready to come out with Conchubar, and some of them did not wait for Conchubar at all, but set out on the track of the army of Ireland.

Then Conchubar and his men set out from Emain, and the first day they went as far as Irard Cuillenn, and there they made a halt. "What are we stopping here for?" said Conchubar. "We are waiting for your own two sons," his men said, "Fiachna and Fiacha, that are gone to meet your grandson Erc, son of Fedelm, and of Cairbre, king of Teamhair, to bring him with us." "By my word," said Conchubar, "I will not make any more delay here, for fear the men of Ireland might hear I am risen from my weakness; for they do not know it up to this," he said, "or even if I am alive at all."

So he himself and Celthair, and thirty hundred fierce
chariot-fighters, went on, and it was not long before
they came on eight times twenty strong men belonging
to Ailell and to Maeve, and each of them bringing away
a woman of the women of Ulster with him. And
Conchubar and Celthair struck their heads off, and set
the women free; and then they went back to Irard
Cuillenn.

Now, as to the men of Ireland, they spent that night at
Sleamhain of Meath. And in the night Cormac Conloingeas started up out of his sleep, and he called out that
there had a warning dream come to him, and that there
was a terrible battle before them. And after a while
Dubthach, the Beetle of Ulster, started up out of his sleep,
and called out the same thing, that there had a warning
dream come to him, and that it would not be long till
there would be a great clashing of shields. And with
these dreams and foretellings, great fear came on the
men of Ireland, and it was an uneasy night they spent
at Sleamhain that time.

And in the morning Ailell said : " We have been harry-
ing Ulster and Cuailgne this long time, and we have
taken the women and the cattle and the goods of the
men of Ulster, and we have cut down hills behind us;
and now," he said, " it is time for us to turn back to
Magh Ai, and they can follow us and fight with us there
if they have a mind to.   But before that," he said, " I will
send a messenger to look out across the great plain of
Meath, to see if any of them are coming against us; and
if they are," he said, " I will not go from this without
giving battle to them, for he would not be a good king
that would be good at running away."

So he sent out Mac Roth, the herald. And he had not
long to wait before he heard a noise that was like the
falling of the sky, or the breaking in of the sea over the
land, or the falling of trees on one another in a great

storm.   And he saw the plain covered with wild creatures that had broken away out of the woods.   Then he went back to Ailell and to Maeve, and told them his story, and they asked him what had he seen ; and he said : " I thought I saw a grey mist far away across the plain, and then I saw something like falling snow, and then through the mist I saw something shining like sparks from a fire, or like the stars on a very frosty night."   " What was it he saw, Fergus ? " said Ailell.   And Fergus said : " The mist he saw was the dust that went up from the march of the men of Ulster, and the flakes of snow were the foam flakes from the bits of their horses ; and what he saw shining like sparks from the fire, or like stars on a frosty night, was the angry light of their eyes shining under their helmets."

" It is little I care for that," said Maeve ; " we have good fighting men to meet them."   " It is a pity for you to think that," said Fergus ; " for there is neither in Alban nor in Ireland an army that can put down the men of Ulster when once their weakness is gone from them and their anger is kindled."

That night the men of Ireland made their camp in Clartha, and they put Mac Roth and another man to keep a good watch, the way the men of Ulster would not fall on them without warning.   Now Conchubar and Celtchair, with their thirty hundred men, had followed them to Slieve Sleamhain, and when they found them gone from there they followed on to Clartha, for they thought to get the start of the rest of Ulster in reddening their hands upon the men of Ireland.   So Mac Roth was not long waiting when he saw men and horses coming from the north-east, and he went back into the camp.   " Well, Mac Roth," said Ailell, " have you seen any of the men of Ulster on our track ? "   " I saw men and horses coming," he said.   " What is the number of them ? " said Ailell.   " Not less than thirty hundred chariots." "Those are the men of Ulster coming with Conchubar," said Ailell; "and what did you mean a while ago, Fergus, threatening us with the dust of a great army in the plain, when a little troop like that is all that can be brought against us?" "You are too quick in complaining of that," said Fergus, "and you will soon know what their number is."

"Let us make some good plan now," said Maeve, "for I am sure it is that hot, rude man, Conchubar, king of Ulster, that is coming to attack us. Let us make a pen before him," she said, "of all the army standing round on three sides, and thirty hundred men ready to shut the mouth of it on him when he comes in. For we must take these fellows alive and not kill them, for it would be unworthy of our name to do more than make prisoners of them, and they so few." Now this was one of the most laughable things that was said in the whole course of the war, Conchubar and his thirty hundred of the best men of Ulster to be taken alive. And when Conchubar's son, Cormac Conloingeas, heard this, there was great anger on him, and it is what he thought: "If I do not get satisfaction now at once from Maeve for this boast of hers, I will never get it again." So he rose up with his three thousand men to make an attack on her, and on Ailell; and they rose up as well, and their sons the Maines along with them, and the sons of Magach But then the Gailiana, and the men of Munster, and of Teamhair, came between them, and made peace, and persuaded them to lay down their arms. But for all that, Maeve did make a pen of the army of Ireland to shut up Conchubar, and she had men ready to close it up when once he would be in. But it is what Conchubar did, he never so much as looked for an opening, but when he saw the army before him, he went straight through it, and he broke open a gap of two hundred on the right hand, and a gap of two hundred on the left, and went through them all, and cut them down in the very middle, so that eight hundred men of them were killed.

And then he went away from them, back to Slieve Sleamhain, to join the army of Ulster.

Then the men of Ulster began to gather upon the plain in their full strength, and when Ailell heard it, he said : " Let some one go up and watch them coming, and bring us a report of the appearance that is on them, and of the chief men that are leading them." "Let Mac Roth go," said Fergus.

So Mac Roth went out and took a post on the plain from the early light of the morning till the fall of evening, and through all that time the men of Ulster were coming, so that the ground was not naked under them, every division under its own chief man, and every troop under its own lord, and each one of them apart from the others, and they came on till they had covered the Hill of Sleamhain.

And when evening came, Mac Roth came back to Ailell and to Maeve, and they questioned him and said : " What sort were the men of Ulster as they came across the plain ? " And Mac Roth said : " The first troop I saw coming had three thousand men in it, and as soon as they got to the hill, they took their armour off, and they began to dig and to make a seat of sods and of earth on the highest part of the hill, for their leader to sit on until the rest of the army would come.

" He had the appearance of a tall, proud man, used to giving orders ; and he had yellow, curling hair on him, and a yellow forked beard, and a red, pleasant face, and blue eyes you would be afraid of. A five-folded crimson cloak he had on him, and a gold pin over his breast, and a white shirt with threads of gold woven into it next his body." " Who was that man, Fergus ? " said Ailell. " He was Conchubar, son of Fachtna and of Ness, High King of Ulster." " There was a man stood beside him,"

said Mac Roth, "with scattered white hair, and a purple
cloak, and a shield with bosses of red brass, and a long
iron sword of foreign make. And he looked up to the
sky, and threw his hand upwards, and with that the
clouds seemed like as if they were rushing at one
another, and fire came from them towards the men of
Ireland." "That was Cathbad the Druid," said Fergus,
"and he trying by his enchantments to know how the
battle would go to-morrow."

"I saw another man with Conchubar," said Mac
Roth, "and he having a smooth, dark face, and white
eyes in his head; a long bronze rod in his hand, and a
little bell beside him, and when he touched it with his
rod, all the people near him began to laugh." "Who is
that man?" said Ailell. "It is easy to know that," said
Fergus; "that is Rocmid, the king's fool. There was
never trouble or tiredness on any man of Ulster that he
would not forget if he saw Rocmid." "There came
another troop then," said Mac Roth, "and it is what I
thought, that the leader they had was the handsomest
and the most comely of all the men of Ireland, tall and
well formed. Deep red-yellow hair he had, his face
wide at the top and narrow below; thin, red lips, and
grey eyes that were laughing. A red and white cloak
on him, that the wind stirred as he walked, a white
shield with gold fastenings at his shoulder, a long,
dark green spear in his hand." "Who was that man,
Fergus?" said Ailell. "That man is himself half an
army, Rochad, son of Fatheman, from Rachlainn, in the
North," said Fergus. Now this was the same Rochad
that Findabair had loved. "There was another troop
came then," said Mac Roth, "and a quiet, grey-haired
man at the head of it. A dark-green, long-woolled cloak
he had about him, and a white shirt, and a silver belt
around his waist, and a bell branch at his shoulder. He
sat before King Conchubar when he came to the hill,

and his whole company sat about him. And the sound of his voice when he spoke before the king, and when he was advising him, was sweeter than a three-cornered harp in the player's hand." "Who was that man, Fergus?" said Ailell. "That was Sencha, the orator, the best-spoken of all the men of the whole world, and the peace-maker of the army of Ulster," said Fergus; "and the whole of the men of the world, from the rising to the setting of the sun, he would pacify with his three fair words. But by my word, it is no cowardly or no peaceful counsel that man will give his king to-day, but counsel of courage, and of strength, and of battle."

"There came another troop," said Mac Roth, "and a man at the head of them, and it would not be easy to find a man with a better appearance, or with hair more like gold than what he has. There was a sword with an ivory hilt in his hand, and he throwing it up and catching it in his hand again, as it was coming on the heads of the people near him." "That is Aithirne, the poet and satirist," said Fergus. It was said now of that man that he was very covetous, and that he would ask the one-eyed man for his one eye, and that the rivers and the lakes went back before him when he made a satire on them, and rose when he praised them. And one time when the men of Ulster were fighting to protect him against the men of Leinster, that he had stirred up, and were shut up in Beinn Etair, he had plenty of cows himself in the fort, but he would not give a drop of milk to man or boy, or to a wounded man itself, but left them without food and without drink, unless they would eat the clay or drink the salt water of the sea.

"I saw another troop coming," said Mac Roth, "wild-looking, and in the middle of it a young little lad, red and freckled. He had a silk shirt on him with a border of red gold, and a shield faced with gold, with a golden rim, and a little bright gold sword at his side." "Who is that, Fergus?" said Ailell. "I do not remember leaving any such boy as that when I left Ulster," said Fergus; "but it is likely it may be Erc, son of Cairbre, that has come without leave of his father to help his grandfather, Conchubar; and the men of Teamhair with him. And if what I think is true," he said, "you will find that troop to be a drowning sea, and it is by that troop and by that little boy the battle will be won against you."

Now that was the same Erc that fought afterwards in the last battle against Cuchulain at Muirthemne, and some said it was he that made an end of Cuchulain, but others said it was only the Grey of Macha he made an end of. And Conall Cearnach killed him afterwards in his red vengeance; and his sister Acaill came to Teamhair where he was buried, and cried for him through nine days, till her heart broke like a nut inside her, and she desired that her grave and her mound should be made in a place where the grave and the mound of Erc could be seen from it. And it was made in the place that used to be called the place of the poet Maine, but that is called now the place of Acaill.

"I saw another company," said Mac Roth, "having at its head a tall, large man, with high looks, with soft brown hair in thin smooth locks on his forehead; a deep grey cloak wrapped around him, having a silver brooch in it; a soft white shirt next his skin." "I know that man," said Fergus; "he is Eoghan, son of Durthact, king of Fernmaige, one of the twelve chief heroes of the Red Branch."

"I saw another company coming," said Mac Roth, "and a great many in it; and they red with the fire of their anger, strong and eager and destroying. At their head an angry man, dreadful to look at, long-nosed, large-eared, with coarse grey hair; a striped cloak on him, an iron skewer in place of a brooch, a coarse striped shirt next his skin, a great spear in his hand."

"I know that man," said Fergus; "Celthair, son of Uthecar; a head of battle in Ulster. And the spear in his hand is the great spear, the Luin, that was brought back from the East by the three sons of Tuireann."

"I saw the troop that came last," said Mac Roth, "and it without a leader. There were thirty hundred in it, of proud, clean, ruddy men; long fair hair they had, and shining eyes, and long shining cloaks with good brooches, blue shining spears, good coverings on their heads, and shirts of striped silk. But they seemed to have some great trouble on them, and to be very down-hearted." "What men are those, Fergus?" said Ailell. "I know them well," said Fergus. "It is well for those on whose side they are, and it is a pity for those they are against; for they are able by themselves," he said, "to fight the whole army of Ireland; for they are Cuchulain's men from Muirthemne."

Now all this time Cuchulain was lying on his bed, with the dint of his wounds. But when he knew by the noise on the plain that the men of Ulster were gathering for the battle, he used all his strength and tried to rise up; and he gave a great shout, that all his own troop heard it, and all the whole army. But his people that were about him laid him down on the bed again by force, and put ropes and fastenings over him, the way he could not move from it to open his wounds again. And as he was lying there, two mocking women came from Ailell's camp, and stood beside his bed, and let on to be crying and lamenting; and it is what they told him, that the men of Ulster were beaten, and that Conchubar was killed, and that Fergus was killed along with him. And in the night the Morrigu came like a lean, grey-haired hag, shrieking from the one army to the other, hopping over the points of their weapons, to stir up anger between them, and she called out that ravens would be picking men's necks on the morrow. And with all this outcry, Cuchulain could not sleep, and when the day began to break he said to Laeg: "Look out now, and bring me word of everything that happens on this day." So Laeg looked out, and he said: "I see a little herd of cattle breaking out from the west of Ailell's camp, and there are lads following after them and trying to bring them back; and I see more lads coming out from the army of Ulster to attack them." "That little herd on the plain is the beginning of a great battle," said Cuchulain, "for it is the Brown Bull of Cuailgne and his heifers are in it, and now the young men of the east and of the west will come out against one another. And go now, Laeg," he said, "for I cannot go out myself, and call to the men of Ulster, and stir them up to the battle." So Laeg went out and called to them in Cuchulain's name to get themselves ready and to come out to the battle.

When the men of Ulster heard that message from Cuchulain, they rose up, and rushed out without stopping to put on their clothing, but only taking their weapons in their hands; and such of them as had the door of their tents facing eastwards did not wait to go through it, but broke out to the west.

But Conchubar was not in such haste to bring his own men out, but he said to Sencha: "Keep them back till the right time will have come, when the sun will have lighted all the valleys and the hills."

Then Laeg went to look out again, and he saw the army of Ireland coming out to meet the men of Ulster, and there began a great fight between them, and it went on a good while without one side getting the better of the other. And when Cuchulain heard it he said: "My grief! I not to be able to go among them!"

Now as to Maeve, she was sending out her men, the three Conaires from Slieve Lis, the three red Luachras, the three nimble Suibhnes, the three sky-like Eochaids, the three bards from Lough Riach, the three Fachtnas from the woods of Navan, the three sad-faced Murroughs, the three boiling Laegaires, the three dove-like Conalls, the three sons of Driscoll that fought together, the three Fintans from beside the sea.   And some say that besides these there were three young men of the Sidhe in shining armour, that mixed through the army to stir up courage, and that none of the men of the army could see among them, Delbhaeth, son of Eithlin, and Cermat Honey-mouth, and Angus Og, son of the Dagda.

But when Maeve saw the battle going on, and neither side getting the victory, she called to Fergus, and she said : "It is time for you, Fergus, to go out and avenge yourself on your enemy Conchubar ; and besides that," she said, " it is right for you to go and to fight for us now, after all the good treatment you got from us in Connaught." "I would go out willingly," said Fergus, "if I had my own sword again, the Caladcholg, the sword that Leite brought from the country of the Sidhe." Then Ailell said to his chariot - driver, Ferloga : "Go now and bring Fergus's sword that I bade you to hide away." So Ferloga brought the sword, and put it in Fergus's hand, and Fergus gave it a great welcome. "Come out now into the battle, Fergus," said Maeve, "and spare no one to-day, unless it might be some very dear friend."

Then Fergus and Maeve and Ailell went out into the battle, and three times they made the army of Ulster go back before them. And when Conchubar heard his people were being driven back, he called out to the household of the Red Branch : "Let you hold the place I am in now, till I go see who has turned back our men against us three times on the north side."

And the men of the Red Branch called back to him : "We will do that, and unless the sky should fall on us, or the earth give way under us, we will not give up one inch of ground before the men of Ireland till you come to us again, or till we get our death."

Then Conchubar went to see who it was that was driving back his army, and it was Fergus he found before him; and Fergus struck three great blows on Conchubar's shield, the Ochain, so that the shield screamed out loud, and all the shields of the army of Ulster screamed with it, and the three great waves of Ireland answered it.

Then Fergus said: "Who is it is holding his shield against me?" And Conchubar knew then who was before him, and he cried out: "It is the man, Fergus, that is greater and more comely and younger and better than yourself, the man whose father and mother were better than your own; the man that put to death the three great candles of the valour of the Gael, the three prosperous sons of Usnach, in spite of your guarantee and your protection; the man that banished you out of your own country; the man that made your house a dwelling-place for deer and foxes; the man that never left you so much as the breadth of your foot of land in Ulster; the man that drove you to the entertainment of a woman; and the man that will drive you back to-day in the presence of the men of Ireland, Conchubar, son of Fachtna Fathach, High King of Ulster, the High King of Ireland."

When Fergus heard that, he took his sword, the Caladcholg, in his two hands, and he was swinging it over his head, that it seemed to have the size and appearance of a rainbow, and he was about to give his three great strokes on the men of Ulster.

But Conchubar's son, Cormac Conloingeas, saw what he was doing, and he made a rush at Fergus, and put his arms about his knees, and he said: "Do not put out your great strength, my master Fergus, to destroy the whole army of Ulster." "Let me go," said Fergus, "for I will not live through the day unless I strike my three blows on the men of Ulster." But Cormac Conloingeas would not leave off from asking him, and then he said: "Tell Conchubar to go back to his own place in the battle, and I will spare the army." So Conchubar went back, and then Fergus struck his three blows on three little hills that were near him, and cut their tops off, and they are called "the three bare hills of Meath" to this day.

But when Cuchulain heard the scream of Conchubar's shield the time Fergus struck it, he called out to Laeg: "Who has dared to strike those three blows upon the Ochain, and I still living?" "It is Fergus, son of Rogh, struck them," said Laeg. "Where is the battle going on now?" said Cuchulain. "The armies are come as far as Gairech," said Laeg. "By my hand of valour," said Cuchulain, "they will not have reached to Ilgairech before I will be with them." With that he put out all his strength, and he broke the ropes that were about him, and threw them off, and he scattered the grass that was on his wounds into the high air. And the two mocking women were there yet, and he dashed them one against the other, and left them there on the ground. And he looked for his arms, but he could see none of them; but only his chariot, that was broken, was lying there. And he took hold of a shaft of it, and rushed, with all his wounds, straight into the battle, till he found Fergus, and he called to him to go back before him now, as he had promised he would do. But Fergus gave him no answer. Then Cuchulain said: "Go back, now, Fergus, or by the oath of my people," he said, "I will grind you to pieces as a mill grinds the malt." Then Fergus said: "Do not be giving out threats to me, for my army is well able for the army of Ulster." "You gave me your promise, Fergus," said Cuchulain, "to go back before me when we would meet in the great battle, and when I would be covered with wounds. You bound yourself to that the time I went back before you, and you without your sword."

Then Fergus, when he heard that, went back three steps, and then he turned, and his men with him, and

gave way before Cuchulain.   And all the men of Ireland
turned when they saw that, and broke out of their ranks,
and ran over the hill westward, and Cuchulain and the
men of Ulster followed after them, making a great
slaughter.   And Cuchulain came up with Maeve, and
she called out: "A gift to me, Cuchulain."   "What is it
you are asking of me?" he said.   "Take what is left of
my army under your protection, and let it pass over the
great ford westward."   So he agreed to do that, and
what was left of the army of Ireland went over the great
ford of the Sionnan at Athluain, and Maeve and Ailell
and Fergus, and the Maines, and the sons of Magach
stopped to the last, and drew their shields of protection
behind the men of Ireland, till they had got back to
Cruachan in Connaught, the place they set out from.

It was mid-day when Cuchulain came into the battle,
and the sun was setting when the last of them went over
the ford.   And then Cuchulain took his sword that Laeg
had brought him, for he had but a few splinters left of
the shaft of the chariot he had used in the fight, and he
made three blows at three rocks, and cut the tops off
them, for an insult to Connaught for ever, the way if
any one should speak of the three bare hills of Meath,
the three bare rocks of Athluain would be there to give
the answer.

And Fergus was watching the army of Ireland going
back over the ford, and it is what he said : " This army is
swept away to-day ; it is wandering and going astray
like a mare among her foals that goes astray in a strange
place, not knowing what path to take.   And it is following the lead of a woman," he said, "has brought it into
this distress."

This then was the end of the battle of Gairech and
Ilgairech, and the end of the war for the Brown Bull of
Cuailgne.

XIII

THE TWO BULLS

THIS, now, is the story of the two bulls, the Brown of
Cuailgne, and the White-horned of Cruachan Ai,
and this is the way it was with them—for they were not
right bulls, but there was enchantment on them. In
the time long ago Bodb was king of the Sidhe of
Munster, and it is in Femen, of Slieve-na-man he was, and
Ochall Ochne was king of the Sidhe of Connaught, and
it is in Cruachan he used to be. They used at one time
to be fighting one against the other, but afterwards they
made peace, and were good friends. Now Bodb had a
swineherd, whose name was Friuch, and Ochall had a
swineherd whose name was Rucht, and they were
friendly with one another the same as their masters.
And they had the knowledge of enchantments, and could
turn themselves to every shape. And when there was a
great plenty of mast in Munster, the swineherd from
Connaught would bring his lean swine to the south, and
in the same way, when mast was plentiful in Connaught,
the swineherd would bring his swine northward, and
would bring them home again fat.

But after a while some bad feeling rose up between
the two, for the men of Connaught and the men of
Munster began to set them one against the other. So
one year when there was great mast in Munster, and
Rucht brought his herd from Connaught, so soon as his
comrade Friuch had bade him welcome, he said : " The

people are all saying your power is greater than mine."
"It is no less any way," said Ochall's herd. "We will
soon know that," said Friuch. "I will put an enchantment on your swine, and even though they eat their
share of mast, they will not be fat, like mine will be."
And so it happened, he put an enchantment on the
Connaught swine, and when Rucht went home with
them they could hardly walk at all, they were so thin
and so weak, and all the people were laughing at the
state they were in. "It was a bad day for you, you went
to the South," they said, "for your comrade has greater
power than what you have." "That is not so," said he.
"Wait till it is our turn to have mast, and I will play
the same trick on him."

So the next year he did as he had said, and the
Munster swine pined away, so that every one said their
power was the same. And when Bodb's swineherd
went back home to Munster with his lean swine, his
master put him out of the place. And Ochall put his
herd out of his place as well, because of the swine
coming back in so bad a state from Munster.

One day, two full years after that, the men of Munster
were gathered together near Femen, and they took
notice of two ravens that were making a great cawing.
"What a noise those birds have been making all through
the year!" they said. "They never stop scolding at one
another." Just then Findell, Ochall's steward from
Cruachan, came towards them on the hill, and they bade
him welcome. "What a noise those birds are making!"
he said; "any one would think them to be the same
two birds we had in Cruachan last year." With that,
they saw the two ravens change into the shape of men,
and they knew them to be the two swineherds, and
they bade them welcome. "It is not right you to
welcome us," said Bodb's swineherd, "for there will be
many dead bodies of friends, and much crying on

account of us two." What has happened you all
through this time?" they asked. "Nothing good," he said.
" Since we went from you we have been all the time in
the shape of birds, and you saw the way we were scolding at one another all through this year.   And we were
quarrelling in the same way the whole of last year at
Cruachan, and the men of the North and of the South
have seen what our power is.   And now," he said, "we
will go into the shape of water beasts, and be under the
water for the length of two years."   And with that one
of them went into the Sionnan, and the other into the
Suir, and they were seen for a year in the Suir, and for
a year in the Sionnan, and they devouring one another.
And one day the men of Connaught had a great
gathering at Ednecha, on the Sionnan, and they saw these
two beasts in the river ; each one of them looked to be
as big as the top of a hill, and they made such a furious
attack on one another that fiery swords seemed to be
coming from their jaws, and the people came round
them on every side.   They came out of the Sionnan
then, and as soon as they touched the shore, they
changed again into the shape of the two swineherds.
Ochall bade them welcome.   "Where have you been
wandering?" he asked them.   "Indeed it is tired we
are with our wanderings," they said.   " You saw what we
were doing before your eyes, and that is what we were
doing through these two years, under seas and waters.
And now we must take new shapes on us, till we try
one another's strength again."   And with that they
went away.

    It happened a good while after that there was a great
gathering of the men of Connaught at Loch Riach, for
Bodb was coming on a friendly visit to Ochall.   And
Bodb brought a great troop with him, the most splendid
ever seen ; speckled horses they had, and green cloaks
with silver brooches, and shoes with clasps of red bronze,

and every one of them had a collar of gold, with a stone worth a newly-calved cow set in it. When Ochall saw what grand clothes and horses they had, he called to his people secretly, and asked could they match Bodb's people in dress and in horses and arms, and they said they could not. Then Ochall said: " That is a pity, and our great name is lost." But just then a troop of men were seen coming from the North, and black horses with them, that you would think had been cast up by the sea, and bridle-bits of gold in their mouths. And the men had black-grey cloaks, and a gold brooch at the breast of each, and a white tunic with crimson stripes, and fifty coils of bright gold round every man. And every man of them had black hair, as smooth as if a cow had licked it. And they stopped a little way off, and then the men of Connaught stood up and gave up their place to them. There was a Druid from Britain there, and when he saw them make way he said : " From this out, to the end of life and time, the Connaught men will be under the yoke, attending on hounds and on sons of kings and queens for ever."

Then after they had been feasting for a while, Bodb asked could any Connaught man be found that would fight against his champion Rinn, that was with him, and that had a great name, but no one knew where he came from. And at first there could no one be found, but then a strange champion came out from among the men of Connaught, and he said, " I will go against him." " That is no welcome news," said Rinn. Then they fought against one another for three days and three nights, and before the end of that time the two armies began to join into the fight, and a troop came from Leinster and joined with Bodb, and another troop came from Meath and joined with Ochall. And four kings were killed there, and Ochall among them, and then Bodb went back to Slieve-na-man. But as to the two champions, they were seen no more, and it was known they were the two swineherds. After that they were for two years with the appearance of shadows, threatening one another, the way that many people died of fright after seeing them.

And after that, they were in the shape of eels, and one went into the river Cruind, in Cuailgne; and after a while a cow belonging to Daire, son of Fachna, drank it down. And the other went into the Spring of Uaran Garad, in Connaught; and one day Maeve went out to the spring, and a small bronze vessel in her hand, and she dipped it in the water, and the little eel went into it, and every colour was to be seen on him. And she was a long time looking at him, she thought the colours so beautiful. Then the water went away, and the eel was alone in the vessel. "It is a pity you cannot speak to me," said Maeve. "What is it you want to know?" said the eel. "I would like to know what way it is with you in that shape of a beast," she said; "and I would like to know what will happen me after I get the sway over Connaught." "Indeed it is a tormented beast I am," he said, "and it is in many shapes I have been. And as to yourself," he said, "handsome as you are, you should take a good man to be with you in your sway." "I have no wish," said Maeve, "to let a man of Connaught get the upper hand over me," and with that she went home again.

But she married Ailell after that, and as for the eel, he was swallowed down by one of Maeve's cows that came to drink at the spring.

And it was from that cow, and from the cow that belonged to Daire, son of Fachna, the two bulls were born, the White-horned and the Brown. They were the finest ever seen in Ireland, and gold and silver were put on their horns by the men of Ulster and Connaught. In Connaught no bull dared bellow before the White-horned, and in Ulster no bull dared bellow before the Brown.

As to the Brown, he that had been Friuch, the Munster swineherd, his lowing when he would be coming home every evening to his yard was good music to the people of the whole of Cuailgne. And wherever he was, neither Bocanachs nor Bananachs nor witches of the valley, could come into the one place with him. And it was on account of him the great war broke out.

Now, when Maeve saw at Ilgaireth that the battle was going against her, she sent eight of her own messengers to bring away the Brown Bull, and his heifers. "For whoever goes back or does not go back," she said, "the Brown Bull must go to Cruachan."

Now when the Brown Bull came into Connaught, and saw the beautiful trackless country before him, he let three great loud bellowings out of him. As soon as the White-horned heard that, he set out for the place those bellowings came from, with his head high in the air.

Then Maeve said that the men of her army must not go to their homes till they would see the fight between the two bulls.

And they all said some one must be put to watch the fight, and to give a fair report of it afterwards. And it is what they agreed, that Bricriu should be sent to watch it, because he had not taken any side in the war; for he had been through the whole length of it under care of physicians at Cruachan, with the dint of the wound he got the day he vexed Fergus, and that Fergus drove the chess-men into his head. " I will go willingly," said Bricriu. So he went out and took his place in a gap, where he could have a good view of the fight.

As soon as the bulls caught sight of one another they pawed the earth so furiously that they sent the sods flying, and their eyes were like balls of fire in

their heads; they locked their horns together, and they
ploughed up the ground under them and trampled it,
and they were trying to crush and to destroy one
another through the whole length of the day.

And once the White-horned went back a little way
and made a rush at the Brown, and got his horn into
his side, and he gave out a great bellow, and they
rushed both together through the gap where Bricriu
was, the way he was trodden into the earth under
their feet. And that is how Bricriu of the bitter
tongue, son of Cairbre, got his death.

Then when the night was coming on, Cormac
Conloingeas took hold of a spear-shaft, and he laid
three great strokes on the Brown Bull from head to
tail, and he said : " This is a great treasure to be boasting of, that cannot get the better of a calf of his own
age." When the Brown Bull heard that insult, great
fury came on him, and he turned on the White-horned
again. And all through the night the men of Ireland
were listening to the sound of their bellowing, and they
going here and there, all through the country.

On the morrow, they saw the Brown Bull coming
over Cruachan from the west, and he carrying what
was left of the White-horned on his horns. Then
Maeve's sons, the Maines, rose up to make an attack
on him on account of the Connaught bull he had destroyed. "Where are those men going :" said Fergus.
"They are going to kill the Brown Bull of Cuailgne."
" By the oath of my people," said Fergus, "if you do
not let the Brown Bull go back to his own country in
safety, all he has done to the White-horned is little to
what I will do now to you."

Then the Brown Bull bellowed three times, and set
out on his way. And when he came to the great ford
of the Sionnan he stopped to drink, and the two loins of
the White-horned fell from his horns into the water.

And that place is called Ath-luain, the ford of the loin, to this day. And its liver fell in the same way into a river of Meath, and it is called Ath-Truim, the ford of the liver, to this day.

Then he went on till he came to the top of Slieve Breagh, and when he looked from it he saw his own home, the hills of Cuailgne; and at the sight of his own country, a great spirit rose up in him, and madness and fury came on him, and he rushed on, killing everyone that came in his way.

And when he got to his own place, he turned his back to a hill and he gave out a loud bellowing of victory. And with that his heart broke in his body, and blood came bursting from his mouth, and he died.

XIV

THE ONLY JEALOUSY OF EMER

IT happened one time, near to the day of Samhain, the men of Ulster came together for games and for feasting upon the plain of Muirthemne.

And they were all of them there but Conall Cearnach and Lugaid of the Red Stripes. "Let the feast be begun," they said. "It shall not be begun," said Cuchulain, "till Conall and Lugaid are here."

Sencha, the poet, said then : "Let us play chess while we are waiting, and let poems be sung for us, and let games be played." And they agreed to that.

While they were doing these things, a flock of birds came down on the lake before them, and in all Ireland there were not birds to be seen that were more beautiful.

A great longing came on the women that were there to have the birds that were on the lake, and they began to quarrel with one another as to who should have them.

King Conchubar's wife said : "I must have a bird of these birds on each of my two shoulders." "We must all have the same," said the other women. "If any one is to get them, it is I that must first get them," said Eithne Inguba, who loved Cuchulain. "What shall we do ? " said the women. "It is I will tell you that," said Levarcham, "for I will go to Cuchulain from you to ask him to get them."

So she went to Cuchulain and said : "The women of

Ulster desire that you will get these birds for them."
Cuchulain put his hand upon his sword as if to strike
her, and he said: "Have the idle women of Ulster
nothing better to do than to send me catching birds to-
day?" "It is not for you," said Levarcham, "to be
angry with the women of Ulster; for there are many
of them are half blind to-day with looking at you, from
the greatness of their love for you."

Then Cuchulain told Laeg to yoke his chariot for him,
and he went in it to the lake, and he gave the birds a
side stroke of his sword, so that their feet and their
wings could not rise from the water.

They caught them all then, and divided them among
the women, so that there was not a woman among them
who did not get two birds, but Eithne Inguba only.
Cuchulain came last to her. "It is vexed you seem to
be," he said. "Is it because I have given the birds to
the other women?" "You have good reason for that,"
she said, "for there is not a woman of them but would
share her love and her friendship with you; while, as to
me, no person shares my love but you alone."

"Do not be vexed then," said Cuchulain; "for whatever birds may come to the plain of Muirthemne, or to
the Boinne, from this out, you shall have the two most
beautiful among them."

It was not long after that, two other birds came on
the lake, and they linked together with a chain of red
gold, and they were singing soft music that went near
to put sleep on the whole gathering.

Cuchulain went over towards the birds, but Laeg said
to him not to go, and Eithne said: "If you would take
our advice, you would not go near them, for there is
enchantment behind these birds; let some other birds be
got for me besides these."

"Do you think you can put me from what I have a
mind to do?" said Cuchulain. And he said to Laeg:

"Put a stone into that sling." Laeg took a stone and put it in a sling, and Cuchulain made a cast, but it missed. "My grief!" he said. Then he took another stone, and made another cast, and it passed by them. "I am good for nothing," he said, "for since I first took arms I never made a bad cast till this day." Then he threw his heavy spear, and it went through the flying wing of one of the birds, and the two of them dived down under the water.

Cuchulain went away then with vexation on him, and he lay down with his head against a rock, and sleep came on him. And he saw two women coming towards him, one of them having a green cloak about her, and the other a five-folded crimson cloak.

The woman with the green cloak went up to him, and smiled at him, and she gave him a stroke of a rod. The other went up to him then, and smiled at him, and gave him a stroke in the same way; and they went on doing this for a long time, each of them striking him in turn, till he was more dead than alive. And then they went away and left him there.

All the men of Ulster saw that something had happened, and they asked if they would awaken him. "Do not," said Conall; "do not move him before night."

After that Cuchulain stood up in his sleep, and the men of Ulster asked him who was it had used him like that, but he could not speak with them. But after a while he said: "Bring me and lay me on my bed, not to Dundealgan, but to the Speckled House at Emain." "Let him be brought to Dundealgan, where Emer his wife is," said Laeg. "Not so," said Cuchulain, "but bring me to the Speckled House." So he was brought there, and he stopped to the end of a year in that place without speaking to any person.

One day before the next feast of Samhain, at the end of the year, Conchubar and the men of Ulster were around him in the house; that is, Laegaire between him and the wall, and Conall Cearnach between him and the door, Lugaid of the Red Stripes beside his pillow, and Eithne Inguba at his feet.

As they were sitting like this, one who had the appearance of a man came into the house to them, and sat down on the side of the bed where Cuchulain was lying.

"What has brought you here?" said Conall. "I will tell you that," said he. "It is to speak with the man lying here on the bed I am come. And if the man lying here were in his health, he would be a protection to all the men of Ulster; but as he is, under great sickness and weakness, he is a better protection to them." And he stood up then, and it is what he said:

"If Cuchulain, son of Sualtim, would take my friendship to-day, all he has seen in his sleep would be his, with no help from his army.

"Liban, she who sits at the right hand of Labraid of the quick sword, has said that the coming of Cuchulain would bring great joy to the heart of Fand her sister.

"O Cuchulain, it is not long your sickness would be on you if they would come, the two daughters of Aedh Abrat. Here to the south, to the plain of Muirthemne, I will send Liban to cure your sickness, Cuchulain."

"Who are you yourself?" they said to him then.

"I am Angus," he said, and with that he went out; and they did not know where he came from, or where he went. And then Cuchulain sat up and spoke to them. "It is time indeed," said the men of Ulster, "for you to tell us all that has happened you." "I saw," he said, "a vision about this time last year": and then he told them all he had seen, and of the women that had come and had struck him with their rods. "And what is to be done now, my master, Conchubar?" he said. "This must be done," said Conchubar: "you must go back till you come to the same rock."

So then Cuchulain set out, and came to the same rock, and there he saw the same woman with the green cloak coming towards him. "That is well, Cuchulain," said she. "It is not well indeed; and tell me what did you want with me when you came last year?" said Cuchulain.

"It was not to harm you, indeed, we came," said the woman, "but to ask your love; and I am come now to speak to you," she said, "from Fand, daughter of Aedh Abrat; for Manannan, Son of the Sea, has left her, and her love has fallen on you; and my own name is Liban, wife of Labraid of the quick sword. And I have a message for you from him," she said, "that he will give all you can wish for, if you will give him one day's help against Senach of the crooked body, and against Eochaid Juil, and against Eoghan of Inver, that is Eoghan of the River's Mouth."

"My weakness is on me yet," said Cuchulain, "and I could not go out fighting against men to-day." "You will not be long so," said Liban; "you will be healed, and what is lost of your strength will be given back to you again; and you ought to do this much for Labraid," she said, "because he is the best of the heroes of the world."

"In what place is he?" said Cuchulain. "He is in Magh Mell, the Happy Plain," she said. "I will not go," said Cuchulain, "until I see Emer, my wife. And you are to go for me, Laeg," he said, "to where she is, and tell her it was the women of the Sidhe came to me from the hills and struck me; and tell her I am getting better now, and bid her come and visit me."

So Laeg went to Emer, and he told her what way Cuchulain was. And Emer said: "It is a bad servant you are, Laeg, you that are coming and going by the hills, and that cannot find a cure for your master; and it is a pity for the men of Ulster," she said, "that they do not find a certain cure for him. If it had been Conchubar that was in bonds, or Fergus that could not sleep, or Conall Cearnach that had wounds on him, it is Cuchulain that would give them relief." And it is what she said:

"My grief! son of Riangabra, you who go early and late among the hills, you are not early but late in bringing a cure for the beautiful son of Dechtire.

"It is a pity for the brave men of Ulster, with all the knowledgeable men and the learners among them, that they have not searched the whole face of the world for a cure for their friend Cuchulain.

"If it was Fergus had lost his sleep, and that any enchantment could cure him, it is the son of Dechtire would not sleep at home till he had found a Druid to do it.

"If it were Conall in the same way was suffering from wounds and from sores, it is the Hound would search the wide world till he would find one that would cure him.

"If it was Laegaire of many gifts was wounded in battle, Cuchulain would have searched through all Ireland to cure the grandson of Iliach.

"If it were on Celthair the revengeful sleep had fallen and long sickness, night and day would see the journeys of Setanta among the hills.

"If it had been Furbaigh, chief of fighters, that lay wasting in his bed, he would have searched the ridge of the world until he had found what would save him.

"The host of the hill of Truin has killed him; they have taken from him his great courage; the Hound of Muirthemne is no better than any other hound since the sleep of the hill of Bruagh came on him.

"My grief! sickness has laid hold of me for the Hound

of the smith of Conchubar; it will be sickness to my heart and my body, I to fail in bringing him a cure.

"My grief! It hurts my heart, sickness to be on the rider of the plain, so that he could not come here, to the gathering at the plain of Muirthemne.

"It is why he does not come from Emain, the appearance he had is gone from him; my voice is weak and dead because of the way he is. A month and a quarter and a year without sleep, that is the way I am, and without hearing any one speak pleasant words, son of Riangabra, O son of Riangabra."

After she had made this complaint, Emer went forward to Emain Macha to attend on Cuchulain, and she sat on the side of the bed where he was, and it is what she was saying:

"Rise up, champion of Ulster, awake from your sleep, in health and happiness. Look at the well-shaped king of Macha; he will not allow your long sleep. Look at his shoulder, smooth like crystal; look at his drinking-horns and battle spoils; look at his chariots that sweep the valleys; look at the movements of his chess-men.

"Think on his heroes in their strength; think on his high, fine women; think on his kings of brave doings; think on their high noble queens.

"Think on the beginning of clear winter; think on its wonders in their turn; think in yourself of what it brings forth—its cold, its length, its want of beauty. This stupor, it is not good wholesome sleep; it is idleness and the fear of battle; long sleep is the same as drunkenness; weakness is only second to death.

"Awake from the sleep of the Sidhe you have drunk; cast it off with all your great strength. You have had your fill of sweet flowery words; rise up, O hero of Ulster."

Cuchulain rose up then, and he drew his hand across his face, and he put his stupor and his heaviness off

him. Then Laeg said : "It is great idleness for a hero
to give in to the sleep of a sick-bed because women
from Magh Mell have appeared to you, who overcame
you, who bound you, who put you within the power
of idle women. Rise up out of death, you who are
wounded by women of the Sidhe, for your strength
has come, the strength of a hero among heroes ; rise
up till you go to the place of fighting men, till you do
great deeds, where Labraid of the quick hand leads
his men. Rise up that you may be great, and leave
this idleness."

Then Cuchulain went again to the rock, and he saw
Liban coming towards him, and she asked him again
to go with her to her country. "What place is Labraid
in at this time ? " said Cuchulain. " I will tell you that,"
said Liban, and it is what she said :

"Labraid is at this time upon a clear lake, where
companies of women come to. It is not tired you
would be coming to his country, if you would but visit
Labraid of the quick sword.

"A happy house ordered by a kind woman ; a
hundred men in it that are masters of learning ; the
beauty of redness is on the cheek of Labraid.

" He shakes a wolf's head before his thin red sword ;
he bruises the armour of rushing hosts ; he breaks the
shields of heroes.

" His appearance in the fight is the delight of the
eye ; he does his brave deeds at all points ; it is he is
worth more than any other man.

" The greatest of fighters, the one told of in stories,
has reached the country of Eochaid Juil ; his hair is
like rings of gold upon him ; his coming is like the
smell of wine.

" A man of many strange deeds, Labraid of the quick
hand at sword ; he does not strike till he is forced ; he
keeps his people in quietness.

"There are bridles and collars of red gold on his horses, and this is not all his riches; the house he lives in is supported by pillars of silver and of crystal."

"I will not go on a woman's asking," said Cuchulain. "Let Laeg come with me then," said Liban, "to see and to know everything." "Let him go then," said Cuchulain.

Then Laeg went along with the women, and they went past Magh Luada, the Racing Plain, and past the Bile Buada, the Tree of Victory, and past Oenach Emna, the gathering-place of Emain, and to Oenach Fidhga, the gathering-place of the woods; and it was there Aedh Abrat used to be with his daughters. And Liban caught Laeg by the shoulder: "You will not escape to-day, Laeg," she said, "unless you are protected by a woman." "That is not what we were much used to up to this," said Laeg, "to be under women protection." "My grief for ever, Cuchulain not to be in your place now!" said Liban. "I would be glad indeed he to be here," said Laeg.

They went away then towards the Island of Labraid, and when they came to the lake they saw a little copper ship upon the water before them. Then they went into the ship, and they came to the island, and there they went to the door of a house. And they saw a man coming towards them, and Liban said to him: "Where is Labraid of the quick sword?" And the man said: "Labraid is putting courage into the people, and he is gathering them for battle. There will be great slaughter made there, that will fill the plain of Fidgha."

Then they went up to the house, and Laeg thought he had seen it before, and yet it was strange. And in it were beds, crimson, green, white and gold; and the great candle there was a bright precious stone. And at the western door, where the sun goes down, there was a stud of horses with grey speckled manes, and others of red-brown. And at the eastern door were three tall trees of pure crimson, with lasting flowers, and birds singing from them for the young men of the king's rath. And there was a tree at the door of the court that there was not the like of for beauty, a silver tree, and when the sun was shining on it, it was like gold. And there were three times twenty other trees there, and the top of every one meeting the other, and three hundred could be fed from every tree with fruit that is different, that is always ripe. And there was a fountain in the great court, and three times fifty striped cloaks, and a shining gold pin in the ear of every cloak. And there was a vat of merry mead for dividing among the household; it is a lasting custom that it is always full, ever and always. And in the house were three times fifty women, and they all bade welcome to Laeg, and it is what they all said to him: "There is a welcome before you, Laeg, for the sake of the woman with whom you come, and for the sake of him from whom you come, and for your own sake."

"What will you do now, Laeg?" said Liban. "Will you go first and speak with Fand?" "I will, if I know the place she is in," said Laeg. "I will tell you that, for she is apart in a room by herself," said Liban. So they went to speak with her, and she bade Laeg welcome in the same way as the others. And the meaning of the name Fand is a tear that passes over the fire of the eye. It was for her purity she was called that, and for her beauty; for there was nothing in life with which she could be compared besides it.

And when she had bade Laeg welcome, she said: "For what reason did Cuchulain not come?" "He had no mind to come on a woman's asking," said Laeg. "And besides that," he said, "he did not know if it was from yourself the message came." "It was from myself indeed," she said, "and let him not be long in coming, for it is on this day the battle is to be fought."

While they were there together, they heard the sound of Labraid's chariot coming to the island. "It is troubled Labraid's mind is to-day," said Liban. "Let us go out before him." So they went out, and Liban bade him welcome, and it is what she said:

"Welcome, Labraid of the quick hand at sword, yourself an army, a destroyer of heroes; welcome, welcome, Labraid."

Labraid made no answer, and Liban spoke again:

"Welcome, Labraid of the quick hand at sword; his hand is open to all; his word is faithful; his justice is right; kind his sway; strong his right arm; gentle to his horses; welcome, welcome, Labraid!"

Still Labraid did not answer, and she spoke again, and it is what she said:

"Welcome, Labraid of the quick sword; lifter up of the weak; subduer of the strong; welcome, Labraid; welcome, Labraid!"

Then Labraid said: "Leave your praises, woman, for it is not pride or happiness or high thoughts of myself I have in my mind to-day. A battle is near, and the striking of swords in right and left hands; the one heart of Eochaid Juil is equal to many. It is not a time for pride."

"There is good news before you," said Liban then. "Laeg, the chariot-driver of Cuchulain, is here, and he has brought a message from him that he will go into the battle with you." Then Labraid bade him welcome as the women had done, and he said: "Go back home now, and tell Cuchulain to make no delay in coming, for it is to-day the battle is to be fought."

So Laeg went away then to Emain Macha, and told his story to Cuchulain, and to all the rest, and it is what he said:

"Labraid is a king of great armies. I saw his country, bright, free, where no lies are spoken, and no bad thing. I saw the masters of music within, giving delight to the daughters of Aedh. If I had not come away quickly, they would have taken my strength from me.

"I saw all this at the hill of the Sidhe. The women there are beautiful, their gifts are beyond counting; as to Fand, the daughter of Aedh Abrat, no one could reach her beauty but the queens of the kings.

"Eithne Inguba is a beautiful woman, but the woman I am speaking of now takes away the wits from whole armies.

"It is a pity, Cuchulain, you did not go a while ago, and every one asking you to do it, that you might see the way it is in the great house I have seen.

"If all Ireland were mine, and I king over the happy hills, I would give it, and that would be no small thing, to live for ever in the place I have been in."

"That is good," said Cuchulain. "It is good," said Laeg, "and it is right to go to reach it, and everything in that country is good."

Then Cuchulain rose up, and he passed his hand over his face, and he spoke pleasantly with Laeg, and he felt that the things the young man was telling him were a strengthening to his mind. And Laeg said: "It is time to come, for the battle is being fought to-day."

Cuchulain went along with him then to that country, and took his chariot with him till they reached the island. Labraid bade them welcome, and all the women; and Fand bade Cuchulain her own welcome.

"What is to be done here now?" said Cuchulain.

"This is what we have to do," said Labraid; "to go and take a turn round the army that is against us."

They went forward then till they reached the gathering-place of the armies, and till they cast an eye over

them, and it seemed as if there was no end to them.
"Go you away for a while," said Cuchulain to Labraid.
So Labraid went away then, and Cuchulain stayed before
the armies. Then two black ravens croaked, and all the
armies laughed. "It is likely," they said, "the ravens
are telling of the coming of the angry man from
Muirthemne." And they hunted them away.

After that Eochaid Juil went to wash his hands at
the spring, and Cuchulain saw his bare shoulder through
the shirt, and he threw a spear at him, and it passed
through him ; and then he attacked the army alone, and
killed a great many. Then he was attacked by Senach
Siabartha the Unearthly, and they fought very hard,
and Cuchulain overcame him in the end. And Labraid
came then, and broke the armies before him, and he
called to Cuchulain to leave off from killing. But Laeg
said : "I am in dread he will spend his rage on us, since
he has not had enough of fighting. And let your people
go," he said, "and let them make ready three vats of
water to put out his heat. The first vat he will go into
will boil over ; the second vat, no person could bear its
heat ; but the heat of the third vat will be fit to bear."

When the women saw Cuchulain coming back, it was
then Fand sang before him : "Stately is the man that
comes in his chariot ; young he is, and without a beard ,
his course is splendid across the plain at evening, at
Senach Fidhga, the gathering-place of the woods.

"It is not the music of the Sidhe would keep him in
a bed ; it is the red colour of blood that is upon him ; I
stand looking at the horses of his chariot ; their like is
not known, they are as fast as the winds of spring.

"It is Cuchulain that is coming, the young hero from
Muirthemne ; it is a pity for the man against whom he
is angered."

Then Liban asked him what he had done in the fight.
And Cuchulain said : "Fair, ruddy-faced men attacked

me on every side from the back of horses, the people of
Manannan, Son of the Sea, called there by Eochaid of
Inver; I gave them wound for wound. I threw my spear
at Eochaid Juil; it was not with the uncertain cast
of a man among mists I threw it. I heard his groan, and
its sound was friendly to me; if those who have spoken
have told the truth, it was that throw won the battle."

It was to the son, now, of this Eochaid Juil of the
Land of Promise, that Aebgreine, the daughter of
Naoise and Deirdre was given afterwards in marriage
by Manannan.

After that, Cuchulain stopped a month in that country
with Fand, and at the end of the month he bade her
farewell, and she said to him: "In whatever place you
tell me to go and meet you, I will go there." And the
place they settled to meet at was at Ibar Cinn Tracta,
the yew at the head of Baile's strand.

But when all this was told to Emer, there was great
anger on her, and she had knives made ready to kill the
woman with, and she came, and fifty young girls with
her, to the place where they had settled to meet.

Cuchulain and Laeg were playing chess there, and they
did not see the women coming. It was Fand saw them
first, and she said to Laeg: "Look, Laeg, at what I see."
"What is that?" said Laeg. Then he looked, and it is
what Fand said: "Look behind you, Laeg; there are
women listening to you, wise, with sharp, green knives in
their right hands, with gold at their well-shaped breasts;
they move as brave men do, going through a battle of
chariots. Well does Emer, daughter of Forgall, change
colour in her anger."

"No harm shall be done to you by her," said Cuchulain;
"and she shall not reach to you at all. Come into the
sunny seat of the chariot, opposite myself, for I will
defend you against all the many women of the four
points of Ulster; for though Forgall's daughter may

threaten," he said, "on the strength of her companions, to do some daring thing, it is surely not against me she will dare it."

Then Cuchulain said to Emer: "It is little I mind you, woman, in spite of my affection for you, more than any other man minds a woman. The spear in your shaking hand does not wound me, nor your weak, thin knife, nor your vain, gathered anger; for it would be a pity my strength to be put down by a woman's strength."

"I ask then," said Emer, "what was it led you, Cuchulain, to dishonour me before all the women of the province, and before all the women of Ireland, and before all honourable people in the same way? For it was under your shelter I came, and on the strength of your faithfulness; for although you threaten a great quarrel in your pride, it is certain, Cuchulain, you cannot put me away, even if you would try to do it."

"I ask you, Emer," said Cuchulain, "why I may not have my turn in the company of this woman; for in the first place she is well-behaved, comely, well-mannered, worthy of a king, this woman from beyond the waves of the great sea; with form and countenance and high descent; with embroidery and handiness, with sense and quickness; for there is not anything under the skies her husband could ask, but she would do it, even if she had not given her promise. And O Emer," he said, "you will never find any brave, comely man so good as myself."

"It is certain," said Emer, "that I will not refuse this woman if you follow her. But all the same, everything red is beautiful, everything new is fair, everything high is lovely, everything common is bitter, everything we are without is thought much of; everything we know is thought little of, till all knowledge is known. And O Cuchulain," she said, "I was at one time in esteem with you and I would be so again, if it were pleasing to you."

And grief came upon her, and overcame her. " By my word, now," said Cuchulain, " you are pleasing to me, and will be pleasing as long as I live."

" Let me be given up," said Fand. " It is better for me to be given up," said Emer. " Not so," said Fand, " it is I that will be given up in the end, and it is I that have been in danger of it all this time."

And great grief and trouble of mind came on Fand, because she was ashamed to be given up, and to have to go back to her home there and then; and the great love she had given Cuchulain troubled her; and so she was lamenting, and she made this complaint:

" It is I will go on the journey; I agree to it with great sorrow; though my father has so great a name, I would sooner stay with Cuchulain. It would be better for me to be here, to be under your rule without grief, than to go, though you may wonder at it, to the sunny house of Aedh Abrat.

" O Emer, the man is yours, and well may you wear him, for you are worthy; what my arm cannot reach, that at least I may wish well to.

" Many were the men asking for me, in the court and in country places; I never went to meet one of them, for it is myself was of right behaviour.

" A pity it is to give love to a man, and he to take no heed to it. It is better to be turned away, if you are not loved as you love.

" It was not right of you, Emer of the yellow hair, to take hold of Fand, to kill her in her misery."

Now all this was told to Manannan, that Fand, daughter of Aedh Abrat was fighting alone against the women of Ulster, and that Cuchulain was putting her away. Manannan came then from the east in search of her, and he was near them, and no one of them saw him but only Fand. And then great fear and trouble of mind came on her at seeing Manannan, and it is what she said:

"Look on the great son of the sea, from the plains of Eoghan of Inver; Manannan, lord of the fair hills of the world; there was a time when he was dear to me.

"He may even to-day be constant; my mind is no friend to jealousy.   There is a road love leads us in.

"The time I and the friend of Lugh were in the sunny palace of Dun Inver, we thought, without a doubt, that we should never be parted from one another.

"When Manannan the great married me, I was a wife worthy of him; he gave me a bracelet of heavy gold, as the price of my beauty.

"I see, coming over the sea, no earthly person sees him, the crested horseman of the high-maned waves; he has no need of long ships.

"As for me myself, because there is foolishness in the minds of women, the man I loved exceedingly has left me here astray.

"Farewell to you, beautiful Cuchulain; I go away from you with a kind heart.   Though I do not come back again, let me have your good will; all things are good in comparison with a parting.

"It is time for me to go away; there is one to whom it is not grief, but for all that, it is a great disgrace to me, O Laeg, son of Riangabra.

"It is with my own husband I will go, because he will do as I desire.   Look now at my going, that it may not be said I went away secretly."

Then Fand went over to Manannan, and Manannan bade her welcome, and he said: "Well, woman, is it after Cuchulain you will be going from this time, or is it with me you will go?"   "By my word now," said she, "there is one of you I would sooner follow than the other; but it is along with you I will go and I will not wait on Cuchulain, because he has left me.   And another thing," she said, "you have not a queen that is fitting for you, and that is what Cuchulain has."

But when Cuchulain saw the woman going away from him with Manannan, he said to Laeg: "What is that?" "It is Fand," said Laeg, "that is going to Manannan, Son of the Sea, because she was not pleasing to you."

It is then there was great anger on Cuchulain, and he went with great leaps southward to Luachair, the place of rushes; and he stopped for a long while without drink, without food, among the mountains, and where he slept every night, was on the road of Midluachan.

And when Emer heard that, she went to visit Conchubar in Emain Macha, and she told him the way Cuchulain was.

Then Conchubar sent the poets and the skilled men and the Druids of Ulster to visit him, that they might lay hold of him, and bring him to Emain Macha along with them. But when they came to him, he would have killed them, but the Druids did enchantment on him, until they had laid hold of him, and until his wits began to come back to him. Then he asked them for a drink, and the Druids gave him a drink of forgetfulness. From the moment he drank that drink, he did not remember Fand, and all the things he had done. And they gave a drink of forgetfulness to Emer as well, that she might forget her jealousy, for the state she was in was no better than his own.

And after that, Manannan shook his cloak between Cuchulain and Fand, the way they should never meet one another again.

XV

ADVICE TO A PRINCE

THERE was a meeting of the three provinces of Ireland held about this time in Teamhair, to try could they find some person to give the High Kingship of Ireland to; for they thought it a pity the Hill of the Lordship of Ireland, that is Teamhair, to be without the rule of a king on it, and the tribes to be without a king's government to judge their houses. For the men of Ireland had been without the government of a High King over them since the death of Conaire at Da Derga's Inn.

And the kings that met now at the court of Cairbre Niafer were Ailell and Maeve of Connaught, and Curoi, and Tigernach, son of Luchta, king of Tuathmumain, and Finn, son of Ross, king of Leinster. But they would not ask the men of Ulster to help them in choosing a king, for they were all of them against the men of Ulster.

There was a bull-feast made ready then, the same way as the time Conaire was chosen, to find out who was the best man to get the kingship.

After a while the dreamer screamed out in his sleep, and told what he saw to the kings. And what he saw this time, was a young strong man, with high looks, and with two red stripes on his body, and he sitting over the pillow of a man that was wasting away in Emain Macha.

294

A message was sent then with this account to Emain Macha. The men of Ulster were gathered at that time about Cuchulain, that was on his sick-bed. The messenger told his story to Conchubar and to the chief men of Ulster.

"There is a young man of good race and good birth with us now that answers to that account," said Conchubar; "that is Lugaid of the Red Stripes, son of Clothru, daughter of Eochaid Feidlech, the pupil of Cuchulain; and he is sitting by his pillow within, caring him, for he is on his sick-bed."

And when it was told Cuchulain that messengers were come for Lugaid, to make him King in Teamhair, he rose up and began to advise him, and it is what he said:

"Do not be a frightened man in a battle; do not be light-minded, hard to reach, or proud. Do not be ungentle, or hasty, or passionate; do not be overcome with the drunkenness of great riches, like a flea that is drowned in the ale of a king's house. Do not scatter many feasts to strangers; do not visit mean people that cannot receive you as a king. Do not let wrongful possession stand because it has lasted long, but let witnesses be searched to know who is the right owner of land. Let the tellers of history tell truth before you; let the lands of brothers and their increase be set down in their lifetime; if a family has increased in its branches, is it not from the one stem they are come? Let them be called up, let the old claims be established by oaths; let the heir be left in lawful possession of the place his fathers lived in; let strangers be driven off it by force.

"Do not use too many words. Do not speak noisily; do not mock, do not give insults, do not make little of old people. Do not think ill of any one; do not ask what is hard to give. Let you have a law of lending, a law of oppression, a law of pledging. Be obedient to the advice of the wise; keep in mind the advice of the old. Be a follower of the rules of your fathers. Do not be cold-hearted to friends; be strong towards your enemies; do not give evil for evil in your battles. Do not be given to too much talking. Do not speak any harm of others. Do not waste, do not scatter, do not do away with what is your own. When you do wrong, take the blame of it; do not give up the truth for any man. Do not be trying to be first, the way you will not be jealous; do not be an idler, that you may not be weak; do not ask too much, that you may not be thought little of. Are you willing to follow this advice, my son?"

Then Lugaid answered Cuchulain, and it is what he said: "As long as all goes well, I will keep to your words, and every one will know that there is nothing wanting in me; all will be done that can be done."

Then Lugaid went away with the messengers to Teamhair, and he was made king, and he slept in Teamhair that night. And after that all the people that had gathered there went to their own homes.

XVI

THE SONS OF DOEL DERMAIT

ONE time Cuchulain was gone west to Carraige, in the province of Connaught, and Lugaid of the Red Stripes with him, and Laeg. And one day they saw a young girl standing on the burial-hill of Tetach. " What is it you are wanting ? " said Lugaid. " I want Cuchulain, son of Sualtim," she said, " for I have set my love on him on account of his great deeds that I have heard of." "There he is, beyond," said Lugaid. Then she went over to him, and put her arms about his neck, and kissed him ; and she told him she was Finnchoem, daughter of Eocho Rond, king of Hy Maine.

Then Cuchulain took her into his keeping, and they travelled northward through the night, towards Emain. And one time in the darkness of the night, towards Fid Manach, they saw three fires in a wood before them, and nine men at every fire; outlaws they were, that were robbing the country. And Cuchulain killed three of them at every fire.

And in the morning they saw a troop of men coming towards them on the plain, and Finnchoem's father, the king of Hy Maine, leading them, and he having on him a four-folded crimson cloak, with four borders of gold, and a shield with eight borders of white bronze, and a gold-hilted sword at his side. And he had light yellow hair falling down on each side to the flanks of his grey-black horse ; and there was a gold chain of the weight of seven ounces hanging from his hair, and it was from that he took his name, Eocho Rond, that is, Eocho of the gold chain. And as soon as he saw Cuchulain, he threw his spear at him. But Cuchulain caught the spear and threw it back again, and it struck the horse in the neck, so that he reared up and threw his master. And Cuchulain lifted Eocho in his arms, and carried him as far as Cruachan, that they were near at the time, to leave him with Ailell and with Maeve. And there was great shame on the king of Hy Maine at what had happened.

And when Cuchulain was leaving him he said: " May you never have rest in sitting, or in lying down, until you find out what it was brought away the three sons of Doel Dermait, the Beetle of Forgetfulness, out of their own country."

And Cuchulain went on to Emain. But when he sat down in his place, it seemed to him the walls of the house and the ground under him to be on fire. Then he said to his people: " I think what Eocho Rond threatened me with is coming on me, and I will get my death if I do not do as he bade me."

Then he went back to his own place, Dundealgan, and out westward to Baile's strand. And there he saw a boat coming, and the king of Alban's son in it, and his people, and they bringing presents for king Conchubar, of purple, and of golden drinking-cups. And when they saw the three men on the strand, Cuchulain and Lugaid and Laeg, they said to them: " It is likely if the king knew we were here, he would send us food and drink by you." " Is it a steward you would make of me? " said Cuchulain, and anger came on him, and he took the sword in his hand to strike them. " Give us our life, Cuchulain, for we did not know you," said the king's son.

" Do you know what was it drove the three sons of Doel Dermait from their own country? " said Cuchulain.

"I do not know that," said the king's son. "But I have a sea charm, and I will set it for you, and I will give it to you, and you will find the knowledge you are looking for."

Then Cuchulain gave him his little spear, and scratched an Ogham on it, and said to him : "Set out now, and go and take my seat at Emain Macha."

Then they took the things out of the boat, and Cuchulain got in, and Lugaid of the Red Stripes, and Laeg ; and they put up the sail, and went on for a day and a night until they came to an island. It was a fine, large, beautiful island, having a silver wall about it, and a paling of bronze.

Then Cuchulain landed, and he saw a house with pillars of white bronze, and three times fifty beds in the house, and a chessboard, and a draughtboard, and a harp hanging over every bed. And he saw a grey king and queen in the house, with purple cloaks on them, worked with dark-coloured gold, and three young girls of the one age, having a dress worked with gold thread on each of them.

And the king gave them a friendly welcome, and he said : "Cuchulain is welcome to us for Lugaid's sake, and Laeg is welcome for his father and his mother's sake."

Then Cuchulain asked him did he know what was it drove the three sons of Doel Dermait out of their own country. "You will soon know that," he said, "for their sister and their sister's husband are in that island there to the south."

Then three pieces of iron were put in the fire, and when they were red-hot, the three young girls took them out, and put them in three vats, and Cuchulain and Lugaid and Laeg bathed in the vats. And they were brought cups of mead. And then they heard a noise of arms and of trumpets, and they saw fifty armed men coming to the house, and every two of them bringing a

pig and an ox, and every one a cup of mead of hazel
nuts. And then every man of them came again, and a
load of firing on his back; and then the oxen and the
pigs were cooked, and a feast for hundreds was given to
Cuchulain and his comrades.

And the next day they went on to the island where
the daughter of Doel Dermait was, and the boat went
on, steering itself, to the island. And Condla, son-in-law
of Doel Dermait, was lying on the strand, and his head
against a pillar at the east of the island, and his feet at
the west of the island, and every time he breathed, he
made a wave in the sea that turned the boat back. But
then he called out to Cuchulain: "Come to land, for
there is no fear of you on us; for however great your
anger may be, it is not in the prophecy that it is by you
this island will be destroyed." Then Cuchulain came to
land, and Condla and his wife bade him welcome. And
Cuchulain asked if they knew what it was had driven
the three sons of Doel Dermait from their own country.
"I know it," said the woman, "and I will show you
where they are, for it is foretold that their healing is to
come by you; and it is glad my true, warm heart would
be, they to be healed." And then she said: "Go to
where that wall is, and you will find Cairpre Cundail,
and he will bring you to the valley where they are kept
by Eocho Glas, the strong man."

So they went on to the wall, and they saw two
women that were cutting rushes, and Cuchulain said
to one of them: "What is the name of this country
I have come to?" And the woman rose up, and it
is what she said: "There are seven princes in this
country, and every one of them has had seven victories;
and there are seven women in this country, every one of
them having a king under her feet. And every one of
them has seven armies; and when a thief comes to this
place, he does not go back again to tell the story of it."

Then Cuchulain struck her down with his hand, and the other woman went away to tell Cairpre Cundail what had happened.

Cairpre Cundail came out then, and he and Cuchulain fought through the day, and neither got the better of the other. But at night Cairpre said: " That is enough, Cuchulain." And they left off for the night. And next morning Cairpre brought Cuchulain to the valley where Eocho Glas was, that he himself was always at war with. And Eocho Glas called out: " Is any one there of your miserable fighters?" "There is some one here," said Cuchulain. At that Eocho said: "That is not a voice that pleases me, for it is the voice of the angry man from Muirthemne."

Then he came out, and they fought together in the valley, and then they fought beside the sea. And in the end Cuchulain took the Gae Bulg and put it through him, and he fell, and Cuchulain struck his head off.

Then the prisoners of Eocho Glas came running from the hills on every side, east and west, and bathed themselves in his blood, for he had been doing them every sort of hurt and harm, and they all got healing.

And the three sons of Doel Dermait came with them, and were healed along with them, and they told their whole story to Cuchulain. And then they set out for their own country.

And Cuchulain went back the same way as he came; and he brought wonderful presents with him from Cairpre Cundail.

And when he got back to Ulster, he went on to Emain Macha, and his share of food and drink were waiting there for him yet. And he told his whole story to Conchubar and to the heroes of the Red Branch, and to Eocho Rond, king of Hy Maine; and that is the way he made his peace with him.

XVII

BATTLE OF ROSNAREE

THERE was a time, now, after the war for the Bull of Cuailgne, when King Conchubar got someway down-hearted, and there was a heaviness on his mind.

And the men of Ulster thought it might be lonesome he was, and fretting after Deirdre yet, and they searched about through the whole province for a wife for him.

And at last they found a beautiful young girl of good race, whose name was Luain, and they brought her to Emain Macha, and a great wedding was made, and great feasting ; and the king grew to be quiet and happy in his mind. But among the men that came to the wedding were the two sons of the poet Aithirne, that had such a bad name for covetousness and for cruelty.

The two sons were poets as well, Cuingedach and Abhartach, and when they saw Luain, Conchubar's queen, and she so beautiful, the two of them fell in love with her there and then. And they stopped at Emain, and after a while each of them tried to gain her secret love. But there was great anger and displeasure on Luain at that, and she drove them from her.

They went home then to their father, Aithirne, and the three of them, to avenge themselves on Luain, made satires on her, that brought blotches out on her face. And when her face that was so beautiful was spoiled like that, she went back and hid herself in her father's

302

house, and with the shame and the sorrow that were on her, she died there.

Then great anger and rage came on Conchubar, and he sent the men of Ulster to Aithirne's house, and they killed himself and his two sons, and they pulled his house down to the ground.

But the rest of the poets of Ulster were not well pleased that Conchubar should put such disrespect on one of themselves and do such a great vengeance on him, and they gathered together and gave Aithirne a great burial and keened him, and it was Amergin that made a lament over his grave.

And then Conchubar stopped in Emain Macha, and the cloud of trouble came on him again, and he used to be thinking of the war for the Bull of Cuailgne, and of all that Maeve's army did when he was in his weakness; and he did not sleep in the night, and there was no food that pleased him.

And then the men of Ulster bid Cathbad, the Druid, go to Conchubar, and rouse him out of his sickness.

So Cathbad went to him, and he cried tears down when he saw him, and he said: "Tell me, Conchubar, what wound it is or what sickness has weakened you and has made your face so pale?" "It is no wonder sickness to be on me," said Conchubar, "when I think of the way the four provinces of Ireland came and destroyed my forts and my duns and my walled towns and the houses of my people, and when I think how Maeve brought away cattle and gold and silver, and how she came as far as Dun Sescind and Dun Sobairce, and brought away Daire's bull out of my own province. And it is what vexes me, Maeve herself to have got away safe from the battle; and it is time for me to go and avenge that time on the men of Ireland," he said. "That is no right thing you are saying," said Cathbad, "for the men of Ulster did a good vengeance on the men of Ireland the time they gained the battle of Ilgaireth." "I do not count any battle to be a battle," said Conchubar, "unless a king or a queen has fallen in it; and I swear by the oath of my people, Cathbad," he said, "that kings and great men will be brought to their death by me, or else I myself will go to my death."

"This is my advice to you," said Cathbad, "not to set out till the winter is gone by; for at this time the winds are rough, and the roads are heavy, and the rivers are full and flooded, and every windy gap is cold. It is best to wait for the summer," he said, "till the fords are shallow and the roads are smooth, till the thick leaves on the bushes will be shelters, till every sod of grass will be a pillow, till our colts will be strong, till the nights will be short for keeping watch against an enemy. It is best to wait," he said, "till you can gather together the men of Ulster, and till you can send messengers to your friends among the Gall." "I am willing to do that," said Conchubar, "but I give my word," he said, "let them come, or let them not come, I will go myself to Teamhair to get satisfaction from Cairbre Niafer, my own son-in-law, that did not come to help me at the gathering at Ilgaireth, and to Lugaid, son of Curoi, and to Eocha, son of Luchta, and to Maeve, and to Ailell, till I throw down the stones over the graves of their chief men, till I destroy and lay waste their country, the same way as the men of Ireland destroyed my province."

So then Conchubar sent out messengers to Conall Cearnach, that was raising his tribute in the islands of Leodus, and of Cadd, and of Orc, and to the countries of the Gall, to Olaib, grandson of the king of Norway, and to Baire of the Scigger islands, and to Siugraid Soga, king of Sudiam; to the seven sons of Romra, and to the son of the king of Alban, and to the king of the island of Orc.

And the first to answer the messengers, and to set out

for Ulster was Conall Cearnach, for there was great anger on him when he heard of all that had happened in Ulster in the war for the Bull of Cuailgne, and he not in it. "And if I had been in it," he said, "the men of Connaught would not have taken spoil from Ulster, without an equal vengeance being measured to them again." And Olaib, grandson of the king of Norway, came with him, and Baire, of the Scigger islands, and their men with them in their ships; and they came through the green waves, and the seals and the sword-fishes rising about them, towards Dundealgan, and the place where they landed was at the Strand of Baile, son of Buan.

This, now, is the story of Baile that was buried at that strand.

He was of the race of Rudraige, and although he had but little land belonging to him, he was the heir of Ulster, and every one that saw him loved him, both man and woman, because he was so sweet-spoken; and they called him Baile of the Honey-Mouth. And the one that loved him best was Aillinn, daughter of Lugaidh, the King of Leinster's son. And one time she herself and Baile settled to meet one another near Dundealgan, beside the sea. Baile was the first to set out, and he came from Emain Macha, over Slieve Fuad, over Muir-themne, to the strand where they were to meet; and he stopped there, and his chariots were unyoked, and his horses were let out to graze. And while he and his people were waiting there they saw a strange, wild-looking man, coming towards them from the South, as fast as a hawk that darts from a cliff or as the wind that blows from off the green sea. "Go and meet him," said Baile to his people, "and ask him news of where he is going and where he comes from, and what is the reason of his haste." So they asked news of him, and he said: "I am going back now to Tuagh Inbhir, from Slieve Suidhe Laighen, and this is all the news I have, that Aillinn daughter of Lugaidh, was on her way to meet Baile, son of Buan, that she loved. And the young men of Leinster overtook her, and kept her back from going to him, and she died of the heartbreak there and then. For it was foretold by Druids that were friendly to them that they would not come together in their lifetime, but that after their death they would meet, and be happy for ever after." And with that he left them, and was gone again like a blast of wind, and they were not able to hinder him.

And when Baile heard that news, his life went out from him, and he fell dead there on the strand.

And at that time the young girl Aillinn was in her sunny parlour to the south, for she had not set out yet. And the same strange man came in to her, and she asked him where he came from. "I come from the North," he said, "from Tuagh Inver, and I am going past this place to Slieve Suidhe Laighen. And all the news I have," he said, "is that I saw the men of Ulster gathered together on the strand near Dundealgan, and they raising a stone, and writing on it the name of Baile, son of Buan, that died there when he was on his way to meet the woman he had given his love to ; for it was not meant for them ever to reach one another alive, or that one of them should see the other alive." And when he had said that he vanished away, and as to Aillinn, her life went from her, and she died the same way that Baile had died.

And an apple-tree grew out of her grave, and a yew-tree out of Baile's grave. And it was near that yew-tree Conall Cearnach landed, and Baire, and the grandson of the king of Norway. And Cuchulain had made ready a great feast for them, and for Conchubar that had come to meet them, at bright-faced Dundealgan.

And the Hound bade them a kind, loving welcome, and he said : " Welcome to those I know, and those I do not know, to the good and the bad, the young and the old among you." And they stopped there a week, and Conchubar was well pleased to see the whole strand full of his friends that were come in their ships. And then he bade farewell to Emer, daughter of Forgall, and he said to Cuchulain : " Go now to the three fifties of old fighting men, that are resting in their age, under Irgalach, son of Macclach, and say to them to come with me to this gathering and to this war, the way I will have their help and their advice." " Let them go to it if they have a mind," said Cuchulain ; " but it is not I that will go and ask it of them."

So then Conchubar himself went to the great house, where the old fighting men used to be living that had laid by their arms. And when he came in, they raised their heads from their places to look at the great king. And then they leaped up, and they said : " What has brought you to us to day, our chief and our lord ? " " Did you get no word," he said, " of the way the four provinces of Ireland came against us, and how they burned down our forts and our houses, and how they brought their makers of poems and of stories along with them, that their deeds might be told, and our disgrace might be the greater. And I am going out against them now," he said, " to get satisfaction from them ; and let you come with me, and I will have your advice." Then the hearts of the old men rose in them, and they caught their old horses and yoked their old chariots. And they went on with the king to the mouth of the Water of Luachann that night.

And the next day Conchubar set out with his own men and his friends from beyond the sea, to Slieve Breagh, that is near Rosnaree on the Boinne. And they made their camp at Cuanglas, the green harbour, and lighted their fires, and music and merry songs were made for them. But Cuchulain stopped behind in

Dundealgan to gather his own people, and to make provision for them on the march.

Now news had been brought to Cairbre Niafer at Teamhair, that Conchubar was gathering his men to get satisfaction for all that had been done to Ulster in the war for the Bull of Cuailgne, and that it was likely he himself would be the first he would come against.

For there was some bad feeling between Cairbre and the men of Ulster, since the time he drove the sons of Umor into Connaught, with the heavy rent he put on them, and that after Conall Cearnach and Cuchulain giving their own security for their good behaviour. They turned on their securities after that, and fought with them, and Conall Cool, the son of their chief, fell ; and Cuchulain, and his father, and his friends, raised the heap of stones over him that is called Carn Chonaill, in the province of Connaught.

And Cairbre sent a message to Cruachan, to say to Ailell and to Maeve : "If it is towards us Conchubar and the men of Ulster are coming, let you come to our help ; but if it is past us they go, into the fair-headed province of Connaught, we will go to your help." So when Conchubar came to Cuanglas, at Rosnaree, there was a good army gathered there to make a stand against him ; the three troops of the children of Deagha, and a great troop of the Collamnachs, and of the men of Bregia, and of the Gailiana. And he rose up early in the morning, and he could see the moving of men and the shining of spears, and he heard the noise of a great army, and he said : "We will send some one of our men to bring us word about them."

And he sent out Feic, son of Follaman. And Feic went up to a hill beside the Boinne, and he began to look at the army and to count it, and it vexed him to see how many were in it. "If I go back now and tell this," he said, "the men of Ulster will come and will begin the

battle, and there will be no better chance for me to get
a great name and do great deeds than for any other
man. And why would I not go and begin a fight now
by myself?" And with that he crossed the river.

But the men that were in front caught sight of him,
and the whole army began shouting around him, and he
had not courage to go against them, but he turned to
cross the river again. But he gave a false leap, just
where the water was deepest, and a wave laughed over
him, and he died.

It seemed a long time to Conchubar that he was
away, and he said to the men of Ulster: "What is
your advice to us about this battle?" "It is what we
advise," they said, "to wait till our strong fighters and
our chief men are come. And they had not long to
wait before they saw troops coming, Cathbad with
twelve hundred men, and Amergin with twelve hundred
men, and Eoghan, king of Fernmaighe, and Laegaire
Buadach, and the three sons of Conall Buide.

And then they saw another troop coming, and in the
front of it a fierce, brown man. Rough, dark hair he
had, and a big nose and hollow cheeks, and his talk
was quick and hurried. A blue cloak about him, and
a brooch of silver as white as a bird, a heavy sword,
and a shield with iron rims. And this is who he was,
Daire of Cuailgne, that was come to get satisfaction for
his bull and for his herds on the men of Ireland.
"What is delaying you here," he said to Conchubar.
"I have good reason for delaying," said Conchubar,
"for there is a great army under Cairbre Niafer before
us at Rosnaree, and there are not enough of us to go
against them. And it is not refusing a battle we are,
but waiting till we get our full number." "By my
word," said Daire, "if you do not go out against them,
it is I will go against them by myself."

Then Conchubar put on his armour, and took his

many-coloured shield, and his sword, the Ochain. And
all the men of Ulster gathered around him, and they
raised their spears and their shields, and it was like a
great river breaking from the side of a mountain, and
breaking what it meets of stones and trees before it, that
they went to meet the men of Leinster at Rosnaree on
the Boinne.

And when Cairbre Niafer and his friends and his
men saw them coming, they made ready for them, and
came towards the river.

And the men of Ulster crossed the river, and the two
armies met, and each of them took to hacking and
destroying the other. And the Gailiana pressed heavily
on the men of Ulster, and came in to the middle of
them, and cut them down like trees are cut in a wood.
And as for Conchubar he did not give back, where he
was, and Celthair on his right hand, and Amergin the
poet on his right hand again, and Eoghan, king of
Fernmaighe, on his left, and Daire of Cuailgne near him.
These few stood against the Gailiana, and fought
against them, stout and proud. But as to the young
men and those that were never in a fight before, they
turned round and burst through the battle northwards.

It was just then Conall Cearnach was coming in
his chariot, and when the young men of Ulster saw
the face of Conall, they came to a stop, and Conall
saw that they were beaten and running from the battle,
and he called out sharp words to them, for there was
anger on him, they to have left the fight, and with no
sign of blood or of wounds upon them.

But they were ashamed then, and content to go back
to the battle, when they had Conall's hand to help them ;
and each one of them tore a green branch off the oak
trees that were near them, and held it up, and they went
with him ; for they knew there would be no running
away in any place where Conall's face would be seen.

And it happened just at that time Conchubar, the High King, was taking three backward steps out of the battle northward, but when he saw the face of Conall coming towards him, he called to him to stop the army from falling back. " I give my word," said Conall, " I think it easier to fight the battle by myself than to stop the rout now."

And just then the three royal poets of the king of Teamhair came to give him their help, Eochaid the Learned, and Diarment of the Songs, and Forgel the Just, and they went into the fight against Conall. And Conall looked at them and he said : " I give my true word," he said, " if you were not poets and men of learning, you would have got your death by me before this ; and now that you are come fighting with your master," he said, " where is there any reason for sparing you ? " And with that he made a blow at them with a heavy stick that was in his hand, that struck the three heads off them.

Then Conall drew his sword out of its sheath, and he played the music of his sword on the armies of Leinster, and the sound of it was heard on every side ; and when the men near him heard it their faces whitened, and each one of them went back to his place in the battle. And at that time Cuchulain came into the battle, and the men of the Gailiana gave wild shouts at him, and anger came on him and he scattered them.

And strength came again into the hearts of the men of Ulster, and their anger rose, and the earth shook under their feet, and there was clashing of swords on both sides, and the shouting of young men, and the screams of old men, and the groaning of chariot-fighters, and the crying of ravens. And there were many lying in cold pools, the white soles of their feet close together, and the red lips turning grey, and the bright faces very pale, and darkness coming on their grey eyes, and confusion on their clear wits.

It is then Cuchulain met with Cairbre Niafer, and he went against him, and put his shield against his shield and there they were face to face. And Cairbre said words of insult to Cuchulain, and Cuchulain answered him back and said: "It is all I ask of you, to fight with me now alone." "I will do that," said Cairbre Niafer, "for I am a king in my way of living, and a champion in battles."

Then each attacked the other, and it was hard for them to hold their feet firm, or to strike with their hands, in the closeness of the fight. And Cairbre broke all his weapons, but nine of his men came and kept up the fight against Cuchulain till more weapons could be brought to him. And then Cuchulain's weapons were broken, and Cairbre and nine of his men came and held up their shields before him till Laeg could bring him his own right weapons, the Dubach, the grim one, his spear, and the Cruaidin, his sword. And then they took to hitting at one another again, and at last Cuchulain took his spear into his left hand, and struck at Cairbre with it, and he lowered his shield to protect his body. And then Cuchulain changed it to his right hand, and struck at him over the rim of his shield, and it went through his heart; and before his body could reach the ground, Cuchulain made a spring and struck his head off. And then he held up the head, and shook it before the two armies.

Then Sencha, son of Ailell, rose up and shook the branch of peace, and the men of Ulster stood still. As to the men of Leinster, when they saw their king was killed, they fell back; but Iriel of the Great Knees, the son of Conall Cearnach, followed after them, and did a great slaughter on the Gailiana and on the rest of the army till they reached to the Rye of Leinster.

And then the men of Ulster went back to their homes. And as to Conchubar, he went back to Emain, and it was not till a good while after that he got the wound in his head that Fintan sewed up with gold thread, to match the colour of his hair, and that brought him to his death in the end.

XVIII

THE ONLY SON OF AOIFE

THE time Cuchulain came back from Alban, after he had learned the use of arms under Scathach, he left Aoife, the queen he had overcome in battle, with child.

And when he was leaving her, he told her what name to give the child, and he gave her a gold ring, and bade her keep it safe till the child grew to be a lad, and till his thumb would fill it; and he bade her to give it to him then, and to send him to Ireland, and he would know he was his son by that token. She promised to do so, and with that Cuchulain went back to Ireland.

It was not long after the child was born, word came to Aoife that Cuchulain had taken Emer to be his wife in Ireland. When she heard that, great jealousy came on her, and great anger, and her love for Cuchulain was turned to hatred; and she remembered her three champions that he had killed, and how he had overcome herself, and she determined in her mind that when her son would come to have the strength of a man, she would get her revenge through him. She told Conlaoch her son nothing of this, but brought him up like any king's son; and when he was come to sensible years, she put him under the teaching of Scathach, to be taught the use of arms and the art of war. He turned out as apt a scholar as his father, and it was not long before he had learnt all Scathach had to teach.

Then Aoife gave him the arms of a champion, and bade him go to Ireland, but first she laid three commands on him: the first never to give way to any living person, but to die sooner than be made turn back; the second, not to refuse a challenge from the greatest champion alive, but to fight him at all risks, even if he was sure to lose his life; the third, not to tell his name on any account, though he might be threatened with death for hiding it. She put him under *geasa*, that is, under bonds, not to do these things.

Then the young man, Conlaoch, set out, and it was not long before his ship brought him to Ireland, and the place he landed at was Baile's Strand, near Dundealgan.

It chanced that at that time Conchubar, the High King, was holding his court there, for it was a convenient gathering-place for his chief men, and they were settling some business that belonged to the government of that district.

When word was brought to Conchubar that there was a ship come to the strand, and a young lad in it armed as if for fighting, and armed men with him, he sent one of the chief men of his household to ask his name, and on what business he was come.

The messenger's name was Cuinaire, and he went down to the strand, and when he saw the young man he said: " A welcome to you, young hero from the east, with the merry face. It is likely, seeing you come armed as if for fighting, you are gone astray on your journey; but as you are come to Ireland, tell me your name and what your deeds have been, and your victories in the eastern bounds of the world."

" As to my name," said Conlaoch, " it is of no great account; but whatever it is, I am under bonds not to tell it to the stoutest man living."

" It is best for you to tell it at the king's desire," said

Cuinaire, "before you get your death through refusing it, as many a champion from Alban and from Britain has done before now." "If that is the order you put on us when we land here, it is I will break it," said Conlaoch, "and no one will obey it any longer from this out."

So Cunaire went back and told the king what the young lad had said. Then Conchubar said to his people: "Who will go out into the field, and drag the name and the story out of this young man?" "I will go," said Conall, for his hand was never slow in fighting. And he went out, and found the lad angry and destroying, handling his arms, and they attacked one another with a great noise of swords and shouts, and they were gripped together, and fought for a while, and then Conall was overcome, and the great name and the praise that was on Conall, it was on the head of Conlaoch it was now.

Word was sent then to where Cuchulain was, in pleasant, bright-faced Dundealgan. And the messenger told him the whole story, and he said: "Conall is lying humbled, and it is slow the help is in coming; it is a welcome there would be before the Hound."

Cuchulain rose up then and went to where Conlaoch was, and he still handling his arms. And Cuchulain asked him his name and said: "It would be well for you, young hero of unknown name, to loosen yourself from this knot, and not to bring down my hand upon you, for it will be hard for you to escape death." But Conlaoch said: "If I put you down in the fight, the way I put down your comrade, there will be a great name on me; but if I draw back now, there will be mockery on me, and it will be said I was afraid of the fight. I will never give in to any man to tell the name, or to give an account of myself. But if I was not held with a command," he said, "there is no man in the world I would

sooner give it to than to yourself, since I saw your face.
But do not think, brave champion of Ireland, that I will
let you take away the fame I have won, for nothing."

With that they fought together, and it is seldom such
a battle was seen, and all wondered that the young lad
could stand so well against Cuchulain.

So they fought a long while, neither getting the
better of the other, but at last Cuchulain was charged
so hotly by the lad that he was forced to give way,
and although he had fought so many good fights, and
killed so many great champions, and understood the
use of arms better than any man living, he was pressed
very hard.

And he called for the Gae Bulg, and his anger came
on him, and the flames of the hero-light began to shine
about his head, and by that sign Conlaoch knew him to
be Cuchulain, his father. And just at that time he was
aiming his spear at him, and when he knew it was
Cuchulain, he threw his spear crooked that it might
pass beside him. But Cuchulain threw his spear, the
Gae Bulg, at him with all his might, and it struck the
lad in the side and went into his body, so that he fell to
the ground.

And Cuchulain said : " Now, boy, tell your name and
what you are, for it is short your life will be, for you will
not live after that wound."

And Conlaoch showed the ring that was on his
hand, and he said : "Come here where I am lying
on the field, let my men from the east come round me.
I am suffering for revenge. I am Conlaoch, son of the
Hound, heir of dear Dundealgan ; I was bound to this
secret in Dun Scathach, the secret in which I have found
my grief."

And Cuchulain said : " It is a pity your mother not
to be here to see you brought down. She might have
stretched out her hand to stop the spear that wounded

you." And Conlaoch said: "My curse be on my mother, for it was she put me under bonds; it was she sent me here to try my strength against yours." And Cuchulain said: "My curse be on your mother, the woman that is full of treachery; it is through her harmful thoughts these tears have been brought on us." And Conlaoch said: "My name was never forced from my mouth till now; I never gave an account of myself to any man under the sun. But, O Cuchulain of the sharp sword, it was a pity you not to know me the time I threw the slanting spear behind you in the fight."

And then the sorrow of death came upon Conlaoch, and Cuchulain took his sword and put it through him, sooner than leave him in the pain and the punishment he was in.

And then great trouble and anguish came on Cuchulain, and he made this complaint:

"It is a pity it is, O son of Aoife, that ever you came into the province of Ulster, that you ever met with the Hound of Cuailgne.

"If I and my fair Conlaoch were doing feats of war on the one side, the men of Ireland from sea to sea would not be equal to us together. It is no wonder I to be under grief when I see the shield and the arms of Conlaoch. A pity it is there is no one at all, a pity there are not hundreds of men on whom I could get satisfaction for his death.

"If it was the king himself had hurt your fair body, it is I would have shortened his days.

"It is well for the House of the Red Branch, and for the heads of its fair army of heroes, it was not they that killed my only son.

"It is well for Laegaire of Victories it is not from him you got your heavy pain.

"It is well for the heroes of Conall they did not join in the killing of you; it is well that travelling across the plain of Macha they did not fall in with me after such a fight.

"It is well for the tall, well-shaped Forbuide; well for Dubthach, your Black Beetle of Ulster.

"It is well for you, Cormac Conloingeas, your share of arms gave no help, that it is not from your weapons he got his wound, the hard-skinned shield or the blade.

"It is a pity it was not one on the plains of Munster, or in Leinster of the sharp blades, or at Cruachan of the rough fighters, that struck down my comely Conlaoch.

"It is a pity it was not in the country of the Cruithne, of the fierce Fians, you fell in a heavy quarrel, or in the country of the Greeks, or in some other place of the world, you died, and I could avenge you.

"Or in Spain, or in Sorcha, or in the country of the Saxons of the free armies; there would not then be this death in my heart.

"It is very well for the men of Alban it was not they that destroyed your fame; and it is well for the men of the Gall.

"Och! It is bad that it happened; my grief! it is on me is the misfortune, O Conlaoch of the Red Spear, I myself to have spilled your blood.

"I to be under defeat, without strength. It is a pity Aoife never taught you to know the power of my strength in the fight.

"It is no wonder I to be blinded after such a fight and such a defeat.

"It is no wonder I to be tired out, and without the sons of Usnach beside me.

"Without a son, without a brother, with none to come after me; without Conlaoch, without a name to keep my strength.

"To be without Naoise, without Ainnle, without Ardan; is it not with me is my fill of trouble?

"I am the father that killed his son, the fine green branch ; there is no hand or shelter to help me.

"I am a raven that has no home ; I am a boat going from wave to wave ; I am a ship that has lost its rudder; I am the apple left on the tree; it is little I thought of falling from it; grief and sorrow will be with me from this time."

Then Cuchulain stood up and faced all the men of Ulster. "There is trouble on Cuchulain," said Conchubar; "he is after killing his own son, and if I and all my men were to go against him, by the end of the day he would destroy every man of us. Go now," he said to Cathbad, the Druid, "and bind him to go down to Baile's Strand, and to give three days fighting against the waves of the sea, rather than to kill us all."

So Cathbad put an enchantment on him, and bound him to go down. And when he came to the strand, there was a great white stone before him, and he took his sword in his right hand, and he said : "If I had the head of the woman that sent her son to his death, I would split it as I split this stone." And he made four quarters of the stone.

Then he fought with the waves three days and three nights, till he fell from hunger and weakness, so that some men said he got his death there. But it was not there he got his death, but on the plain of Muirthemne.

XIX

THE GREAT GATHERING AT MUIRTHEMNE

NOW after all the battles Cuchulain had fought, and
all the men he had killed, it is no wonder he had
a good share of enemies watching to get the upper hand
of him.   And besides Maeve, those that had their minds
most set against him were Erc, son of Cairbre Niafer,
that he had killed at Rosnaree, and Lugaid, son of
Curoi, that he had killed at his own house in Munster,
and the three daughters of Calatin.

This, now, was the way it happened that Curoi got
his death by him.   He met with Blanad one time, a
good while after Curoi had given him the championship
of Ulster, and it is what she told him that there was not
a man on the face of the earth she loved more than himself.   And she bade him come, near Samhain time,
to Curoi's dun at Finglas, and his men with him, and to
bring her away by force.

So when the time came, Cuchulain set out, and his
men with him, and they came to a wood near the dun,
that had a stream running through it, and he sent word
to Blanad he was waiting there.   And Blanad sent him
back word to come and bring her away at whatever time
he would see the stream in the wood turning white.   And
when what she thought to be a good time came, when
all the men of the place were sent out looking for stones
to build a great new dun, she milked the three white

cows with red ears Curoi had brought away by force
from her father, Midhir, into the cauldron he had
brought away with them, and she poured a great vessel
of new milk into the stream, where it ran by the dun.
And when Cuchulain saw the stream turning white, he
went up to the dun. But he found Curoi there before
him, and they fought, and Curoi was killed, the son of
Daire, lord of the southern sea, that had a great name
and great praise on him before Blanad was his wife.

Then Cuchulain brought Blanad away with him to
Ulster. But Curoi's poet, Feirceirtne, followed after
them to avenge his master's death. And when they
were come as far as the headland of Cian Beara, he
saw Blanad standing on the edge of a high rock, and
she alone. And he went up to her, and took her in his
arms, and threw her, and himself along with her, over
the rock, and they both got their death by the fall on
the moment.

And as to the children of Calatin, this is the way it
was with them. At the time Cuchulain made an end of
Calatin at the ford, and of all his sons with him, Calatin's
wife was with child. And when her time came, there
were three daughters born at the one birth, and they deformed, and each of them having but one eye.

Then Maeve came from Cruachan to visit them, and
she brought away the children with her, and took the
charge of them. And when they were come to sensible
years, she came to see them, and she said : " Do you know
who it was killed your father ? " " We know well," they
said, " it was Cuchulain, son of Sualtim, killed him."
" That is so," said Maeve, " and let you make a journey
now," she said, " through the whole world, to get knowledge of spells and enchantments from them that have it,
the way you will be able to avenge your father when the
time comes."

When the three one-eyed daughters of Calatin heard

that, they went out into Alban, and to every other country, from the rising to the setting of the sun, and they were learning every sort of enchantment and of witchcraft. And at the end they came back to Cruachan.

And as to Maeve, she went up one morning to her sunny parlour, and from there she saw the three daughters of Calatin sitting outside on the lawn. So she took her cloak, that had beautiful embroidery on it, and put it about her, and she went out on the lawn and bade them welcome, and she sat down before them, and asked news of all they had done since they left Ireland. And they told her all they had learned. "Do you remember it all?" said Maeve. "We remember it well," they said, "and we can do many things, and we can make the appearance of terrible battles by secret words."

Maeve brought them then into the royal house, and they were attended on, and they were given every sort of food and of drink, and of good treatment.

And then Maeve sent word to Lugaid, and he came to Cruachan, and himself and Maeve began to talk together. "Do you remember," she said, "who it was killed Curoi your father?" "I remember it well," he said; "it was Cuchulain killed him." Then Erc came to her, and she asked him the same question about his father Cairbre Niafer, and he made the same answer. "What you say is true," Maeve said then, "and the children of Calatin are come back to me now, after going through the whole world, to fight against Cuchulain with their enchantments. And there is no king or chief man, or fighting man in the four provinces of Ireland, but lost his friend or his comrade, his father or his brother, by him in the war for the Bull of Cuailgne, or at some other time. And now," she said, "it is best for us to gather together a great army of the men of Ireland to make an attack on him, for the men of Ulster have their weakness coming on them, and it is likely they will not be able to help him."

With that, Lugaid went away southward to the king of Munster, to bid him come, and bring his men with him; and Erc went and called to the chief men of Leinster in the same way.

Then all the provinces gathered together to Cruachan, and they stopped there with feasting and merriment for three days and three nights. And at the end of that time they went out of Cruachan. But Maeve did not bring Fergus with them this time, for she was sure the men of Ireland would never be able to make an end of Cuchulain if Fergus was along with them.

And this is the way they went, beyond Magh Finn to Athluain, and they rested there that night.

And the next day they went on their road till they came to Glean-na-loin, and from that to Glean-mor, and from that to Tailtin, and they stopped the night there; and then they went on by the borders of Magh Breagh, and Midhe, and Treathfa, and Cuailgne.

It is then Conchubar, King of Ulster, got word that the borders of his province were being robbed and destroyed by the men of Munster and Leinster, and of Connaught.

"Where is Levarcham?" said Conchubar. "I am here," she said. "Go out for me now," said Conchubar, "and bring Cuchulain here to Emain; for it is against him this army we have news of is gathered. Bid him to make no delay, but to leave Dundealgan and Muirthemne and to come here to advise with myself, and with Cathbad and Amergin, and all the knowledgeable men. For if he can put off this battle till I myself, and Conall, and all the men of Ulster, will be ready to go out with him, we will give them a great defeat, the way they will not come into my province again. For there are many bear him ill-will," he said, "on account of all he killed. Finn, son of Ross, Fraoch, son of Idath, and Dearg, son of Conroi, and many of the best men of Ulster; and

Cairbre Niafer at the battle of Rosnaree ; and Curoi, son
of Daire, High King of Munster, and many of the men of
Munster besides him ; Fircearna, and Fiamain, and Niall,
and Laoc Leathbuine, and many more along with them."

Levarcham went quickly then with that message, and
it is where she found Cuchulain, between sea and land,
on Baile's Strand, and he trying to bring down sea-birds
with his sling ; but with all the birds that were flying
over him and past him, he could not bring one down,
but they all escaped him.

And there was heaviness on him, not to be able to hit
them, for he knew it had some bad meaning. And indeed he had never been very happy in his mind since the
death of the blossomed branch, Aoife's son, there on that
strand. Then he saw Levarcham coming, and he bade
her welcome. "I am glad of that welcome," said
Levarcham, "and it with news from Conchubar I am
come to you." "What is your news?" said Cuchulain.
"I have news indeed," she said. And then she told him
all that Conchubar had said, from beginning to end.
"And it is what all are asking of you," she said : "chief
men and fighting men, poets and learned men, women
and young girls, to keep aside from the men of Ireland
that are coming here to Muirthemne, and not to go out
alone against that great army." "I would sooner stop
here and defend my own place," said Cuchulain. "It is
best for you to go to Emain," said Laeg. So after a while
he gave in to them, and they went back to Dundealgan,
and Emer came out on the lawn to meet them, and they
gave her the same advice, to go to Emain Macha where
Conchubar and his chief men were gathered together.
Then Emer got her chariot, and she sent her servants
and the herds, and the cattle to Slieve Cuilenn in the
North, and herself and Cuchulain set out for Emain.
And that was the first time Dundealgan was emptied
since Cuchulain had the sway over it.

And when Cuchulain came to Emain Macha, they brought him to the bright, sunny house. And when the women of the place heard he was there, they came and spoke sweet words, and the poets and the harpers came, and the skilled men, and they all made music, and feasting, and pleasant talk round about Cuchulain, in the wide, white, sunny house of the Red Branch ; for what always quieted Cuchulain best was the singing of songs and rhymes before him. It is that way Scumac, the story-teller, quieted him one time he was vexed, and had a mind to set fire to Emain, because Conchubar had gone to a feast given by Conall, son of Gleo Glas, in Cuailgne, and had left no word for him to follow.

And Conchubar bade Cathbad, and the learned men, and the women, to keep a good watch on Cuchulain, and to mind him well. "For I leave the charge of him on you," he said, "to save him from the plans Maeve has made against him, and from the power of the children of Calatin. For if he should fall," he said, "it is certain the safety and the prosperity of Ulster will fall with him for ever." "That is true," said Cathbad, and all the others said the same.

"Well," said Geanann, Cathbad's son, " I will go now and see him." He went then to the place Cuchulain and Emer were, and the poets, and the women, and the learned men with them, and a feast laid out on the table, and all of them at drinking and pleasantness and games.

Now as to the men of Ireland, they came to the plain of Muirthemne, and they made their camp there, and they began to destroy and to take all they could find there, and in Macaire Conall ; and when they knew Cuchulain had left Dundealgan, it is then the three daughters of Calatin went with the lightness and the quickness of the wind to Emain Macha. And they sat down on the lawn outside the house where Cuchulain was, and they began to tear up the earth and the grass, and by means

of their witchcraft they put the appearance of troops of
men and of armies on stalks and coloured oak-leaves,
and little fuzz-balls ; and the sounds of fighting and striking, and the shouting of a great army were heard on
every side, as if there was an attack being made on the
dun.

It was bright-faced Geanann, son of Cathbad, was
keeping a watch on Cuchulain that day, and he saw
him sit up and look out on the lawn, and redness and
shame came on his face, when he saw, as he thought,
two armies fighting one another, and he put out his
hand as if to take his sword, but Geanann threw his two
arms about him and hindered him, and told him there
was nothing before him but witchcraft and enchantment,
and the appearance of fighting made up by the children
of Calatin to bring him out to his death. And Cathbad
and all the learned men came then and told him the
same thing. But after all that, it was hardly they were
able to hold him back and to persuade him.

The next day Cathbad himself came to keep a watch
on him with the rest, and after a while the noise of
shouting began again, and for all they could do, Cuchulain went and looked out at the window. And the first
thing he thought he saw was the army of Ireland standing there upon the plain. And then he thought he saw
Gradh, son of Lir, standing there ; and after that he
thought he heard the harp of the son of Meardha playing
the sweet music of the Sidhe, and he knew when he
heard those sounds that his time was come, and that his
courage and his strength would soon be made an end
of. And then one of the daughters of Calatin took the
appearance of a crow, and came flying over him and
saying mocking words, and she bade him go out and
save his own house and his lands from the enemies that
were destroying them. And though Cuchulain knew
well by this time it was witchcraft was being worked

against him, he was as ready as before to rush out when
he heard the sounds and the shouting of battle ; and
there came trouble and confusion on his mind with the
noise of striking and of fighting, and with the sweet
sounds of the harp of the Sidhe. But Cathbad did his
best with him, and it is what he told him, that if he
would but stop quiet for another three days in Emain,
the power of the enchantments would be broken, and
Conall Cearnach would have come to his help, and he
could go out again, and the whole world would be
full of his name and of his lasting victories.

And the women of Emain and the musicians closed
round him, and they sang sweet songs, and led away
his mind from what he had heard, until the day drew
to a close.

And on the morning of the morrow, Conchubar called
for Cathbad and Bright-Faced Geanann, and the rest
of the Druids. And Emer came along with them, and
Celthair's daughter, Niamh, that Cuchulain loved, and
the rest of the women of the House of the Red Branch.
And Conchubar asked them in what way they could
best keep a watch on Cuchulain through the day. "We
do not know that," they said. "I will tell you what is
best to do," said Conchubar then. "Bring him away
with you to Glean-na-Bodhar, the Deaf Valley. For
if all the men of Ireland were letting out shouts and
cries of war around it, no one that would be in that valley
would hear any sound at all. Bring Cuchulain there,
then," he said, "and keep him there with you till their
enchantments will be spent, and till Conall Cearnach
will come to his help out of the island of Leodus."
"King," said Niamh, "we were asking him and persuading
him all through yesterday to go to that valley, but he
would not go there, for all I myself or the rest of the
women of Ireland could say. And let you yourself go to
him now," she said, "with Cathbad, and Geanann, and the

poets, and with Emer, and let you bring him into that valley, and let there be music and pleasantness made about him there, the way he will not hear the shouts and the mocking words of the children of Calatin." It is not I will go with him," said Emer, "but let Niamh go, and my blessing with her, for it will be hard for him to refuse her." So they agreed to that, and they went to where Cuchulain was, and Conchubar's harper, Cobhtach, went along with them, making sweet music. Then Cathbad went out to Cuchulain where he was lying on the bed, and he began to ask him and to persuade him. "Dear son," he said, "come with me to-day to use the feast I am making, and all the women and the poets will come with us. And there are bonds on you not to refuse my feast." "My grief for that," said Cuchulain. "This is no fit time for me to be feasting and making merry, and the four provinces of Ireland burning and destroying Ulster, and the men of Ulster in their weakness, and Conall away, and the men of Ireland putting insults on me and reproaches, and saying I have run away before them. And but for yourself and Conchubar," he said, "and for Geanann and Amergin, I would fall on them and scatter them, that their dead would be more than their living." Then all the women persuaded him, and Emer spoke to him, and it is what she said : "Little Hound, I never hindered you until this hour from any deed or any adventure you had a mind for. So now, for my sake, my choice sweetheart, my first love and first darling of the men of the world, go with Cathbad and with Geanann, with Niamh and with the poets, to share Cathbad's feast."

Then Niamh went over to him and gave him three fond, loving kisses ; and then they all rose up, and he rose along with them, heavy and sorrowful, and in that way he went in their company into Glean-na-Bodhar. And when they came into it, he said : "My grief! I ever to have come here, and I never came to any place I liked less than this: for now the men of Ireland will be saying it was to escape them I came here." "You gave me your word," said Niamh, "you would not go out to meet the men of Ireland without leave from me." If I gave it," said Cuchulain, "it is right for me to hold to it."

Their chariots were unyoked then, and the Grey of Macha and the Black Sainglain were let loose to graze in the valley, and they all went to the house Cathbad had made ready. And there was a great feast laid out, and Cuchulain was put in the chief place, and to his right hand were Cathbad and Geanann and the poets, and on the left was Niamh, daughter of Celthair, with the women. And opposite them were the musicians and the reciters. And then they all took to feasting and drinking and to games, and they made a great show of mirth and pleasantness before Cuchulain.

But as to the three deformed, one-eyed children of Calatin, they came quickly and lightly, the way they had come on the other days, to the lawn at Emain, to the place where they had got sight of Cuchulain in the house. And when they did not see him there, they searched through the whole of Emain, but when they did not find him with Conchubar, or with the men of the Red Branch, there was great wonder on them. And then they began to think it was Cathbad was hiding him from them, and they rose up high in the air, on a blast of moaning wind they made by their enchantments, and on it they went over the whole province, searching out every wood and valley, every cave and secret path. But they found nothing, till at last they came over Glean-na-Bodhar, and there in the middle of the valley they saw the Grey of Macha and the Black Sainglain and Laeg, son of Riangabra, beside them.

They knew then that Cuchulain must be in the valley, and presently they heard the sounds of music and of laughter and of women's voices, where all the people in the feasting-house were trying their best to raise the cloud and the heaviness off Cuchulain's mind.

Then the children of Calatin came down into the valley, and the same way as before they took thistle-stalks and little fuzz-balls and withered leaves, and put on them the appearance of troops of armed men, so that there seemed to be no hill or no place outside the whole valley but was filled with battalions, coming hundred by hundred. And the air was all filled with sounds of battle and shouts, and of trumpets and dreadful laughter, and the cries of wounded men. And there seemed to be fires in the country about, and a noise of the crying of women. And great dread came on all that heard that outcry, both men and women, and dogs of every kind.

But when the women that were with Cuchulain heard those shouts, they shouted back again and raised their voices, but with all they could do, they did not keep the outcry from reaching to Cuchulain. " My grief ! " he said, " I hear the shouts of the men of Ireland that are spoiling the whole of the province ; my fame is at an end, my great name is gone from me, Ulster is put down for ever." "Let the noise pass by," said Cathbad ; " it is only the noise made by the children of Calatin, that want to draw you out from where you are, to make an end of you. Stop here with us now, and put the trouble off your mind."

Cuchulain stayed quiet then, but the children of Calatin went on a long time filling the air with battle noises. But they tired of it at last, for they saw that Cathbad and the women were too much for them.

Then anger came on Badb, one of Calatin's daughters, and she said : "Go on now, making sounds of fighting in the air, and I myself will go into the valley ; for even if I get my death by it, I will speak with Cuchulain."

With that, she went on in the madness of her anger

to the very house where the feast was going on, and there she took the appearance of a woman of Niamh's women, and she beckoned Niamh out to speak with her.

So Niamh came out, thinking she had news to give her, and a good many of the other women of Emain with her, and Badb bade them follow her. And she led them a long way down the valley, and then by her enchantments she raised a thick mist between them and the house, so that they could not find their way, but were astray in the valley, not knowing where they were.

Then she went back to the feasting-house, and she put on herself the appearance of Niamh, and she came in to where Cuchulain was and called out: "Rise up, Cuchulain; Dundealgan is burned, Muirthemne is destroyed, and Conaille Muirthemne. The whole province is trampled down by the men of Ireland. And it is on myself the blame will be laid," she said, "and all Ulster will say that I hindered you, and kept you back from going out to check the army, and to get satisfaction from the men of Ireland. And it is from Conchubar himself I will get my death on account of that," she said. For she knew Cuchulain had given Niamh his promise that without leave from her, he would not go out to face the men of Ireland.

"My grief!" said Cuchulain then, "it is hard to trust in women. For I thought," he said, "that you would not have given me that leave for the whole riches of the world. But since you yourself give me leave to go out and face the men of Ireland, I will do it." And with that he rose up to go out. And as he rose up, he threw his cloak about him, and his foot caught in the cloak, and the gold brooch that was in the cloak fell on his foot and pierced it. "Truly the brooch is a friend that gives me a warning," said Cuchulain.

He went out then, and he bade Laeg to yoke the horses and to make ready the chariot. And Cathbad,

and Geanann, and the women followed him out, and took
hold of him, but they were not able to stop him. For
the cries of battle were still in the air, and he thought he
saw a great army standing on the lawn at Emain, and
the whole plain filled up and crowded with troops and
bands of men, with horses and arms and armour, and he
thought he heard great shouts, and that he saw all
Conchubar's city burning, and all the hills round about
Emain full of things brought away, and he thought he
saw Emer's sunny house thrown down, and the House of
the Red Branch in one blaze, and all Emain under fire
and smoke. And Cathbad tried to quiet him. "Dear
son," he said, "for this day only, follow my advice, and
do not go out against the men of Ireland, and I will be
able to save you from all the enchantments of the
children of Calatin." But Cuchulain said: "Dear master,
there is no reason for me to care for my life from this
out, for my time is at an end, and Niamh has given me
leave to go and face the men of Ireland." And then
Niamh herself came up to him and said: "My grief!
my little Hound, I would never have given you that
leave for all the riches of the world; and it was not I
that gave you leave, but Badb, the daughter of Calatin,
that took my shape on her. And stay with me now," she
said, "my friend, my darling." But Cuchulain would not
believe her, and he bade Laeg yoke the chariot, and put
his arms in order. Laeg went to do that, but indeed
that time above all others he had no mind for the work.
And when he shook the bridles towards the horses as he
was used to do, they went away from him; and the Grey
of Macha would not let him come near him at all.
"Truly," said Laeg, "this is a warning of some bad
thing. And indeed, my life," he said to the Grey, "it
is seldom you would not come to meet the bridle and
to meet myself, up to this day." Then he went to
Cuchulain and said: "I swear by the gods my people

swear by, that if all the men in the province of Ulster
were round about the Grey of Macha, they would not
be able to bring him as far as the chariot, and I never
refused you up to this," he said, "and come out now and
speak to the Grey yourself."

So Cuchulain went out, and the horse turned his left
side three times to his master. Then he reproached the
horse. "You were not used," he said, "to behave like
that to me." Then the Grey of Macha came up to him
and he let big, round tears of blood fall on Cuchulain's
feet.

Then the chariot was yoked; and it was the Morrigu
had unyoked it and had broken it the night before, for she
did not like Cuchulain to go out and to get his death in
the battle. And Cuchulain set out and came to Emain,
and to the house where Emer was, and she came out and
bade him come down from his chariot. "I will not," he
said, "until I go first to Muirthemne, to attack the four
great provinces of Ireland, and to avenge all the hurts
and the insults they have put on me, and on Ulster, for
I have seen their gatherings and their armies." "Those
were made up by enchantments," said Emer. "I tell
you, woman," he said, "and I swear by my word, I will
never come back here until I have made an attack upon
them in their camp."

Then he turned his chariot towards the south, by the
road of Meadhon Luachair, and Levarcham cried out
after him, and the three times fifty queens that were in
Emain Macha, and that loved him, cried out upon him
miserably, and struck their hands together, for they knew
he would not come back to them again.

XX

DEATH OF CUCHULAIN

CUCHULAIN went on then to the house of his mother, Dechtire, to bid her farewell. And she came out on the lawn to meet him, for she knew well he was going out to face the men of Ireland, and she brought out wine in a vessel to him, as her custom was when he passed that way. But when he took the vessel in his hand, it was red blood that was in it. "My grief!" he said, "my mother Dechtire, it is no wonder others to forsake me, when you yourself offer me a drink of blood." Then she filled the vessel a second, and a third time, and each time when she gave it to him, there was nothing in it but blood.

Then anger came on Cuchulain, and he dashed the vessel against a rock, and broke it, and he said: "The fault is not in yourself, my mother Dechtire, but my luck is turned against me, and my life is near its end, and I will not come back alive this time from facing the men of Ireland." Then Dechtire tried hard to persuade him to go back and to wait till he would have the help of Conall. "I will not wait," he said, "for anything you can say; for I would not give up my great name and my courage for all the riches of the world. And from the day I first took arms till this day, I have never drawn back from a fight or a battle. And it is not now I will begin to draw back," he said, "for a great name outlasts life."

Then he went on his way, and Cathbad, that had followed him, went with him. And presently they came to a ford, and there they saw a young girl, thin and white-skinned and having yellow hair, washing and ever washing, and wringing out clothing that was stained crimson red, and she crying and keening all the time. "Little Hound," said Cathbad, "do you see what it is that young girl is doing? It is your red clothes she is washing, and crying as she washes, because she knows you are going to your death against Maeve's great army. And take the warning now and turn back again." "Dear master," said Cuchulain, "you have followed me far enough; for I will not turn back from my vengeance on the men of Ireland that are come to burn and to destroy my house and my country. And what is it to me, the woman of the Sidhe to be washing red clothing for me? It is not long till there will be clothing enough, and armour and arms, lying soaked in pools of blood, by my own sword and my spear. And if you are sorry and loth to let me go into the fight, I am glad and ready enough myself to go into it, though I know as well as you yourself I must fall in it. Do not be hindering me any more, then," he said, "for, if I stay or if I go, death will meet me all the same. But go now to Emain, to Conchubar and to Emer, and bring them life and health from me, for I will never go back to meet them again. It is my grief and my wound, I to part from them! And O Laeg!" he said, "we are going away under trouble and under darkness from Emer now, as it is often we came back to her with gladness out of strange places and far countries."

Then Cathbad left him, and he went on his way. And after a while he saw three hags, and they blind of the left eye, before him in the road, and they having a venomous hound they were cooking with charms on rods of the rowan tree. And he was going by them, for he knew it was not for his good they were there.

But one of the hags called to him : " Stop a while with us, Cuchulain." " I will not stop with you," said Cuchulain. " That is because we have nothing better than a dog to give you," said the hag. " If we had a grand, big cooking-hearth, you would stop and visit us ; but because it is only a little we have to offer you, you will not stop. But he that will not show respect for the small, though he is great, he will get no respect himself."

Then he went over to her, and she gave him the shoulder-blade of the hound out of her left hand, and he ate it out of his left hand. And he put it down on his left thigh, and the hand that took it was struck down, and the thigh he put it on was struck through and through, so that the strength that was in them before left them.

Then he went down the road of Meadhon-Luachair, by Slieve Fuad, and his enemy, Erc, son of Cairbre, saw him in the chariot, and his sword shining red in his hand, and the light of his courage plain upon him, and his hair spread out like threads of gold that change their colour on the edge of the anvil under the smith's hand, and the Crow of Battle in the air over his head.

" Cuchulain is coming at us," said Erc to the men of Ireland, " and let us be ready for him." So they made a fence of shields linked together, and Erc put a couple of the men that were strongest here and there, to let on to be fighting one another, that they might call Cuchulain to them ; and he put a Druid with every couple of them, and he bid the Druid to ask Cuchulain's spears of him, for it would be hard for him to refuse a Druid. For it was in the prophecy of the children of Calatin that a king would be killed by each one of those spears in that battle.

And he bid the men of Ireland to give out shouts, and Cuchulain came against them in his chariot, doing his three thunder feats, and he used his spear and his sword in such a way, that their heads, and their hands, and their feet, and their bones, were scattered through the plain of Muirthemne, like the sands on the shore, like the stars in the sky, like the dew in May, like snow-flakes and hailstones, like leaves of the trees, like buttercups in a meadow, like grass under the feet of cattle on a fine summer day. It is red that plain was with the slaughter Cuchulain made when he came crashing over it.

Then he saw one of the men that was put to quarrel with the other, and the Druid called to him to come and hinder them, and Cuchulain leaped towards them. "Your spear to me," cried the Druid. "I swear by the oath of my people," said Cuchulain, "you are not so much in want of it as I am in want of it myself. The men of Ireland are upon me," he said, "and I am upon them." "I will put a bad name on you if you refuse it to me," said the Druid. "There was never a bad name put on me yet, on account of any refusal of mine," said Cuchulain, and with that he threw the spear at him, and it went through his head, and it killed the men that were on the other side of him.

Then Cuchulain drove through the host, and Lugaid, son of Curoi, got the spear. "Who is it will fall by this spear, children of Calatin?" said Lugaid. "A king will fall by it," said they. Then Lugaid threw the spear at Cuchulain's chariot, and it went through and hit the driver, Laeg, son of Riangabra, and he fell back, and his bowels came out on the cushions of the chariot. "My grief!" said Laeg, "it is hard I am wounded." Then Cuchulain drew the spear out, and Laeg said his farewell to him, and Cuchulain said: "To-day I will be a fighter and a chariot-driver as well."

Then he saw the other two men that were put to quarrel with one another, and one of them called out it would be a great shame for him not to give him his help. Then Cuchulain leaped towards them. "Your spear to me, Cuchulain," said the Druid. "I swear by the oath my people swear by," said he, "you are not in such want of the spear as I am myself, for it is by my courage, and by my arms, that I have to drive out the four provinces of Ireland that are sweeping over Muirthemne to-day." "I will put a bad name upon you," said the Druid. "I am not bound to give more than one gift in the day, and I have paid what is due to my name already," said Cuchulain. Then the Druid said: "I will put a bad name on the province of Ulster, because of your refusal."

"Ulster was never dispraised yet for any refusal of mine," said Cuchulain, "or for anything I did unworthily. Though little of my life should be left to me, Ulster will not be reproached for me to-day." With that he threw his spear at him, and it went through his head, and through the heads of the nine men that were behind him, and Cuchulain went through the host as he did before.

Then Erc, son of Cairbre Niafer, took up his spear. "Who will fall by this?" he asked the children of Calatin. "A king will fall by it," they said. "I heard you say the same thing of the spear that Lugaid threw a while ago," said Erc. "That is true," said they, "and the king of the chariot-drivers of Ireland fell by it, Cuchulain's driver Laeg, son of Riangabra."

With that, Erc threw the spear, and it went through the Grey of Macha. Cuchulain drew the spear out, and they said farewell to one another. And then the Grey went away from him, with half his harness hanging from his neck, and he went into Glas-linn, the grey pool in Slieve Fuad.

Then Cuchulain drove through the host, and he saw the third couple disputing together, and he went between them as he did before. And the Druid asked his spear of him, but he refused him. "I will put a bad name on you," said the Druid. " I have paid what is due to my name to-day," said he; " my honour does not bind me to give more than one request in a day." " I will put a bad name upon Ulster because of your refusal." " I have paid what is due for the honour of Ulster," said Cuchulain. " Then I will put a bad name on your kindred," said the Druid. " The news that I have been given a bad name shall never go back to that place I am never to go back to myself; for it is little of my life that is left to me," said Cuchulain. With that he threw the spear at him, and it went through him, and through the heads of the men that were along with him.

" You do your kindness unkindly, Cuchulain," said the Druid, as he fell. Then Cuchulain drove for the last time through the host, and Lugaid took the spear, and he said : " Who will fall by this spear, children of Calatin ?" " A king will fall by it," said they. " I heard you saying that a king would fall by the spear Erc threw a while ago." " That is true," they said, " and the Grey of Macha fell by it, that was the king of the horses of Ireland."

Then Lugaid threw the spear, and it went through and through Cuchulain's body, and he knew he had got his deadly wound ; and his bowels came out on the cushions of the chariot, and his only horse went away from him, the Black Sainglain, with half the harness hanging from his neck, and left his master, the king of the heroes of Ireland, to die upon the plain of Muirthemne.

Then Cuchulain said : " There is great desire on me to go to that lake beyond, and to get a drink from it."

" We will give you leave to do that," they said, " if you will come back to us after."

" I will bid you come for me if I am not able to come back myself," said Cuchulain.

Then he gathered up his bowels into his body, and he went down to the lake. He drank a drink, and he washed himself, and he turned back again to his death, and he called to his enemies to come and meet him.

There was a pillar-stone west of the lake, and his eye lit on it, and he went to the pillar-stone, and he tied himself to it with his breast-belt, the way he would not meet his death lying down, but would meet it standing up. Then his enemies came round about him, but they were in dread of going close to him, for they were not sure but he might be still alive.

"It is a great shame for you," said Erc, son of Cairbre, "not to strike the head off that man, in revenge for his striking the head off my father."

Then the Grey of Macha came back to defend Cuchulain as long as there was life in him, and the hero-light was shining above him. And the Grey of Macha made three attacks against them, and he killed fifty men with his teeth, and thirty with each of his hoofs. So there is a saying : "It is not sharper work than this was done by the Grey of Macha, the time of Cuchulain's death."

Then a bird came and settled on his shoulder. "It is not on that pillar birds were used to settle," said Erc.

Then Lugaid came and lifted up Cuchulain's hair from his shoulders, and struck his head off, and the men of Ireland gave three great heavy shouts, and the sword fell from Cuchulain's hand, and as it fell, it struck off Lugaid's right hand, so that it fell to the ground. Then they cut off Cuchulain's hand, in satisfaction for it, and then the light faded away from about Cuchulain's head, and left it as pale as the snow of a single night. Then all the men of Ireland said that as it was Maeve had gathered the army, it would be right for her to bring away the head to Cruachan. "I will not bring it with me; it is for Lugaid that struck it off to bring it with him," said Maeve. And then Lugaid and his men went away, and they brought away Cuchulain's head and his right hand with them, and they went south, towards tne Lifé river.

At that time the army of Ulster was gathering to attack its enemies, and Conall was out before them, and he met the Grey of Macha, and his share of blood dripping from him. And then he knew that Cuchulain was dead, and himself and the Grey of Macha went looking for Cuchulain's body. And when they saw his body at the pillar-stone, the Grey of Macha went and laid his head in Cuchulain's breast: "That body is a heavy care to the Grey of Macha," said Conall.

Then Conall went after the army, thinking in his own mind what way he could get satisfaction for Cuchulain's death. For it was a promise between himself and Cuchulain that whichever of them would be killed the first, the other would get satisfaction for his death.

"And if I am the first that is killed," said Cuchulain at that time, "how long will it be before you get satisfaction for me?"

"Before the evening of the same day," said Conall, "I will have got satisfaction for you. And if it is I that will die before you," he said, "how long will it be before you get satisfaction for me?"

"Your share of blood will not be cold on the ground," said Cuchulain, "when I will have got satisfaction for you."

So Conall followed after Lugaid to the river Lifé.

Lugaid was going down to bathe in the water, but he said to his chariot-driver: "Look out there over the plain, for fear would any one come at us unknown."

The chariot-driver looked around him. "There is a man coming on us," he said, "and it is in a great hurry he is coming; and you would think he has all the ravens in Ireland flying over his head, and there are flakes of snow speckling the ground before him."

"It is not in friendship the man comes that is coming

like that," said Lugaid. "It is Conall Cearnach it is, with Dub-dearg, and the birds that you see after him, they are the sods the horse has scattered in the air from his hoofs, and the flakes of snow that are speckling the ground before him, they are the froth that he scatters from his mouth and from the bit of his bridle. Look again," said Lugaid, "and see what way is he coming." "It is to the ford he is coming, the same way the army passed over," said the chariot-driver. "Let him pass by us," said Lugaid, "for I have no mind to fight with him."

But when Conall came to the middle of the ford, he saw Lugaid and his chariot-driver, and he went over to them. "Welcome is the sight of a debtor's face," said Conall. "The man you owe a debt to is asking payment of you now, and I myself am that man," he said, "for the sake of my comrade, Cuchulain, that you killed. And I am standing here now, to get that debt paid."

They agreed then to fight it out on the plain of Magh Argetnas, and in the fight Conall wounded Lugaid with his spear. From that they went to a place called Ferta Lugdac. "I would like that you would give me fair play," said Lugaid. "What fair play?" said Conall Cearnach.

"That you and I should fight with one hand, said he, "for I have the use of but one hand."

"I will do that," said Conall. Then Conall's hand was bound to his side with a cord, and then they fought for a long time, and one did not get the better of the other. And when Conall was not gaining on him, his horse, Dub-dearg, that was near by, came up to Lugaid, and took a bite out of his side.

"Misfortune on me," said Lugaid, "it is not right or fair that is of you, Conall."

"It was for myself I promised to do what is right and fair," said Conall. "I made no promise for a beast, that is without training and without sense."

"It is well I know you will not leave me till you take my head, as I took Cuchulain's head from him," said Lugaid. "Take it, then, along with your own head. Put my kingdom with your kingdom, and my courage with your courage; for I would like that you would be the best champion in Ireland."

Then Conall made an end of him, and he went back, bringing Cuchulain's head along with him to the pillar-stone where his body was.

And by that time Emer had got word of all that had happened, and that her husband had got his death by the men of Ireland, and by the powers of the children of Calatin. And it was Levarcham brought her the story, for Conall Cearnach had met her on his way, and had bade her go and bring the news to Emain Macha; and there she found Emer, and she sitting in her upper room, looking over the plain for some word from the battle.

And all the women came out to meet Levarcham, and when they heard her story, they made an outcry of grief and sharp cries, with loud weeping and burning tears; and there were long dismal sounds going through Emain, and the whole country round was filled with crying. And Emer and her women went to the place where Cuchulain's body was, and they gathered round it there, and gave themselves to crying and keening.

And when Conall came back to the place, he laid the head with the body of Cuchulain, and he began to lament along with them, and it is what he said: "It is Cuchulain had prosperity on him, a root of valour from the time he was but a soft child; there never fell a better hero than the hero that fell by Lugaid of the Lands. And there are many are in want of you," he said, "and until all the chief men of Ireland have fallen by me, it is not fitting there should ever be peace.

"It is grief to me, he to have gone into the battle

without Conall being at his side; it was a pity for him
to go there without my body beside his body.   Och!
it is he was my foster-son, and now the ravens are
drinking his blood; there will not be either laughter or
mirth, since the Hound has gone astray from us."

"Let us bury Cuchulain now," said Emer.   "It is not
right to do that," said Conall, "until I have avenged
him on the men of Ireland.   And it is a great shouting
I hear about the plain of Muirthemne, and it is full the
country is of crying after Cuchulain; and it is good at
keeping the country and watching the boundaries the
man was that is here before me, a cross-hacked body in
a pool of blood.   And it is well it pleased Lugaid, son of
Curoi, to be at the killing of Cuchulain, for it was Cuchulain killed the chiefs and the children of Deaguid round
Famain, son of Foraoi, and round Curoi, son of Daire
himself.   And this shouting has taken away my wits
and my memory from me," he said, "and it is hard for
me, Cuchulain not to answer these cries, and I to be
without him now; for there is not a champion in Ireland
that was not in dread of the sword in his hand.   And it is
broken in halves my heart is for my brother, and I will
bring my revenge through Ireland now, and I will not
leave a tribe without wounding, or true blood without
spilling, and the whole world will be told of my rout to
the end of life and time, until the men of Munster and
Connaught and Leinster will be crying for the rising
they made against him.   And without the spells of
the children of Calatin, the whole of them would not
have been able to do him to death."

After that complaint, rage and madness came on
Conall, and he went forward in his chariot to follow after
the rest of the men of Ireland, the same way as he had
followed after Lugaid.

And Emer took the head of Cuchulain in her hands,
and she washed it clean, and put a silk cloth about it,

and she held it to her breast; and she began to cry heavily over it, and it is what she said:

"Ochone!" said she, "it is good the beauty of this head was, though it is low this day, and it is many of the kings and princes of the world would be keening it if they knew the way it is now, and the poets and the Druids of Ireland and of Alban; and many were the goods and the jewels and the rents and the tributes that you brought home to me from the countries of the world, with the courage and the strength of your hands!"

And she made this complaint:

"Och, head! Ochone, O head! you gave death to great heroes, to many hundreds; my head will lie in the same grave, the one stone will be made for both of us

"Och, hand! Ochone, hand that was once gentle. It is often it was put under my head; it is dear that hand was to me!

"Dear mouth! Ochone, kind mouth that was sweet-voiced telling stories; since the time love first came on your face, you never refused either weak or strong!

"Dear the man, dear the man, that would kill the whole of a great host; dear his cold bright hair, and dear his bright cheeks!

"Dear the king, dear the king, that never gave a refusal to any; thirty days it is to-night since my body lay beside your body.

"Och, two spears! Ochone, two spears! Och, shield! Och, deadly sword! Let them be given to Conall of the battles; there was never any wage given like that.

"I am glad, I am glad, Cuchulain of Muirthemne, I never brought red shame on your face, for any unfaithfulness against you.

"Happy are they, happy are they, who will never

hear the cuckoo again for ever, now that the Hound has died from us.

"I am carried away like a branch on the stream; I will not bind up my hair to-day. From this day I have nothing to say that is better than Ochone!"

And then she said: "It is long that it was showed to me in a vision of the night, that Cuchulain would fall by the men of Ireland, and it appeared to me Dundealgan to be falling to the ground, and his shield to be split from lip to border, and his sword and his spears broken in the middle, and I saw Conall doing deeds of death before me, and myself and yourself in the one death. And oh! my love," she said, "we were often in one another's company, and it was happy for us; for if the world had been searched from the rising of the sun to sunset, the like would never have been found in one place, of the Black Sainglain and the Grey of Macha, and Laeg the chariot-driver, and myself and Cuchulain. And it is breaking my heart is in my body, to be listening to the pity and the sorrowing of women and men, and the harsh crying of the young men of Ulster keening Cuchulain, and Ulster to be in its weakness, and without strength to revenge itself upon the men of Ireland."

And after she had made that complaint, she brought Cuchulain's body to Dundealgan; and they all cried and keened about him until such time as Conall Cearnach came back from making his red rout through the army of the men of Ireland.

For he was not satisfied to make a slaughter of the men of Munster and Connaught, without reddening his hand in the blood of the men of Leinster as well.

And when he had done that, he came to Dundealgan, and his men along with him, but they made no rejoicing when they went back that time. And he brought the heads of the men of Ireland along with him in a gad, and he laid them out on the green lawn, and the people of the house gave three great shouts when they saw the heads.

And Emer came out, and when she saw Conall Cearnach, she said: "My great esteem and my welcome before you, king of heroes, and may your many wounds not be your death; for you have avenged the treachery done on Ulster, and now what you have to do is to make our grave, and to lay us together in the grave, for I will not live after Cuchulain.

"And tell me, Conall," she said, "whose are those heads all around on the lawn, and which of the great men of Ireland did they belong to?"

And she was asking, and Conall was answering, and it is what she said:

"Tell me, Conall, whose are those heads, for surely you have reddened your arms with them. Tell me the names of the men whose heads are there upon the ground."

And Conall said: "Daughter of Forgall of the Horses, young Emer of the sweet words, it is in revenge for the Hound of Feats I brought these heads here from the south."

"Whose is the great black head, with the smooth cheek redder than a rose; it is at the far end, on the left side, the head that has not changed its colour?"

"It is the head of the king of Meath, Erc, son of Cairbre of Swift Horses; I brought his head with me from far off, in revenge for my own foster-son."

"Whose is that head there before me, with soft hair, with smooth eyebrows, its eyes like ice, its teeth like blossoms; that head is more beautiful in shape than the others?"

"A son of Maeve; a destroyer of harbours, yellow-haired Maine, man of horses; I left his body without a head; all his people fell by my hand."

"O great Conall, who did not fail us, whose head is
this you hold in your hand? Since the Hound of Feats
is not living, what do you bring in satisfaction for his
head?"

"The head of the son of Fergus of the Horses, a
destroyer in every battle-field, my sister's son of the
narrow tower; I have struck his head from his body."

"Whose is that head to the west, with fair hair, the
head that is spoiled with grief? I used to know his
voice; I was for a while his friend."

"That is he that struck down the Hound, Lugaid, son
of Curoi of the Rhymes. His body was laid out straight
and fair, I struck his head off afterwards."

"Whose are those two heads farther out, great Conall
of good judgment? For the sake of your friendship,
do not hide the names of the men put down by your
arms."

"The heads of Laigaire and Clar Cuilt, two men that
fell by my wounds. It was they wounded faithful Cuchulain; I made my weapons red in their blood."

"Whose are those heads farther to the east, great
Conall of bright deeds? The hair of the two is of
the one colour; their cheeks are redder than a calf's
blood."

"Brave Cullain and hardy Cunlaid, two that were
used to overcome in their anger. There to the east,
Emer, are their heads; I left their bodies in a red
pool."

"Whose are those three heads with evil looks I see
before me to the north? Their faces blue, their hair
black; even hard Conall's eye turns from them."

"Three of the enemies of the Hound, daughters of
Calatin, wise in enchantments; they are the three witches
killed by me, their weapons in their hands."

'O great Conall, father of kings, whose is that head
that would overcome in the battle? His bushy hair is

gold-yellow; his head-dress is smooth and white like silver."

"It is the head of the son of Red-Haired Ross, son of Necht Min, that died by my strength. This, Emer, is his head; the high king of Leinster of Speckled Swords."

"O great Conall, change the story. How many of the men that harmed him fell by your hand that does not fail, in satisfaction for the head of Cuchulain?"

"It is what I say, ten and seven scores of hundreds is the number that fell, back to back, by the anger of my hard sword and of my people."

"O Conall, what way are they, the women of Ireland, after the Hound? Are they mourning the son of Sualtim? are they showing respect through their grief?"

"O Emer, what shall I do without my Cuchulain, my fine nurseling, going in and out from me, to-night?"

"O Conall, lift me to the grave. Raise my stone over the grave of the Hound; since it is through grief for him I go to death, lay my mouth to the mouth of Cuchulain.

"I am Emer of the Fair Form; there is no more vengeance for me to find; I have no love for any man. It is sorrowful my stay is after the Hound."

And after that Emer bade Conall to make a wide, very deep grave for Cuchulain; and she laid herself down beside her gentle comrade, and she put her mouth to his mouth, and she said: "Love of my life, my friend, my sweetheart, my one choice of the men of the earth, many is the woman, wed or unwed, envied me till to-day: and now I will not stay living after you."

And her life went out from her, and she herself and Cuchulain were laid in the one grave by Conall. And he raised the one stone over them, and he wrote their names in Ogham, and he himself and all the men of Ulster keened them.

But the three times fifty queens that loved Cuchulain saw him appear in his Druid chariot, going through Emain Macha; and they could hear him singing the music of the Sidhe.

THE END

NOTE BY W. B. YEATS ON THE CONVER-SATION OF CUCHULAIN AND EMER. (Page 23).

THIS conversation, so full of strange mythological information, is an example of the poet speech of ancient Ireland. One comes upon this speech here and there in other stories and poems. One finds it in the poem attributed to Ailbhe, daughter of Cormac Mac Art, and quoted by O'Curry in "MS. Materials," of which one verse is an allusion to a story given in Lady Gregory's book:

> "The apple tree of high Aillinn,
> The yew of Baile of little land,
> Though they are put into lays,
> Rough people do not understand them."

One finds it too in the poems which Brian, Son of Tuireann, chanted when he did not wish to be wholly understood. "That is a good poem, but I do not understand a word of its meaning," said the kings before whom he chanted; but his obscurity was more in a roundabout way of speaking than in mythological allusions. There is a description of a banquet, quoted by Professor Kuno Meyer, where hens' eggs are spoken of as "gravel of Glenn Ai," and leek, as "a tear of a fair woman," and some eatable sea-weed, dulse, perhaps, as a "net of the plains of Rein"—that is to say, of the sea—and so on. He quotes also a poem that calls the sallow, "the strength of bees," and the hawthorn "the barking of hounds," and the gooseberry bush "the sweetest of trees," and the yew, "the oldest of trees."

This poet speech somewhat resembles the Icelandic court poetry, as it is called, which certainly required alike for the writing and understanding of it a great traditional culture. Its descriptions of shields and tapestry, and its praises of Kings, that were first written, it seems, about the tenth century, depended for their effects on just this heaping up of mythological allusions, and the "Eddas"

were written to be a granary for the makers of such poems. But
by the fourteenth and fifteenth centuries they have come to be as
irritating to the new Christian poets and writers who stood outside
their tradition, as are the more esoteric kinds of modern verse to
unlettered readers. They were called "obscure," and "speaking
in riddles," and the like.

It has sometimes been thought that the Irish poet speech was
indeed but a copy of this court poetry, but Professor York Powell
contradicts this, and thinks it is not unlikely that the Irish poems
influenced the Icelandic, and made them more mythological and
obscure.

I am not scholar enough to judge the Scandinavian verse, but
the Irish poet speech seems to me at worst an over-abundance
of the esoterism which is an essential element in all admirable
literature, and I think it a folly to make light of it, as a recent
writer has done. Even now, verse no less full of symbol and myth
seems to me as legitimate as, let us say, a religious picture full
of symbolic detail, or the symbolic ornament of a Cathedral.

Nash's—

> "Brightness falls from the air,
> Queens have died young and fair,
> Dust hath closed Helen's eye"—

must seem as empty as a Scald's song, or the talk of Cuchulain
and Emer, to one who has never heard of Helen, or even to one
who did not fall in love with her when he was a young man. And
if we were not accustomed to be stirred by Greek myth, even without remembering it very fully, "Berenice's ever burning hair' would
not stir the blood, and especially if it were put into some foreign
tongue, losing those resounding "b's" on the way.

The mythological events Cuchulain speaks of give mystery to
the scenery of the tales, and when they are connected with the
battle of Magh Tuireadh, the most tremendous of mythological
battles, or anything else we know much about, they are full of
poetic meaning or historical interest. The hills that had the shape
of a sow's back at the coming of the Children of Miled, remind
one of Borlase's conviction that the pig was the symbol of the
mythological ancestry of the Firbolg, which the Children of Miled
were to bring into subjection, and of his suggestion that the
magical pigs that Maeve numbered were some Firbolg tribe that
Maeve put down in war. And everywhere that esoteric speech
brings the odour of the wild woods into our nostrils.

The earlier we get, the more copious does this traditional and
symbolical element in literature become. Till Greece and Rome

created a new culture, a sense of the importance of man, all that we understand by humanism, nobody wrote history, nobody described anything as we understand description. One called up the image of a thing by comparing it with something else, and partly because one was less interested in man, who did not seem to be important, than in divine revelations, in changes among the heavens and the gods, which can hardly be expressed at all, and only by myth, by symbol, by enigma. One was always losing oneself in the unknown, and rushing to the limits of the world. Imagination was all in all. Is not poetry, when all is said, but a little of this habit of mind caught as in the beryl stone of a Wizard?

NOTES

THE Irish text, from which the greater number of the stories in this book have been taken, has been published either in *Irische Texte* or the *Revue Celtique*, or by O'Curry in *Atlantis* and elsewhere, and I have worked from this text, comparing it with the translations that have been already made. In some cases, as in the greater part of "The War for the Bull of Cuailgne," a very small part of the Irish text has as yet been printed, and I have had to work by comparing and piecing together various translations.

I have had to put a connecting sentence of my own here and there, and I have condensed many passages, and I have sometimes tried to give the meaning of a formula that has lost its old meaning. Thus I have exchanged for the grotesque accounts of Cuchulain's distortion—which no doubt merely meant that in time of great strain or anger he had more than human strength—the more simple formula that his appearance changed to the appearance of a god. In the same way, I have left out Levarcham's distortion, which was the recognised way of saying she was a swift messenger.

As to the date of the stories, I cannot do better than quote from Mr Alfred Nutt's "Cuchulain, the Irish Achilles":—

"It suffices to say that we possess a MS. literature of which Cuchulain and his contemporaries are the subject, the extent of which may be roughly reckoned at 2000 8vo pages. The great bulk of this is contained in MSS. which are older than the twelfth century, or which demonstrably are copied from pre-twelfth-century MSS.; where post-twelfth-century versions alone remain, the story itself is nearly always known from earlier sources; in fact, there is hardly a single scene or incident in the whole cycle which has reached us only in MSS. of the thirteenth and following centuries. At the same time a not inconsiderable portion of the cycle comes before us altered in language, and to some extent in content, style of narrative, and characterisation, showing that the saga as a whole remained a living element of Irish culture and participated in the accidents of its evolution.

"The great bulk of this literature is, as I have said, certainly older than the twelfth century; but we can carry it back much farther, apart from any considerations based upon the subject-matter. Arguments of a nature purely philological, based upon the language of the texts, or critical, based upon the relations of the various MSS. to each other, not only allow, but compel us to date the *redaction* of the principal Cuchulain stories, substantially in the form under which they have survived, back to the seventh to ninth centuries. Whether or no they are older yet, is a question that cannot be answered without preliminary examination of the subject-matter. In the meantime it is something to know that the Cuchulain stories were put into permanent literary form at about the same date as Beowulf, some 100 to 250 years before the Scandinavian mythology crystallised into its present form, at least 200 years before the oldest Charlemagne romances, and probably 300 years before the earliest draft of the Nibelungenlied. Irish is the most ancient *vernacular* literature of modern Europe, a fact which of itself commends it to the attention of the student."

A critical account of this and the other Irish cycles is also given in Dr Douglas Hyde's "Literary History of Ireland."

The Tuatha de Danaan, or the Sidhe, so often mentioned, were the divine race, the people of the Gods of Dana, who conquered the Fomor, the powers of darkness and their helpers the Firbolgs, in the battle of Magh Tuireadh, and possessed Ireland until they were in their turn conquered by the children of the Gael, under the leadership of the Sons of Miled. Then they became invisible, and made their home in hills and raths.

The Morrigu was their goddess of battle, and Angus Og, Son of the Dagda, their god of youth and love, and Lugh, the Master of many Arts, their Hermes, their Apollo, and Manannan, Son of Lir, their Sea-God, or, as some say, the sea itself.

The spelling of Irish names for English readers is always a difficulty. I have not gone by any fixed rule, but have taken the spelling of names from various good authorities. As to pronunciation, the modern is generally used, but we know so little what the ancient pronunciation was, that we are left some freedom, and some words have taken a shape from English-speaking generations, that it is hard to change. Teamhair, for instance, has become Tara through a mistaken use of the genitive; Muirthemne is called by Irish speakers "Mur-hev-na," but others call it Muir'them-né,

and I am inclined to prefer this for the charm of its sound, and I
do not see any stronger reason against using it than against
sounding as we do the "s" in Paris. After all, it has not yet been
definitely settled whether Trafalgar is to be spoken in the Spanish
or the English way; English poets have given it one or the other
emphasis. This is the approximate pronunciation of some of the
more difficult names :—

Aedh	.	.	Ae (rhyming to "day").
Aoife	.	.	Eefa.
Badb	.	.	Bibe (as "jibe").
Bodb	.	.	Bove.
Cliodna	.	.	Cleevna.
Cobhthach .	.	.	Cowhach.
Conchubar .	.	.	Conachoor.
Cuailgne	.	.	Cooley.
Cuchulain .	.	.	Cuhoolin, or Cu-hullin.
Dun Sobairce	.	.	Dom Sĕvĕrka.
Emain	.	.	Avvin.
Eochaid	.	.	Yohee.
Eocho	.	.	Yŭchŏ.
Eoghan	.	.	Owen.
Fernmaighe	.	.	Farney.
Glen na (m) Bodhar	.		Glen na Mower (as "bower").
Inbhir	.	.	Inver.
Lugh	.	.	Loo.
Magh Tuireadh	.	.	Moytirra.
Muirthemne	.	.	Mŭr-hĕv-na.
Niamh	.	.	Nee-av.
Rudraige .	.	.	Rury.
Sidhe	.	.	Shee.
Slieve Suidhe Laighen	.		Slieve see lihon.
Suibnes	.	.	Sivness.
Teamhair .	.	.	T'yower.
Tuathmumain	.	.	Too-moon.

I give below some names of places that can still be identified—

Ard Inver .	.	.	Mouth of the Avoca, Co. Wicklow.
Argatros .	.	.	On the Nore, Co. Kilkenny.
Ath Cliath .	.	.	Dublin.
Ath Firdiadh	.	.	(Ferdiad's Ford) Ardee.
Ath Truim .	.	.	Trim.
Beinn Edair	.	.	Howth.
Boinne River	.	.	The Boyne.
Bregia	.	.	Bray.

Bri Leith . . .	In Co. Longford.
Brug na Boinne . .	On the Boyne.
Carraige . . .	Kerry.
Cerna . . .	Probably River Muilchean, Co. Limerick.
Clarthe . . .	Clara, near Mullingar.
Cleitech . . .	On the Boyne.
Conaille-Muirthemne .	Between the Cooley Mountains and the Boyne.
Cruachan . . .	In Co. Roscommon.
Cuailgne . . .	Cooley, Co. Louth.
Cuilsilinne . . .	South-west of Kells.
Drium Criadh . .	Drumcree, Co. Westmeath.
Dundealgan . .	Dundalk.
Dun Rudraige . .	Dundrum, Co. Down.
Dun Scathach . .	Isle of Skye.
Dun Sobairce . .	Dunseverick, Co. Antrim.
Emain Macha . .	Navan fort, near Armagh. A description and plan of Emain Macha are given by D'Arbois de Jubainville in *Revue Celtique*, vol. xvi.
Esro . . .	Ballyshannon.
Fearbile . . .	In Co. Westmeath.
Femen . . .	At Slieve na Man, Co. Tipperary.
Gairech and Ilgaireth .	Two hills near Mullingar.
Hill of Brughean Mor .	In Parish of Drumany, Co. Westmeath.
Hy Maine . . .	A part of Roscommon, bordering Sligo and Mayo.
Inver Colptha . .	Estuary of the Boyne.
Loch Cuan . . .	Strangford Loch.
Loch Riach . . .	In Co. Galway.
Leodus, Cadd, and Ork	Lewis, Shetland, and Orkney.
Magh Ai . . .	In Co. Roscommon.
Magh Breagh . .	In East Meath.
Magh Mucrime . .	Near Athenry, Co. Galway.
Magh Slecht . .	Near Ballymagauran, Co. Cavan.
Muirthemne . .	The part of Co. Louth bordering the sea, between the Boyne and Dundalk.
Road of Midluachair .	The north-eastern road from Teamhair.
Sionnan . . .	The Shannon.
Sleamhain of Meath .	Near Mullingar.
Slieve Breagh . .	Co. Louth.
Slieve Cuilinn . .	Co. Londonderry.
Slieve Fuad . .	Co. Armagh.

Slieve Mis .	. .	Co. Kerry.
Slieve Suidhe Laighen	.	Mount Leinster.
Scigger Isles	. .	Faröe Isles.
Sudiam .	. .	Sweden.
Tailltin .	. .	Telltown.
Teamhair .	. .	Tara, Oo. Meath.
Tuathmumain	. .	Thomond.
Uaran Garad	. .	River Cruind.
Usnech .	. .	{ The Hill of Usnogh in West Meath.
Wave of Assaroe .	.	At Ballyshannon.
Wave of Oliodna .	.	At Glandore, Co. Cork.
Wave of Inbhir .	.	Mouth of the Bann.

The following is a list of the authorities I have been chiefly helped by in putting these stories together. But I cannot make it quite accurate, for I have sometimes transferred a mere phrase, sometimes a whole passage from one story to another, where it seemed to fit better. I have occasionally used Scottish Gaelic versions, as in the account of Deirdre's birth, and the manner of her death, and in a part of "The Only Son of Aoife." "O'Curry" stands for his two books, "The Manners and Customs of Ancient Ireland," and "MS. Materials for Ancient Irish History," and his contributions to *Atlantis*.

BIRTH OF CUCHULAIN.—O'Curry; De Jubainville, *Epopée Celtique*; Nutt, *Voyage of Bran*; Kuno Meyer, *Revue Celtique*; Duvau, *Revue Celtique*; Windisch, *Irische Texte*; Stokes, *Irische Texte*.

BOY DEEDS OF CUCHLAIN.—Same as "War for the Bull of Ouailgne."

COURTING OF EMER.—Kuno Meyer, *Revue Celtique*; Kuno Meyer, *Archæological Review*; Dr Douglas Hyde, *Literary History of Ireland*; De Jubainville, *Epopée Celtique*; O'Curry.

BRICRIU'S FEAST, and THE CHAMPIONSHIP OF ULSTER.—Text, with Henderson's translation, published by Irish Texts Society; De Jubainville, *Epopée Celtique*; O'Curry; Windisch, *Irische Texte*.

THE HIGH KING OF IRELAND.—Whitley Stokes, *Revue Celtique*; O'Ourry; Zimmer, *Keltische Studien*.

FATE OF THE CHILDREN OF USNECH.—Text and Translations published by the Society for the Preservation of the Irish Language; Hyde, *Literary History of Ireland*; Hyde, *Zeitschrift Celt. Philologie*; O'Curry; Whitley Stokes, *Irische Texte*; Windisch, *Irische Texte*; Cameron, *Reliquae Celticae*; O'Flanagan, *Transactions of Gaelic*

Society ; O'Flanagan, *Reliquae Celticae ;* Carmichael, *Transactions of Gaelic Society ; Ultonian Ballads ;* De Jubainville, *Epopée Celtique ;* Dottin, *Revue Celtique.*

THE DREAM OF ANGUS.—Müller, *Revue Celtique.*

RUACHAN.—Kuno Meyer, *Revue Celtique ;* O'Beirne Crowe, *Proceedings of Royal Irish Academy ;* O'Curry ; Rhys, *Celtic Heathendom.*

WEDDING OF MAINE MORGOR.—Windisch, *Irische Texte.*

WAR FOR THE BULL OF CUAILGNE, and AWAKENING OF ULSTER.—MS. translations by O'Daly in Royal Irish Academy; MS. translation by O'Looney in Royal Irish Academy ; O'Curry : Standish Hayes O'Grady's Synopsis in Miss Hull's *Cuchulain Saga ;* Zimmer, Synopsis in *Zeitschrift für Vergleichende Sprachforschung.*

THE TWO BULLS.—Windisch, *Irische Texte ;* Nutt, *Voyage of Bran ;* O'Curry.

THE ONLY JEALOUSY OF EMER, and INSTRUCTION TO A PRINCE.— O'Curry, *Atlantis ;* De Jubainville, *Epopée Celtique.*

THE SONS OF DOEL DERMAIT.—Windisch, *Irische Texte ;* Rhys, *Hibbert Lectures.*

BATTLE OF ROSNAREE.—Text with Father Hogan's translation ; Todd Lecture Series ; O'Curry ; Kuno Meyer, *Revue Celtique.*

ONLY SON OF AOIFE.—Keating's *History of Ireland ;* Miss Brooke's *Reliques ;* Curtain's *Folk Tales ;* Some Gaelic Ballads.

GATHERING AT MUIRTHEMNE, and DEATH OF CUCHULAIN.—"Brislech Mor Magh Muirthemne," and "Deargruatar Conaill Cearnaig"— published in *Gaelic Journal,* 1901; S. Hayes O'Grady in Miss Hull's *Cuchulain Saga ;* Whitley Stokes, *Revue Celtique ;* an unpublished MS. in Dr Hyde's possession.

We must be grateful to all these scholars, workers, or compilers, those who have passed away, and those who are living. And I am personally grateful to my friend Douglas Hyde for patient answering of many questions ; and to my friend and critic, W. B. Yeats, for his kindness and for his severity.

A. G.

A CATALOG OF SELECTED
DOVER BOOKS
IN ALL FIELDS OF INTEREST

A CATALOG OF SELECTED DOVER BOOKS IN ALL FIELDS OF INTEREST

100 BEST-LOVED POEMS, Edited by Philip Smith. "The Passionate Shepherd to His Love," "Shall I compare thee to a summer's day?" "Death, be not proud," "The Raven," "The Road Not Taken," plus works by Blake, Wordsworth, Byron, Shelley, Keats, many others. 96pp. 5$\frac{3}{16}$ x 8$\frac{1}{4}$. 0-486-28553-7

100 SMALL HOUSES OF THE THIRTIES, Brown-Blodgett Company. Exterior photographs and floor plans for 100 charming structures. Illustrations of models accompanied by descriptions of interiors, color schemes, closet space, and other amenities. 200 illustrations. 112pp. 8$\frac{3}{8}$ x 11. 0-486-44131-8

1000 TURN-OF-THE-CENTURY HOUSES: With Illustrations and Floor Plans, Herbert C. Chivers. Reproduced from a rare edition, this showcase of homes ranges from cottages and bungalows to sprawling mansions. Each house is meticulously illustrated and accompanied by complete floor plans. 256pp. 9$\frac{3}{8}$ x 12$\frac{1}{4}$. 0-486-45596-3

101 GREAT AMERICAN POEMS, Edited by The American Poetry & Literacy Project. Rich treasury of verse from the 19th and 20th centuries includes works by Edgar Allan Poe, Robert Frost, Walt Whitman, Langston Hughes, Emily Dickinson, T. S. Eliot, other notables. 96pp. 5$\frac{3}{16}$ x 8$\frac{1}{4}$. 0-486-40158-8

101 GREAT SAMURAI PRINTS, Utagawa Kuniyoshi. Kuniyoshi was a master of the warrior woodblock print — and these 18th-century illustrations represent the pinnacle of his craft. Full-color portraits of renowned Japanese samurais pulse with movement, passion, and remarkably fine detail. 112pp. 8$\frac{3}{8}$ x 11. 0-486-46523-3

ABC OF BALLET, Janet Grosser. Clearly worded, abundantly illustrated little guide defines basic ballet-related terms: arabesque, battement, pas de chat, relevé, sissonne, many others. Pronunciation guide included. Excellent primer. 48pp. 4$\frac{3}{16}$ x 5$\frac{3}{4}$. 0-486-40871-X

ACCESSORIES OF DRESS: An Illustrated Encyclopedia, Katherine Lester and Bess Viola Oerke. Illustrations of hats, veils, wigs, cravats, shawls, shoes, gloves, and other accessories enhance an engaging commentary that reveals the humor and charm of the many-sided story of accessorized apparel. 644 figures and 59 plates. 608pp. 6 $\frac{1}{8}$ x 9$\frac{1}{4}$. 0-486-43378-1

ADVENTURES OF HUCKLEBERRY FINN, Mark Twain. Join Huck and Jim as their boyhood adventures along the Mississippi River lead them into a world of excitement, danger, and self-discovery. Humorous narrative, lyrical descriptions of the Mississippi valley, and memorable characters. 224pp. 5$\frac{3}{16}$ x 8$\frac{1}{4}$. 0-486-28061-6

ALICE STARMORE'S BOOK OF FAIR ISLE KNITTING, Alice Starmore. A noted designer from the region of Scotland's Fair Isle explores the history and techniques of this distinctive, stranded-color knitting style and provides copious illustrated instructions for 14 original knitwear designs. 208pp. 8$\frac{3}{8}$ x 10$\frac{7}{8}$. 0-486-47218-3

Browse over 9,000 books at www.doverpublications.com

ALICE'S ADVENTURES IN WONDERLAND, Lewis Carroll. Beloved classic about a little girl lost in a topsy-turvy land and her encounters with the White Rabbit, March Hare, Mad Hatter, Cheshire Cat, and other delightfully improbable characters. 42 illustrations by Sir John Tenniel. 96pp. 5³⁄₁₆ x 8¼. 0-486-27543-4

AMERICA'S LIGHTHOUSES: An Illustrated History, Francis Ross Holland. Profusely illustrated fact-filled survey of American lighthouses since 1716. Over 200 stations — East, Gulf, and West coasts, Great Lakes, Hawaii, Alaska, Puerto Rico, the Virgin Islands, and the Mississippi and St. Lawrence Rivers. 240pp. 8 x 10¾.
0-486-25576-X

AN ENCYCLOPEDIA OF THE VIOLIN, Alberto Bachmann. Translated by Frederick H. Martens. Introduction by Eugene Ysaye. First published in 1925, this renowned reference remains unsurpassed as a source of essential information, from construction and evolution to repertoire and technique. Includes a glossary and 73 illustrations. 496pp. 6⅛ x 9¼. 0-486-46618-3

ANIMALS: 1,419 Copyright-Free Illustrations of Mammals, Birds, Fish, Insects, etc., Selected by Jim Harter. Selected for its visual impact and ease of use, this outstanding collection of wood engravings presents over 1,000 species of animals in extremely lifelike poses. Includes mammals, birds, reptiles, amphibians, fish, insects, and other invertebrates. 284pp. 9 x 12. 0-486-23766-4

THE ANNALS, Tacitus. Translated by Alfred John Church and William Jackson Brodribb. This vital chronicle of Imperial Rome, written by the era's great historian, spans A.D. 14-68 and paints incisive psychological portraits of major figures, from Tiberius to Nero. 416pp. 5³⁄₁₆ x 8¼. 0-486-45236-0

ANTIGONE, Sophocles. Filled with passionate speeches and sensitive probing of moral and philosophical issues, this powerful and often-performed Greek drama reveals the grim fate that befalls the children of Oedipus. Footnotes. 64pp. 5³⁄₁₆ x 8 ¼. 0-486-27804-2

ART DECO DECORATIVE PATTERNS IN FULL COLOR, Christian Stoll. Reprinted from a rare 1910 portfolio, 160 sensuous and exotic images depict a breathtaking array of florals, geometrics, and abstracts — all elegant in their stark simplicity. 64pp. 8⅜ x 11. 0-486-44862-2

THE ARTHUR RACKHAM TREASURY: 86 Full-Color Illustrations, Arthur Rackham. Selected and Edited by Jeff A. Menges. A stunning treasury of 86 full-page plates span the famed English artist's career, from *Rip Van Winkle* (1905) to masterworks such as *Undine, A Midsummer Night's Dream,* and *Wind in the Willows* (1939). 96pp. 8⅜ x 11.
0-486-44685-9

THE AUTHENTIC GILBERT & SULLIVAN SONGBOOK, W. S. Gilbert and A. S. Sullivan. The most comprehensive collection available, this songbook includes selections from every one of Gilbert and Sullivan's light operas. Ninety-two numbers are presented uncut and unedited, and in their original keys. 410pp. 9 x 12.
0-486-23482-7

THE AWAKENING, Kate Chopin. First published in 1899, this controversial novel of a New Orleans wife's search for love outside a stifling marriage shocked readers. Today, it remains a first-rate narrative with superb characterization. New introductory Note. 128pp. 5³⁄₁₆ x 8¼. 0-486-27786-0

BASIC DRAWING, Louis Priscilla. Beginning with perspective, this commonsense manual progresses to the figure in movement, light and shade, anatomy, drapery, composition, trees and landscape, and outdoor sketching. Black-and-white illustrations throughout. 128pp. 8⅜ x 11. 0-486-45815-6

Browse over 9,000 books at www.doverpublications.com

THE BATTLES THAT CHANGED HISTORY, Fletcher Pratt. Historian profiles 16 crucial conflicts, ancient to modern, that changed the course of Western civilization. Gripping accounts of battles led by Alexander the Great, Joan of Arc, Ulysses S. Grant, other commanders. 27 maps. 352pp. 5⅜ x 8½. 0-486-41129-X

BEETHOVEN'S LETTERS, Ludwig van Beethoven. Edited by Dr. A. C. Kalischer. Features 457 letters to fellow musicians, friends, greats, patrons, and literary men. Reveals musical thoughts, quirks of personality, insights, and daily events. Includes 15 plates. 410pp. 5⅜ x 8½. 0-486-22769-3

BERNICE BOBS HER HAIR AND OTHER STORIES, F. Scott Fitzgerald. This brilliant anthology includes 6 of Fitzgerald's most popular stories: "The Diamond as Big as the Ritz," the title tale, "The Offshore Pirate," "The Ice Palace," "The Jelly Bean," and "May Day." 176pp. 5⅜ x 8½. 0-486-47049-0

BESLER'S BOOK OF FLOWERS AND PLANTS: 73 Full-Color Plates from Hortus Eystettensis, 1613, Basilius Besler. Here is a selection of magnificent plates from the *Hortus Eystettensis,* which vividly illustrated and identified the plants, flowers, and trees that thrived in the legendary German garden at Eichstätt. 80pp. 8⅜ x 11.
0-486-46005-3

THE BOOK OF KELLS, Edited by Blanche Cirker. Painstakingly reproduced from a rare facsimile edition, this volume contains full-page decorations, portraits, illustrations, plus a sampling of textual leaves with exquisite calligraphy and ornamentation. 32 full-color illustrations. 32pp. 9⅜ x 12¼. 0-486-24345-1

THE BOOK OF THE CROSSBOW: With an Additional Section on Catapults and Other Siege Engines, Ralph Payne-Gallwey. Fascinating study traces history and use of crossbow as military and sporting weapon, from Middle Ages to modern times. Also covers related weapons: balistas, catapults, Turkish bows, more. Over 240 illustrations. 400pp. 7¼ x 10⅛. 0-486-28720-3

THE BUNGALOW BOOK: Floor Plans and Photos of 112 Houses, 1910, Henry L. Wilson. Here are 112 of the most popular and economic blueprints of the early 20th century — plus an illustration or photograph of each completed house. A wonderful time capsule that still offers a wealth of valuable insights. 160pp. 8⅜ x 11.
0-486-45104-6

THE CALL OF THE WILD, Jack London. A classic novel of adventure, drawn from London's own experiences as a Klondike adventurer, relating the story of a heroic dog caught in the brutal life of the Alaska Gold Rush. Note. 64pp. 5³⁄₁₆ x 8¼.
0-486-26472-6

CANDIDE, Voltaire. Edited by Francois-Marie Arouet. One of the world's great satires since its first publication in 1759. Witty, caustic skewering of romance, science, philosophy, religion, government — nearly all human ideals and institutions. 112pp. 5³⁄₁₆ x 8¼. 0-486-26689-3

CELEBRATED IN THEIR TIME: Photographic Portraits from the George Grantham Bain Collection, Edited by Amy Pastan. With an Introduction by Michael Carlebach. Remarkable portrait gallery features 112 rare images of Albert Einstein, Charlie Chaplin, the Wright Brothers, Henry Ford, and other luminaries from the worlds of politics, art, entertainment, and industry. 128pp. 8⅜ x 11. 0-486-46754-6

CHARIOTS FOR APOLLO: The NASA History of Manned Lunar Spacecraft to 1969, Courtney G. Brooks, James M. Grimwood, and Loyd S. Swenson, Jr. This illustrated history by a trio of experts is the definitive reference on the Apollo spacecraft and lunar modules. It traces the vehicles' design, development, and operation in space. More than 100 photographs and illustrations. 576pp. 6¾ x 9¼. 0-486-46756-2

A CHRISTMAS CAROL, Charles Dickens. This engrossing tale relates Ebenezer Scrooge's ghostly journeys through Christmases past, present, and future and his ultimate transformation from a harsh and grasping old miser to a charitable and compassionate human being. 80pp. 5³⁄₁₆ x 8¼.　　0-486-26865-9

COMMON SENSE, Thomas Paine. First published in January of 1776, this highly influential landmark document clearly and persuasively argued for American separation from Great Britain and paved the way for the Declaration of Independence. 64pp. 5³⁄₁₆ x 8¼.　　0-486-29602-4

THE COMPLETE SHORT STORIES OF OSCAR WILDE, Oscar Wilde. Complete texts of "The Happy Prince and Other Tales," "A House of Pomegranates," "Lord Arthur Savile's Crime and Other Stories," "Poems in Prose," and "The Portrait of Mr. W. H." 208pp. 5³⁄₁₆ x 8¼.　　0-486-45216-6

COMPLETE SONNETS, William Shakespeare. Over 150 exquisite poems deal with love, friendship, the tyranny of time, beauty's evanescence, death, and other themes in language of remarkable power, precision, and beauty. Glossary of archaic terms. 80pp. 5³⁄₁₆ x 8¼.　　0-486-26686-9

THE COUNT OF MONTE CRISTO: Abridged Edition, Alexandre Dumas. Falsely accused of treason, Edmond Dantès is imprisoned in the bleak Chateau d'If. After a hair-raising escape, he launches an elaborate plot to extract a bitter revenge against those who betrayed him. 448pp. 5³⁄₁₆ x 8¼.　　0-486-45643-9

CRAFTSMAN BUNGALOWS: Designs from the Pacific Northwest, Yoho & Merritt. This reprint of a rare catalog, showcasing the charming simplicity and cozy style of Craftsman bungalows, is filled with photos of completed homes, plus floor plans and estimated costs. An indispensable resource for architects, historians, and illustrators. 112pp. 10 x 7.　　0-486-46875-5

CRAFTSMAN BUNGALOWS: 59 Homes from "The Craftsman," Edited by Gustav Stickley. Best and most attractive designs from Arts and Crafts Movement publication — 1903–1916 — includes sketches, photographs of homes, floor plans, descriptive text. 128pp. 8¼ x 11.　　0-486-25829-7

CRIME AND PUNISHMENT, Fyodor Dostoyevsky. Translated by Constance Garnett. Supreme masterpiece tells the story of Raskolnikov, a student tormented by his own thoughts after he murders an old woman. Overwhelmed by guilt and terror, he confesses and goes to prison. 480pp. 5³⁄₁₆ x 8¼.　　0-486-41587-2

THE DECLARATION OF INDEPENDENCE AND OTHER GREAT DOCUMENTS OF AMERICAN HISTORY: 1775-1865, Edited by John Grafton. Thirteen compelling and influential documents: Henry's "Give Me Liberty or Give Me Death," Declaration of Independence, The Constitution, Washington's First Inaugural Address, The Monroe Doctrine, The Emancipation Proclamation, Gettysburg Address, more. 64pp. 5³⁄₁₆ x 8¼.　　0-486-41124-9

THE DESERT AND THE SOWN: Travels in Palestine and Syria, Gertrude Bell. "The female Lawrence of Arabia," Gertrude Bell wrote captivating, perceptive accounts of her travels in the Middle East. This intriguing narrative, accompanied by 160 photos, traces her 1905 sojourn in Lebanon, Syria, and Palestine. 368pp. 5⅜ x 8½.
0-486-46876-3

A DOLL'S HOUSE, Henrik Ibsen. Ibsen's best-known play displays his genius for realistic prose drama. An expression of women's rights, the play climaxes when the central character, Nora, rejects a smothering marriage and life in "a doll's house." 80pp. 5³⁄₁₆ x 8¼.　　0-486-27062-9

DOOMED SHIPS: Great Ocean Liner Disasters, William H. Miller, Jr. Nearly 200 photographs, many from private collections, highlight tales of some of the vessels whose pleasure cruises ended in catastrophe: the *Morro Castle, Normandie, Andrea Doria, Europa,* and many others. 128pp. 8⅞ x 11¾.　　0-486-45366-9

THE DORÉ BIBLE ILLUSTRATIONS, Gustave Doré. Detailed plates from the Bible: the Creation scenes, Adam and Eve, horrifying visions of the Flood, the battle sequences with their monumental crowds, depictions of the life of Jesus, 241 plates in all. 241pp. 9 x 12.　　0-486-23004-X

DRAWING DRAPERY FROM HEAD TO TOE, Cliff Young. Expert guidance on how to draw shirts, pants, skirts, gloves, hats, and coats on the human figure, including folds in relation to the body, pull and crush, action folds, creases, more. Over 200 drawings. 48pp. 8¼ x 11.　　0-486-45591-2

DUBLINERS, James Joyce. A fine and accessible introduction to the work of one of the 20th century's most influential writers, this collection features 15 tales, including a masterpiece of the short-story genre, "The Dead." 160pp. 5³⁄₁₆ x 8¼.

0-486-26870-5

EASY-TO-MAKE POP-UPS, Joan Irvine. Illustrated by Barbara Reid. Dozens of wonderful ideas for three-dimensional paper fun — from holiday greeting cards with moving parts to a pop-up menagerie. Easy-to-follow, illustrated instructions for more than 30 projects. 299 black-and-white illustrations. 96pp. 8⅜ x 11.

0-486-44622-0

EASY-TO-MAKE STORYBOOK DOLLS: A "Novel" Approach to Cloth Dollmaking, Sherralyn St. Clair. Favorite fictional characters come alive in this unique beginner's dollmaking guide. Includes patterns for Pollyanna, Dorothy from *The Wonderful Wizard of Oz,* Mary of *The Secret Garden,* plus easy-to-follow instructions, 263 black-and-white illustrations, and an 8-page color insert. 112pp. 8¼ x 11.　　0-486-47360-0

EINSTEIN'S ESSAYS IN SCIENCE, Albert Einstein. Speeches and essays in accessible, everyday language profile influential physicists such as Niels Bohr and Isaac Newton. They also explore areas of physics to which the author made major contributions. 128pp. 5 x 8.　　0-486-47011-3

EL DORADO: Further Adventures of the Scarlet Pimpernel, Baroness Orczy. A popular sequel to *The Scarlet Pimpernel,* this suspenseful story recounts the Pimpernel's attempts to rescue the Dauphin from imprisonment during the French Revolution. An irresistible blend of intrigue, period detail, and vibrant characterizations. 352pp. 5³⁄₁₆ x 8¼.　　0-486-44026-5

ELEGANT SMALL HOMES OF THE TWENTIES: 99 Designs from a Competition, Chicago Tribune. Nearly 100 designs for five- and six-room houses feature New England and Southern colonials, Normandy cottages, stately Italianate dwellings, and other fascinating snapshots of American domestic architecture of the 1920s. 112pp. 9 x 12.　　0-486-46910-7

THE ELEMENTS OF STYLE: The Original Edition, William Strunk, Jr. This is the book that generations of writers have relied upon for timeless advice on grammar, diction, syntax, and other essentials. In concise terms, it identifies the principal requirements of proper style and common errors. 64pp. 5⅜ x 8½.　　0-486-44798-7

THE ELUSIVE PIMPERNEL, Baroness Orczy. Robespierre's revolutionaries find their wicked schemes thwarted by the heroic Pimpernel — Sir Percival Blakeney. In this thrilling sequel, Chauvelin devises a plot to eliminate the Pimpernel and his wife. 272pp. 5³⁄₁₆ x 8¼.　　0-486-45464-9

AN ENCYCLOPEDIA OF BATTLES: Accounts of Over 1,560 Battles from 1479 B.C. to the Present, David Eggenberger. Essential details of every major battle in recorded history from the first battle of Megiddo in 1479 B.C. to Grenada in 1984. List of battle maps. 99 illustrations. 544pp. 6½ x 9¼. 0-486-24913-1

ENCYCLOPEDIA OF EMBROIDERY STITCHES, INCLUDING CREWEL, Marion Nichols. Precise explanations and instructions, clearly illustrated, on how to work chain, back, cross, knotted, woven stitches, and many more — 178 in all, including Cable Outline, Whipped Satin, and Eyelet Buttonhole. Over 1400 illustrations. 219pp. 8⅜ x 11¼. 0-486-22929-7

ENTER JEEVES: 15 Early Stories, P. G. Wodehouse. Splendid collection contains first 8 stories featuring Bertie Wooster, the deliciously dim aristocrat and Jeeves, his brainy, imperturbable manservant. Also, the complete Reggie Pepper (Bertie's prototype) series. 288pp. 5⅜ x 8½. 0-486-29717-9

ERIC SLOANE'S AMERICA: Paintings in Oil, Michael Wigley. With a Foreword by Mimi Sloane. Eric Sloane's evocative oils of America's landscape and material culture shimmer with immense historical and nostalgic appeal. This original hardcover collection gathers nearly a hundred of his finest paintings, with subjects ranging from New England to the American Southwest. 128pp. 10⅝ x 9. 0-486-46525-X

ETHAN FROME, Edith Wharton. Classic story of wasted lives, set against a bleak New England background. Superbly delineated characters in a hauntingly grim tale of thwarted love. Considered by many to be Wharton's masterpiece. 96pp. 5³⁄₁₆ x 8 ¼. 0-486-26690-7

THE EVERLASTING MAN, G. K. Chesterton. Chesterton's view of Christianity — as a blend of philosophy and mythology, satisfying intellect and spirit — applies to his brilliant book, which appeals to readers' heads as well as their hearts. 288pp. 5⅜ x 8½. 0-486-46036-3

THE FIELD AND FOREST HANDY BOOK, Daniel Beard. Written by a co-founder of the Boy Scouts, this appealing guide offers illustrated instructions for building kites, birdhouses, boats, igloos, and other fun projects, plus numerous helpful tips for campers. 448pp. 5³⁄₁₆ x 8¼. 0-486-46191-2

FINDING YOUR WAY WITHOUT MAP OR COMPASS, Harold Gatty. Useful, instructive manual shows would-be explorers, hikers, bikers, scouts, sailors, and survivalists how to find their way outdoors by observing animals, weather patterns, shifting sands, and other elements of nature. 288pp. 5⅜ x 8½. 0-486-40613-X

FIRST FRENCH READER: A Beginner's Dual-Language Book, Edited and Translated by Stanley Appelbaum. This anthology introduces 50 legendary writers — Voltaire, Balzac, Baudelaire, Proust, more — through passages from *The Red and the Black, Les Misérables, Madame Bovary,* and other classics. Original French text plus English translation on facing pages. 240pp. 5⅜ x 8½. 0-486-46178-5

FIRST GERMAN READER: A Beginner's Dual-Language Book, Edited by Harry Steinhauer. Specially chosen for their power to evoke German life and culture, these short, simple readings include poems, stories, essays, and anecdotes by Goethe, Hesse, Heine, Schiller, and others. 224pp. 5⅜ x 8½. 0-486-46179-3

FIRST SPANISH READER: A Beginner's Dual-Language Book, Angel Flores. Delightful stories, other material based on works of Don Juan Manuel, Luis Taboada, Ricardo Palma, other noted writers. Complete faithful English translations on facing pages. Exercises. 176pp. 5⅜ x 8½. 0-486-25810-6

Browse over 9,000 books at www.doverpublications.com

FIVE ACRES AND INDEPENDENCE, Maurice G. Kains. Great back-to-the-land classic explains basics of self-sufficient farming. The one book to get. 95 illustrations. 397pp. 5⅜ x 8½. 0-486-20974-1

FLAGG'S SMALL HOUSES: Their Economic Design and Construction, 1922, Ernest Flagg. Although most famous for his skyscrapers, Flagg was also a proponent of the well-designed single-family dwelling. His classic treatise features innovations that save space, materials, and cost. 526 illustrations. 160pp. 9⅜ x 12¼. 0-486-45197-6

FLATLAND: A Romance of Many Dimensions, Edwin A. Abbott. Classic of science (and mathematical) fiction — charmingly illustrated by the author — describes the adventures of A. Square, a resident of Flatland, in Spaceland (three dimensions), Lineland (one dimension), and Pointland (no dimensions). 96pp. 5$\frac{3}{16}$ x 8¼. 0-486-27263-X

FRANKENSTEIN, Mary Shelley. The story of Victor Frankenstein's monstrous creation and the havoc it caused has enthralled generations of readers and inspired countless writers of horror and suspense. With the author's own 1831 introduction. 176pp. 5$\frac{3}{16}$ x 8¼. 0-486-28211-2

THE GARGOYLE BOOK: 572 Examples from Gothic Architecture, Lester Burbank Bridaham. Dispelling the conventional wisdom that French Gothic architectural flourishes were born of despair or gloom, Bridaham reveals the whimsical nature of these creations and the ingenious artisans who made them. 572 illustrations. 224pp. 8⅜ x 11. 0-486-44754-5

THE GIFT OF THE MAGI AND OTHER SHORT STORIES, O. Henry. Sixteen captivating stories by one of America's most popular storytellers. Included are such classics as "The Gift of the Magi," "The Last Leaf," and "The Ransom of Red Chief." Publisher's Note. 96pp. 5$\frac{3}{16}$ x 8¼. 0-486-27061-0

THE GOETHE TREASURY: Selected Prose and Poetry, Johann Wolfgang von Goethe. Edited, Selected, and with an Introduction by Thomas Mann. In addition to his lyric poetry, Goethe wrote travel sketches, autobiographical studies, essays, letters, and proverbs in rhyme and prose. This collection presents outstanding examples from each genre. 368pp. 5⅜ x 8½. 0-486-44780-4

GREAT EXPECTATIONS, Charles Dickens. Orphaned Pip is apprenticed to the dirty work of the forge but dreams of becoming a gentleman — and one day finds himself in possession of "great expectations." Dickens' finest novel. 400pp. 5$\frac{3}{16}$ x 8¼. 0-486-41586-4

GREAT WRITERS ON THE ART OF FICTION: From Mark Twain to Joyce Carol Oates, Edited by James Daley. An indispensable source of advice and inspiration, this anthology features essays by Henry James, Kate Chopin, Willa Cather, Sinclair Lewis, Jack London, Raymond Chandler, Raymond Carver, Eudora Welty, and Kurt Vonnegut, Jr. 192pp. 5⅜ x 8½. 0-486-45128-3

HAMLET, William Shakespeare. The quintessential Shakespearean tragedy, whose highly charged confrontations and anguished soliloquies probe depths of human feeling rarely sounded in any art. Reprinted from an authoritative British edition complete with illuminating footnotes. 128pp. 5$\frac{3}{16}$ x 8¼. 0-486-27278-8

THE HAUNTED HOUSE, Charles Dickens. A Yuletide gathering in an eerie country retreat provides the backdrop for Dickens and his friends — including Elizabeth Gaskell and Wilkie Collins — who take turns spinning supernatural yarns. 144pp. 5⅜ x 8½. 0-486-46309-5

Browse over 9,000 books at www.doverpublications.com

HEART OF DARKNESS, Joseph Conrad. Dark allegory of a journey up the Congo River and the narrator's encounter with the mysterious Mr. Kurtz. Masterly blend of adventure, character study, psychological penetration. For many, Conrad's finest, most enigmatic story. 80pp. 5³⁄₁₆ x 8¼. 0-486-26464-5

HENSON AT THE NORTH POLE, Matthew A. Henson. This thrilling memoir by the heroic African-American who was Peary's companion through two decades of Arctic exploration recounts a tale of danger, courage, and determination. "Fascinating and exciting." — *Commonweal.* 128pp. 5⅜ x 8½. 0-486-45472-X

HISTORIC COSTUMES AND HOW TO MAKE THEM, Mary Fernald and E. Shenton. Practical, informative guidebook shows how to create everything from short tunics worn by Saxon men in the fifth century to a lady's bustle dress of the late 1800s. 81 illustrations. 176pp. 5⅜ x 8½. 0-486-44906-8

THE HOUND OF THE BASKERVILLES, Arthur Conan Doyle. A deadly curse in the form of a legendary ferocious beast continues to claim its victims from the Baskerville family until Holmes and Watson intervene. Often called the best detective story ever written. 128pp. 5³⁄₁₆ x 8¼. 0-486-28214-7

THE HOUSE BEHIND THE CEDARS, Charles W. Chesnutt. Originally published in 1900, this groundbreaking novel by a distinguished African-American author recounts the drama of a brother and sister who "pass for white" during the dangerous days of Reconstruction. 208pp. 5⅜ x 8½. 0-486-46144-0

THE HUMAN FIGURE IN MOTION, Eadweard Muybridge. The 4,789 photographs in this definitive selection show the human figure — models almost all undraped — engaged in over 160 different types of action: running, climbing stairs, etc. 390pp. 7⅞ x 10⅝. 0-486-20204-6

THE IMPORTANCE OF BEING EARNEST, Oscar Wilde. Wilde's witty and buoyant comedy of manners, filled with some of literature's most famous epigrams, reprinted from an authoritative British edition. Considered Wilde's most perfect work. 64pp. 5³⁄₁₆ x 8¼. 0-486-26478-5

THE INFERNO, Dante Alighieri. Translated and with notes by Henry Wadsworth Longfellow. The first stop on Dante's famous journey from Hell to Purgatory to Paradise, this 14th-century allegorical poem blends vivid and shocking imagery with graceful lyricism. Translated by the beloved 19th-century poet, Henry Wadsworth Longfellow. 256pp. 5³⁄₁₆ x 8¼. 0-486-44288-8

JANE EYRE, Charlotte Brontë. Written in 1847, *Jane Eyre* tells the tale of an orphan girl's progress from the custody of cruel relatives to an oppressive boarding school and its culmination in a troubled career as a governess. 448pp. 5³⁄₁₆ x 8¼.

0-486-42449-9

JAPANESE WOODBLOCK FLOWER PRINTS, Tanigami Kônan. Extraordinary collection of Japanese woodblock prints by a well-known artist features 120 plates in brilliant color. Realistic images from a rare edition include daffodils, tulips, and other familiar and unusual flowers. 128pp. 11 x 8¼. 0-486-46442-3

JEWELRY MAKING AND DESIGN, Augustus F. Rose and Antonio Cirino. Professional secrets of jewelry making are revealed in a thorough, practical guide. Over 200 illustrations. 306pp. 5⅜ x 8½. 0-486-21750-7

JULIUS CAESAR, William Shakespeare. Great tragedy based on Plutarch's account of the lives of Brutus, Julius Caesar and Mark Antony. Evil plotting, ringing oratory, high tragedy with Shakespeare's incomparable insight, dramatic power. Explanatory footnotes. 96pp. 5³⁄₁₆ x 8¼. 0-486-26876-4

THE JUNGLE, Upton Sinclair. 1906 bestseller shockingly reveals intolerable labor practices and working conditions in the Chicago stockyards as it tells the grim story of a Slavic family that emigrates to America full of optimism but soon faces despair. 320pp. $5\frac{3}{16} \times 8\frac{1}{4}$. 0-486-41923-1

THE KINGDOM OF GOD IS WITHIN YOU, Leo Tolstoy. The soul-searching book that inspired Gandhi to embrace the concept of passive resistance, Tolstoy's 1894 polemic clearly outlines a radical, well-reasoned revision of traditional Christian thinking. 352pp. $5\frac{3}{16} \times 8\frac{1}{4}$. 0-486-45138-0

THE LADY OR THE TIGER?: and Other Logic Puzzles, Raymond M. Smullyan. Created by a renowned puzzle master, these whimsically themed challenges involve paradoxes about probability, time, and change; metapuzzles; and self-referentiality. Nineteen chapters advance in difficulty from relatively simple to highly complex. 1982 edition. 240pp. $5\frac{3}{8} \times 8\frac{1}{2}$. 0-486-47027-X

LEAVES OF GRASS: The Original 1855 Edition, Walt Whitman. Whitman's immortal collection includes some of the greatest poems of modern times, including his masterpiece, "Song of Myself." Shattering standard conventions, it stands as an unabashed celebration of body and nature. 128pp. $5\frac{3}{16} \times 8\frac{1}{4}$. 0-486-45676-5

LES MISÉRABLES, Victor Hugo. Translated by Charles E. Wilbour. Abridged by James K. Robinson. A convict's heroic struggle for justice and redemption plays out against a fiery backdrop of the Napoleonic wars. This edition features the excellent original translation and a sensitive abridgment. 304pp. $6\frac{1}{8} \times 9\frac{1}{4}$. 0-486-45789-3

LILITH: A Romance, George MacDonald. In this novel by the father of fantasy literature, a man travels through time to meet Adam and Eve and to explore humanity's fall from grace and ultimate redemption. 240pp. $5\frac{3}{8} \times 8\frac{1}{2}$. 0-486-46818-6

THE LOST LANGUAGE OF SYMBOLISM, Harold Bayley. This remarkable book reveals the hidden meaning behind familiar images and words, from the origins of Santa Claus to the fleur-de-lys, drawing from mythology, folklore, religious texts, and fairy tales. 1,418 illustrations. 784pp. $5\frac{3}{8} \times 8\frac{1}{2}$. 0-486-44787-1

MACBETH, William Shakespeare. A Scottish nobleman murders the king in order to succeed to the throne. Tortured by his conscience and fearful of discovery, he becomes tangled in a web of treachery and deceit that ultimately spells his doom. 96pp. $5\frac{3}{16} \times 8\frac{1}{4}$. 0-486-27802-6

MAKING AUTHENTIC CRAFTSMAN FURNITURE: Instructions and Plans for 62 Projects, Gustav Stickley. Make authentic reproductions of handsome, functional, durable furniture: tables, chairs, wall cabinets, desks, a hall tree, and more. Construction plans with drawings, schematics, dimensions, and lumber specs reprinted from 1900s *The Craftsman* magazine. 128pp. $8\frac{1}{8} \times 11$. 0-486-25000-8

MATHEMATICS FOR THE NONMATHEMATICIAN, Morris Kline. Erudite and entertaining overview follows development of mathematics from ancient Greeks to present. Topics include logic and mathematics, the fundamental concept, differential calculus, probability theory, much more. Exercises and problems. 641pp. $5\frac{3}{8} \times 8\frac{1}{2}$. 0-486-24823-2

MEMOIRS OF AN ARABIAN PRINCESS FROM ZANZIBAR, Emily Ruete. This 19th-century autobiography offers a rare inside look at the society surrounding a sultan's palace. A real-life princess in exile recalls her vanished world of harems, slave trading, and court intrigues. 288pp. $5\frac{3}{8} \times 8\frac{1}{2}$. 0-486-47121-7

CATALOG OF DOVER BOOKS

THE METAMORPHOSIS AND OTHER STORIES, Franz Kafka. Excellent new English translations of title story (considered by many critics Kafka's most perfect work), plus "The Judgment," "In the Penal Colony," "A Country Doctor," and "A Report to an Academy." Note. 96pp. $5\frac{3}{16} \times 8\frac{1}{4}$. 0-486-29030-1

MICROSCOPIC ART FORMS FROM THE PLANT WORLD, R. Anheisser. From undulating curves to complex geometrics, a world of fascinating images abound in this classic, illustrated survey of microscopic plants. Features 400 detailed illustrations of nature's minute but magnificent handiwork. The accompanying CD-ROM includes all of the images in the book. 128pp. 9 x 9. 0-486-46013-4

A MIDSUMMER NIGHT'S DREAM, William Shakespeare. Among the most popular of Shakespeare's comedies, this enchanting play humorously celebrates the vagaries of love as it focuses upon the intertwined romances of several pairs of lovers. Explanatory footnotes. 80pp. $5\frac{3}{16} \times 8\frac{1}{4}$. 0-486-27067-X

THE MONEY CHANGERS, Upton Sinclair. Originally published in 1908, this cautionary novel from the author of *The Jungle* explores corruption within the American system as a group of power brokers joins forces for personal gain, triggering a crash on Wall Street. 192pp. $5\frac{3}{8} \times 8\frac{1}{2}$. 0-486-46917-4

THE MOST POPULAR HOMES OF THE TWENTIES, William A. Radford. With a New Introduction by Daniel D. Reiff. Based on a rare 1925 catalog, this architectural showcase features floor plans, construction details, and photos of 26 homes, plus articles on entrances, porches, garages, and more. 250 illustrations, 21 color plates. 176pp. $8\frac{3}{8} \times 11$. 0-486-47028-8

MY 66 YEARS IN THE BIG LEAGUES, Connie Mack. With a New Introduction by Rich Westcott. A Founding Father of modern baseball, Mack holds the record for most wins — and losses — by a major league manager. Enhanced by 70 photographs, his warmhearted autobiography is populated by many legends of the game. 288pp. $5\frac{3}{8} \times 8\frac{1}{2}$. 0-486-47184-5

NARRATIVE OF THE LIFE OF FREDERICK DOUGLASS, Frederick Douglass. Douglass's graphic depictions of slavery, harrowing escape to freedom, and life as a newspaper editor, eloquent orator, and impassioned abolitionist. 96pp. $5\frac{3}{16} \times 8\frac{1}{4}$. 0-486-28499-9

THE NIGHTLESS CITY: Geisha and Courtesan Life in Old Tokyo, J. E. de Becker. This unsurpassed study from 100 years ago ventured into Tokyo's red-light district to survey geisha and courtesan life and offer meticulous descriptions of training, dress, social hierarchy, and erotic practices. 49 black-and-white illustrations; 2 maps. 496pp. $5\frac{3}{8} \times 8\frac{1}{2}$. 0-486-45563-7

THE ODYSSEY, Homer. Excellent prose translation of ancient epic recounts adventures of the homeward-bound Odysseus. Fantastic cast of gods, giants, cannibals, sirens, other supernatural creatures — true classic of Western literature. 256pp. $5\frac{3}{16} \times 8\frac{1}{4}$. 0-486-40654-7

OEDIPUS REX, Sophocles. Landmark of Western drama concerns the catastrophe that ensues when King Oedipus discovers he has inadvertently killed his father and married his mother. Masterly construction, dramatic irony. Explanatory footnotes. 64pp. $5\frac{3}{16} \times 8\frac{1}{4}$. 0-486-26877-2

ONCE UPON A TIME: The Way America Was, Eric Sloane. Nostalgic text and drawings brim with gentle philosophies and descriptions of how we used to live — self-sufficiently — on the land, in homes, and among the things built by hand. 44 line illustrations. 64pp. $8\frac{3}{8} \times 11$. 0-486-44411-2

Browse over 9,000 books at www.doverpublications.com

ONE OF OURS, Willa Cather. The Pulitzer Prize–winning novel about a young Nebraskan looking for something to believe in. Alienated from his parents, rejected by his wife, he finds his destiny on the bloody battlefields of World War I. 352pp. 5$\frac{3}{16}$ x 8¼. 0-486-45599-8

ORIGAMI YOU CAN USE: 27 Practical Projects, Rick Beech. Origami models can be more than decorative, and this unique volume shows how! The 27 practical projects include a CD case, frame, napkin ring, and dish. Easy instructions feature 400 two-color illustrations. 96pp. 8¼ x 11. 0-486-47057-1

OTHELLO, William Shakespeare. Towering tragedy tells the story of a Moorish general who earns the enmity of his ensign Iago when he passes him over for a promotion. Masterly portrait of an archvillain. Explanatory footnotes. 112pp. 5$\frac{3}{16}$ x 8¼. 0-486-29097-2

PARADISE LOST, John Milton. Notes by John A. Himes. First published in 1667, *Paradise Lost* ranks among the greatest of English literature's epic poems. It's a sublime retelling of Adam and Eve's fall from grace and expulsion from Eden. Notes by John A. Himes. 480pp. 5$\frac{3}{16}$ x 8¼. 0-486-44287-X

PASSING, Nella Larsen. Married to a successful physician and prominently ensconced in society, Irene Redfield leads a charmed existence — until a chance encounter with a childhood friend who has been "passing for white." 112pp. 5⅜ x 8½. 0-486-43713-2

PERSPECTIVE DRAWING FOR BEGINNERS, Len A. Doust. Doust carefully explains the roles of lines, boxes, and circles, and shows how visualizing shapes and forms can be used in accurate depictions of perspective. One of the most concise introductions available. 33 illustrations. 64pp. 5⅜ x 8½. 0-486-45149-6

PERSPECTIVE MADE EASY, Ernest R. Norling. Perspective is easy; yet, surprisingly few artists know the simple rules that make it so. Remedy that situation with this simple, step-by-step book, the first devoted entirely to the topic. 256 illustrations. 224pp. 5⅜ x 8½. 0-486-40473-0

THE PICTURE OF DORIAN GRAY, Oscar Wilde. Celebrated novel involves a handsome young Londoner who sinks into a life of depravity. His body retains perfect youth and vigor while his recent portrait reflects the ravages of his crime and sensuality. 176pp. 5$\frac{3}{16}$ x 8¼. 0-486-27807-7

PRIDE AND PREJUDICE, Jane Austen. One of the most universally loved and admired English novels, an effervescent tale of rural romance transformed by Jane Austen's art into a witty, shrewdly observed satire of English country life. 272pp. 5$\frac{3}{16}$ x 8¼. 0-486-28473-5

THE PRINCE, Niccolò Machiavelli. Classic, Renaissance-era guide to acquiring and maintaining political power. Today, nearly 500 years after it was written, this calculating prescription for autocratic rule continues to be much read and studied. 80pp. 5$\frac{3}{16}$ x 8¼. 0-486-27274-5

QUICK SKETCHING, Carl Cheek. A perfect introduction to the technique of "quick sketching." Drawing upon an artist's immediate emotional responses, this is an extremely effective means of capturing the essential form and features of a subject. More than 100 black-and-white illustrations throughout. 48pp. 11 x 8¼. 0-486-46608-6

RANCH LIFE AND THE HUNTING TRAIL, Theodore Roosevelt. Illustrated by Frederic Remington. Beautifully illustrated by Remington, Roosevelt's celebration of the Old West recounts his adventures in the Dakota Badlands of the 1880s, from roundups to Indian encounters to hunting bighorn sheep. 208pp. 6¼ x 9¼. 0-486-47340-6

THE RED BADGE OF COURAGE, Stephen Crane. Amid the nightmarish chaos of a Civil War battle, a young soldier discovers courage, humility, and, perhaps, wisdom. Uncanny re-creation of actual combat. Enduring landmark of American fiction. 112pp. 5$\frac{3}{16}$ x 8$\frac{1}{4}$. 0-486-26465-3

RELATIVITY SIMPLY EXPLAINED, Martin Gardner. One of the subject's clearest, most entertaining introductions offers lucid explanations of special and general theories of relativity, gravity, and spacetime, models of the universe, and more. 100 illustrations. 224pp. 5$\frac{3}{8}$ x 8$\frac{1}{2}$. 0-486-29315-7

REMBRANDT DRAWINGS: 116 Masterpieces in Original Color, Rembrandt van Rijn. This deluxe hardcover edition features drawings from throughout the Dutch master's prolific career. Informative captions accompany these beautifully reproduced landscapes, biblical vignettes, figure studies, animal sketches, and portraits. 128pp. 8$\frac{3}{8}$ x 11. 0-486-46149-1

THE ROAD NOT TAKEN AND OTHER POEMS, Robert Frost. A treasury of Frost's most expressive verse. In addition to the title poem: "An Old Man's Winter Night," "In the Home Stretch," "Meeting and Passing," "Putting in the Seed," many more. All complete and unabridged. 64pp. 5$\frac{3}{16}$ x 8$\frac{1}{4}$. 0-486-27550-7

ROMEO AND JULIET, William Shakespeare. Tragic tale of star-crossed lovers, feuding families and timeless passion contains some of Shakespeare's most beautiful and lyrical love poetry. Complete, unabridged text with explanatory footnotes. 96pp. 5$\frac{3}{16}$ x 8$\frac{1}{4}$. 0-486-27557-4

SANDITON AND THE WATSONS: Austen's Unfinished Novels, Jane Austen. Two tantalizing incomplete stories revisit Austen's customary milieu of courtship and venture into new territory, amid guests at a seaside resort. Both are worth reading for pleasure and study. 112pp. 5$\frac{3}{8}$ x 8$\frac{1}{2}$. 0-486-45793-1

THE SCARLET LETTER, Nathaniel Hawthorne. With stark power and emotional depth, Hawthorne's masterpiece explores sin, guilt, and redemption in a story of adultery in the early days of the Massachusetts Colony. 192pp. 5$\frac{3}{16}$ x 8$\frac{1}{4}$.
0-486-28048-9

THE SEASONS OF AMERICA PAST, Eric Sloane. Seventy-five illustrations depict cider mills and presses, sleds, pumps, stump-pulling equipment, plows, and other elements of America's rural heritage. A section of old recipes and household hints adds additional color. 160pp. 8$\frac{3}{8}$ x 11. 0-486-44220-9

SELECTED CANTERBURY TALES, Geoffrey Chaucer. Delightful collection includes the General Prologue plus three of the most popular tales: "The Knight's Tale," "The Miller's Prologue and Tale," and "The Wife of Bath's Prologue and Tale." In modern English. 144pp. 5$\frac{3}{16}$ x 8$\frac{1}{4}$. 0-486-28241-4

SELECTED POEMS, Emily Dickinson. Over 100 best-known, best-loved poems by one of America's foremost poets, reprinted from authoritative early editions. No comparable edition at this price. Index of first lines. 64pp. 5$\frac{3}{16}$ x 8$\frac{1}{4}$. 0-486-26466-1

SIDDHARTHA, Hermann Hesse. Classic novel that has inspired generations of seekers. Blending Eastern mysticism and psychoanalysis, Hesse presents a strikingly original view of man and culture and the arduous process of self-discovery, reconciliation, harmony, and peace. 112pp. 5$\frac{3}{16}$ x 8$\frac{1}{4}$. 0-486-40653-9

SKETCHING OUTDOORS, Leonard Richmond. This guide offers beginners step-by-step demonstrations of how to depict clouds, trees, buildings, and other outdoor sights. Explanations of a variety of techniques include shading and constructional drawing. 48pp. 11 x 8$\frac{1}{4}$. 0-486-46922-0

SMALL HOUSES OF THE FORTIES: With Illustrations and Floor Plans, Harold E. Group. 56 floor plans and elevations of houses that originally cost less than $15,000 to build. Recommended by financial institutions of the era, they range from Colonials to Cape Cods. 144pp. 8⅜ x 11. 0-486-45598-X

SOME CHINESE GHOSTS, Lafcadio Hearn. Rooted in ancient Chinese legends, these richly atmospheric supernatural tales are recounted by an expert in Oriental lore. Their originality, power, and literary charm will captivate readers of all ages. 96pp. 5⅜ x 8½. 0-486-46306-0

SONGS FOR THE OPEN ROAD: Poems of Travel and Adventure, Edited by The American Poetry & Literacy Project. More than 80 poems by 50 American and British masters celebrate real and metaphorical journeys. Poems by Whitman, Byron, Millay, Sandburg, Langston Hughes, Emily Dickinson, Robert Frost, Shelley, Tennyson, Yeats, many others. Note. 80pp. 5³⁄₁₆ x 8¼. 0-486-40646-6

SPOON RIVER ANTHOLOGY, Edgar Lee Masters. An American poetry classic, in which former citizens of a mythical midwestern town speak touchingly from the grave of the thwarted hopes and dreams of their lives. 144pp. 5³⁄₁₆ x 8¼. 0-486-27275-3

STAR LORE: Myths, Legends, and Facts, William Tyler Olcott. Captivating retellings of the origins and histories of ancient star groups include Pegasus, Ursa Major, Pleiades, signs of the zodiac, and other constellations. "Classic." — *Sky & Telescope.* 58 illustrations. 544pp. 5⅜ x 8½. 0-486-43581-4

THE STRANGE CASE OF DR. JEKYLL AND MR. HYDE, Robert Louis Stevenson. This intriguing novel, both fantasy thriller and moral allegory, depicts the struggle of two opposing personalities — one essentially good, the other evil — for the soul of one man. 64pp. 5³⁄₁₆ x 8¼. 0-486-26688-5

SURVIVAL HANDBOOK: The Official U.S. Army Guide, Department of the Army. This special edition of the Army field manual is geared toward civilians. An essential companion for campers and all lovers of the outdoors, it constitutes the most authoritative wilderness guide. 288pp. 5³⁄₁₆ x 8¼. 0-486-46184-X

A TALE OF TWO CITIES, Charles Dickens. Against the backdrop of the French Revolution, Dickens unfolds his masterpiece of drama, adventure, and romance about a man falsely accused of treason. Excitement and derring-do in the shadow of the guillotine. 304pp. 5³⁄₁₆ x 8¼. 0-486-40651-2

TEN PLAYS, Anton Chekhov. *The Sea Gull, Uncle Vanya, The Three Sisters, The Cherry Orchard,* and *Ivanov,* plus 5 one-act comedies: *The Anniversary, An Unwilling Martyr, The Wedding, The Bear,* and *The Proposal.* 336pp. 5³⁄₁₆ x 8¼. 0-486-46560-8

THE FLYING INN, G. K. Chesterton. Hilarious romp in which pub owner Humphrey Hump and friend take to the road in a donkey cart filled with rum and cheese, inveighing against Prohibition and other "oppressive forms of modernity." 320pp. 5⅜ x 8½. 0-486-41910-X

THIRTY YEARS THAT SHOOK PHYSICS: The Story of Quantum Theory, George Gamow. Lucid, accessible introduction to the influential theory of energy and matter features careful explanations of Dirac's anti-particles, Bohr's model of the atom, and much more. Numerous drawings. 1966 edition. 240pp. 5⅜ x 8½. 0-486-24895-X

TREASURE ISLAND, Robert Louis Stevenson. Classic adventure story of a perilous sea journey, a mutiny led by the infamous Long John Silver, and a lethal scramble for buried treasure — seen through the eyes of cabin boy Jim Hawkins. 160pp. 5³⁄₁₆ x 8¼. 0-486-27559-0

THE TRIAL, Franz Kafka. Translated by David Wyllie. From its gripping first sentence onward, this novel exemplifies the term "Kafkaesque." Its darkly humorous narrative recounts a bank clerk's entrapment in a bureaucratic maze, based on an undisclosed charge. 176pp. 5³⁄₁₆ x 8¼. 0-486-47061-X

THE TURN OF THE SCREW, Henry James. Gripping ghost story by great novelist depicts the sinister transformation of 2 innocent children into flagrant liars and hypocrites. An elegantly told tale of unspoken horror and psychological terror. 96pp. 5³⁄₁₆ x 8¼. 0-486-26684-2

UP FROM SLAVERY, Booker T. Washington. Washington (1856-1915) rose to become the most influential spokesman for African-Americans of his day. In this eloquently written book, he describes events in a remarkable life that began in bondage and culminated in worldwide recognition. 160pp. 5³⁄₁₆ x 8¼. 0-486-28738-6

VICTORIAN HOUSE DESIGNS IN AUTHENTIC FULL COLOR: 75 Plates from the "Scientific American – Architects and Builders Edition," 1885-1894, Edited by Blanche Cirker. Exquisitely detailed, exceptionally handsome designs for an enormous variety of attractive city dwellings, spacious suburban and country homes, charming "cottages" and other structures — all accompanied by perspective views and floor plans. 80pp. 9¼ x 12¼. 0-486-29438-2

VILLETTE, Charlotte Brontë. Acclaimed by Virginia Woolf as "Brontë's finest novel," this moving psychological study features a remarkably modern heroine who abandons her native England for a new life as a schoolteacher in Belgium. 480pp. 5³⁄₁₆ x 8¼. 0-486-45557-2

THE VOYAGE OUT, Virginia Woolf. A moving depiction of the thrills and confusion of youth, Woolf's acclaimed first novel traces a shipboard journey to South America for a captivating exploration of a woman's growing self-awareness. 288pp. 5³⁄₁₆ x 8¼. 0-486-45005-8

WALDEN; OR, LIFE IN THE WOODS, Henry David Thoreau. Accounts of Thoreau's daily life on the shores of Walden Pond outside Concord, Massachusetts, are interwoven with musings on the virtues of self-reliance and individual freedom, on society, government, and other topics. 224pp. 5³⁄₁₆ x 8¼. 0-486-28495-6

WILD PILGRIMAGE: A Novel in Woodcuts, Lynd Ward. Through startling engravings shaded in black and red, Ward wordlessly tells the story of a man trapped in an industrial world, struggling between the grim reality around him and the fantasies his imagination creates. 112pp. 6⅛ x 9¼. 0-486-46583-7

WILLY POGÁNY REDISCOVERED, Willy Pogány. Selected and Edited by Jeff A. Menges. More than 100 color and black-and-white Art Nouveau–style illustrations from fairy tales and adventure stories include scenes from Wagner's "Ring" cycle, *The Rime of the Ancient Mariner, Gulliver's Travels,* and *Faust.* 144pp. 8⅜ x 11. 0-486-47046-6

WOOLLY THOUGHTS: Unlock Your Creative Genius with Modular Knitting, Pat Ashforth and Steve Plummer. Here's the revolutionary way to knit — easy, fun, and foolproof! Beginners and experienced knitters need only master a single stitch to create their own designs with patchwork squares. More than 100 illustrations. 128pp. 6½ x 9¼. 0-486-46084-3

WUTHERING HEIGHTS, Emily Brontë. Somber tale of consuming passions and vengeance — played out amid the lonely English moors — recounts the turbulent and tempestuous love story of Cathy and Heathcliff. Poignant and compelling. 256pp. 5³⁄₁₆ x 8¼. 0-486-29256-8